Extending Professional Practice in the
Early Years

This Reader forms part of the Open University module *Extending professional practice in the early years* (E210). This is a 60 point, level 2 module for anyone working with young children in public, private, voluntary and independent childcare and education settings. It is the final module in the Open University Foundation Degree in Early Years.

Details of this and other Open University modules and qualifications can be obtained from the Student Registration and Enquiry Service, The Open University, PO Box 197, Milton Keynes MK7 6BJ, United Kingdom; telephone: +44 (0) 845 300 6090; e-mail: general-enquiries@open.ac.uk.

Alternatively, you may wish to visit the Open University website at www.open.ac.uk, where you can learn more about the wide range of modules and qualifications offered at all levels by The Open University.

Extending Professional Practice in the Early Years

Edited by

Linda **Miller**, Rose **Drury** and Carrie **Cable**

The Open University

Los Angeles | London | New Delhi
Singapore | Washington DC

The Open University
Walton Hall
Milton Keynes
MK7 6AA
United Kingdom
www.open.ac.uk

First published 2012

SAGE Publications Ltd
1 Oliver's Yard
55 City Road
London EC1Y 1SP

SAGE Publications Inc.
2455 Teller Road
Thousand Oaks, California 91320

SAGE Publications India Pvt Ltd
B 1/I 1 Mohan Cooperative Industrial Area
Mathura Road
New Delhi 110 044

SAGE Publications Asia-Pacific Pte Ltd
33 Pekin Street #02-01
Far East Square
Singapore 048763

Library of Congress Control Number: 2011921691

British Library Cataloguing in Publication data

A catalogue record for this book is available from the British Library

ISBN 978-1-4462-0751-2
ISBN 978-1-4462-0752-9 (pbk)

Typeset by C & M Digitals (P) Ltd, Chennai, India
Printed in Great Britain by TJ International Ltd, Padstow, Cornwall
Printed on paper from sustainable resources

Contents

Acknowledgements

We wish to thank those who have given permission for us to edit and reprint text from other publications for this Reader. We would particularly like to thank Naima Browne, Natalie Canning, Alison Clark, Victoria Cooper, Caroline Jones and Mary Whalley for their contribution to editing chapters in this book.

Special thanks go to Kathy Simms for her invaluable secretarial and administrative support and to Gill Gowans (Co-publishing Executive) for her help in preparing the manuscript.

Grateful acknowledgement is made to the following sources for permission to reproduce material in this book:

Chapter 1
Clark, A. (2005) 'Ways of seeing: using the Mosaic approach to listen to young children's perspectives', in Clark, A. and Moss, P. (eds) *Beyond Listening*, London: National Children's Bureau and Joseph Rowntree Foundation, pp. 29–48. Reprinted by permission of the Policy Press.

Chapter 2
Guisti, D., Hart, R. and Iltus, S. (2009) 'Is my city or community child-friendly?' *Early Childhood Matters*, November, pp. 29–35. Reprinted by permission of the Bernard van Leer Foundation.

Chapter 3
Stephenson, A. (2009) 'Horses in the sandpit: photography, prolonged involvement and "stepping back" as strategies for listening to children's voices', *Early Child Development and Care*, vol. 179, no. 2, pp. 131–41. Reprinted by permission of the publisher Taylor & Francis Group, http://www.informaworld.com

Chapter 4
Flewitt, R. (2005) 'Conducting research with young children: some ethical considerations', *Early Child Development and Care*, vol. 175, no. 6, pp. 553–65. Reprinted by permission of the publisher Taylor & Francis Group, http://www.informaworld.com

Chapter 5
Woodhead, M. (2008) 'Promoting young children's development: implications of the UN Convention on the Rights of the Child', in Miller, L. and Cable, C. (eds) *Professionalism in the Early Years*, London: Hodder/Arnold Publishers, pp. 154–66. Reprinted by permission of Hodder.

Chapter 6
Rhedding-Jones, J. (2005) 'Questioning diversity', in Yelland, N. (ed.) *Critical Issues in Early Childhood*, Buckingham: Open University Press, pp. 130–45. Reproduced with the kind permission of Open University Press. All rights reserved.

Chapter 7
Hickman, C. and Jones, K. (2005) 'Inclusive practice for children with Special Educational Needs (SEN)', in Waller, T. (ed.) *An Introduction to Early Childhood*, London: Sage, pp. 26–38.

Chapter 8
Peeters, J. and Vandenbroeck, M. (2010) 'Childcare practitioners and the process of professionalization', in Miller, L. and Cable, C. (eds) *Professionalization, Leadership and Management in the Early Years*, London: Sage, pp. 62–76.

Chapter 9
Paige-Smith, A., Rix, J. and Craft, A. (2008) 'Reflective family-centred practices: parents' perspectives and early intervention', in Paige-Smith, A. and Craft, A. (eds) *Developing Reflective Practice in the Early Years*, Maidenhead: McGraw Hill/Open University Press, pp. 145–59. Reproduced with the kind permission of Open University Press. All rights reserved.

Chapter 10
Wyn Siencyn, S. (2010) 'The challenges for children experiencing rural poverty in Wales', in Clark, M.M. and Tucker, S. (eds) *Early Childhoods in a Changing World*, Stoke-on-Trent: Trentham Books, pp. 45–55. Reprinted by permission of Trentham Books.

Chapter 11
Brooker, L. (2009) 'Just like having a best friend: how babies and toddlers construct relationships with their key workers in nurseries', in Papatheodorou, T. and Moyles, J. (eds) *Learning Together in the Early Years*, London: Routledge, pp. 98–108. Reproduced by permission of Taylor & Francis Books UK.

Chapter 12
Peters, S. (2003) '"I didn't expect that I would get tons of friends … more each day": children's experiences of friendship during the transition to school', *Early Years: An International Journal of Research and Development*, vol. 23, no. 1, pp. 45–53. Reprinted by permission of Taylor & Francis Ltd, http://www.tandf.co.uk/journals on behalf of TACTYC.

Chapter 13
Albon, D. (2010) 'Postmodern and post-structuralist perspectives on early childhood education', in Miller, L. and Pound, L. (eds) *Theories and Approaches to Learning in the Early Years*. London: Sage, pp. 38–52.

Chapter 14
Jones, L., Holmes, R., MacRae, S. and MacLure, M. (2010) '"Improper" children', in Yelland, N. (ed.) *Contemporary Perspectives on Early Childhood Education*, New York: McGraw Hill, pp. 177–91. Reproduced with the kind permission of Open University Press. All rights reserved.

Chapter 15
Stephen, C., McPake, J. and Plowman, L. (2010) 'Digital technologies at home: the experiences of 3 and 4 years olds in Scotland', in Clark, M.M. and Tucker, S. (eds) *Early Childhoods in a Changing World*, Stoke-on-Trent: Trentham Books, pp. 145–54. Reprinted by permission of Trentham Books.

Chapter 16
Hedegaard, M. (2008) 'A cultural-historical theory of children's development', in Hedegaard, M. and Fleer, M. (eds) *Studying Children: A Cultural–Historical Approach*, Maidenhead: OUP/McGraw Hill, pp. 10–29. Reproduced with the kind permission of Open University Press. All rights reserved.

Chapter 17
Maynard, T. and Chicken, S. (2010) 'Through a different lens: exploring Reggio Emilia in a Welsh context', in *Early Years*, vol. 30, no. 1, March, pp. 29–39. Reprinted by permission of Taylor & Francis Ltd, http://www.tandf.co.uk/journals on behalf of TACTYC.

Chapter 18
Petrie, P., Boddy, J., Cameron, C., Heptinstall, E., McQuail, S. and Wigfal, V. (2009) *Pedagogy – A Holistic, Personal Approach to Work with Children and Young People, Across Services*, Institute of Education, University of London, Thomas Coram Research Unit, pp. 1–13. www.ioe.ac.uk/publications. Note that this article has been shortened by the editors of the Reader. Reprinted by permission of the IOE.

Chapter 19
McGillivray, G. (2011) 'Constructions of professional identity', in Miller, L. and Cable, C. (eds) *Professionalization, Leadership and Management in the Early Years*, London: Sage, pp. 93–106.

Chapter 20
Whalley, M.E. (2010) 'Leading and managing in the early years: towards a new understanding', in Miller, L. and Cable, C. (eds) *Professionalization, Leadership and Management in the Early Years*, London: Sage, pp. 13–28.

Chapter 21
Rodd, J. (2008) 'Building and leading a team' (Chapter 8), in *Leadership in Early Childhood*, 4th edition, Buckingham: Open University Press, pp. 145–64. Reproduced with the kind permission of Open University Press. All rights reserved.

Chapter 22
Siraj-Blatchford, I. and Manni, L. (2007) *Effective Leadership in the Early Years Sector (ELEYS) Study*, London: Institute of Education, University of London, pp. 1–31. www.ioe.ac.uk/publications. Note that this article has been shortened by the editors of the Reader. Reprinted by permission of the IOE.

Chapter 23
Whitmarsh, J. (2007) 'Negotiating the moral maze: developing ethical literacy in multi-agency settings', in Siraj-Blatchford, I., Clarke, K. and Needham, M. (eds) *The Team Around the Child: Multi-agency Working in the Early Years*, Stoke-on-Trent: Trentham Books, pp. 87–103. Reprinted by permission of Trentham Books.

General introduction

Linda Miller, Rose Drury and Carrie Cable

The chapters in this book comprise a range of edited articles, chapters from books and practitioner-focused and research-based journals, and so encompass different levels of accessibility, challenge and different foci. The book has been compiled for early years practitioners engaged in ongoing learning and working in a diverse range of settings such as day nurseries, playgroups, Children's Centres and schools, and for childminders in home-based settings, but who are likely to be at different points on a continuum of professional development.

The selected readings are written by researchers, academics and authorities in the field of early years, often as an outcome of working closely with children, parents and practitioners. The chapters cover a wide range of themes and issues which we consider to be key considerations for early years practitioners and other professionals working with young children and their families and carers. These critical issues are reflected in the four parts of this book and are grouped under four overarching themes:

1. Listening to children
2. Diversity and transitions
3. Pedagogy and practice
4. Leadership and change

For each of these four parts of the book, you will find a separate introduction outlining the particular content and perspectives of the selected edited readings.

The terms early years, early childhood education and care (ECEC) and early childhood education (ECE) are used interchangeably throughout the chapters in this book. The three terms reflect the diversity of ECEC services internationally which tended historically to be organized in either split or integrated systems, reflecting a focus on care, education or attempts at integration. In split systems, services for the youngest children (up to 4 years old) are separate from pre-school or early education programmes and are usually under the auspices of separate national or local government departments such as education, health or social welfare. In England, the term 'early years' has been adopted to reflect attempts to provide more integrated services, as exemplified in Children's Centres. However, as some chapters reflect, in areas such as funding for services and workforce roles, the reality of such policy initiatives is yet to be realized (OECD, 2006; Miller and Cable, 2011).

As editors, we take the view that it is 'impossible to educate without caring, or care without promoting children's learning' (Owen and Haynes, 2008: 10). At the same time, we would support a view reiterated in a number of chapters in this book (see Part 4), that to do this requires well-qualified, experienced and reflective practitioners.

Background

A changing policy scene

In the last decade, there have been unparalleled developments in the field of early years in all four countries of the United Kingdom (UK): England, Scotland, Wales and Northern Ireland. All have devolved responsibilities, including for education, social services and health. Some aspects of early childhood policy, such as parental leave and subsidies for childcare, rest with the UK government, but the national governments are responsible for policies regarding provision. England is the largest of four countries of the United Kingdom, with 84 per cent of the UK population.

This book has been compiled at a time of change and uncertainty, particularly in England, where a coalition government replaced the former Labour government in 2010. Under the Labour government (1997–2010), services for children, young people and families were brought together under a new Department for Children, Schools and Families (DCSF) as part of a drive to unite the historically separate care and education services. However, the integration of this policy had limits – for example, the Department of Health retains responsibility for children's health, and more recently 'well being' has entered the policy vocabulary. At local authority level, Directors of Children's Services, usually from an education background, integrate planning and delivery of services. The Children's Plan (DCSF, 2007) introduced the idea of 'progressive universalism'. The intention was that all children were to have services designed around their needs, and that services would have a key role in supporting children (and families) with 'additional' needs, be they educational, social or health related. It also supported the use of a Common Assessment Framework (CAF) for early assessment and identification of children's additional needs. This framework is used by practitioners across all children's services (i.e. health, education, social welfare). The purpose and rationale for the CAF is set out on the Every Child Matters website (www.cwdcouncil.org.uk/caf).

The early years workforce

As discussed in Part 4 of this book, increasing the skills, confidence and competence of the early years workforce has been seen by governments in many countries as critical to providing quality provision and positive outcomes for young children and their families (OECD, 2006). Under the Labour government in England, there was a commitment to 'reform' and 'professionalize' the children's workforce (DfES, 2006). This agenda was enshrined in major policy documents and in the establishment of a Children's Workforce Development Council (CWDC) whose stated aims is:

> to improve the lives of children, young people, their families and carers by ensuring that all people working with them have the best possible training, qualifications, support and advice. (2010)

However, funding has been withdrawn for this body and most of its functions will be taken over by the new Department for Education in 2011, although the indications are that it will continue as a sector skills agency. Consequently, there is a high degree of uncertainty in the sector.

As part of the reform process, a Common Core of Skills and Knowledge was developed for all those who work with children, young people and families, for providers to take account of in developing training and qualifications (DfES, 2005; CWDC, 2010). An Integrated Qualifications Framework (IQF) for the children's workforce is also under development for both England and Scotland, to promote skills acquisition and to enable career progression and work across professional boundaries (http://cwdccouncil.org.uk/projects/integratedqualificationsframework.htm). Developments to improve training and qualifications are taking place across all UK countries which reflect the particular situation in each country (Clark and Waller, 2007).

Curriculum guidance and the early years curriculum

Curriculum guidance for early childhood education has become increasingly centralized in a number of countries, which has enhanced debates about what and how young children learn (Bennett, 2001). However, alongside the development of these more centralized systems, many practitioners have retained and woven ideas and influences from other approaches and models into their practice. Developing early childhood curricula involves making decisions and choices about what children should learn. Making these choices involves different people including early childhood practitioners, teachers, educational experts and policy makers. Early childhood curricula may be based on official guidance issued by government and ministers, or may be more locally generated, as in the nurseries of Reggio Emilia in Italy, or it may stem from the distinctive vision and philosophy of key educators (Miller and Pound, 2011).

Since 2008, all providers of early years services in England are required to work to a curriculum framework – The Early Years Foundation Stage (EYFS) – for children from birth to 5 (DCSF, 2008). The framework encompasses key areas of learning, learning goals and a sequential approach to progression and achievement. This approach has been criticized as the 'schoolification' of early childhood because of its strong links to the primary curriculum for children aged 5 to 11 years (OECD, 2006: 62), and as encouraging practitioners to focus on 'strategic compliance' with national requirements (Goouch, 2008: 93). With a new coalition government, the EYFS is under review with the stated aim of making it less bureaucratic and more focused on young children's learning and development (DFE, 2010). However, recent research indicates that practitioners like working with the EYFS as they 'welcome the play-based and child-led nature of the guidance' (Brooker et al., 2010: 1). Interestingly, this research suggests that practitioners can develop a sense of agency in working with a prescribed framework. In this book, the chapter authors look at examples of working in different ways with young children, including the challenge of 'transplanting' a particular curricular model into a new and different context (see Part 3).

International perspectives

Some of the chapters in this book are written by authors outside the UK, but reflect common concerns such as the rights of children, diversity, and a more holistic approach to child development and to working with young children through a 'social pedagogy' model.

ECEC is becoming a growing priority internationally and has received the attention of policy makers in many countries over the last few years. The contribution of ECEC to broader economic and social and education goals is increasingly recognized (OECD, 2006), although services and provision remain underdeveloped in many countries and, as a result, progress is variable (Urban, 2009). The professional development of the ECEC workforce has become a high priority on government agendas (OECD, 2006). Research over the last decade supports the view that quality of provision in the ECEC field is linked to the quality of staff (OECD, 2006; Sylva et al., 2010). However, Oberheumer and Scheryer (2008) – in a study of changes taking place across 27 European countries in the professionalization strategies for work in early childhood provision – raise issues familiar to practitioners working in the UK context, including the traditional demarcation lines between early childhood workers, primary school teachers and early years pedagogues. This research reveals no agreement across Europe on the competence requirements for working with young children up to the age of school entry, and therefore no common understanding of what 'professionalism' in the early years means.

There is therefore both a national and international interest in developing professionals who can work at a high level with young children and lead and manage within the early years. The chapters in this book reflect this challenging policy agenda and aim to support the professional development of practitioners who work in this field.

References

Bennett, J. (2001) 'Goals and curricula in early childhood', in Kamerman, S. (ed.) *Early Childhood Education and Care: International Perspectives*. New York: The Institute for Child and Family Policy at Columbia University.

Brooker, L., Rogers, S., Ellis, D., Hallet, E. and Roberts-Holmes, G. (2010) *Practitioners' Experiences of the Early Years Foundation Stage*. Ref. DFE-RR029. London Department for Education.

Children's Workforce Development Council (CWDC) (2010) *Refreshing the Common Core of Skills and Knowledge for the Children's Workforce*. Leeds: CWDC. Available at: www.cwdcouncil.org.uk/index.asp (accessed 11 May 2010).

Clark, M. and Waller, T. (eds) (2007) *Early Childhood Education and Care*. London: Sage.

Department for Children, Schools and Families (DCSF) (2007) *The Children's Plan*. Available at: www.dcsf.gov.uk/childrensplan (accessed 17 January 2011).

Department for Children, Schools and Families (DCSF) (2008) *Statutory Framework for the Early Years Foundation Stage*. Nottingham: DCSF Publications.

Department for Education (DfE) (2010) *Review of the Early Years Foundation Stage*. Available at: www.direct.gov.uk/en/Nl1/Newsroom/DG_189908 (accessed 17 January 2011).

Department for Education and Skills (DfES) (2005) *Common Core of Skills and Knowledge for the Children's Workforce*. Nottingham: DfES Publications.

Department for Education and Skills (DfES) (2006) *Children's Workforce Strategy: Building a World-class Workforce for Children and Young People*. Nottingham: DfES Publications.

Goouch, K. (2008) 'Understanding playful pedagogies, play narratives and play spaces', *Early Years: An International Journal of Research and Development*, 28(1): 93–102.

Miller, L. and Cable, C. (eds) (2011) *Professionalization, Leadership and Management in the Early Years*. London: Sage

Miller, L. and Pound, L. (eds) (2011) *Theories and Approaches to Learning in the Early Years*. London: Sage

Oberheumer, P. and Scheryer, I. (2008) 'What professional?', *Children in Europe. Aiming High: a Professional Workforce for the Early Years*, 15: 9–12.

OECD (2006) *Starting Strong II: Early Childhood Education and Care*. Paris: Organisation for Economic Co-operation and Development.

Owen, S. and Haynes, G. (2008) 'Developing professionalism in the early years: from policy to practice', in L. Miller and C. Cable (eds) *Professionalism in the Early Years*. Abingdon: Hodder Education.

Sylva, K., Melhuish, E., Sammons, P., Siraj-Blatchford, I. and Taggart, B. (2010) *Early Childhood Matters: Evidence from the Effective Preschool and Primary Education Project*. London: Routledge.

Urban, M. (2009) *Early Childhood Education in Europe: Achievements, Challenges and Possibilities*. Brussels: Education International.

Part 1
Listening to children

Introduction

Rose Drury

A growing interest in children's voice and participation has come to occupy a central place in the children's rights movement. Much of the current focus on listening to children is motivated by a broader, underlying approach to early childhood provision which involves a way of being, living and interacting that permeates all practice and relationships (Clark et al., 2005). Giving voice through 'listening' is part of the underpinning ethos of many early childhood research approaches, as well as some pedagogical practices. In the first part of this book, the focus is on the importance of recognizing and listening to the 'voice of the child' and ways in which practitioners can engage and research with children in developing their own provision and practice. The chapters provide insights into the crucial role of participatory research with young children. Themes which run through the chapters include: listening to young children using a research approach to include the 'voice of the child'; understanding children's perspectives through the process of 'stepping back' from the research process; the importance of 'child consent' in listening to and respecting all research participants' wishes; the fulfilment of children's rights at the local level; and the significance of the United Nations Convention on the Rights of the Child (UNCRC, 1989) and the implications for professional work with young children and developments in policy and services in England.

The first chapter introduces a way of listening which can also be understood as a means of enhancing children's participation as 'experts in their own lives'. In adopting listening as a principle and practice, the distinction between 'practice' and 'research' also becomes blurred. Alison Clark, as the originator of the Mosaic approach, examines the approach as a framework for listening to young children which plays to children's strengths. Starting from this viewpoint, the Mosaic approach brings together a range of methods, including observation and other participatory tools. In the chapter, Clark introduces a number of different research methods that have been adopted for listening to young children, that also contribute to work by practitioners towards the development of a pedagogy of listening. A key influence on the development of the Mosaic approach has been the active view of the child in the research process. Clark argues that using the approach enables multiple listening to take place between children, their peers and adults.

There have been significant developments in recognizing children's rights and participatory research over the past 10 years. In Chapter 2, Dora Giusti, Roger Hart and Selim Iltus describe how the Child Friendly Cities (CFC) approach is committed to fulfilling the rights of children at the local level. The innovative action research project summarized in this chapter has led to practitioners and researchers developing tools which enable communities and cities to assess their child friendliness, foregrounding a participatory approach involving children.

Understanding young children's experiences (aged from 2 to 4 years) of the curriculum in a New Zealand early childhood education centre is the focus of Chapter 3. Drawing on data from a wider ethnographic study, Alison Stephenson describes how research activities using photographs have been found to be an effective way of enabling young children to share their thoughts about their experiences, She illustrates the importance of prolonged involvement in the research experiences and of learning to 'step back' from the data, which allows other possible layers of meaning to be 'heard' and thus emphasizes the importance of reflexive listening.

In Chapter 4, Rosie Flewitt reflects on the relatively recent move in early childhood education towards the respectful involvement of young children in the research process. She argues that established educational guidelines provide no more than a loose ethical framework and proposes that by adopting a flexible, reflective stance, researchers can learn much from children, not only about their perspectives, but also about their inclusion in the research process. Drawing on her experiences of conducting ethnographic video case studies with 3-year-old children, their parents and pre-school practitioners, Flewitt reflects upon the processes of negotiating initial and ongoing consent. The notion of 'informed' consent in exploratory research with young children is problematized and questions of anonymity are raised when collecting and reporting on visual data. She concludes that researchers have a responsibility towards participants, highlighting how the relationship of trust is established and how this relationship shapes the nature and quality of data collected.

The focus of the final chapter in this part of the book is on the implications of the United Nations Convention on the Rights of the Child, 1989 (UNCRC) for recent developments in policy and services in England. In Chapter 5, Martin Woodhead considers the key debates surrounding what 'the development of the child' (which is also one of the six elements of the Common Core of Skills and Knowledge for the Children's Workforce [DfES, 2005]) entails within a framework of rights. In a discussion of the universality of child development processes, he focuses on what he terms the three 'Cs' – thinking about development in ways that are 'Contextual', 'Cultural' and based on respect for children's 'Competencies'. In summary, he argues that implementing the UNCRC not only alters the status of children, but also the status of adults, professionals, parents and others.

References

Clark, A., Kjorholt, A.T. and Moss, P. (eds) (2005) *Beyond Listening: Children's Perspectives on Early Childhood Services*. Bristol: The Policy Press.

Department for Education and Skills (DfES) (2005) *Common Core of Skills and Knowledge for the Children's Workforce*. London: DfES.

UNCRC (1989) *United Nations Convention on the Rights of the Child*. Geneva: Office of the United Nations High Commissioner for Human Rights.

1

Ways of seeing: using the Mosaic approach to listen to young children's perspectives

Alison Clark

Overview

How can young children's perspectives become the focus for an exchange of meanings between children, practitioners, parents and researchers? In this chapter, Alison Clark explores how the Mosaic approach provides a way of facilitating such exchanges. Starting from the viewpoint of young children as competent meaning makers and explorers of their environment, the Mosaic approach brings together a range of methods for listening to young children about their lives. The chapter explores this approach in the context of involving young children in changes to an outdoor play area. Wider questions are raised about adult–child power relations and the status of young children.

[...]

The Mosaic approach was developed during a research study to include the 'voice of the child' in an evaluation of a multiagency network of services for children and families The process is explained in detail elsewhere (Clark and Moss, 2001; Clark, 2003). A second study, *Spaces to play,* adapted the Mosaic approach to listen to young children about their outdoor environment (Clark and Moss, 2005). This chapter will

Clark, A. (2005) 'Ways of seeing: using the Mosaic approach to listen to young children's perspectives', in Clark, A. and Moss, P. (eds) *Beyond Listening*, London: National Children's Bureau and Joseph Rowntree Foundation, pp. 29–48.

refer to case studies from this second study in order to illustrate the complex, multifaceted and sometimes surprising process of listening to young children.

The Mosaic approach was developed in the context of research. But subsequent discussions with practitioners through conferences and workshops have led to its use by early years practitioners. This illustrates how the distinctions between research and teaching can blur. The distinction is also questioned in Reggio Emilia[1]. Discussing the roles of the municipal schools of Reggio Emilia and a team of American researchers, one of the researchers comments that 'the actions of instruction, assessment, documentation and research come to contain each other. They cannot be pulled apart in any practical sense; they are a piece. No dichotomy between teaching and research remains' (Seidel, 2001, p. 333). While within the Reggio schools, they emphasise the teacher as researcher, engaged in a constant process of constructing knowledge about children and learning: 'That is why [Rinaldi says] I have written so often about the teacher as a researcher ... [I]t's not that we don't recognise your [academic] research, but we want our research, as teachers, to be recognised. And to recognise research as a way of thinking, of approaching life, of negotiating, of documenting' (Rinaldi, 2006, p. 192).

Starting points

Concepts of competence are a key feature of the theoretical perspectives that have influenced the development of the Mosaic approach (Clark, 2003). One source has been the active view of the child promoted through the sociology of (or for) childhood (Mayall, 2002). Children are seen not as passive objects in the research process or in society in general but as social actors who are 'beings *not* becomings' (Qvortrup et al, 1994, p. 2). This places an emphasis on exploring children's perceptions of their lives, their interests, priorities and concerns (for example, Christensen and James, 2000).

A second influence has been theoretical perspectives about 'voice' as explored in the field of international development, and through Participatory Appraisal techniques in particular (for example, Hart, 1997; Johnson et al, 1998). These methodologies have been devised in order to make visible the voices of the least powerful adult members of communities, as a catalyst for change. This begins with an expectation of competency: local people are presumed to have a unique body of knowledge about living in their community. The techniques developed include visual and verbal tools. Despite some criticism about the genuine benefits to communities of these approaches (Cooke and Kothari, 2001), the ideas remain of interest to debates about listening.

Third, and most importantly, the theoretical perspectives explored in the municipal preschools[2] of Reggio Emilia have inspired the Mosaic approach. These have hinged around the notion of the competent child and of the pedagogy of listening and the pedagogy of relationships. Malaguzzi, the first pedagogical director of the preschools, focused his work around the view of a rich active child (Edwards et al, 1998) in contrast to viewing children as passive and in need. This change in expectation seems key to understanding the critical thinking and creativity the children attending the schools have consistently demonstrated (for example, through 'The Hundred Languages of Children' touring exhibition).

These perspectives informed the framework for listening that led to the development of the Mosaic approach. The elements of this approach are:

- *multi-method*: recognises the different 'voices' or languages of children;
- *participatory*: treats children as experts and agents in their own lives;
- *reflexive*: includes children, practitioners and parents in reflecting on meanings, and addresses the question of interpretation;
- *adaptable*: can be applied in a variety of early childhood institutions;
- *focused on children's lived experiences*: can be used for a variety of purposes including looking at lives lived rather than knowledge gained or care received;
- *embedded into practice*: a framework for listening that has the potential to be both used as an evaluative tool and to become embedded into early years practice.

Developing the Mosaic approach

The development of the Mosaic approach has taken place through two studies and an international review. The aim of the original study was to develop methodologies for including the voices of young children in the evaluation of early childhood services. The name, the Mosaic approach, was chosen to represent the bringing together of different pieces or perspectives in order to create an image of children's worlds, both individual and collective. The Mosaic approach combines the traditional methodology of observation and interviewing with the introduction of participatory tools. Children use cameras to document 'what is important here'; they take the researcher on a tour and are in charge of how this is recorded, and make maps using their photographs and drawings. Each tool forms one piece of the mosaic. There were two stages in the original study. Stage One focused on gathering material using these varied methods. In Stage Two, these pieces of documentation were brought together with parents' and practitioners' comments to form the basis of dialogue, reflection and interpretation, a process involving children and adults.

An international review of listening to and consulting with young children (Clark et al, 2003), provided a wider perspective on current practice, policy and research developments. The review focused on young children's views and experiences of education and childcare. Young children's participation in the planning, designing and developing of indoor and outdoor spaces was one area identified for future research. The review ends with this remark: 'Young children will best be served by changes to policy and practice which remain alert to their differing perspectives and interests as well as their needs' (Clark et al, 2003, p. 48).

The review led to the outdoor environment being chosen as the focus for the second study, *Spaces to play* (see Clark and Moss, 2005 for a full account of this research). This set out to make young children's perspectives the starting point for change to the physical environment. The study was a collaboration with Learning through Landscapes, a charity based in England that works to promote the use, development and maintenance of school playgrounds. This was part of a wider initiative by Learning through Landscapes to work with a local authority and 15 early years settings to develop accessible, replicable, 'low tech' and affordable solutions to developing their outdoor environment.

The study was based in a preschool for three- to four-year-olds. Twenty-eight children were involved, together with parents and practitioners. The preschool included a number of children with special physical or behavioural needs, including several with speech and language difficulties. It served a mixed locality including an area of social disadvantage.

The manager, practitioners and a group of parents wanted to take more advantage of the small outdoor space available to the preschool. This included a soft play surface, a small area of decking, a muddy bank and 'boggy' ground where there was an underground spring. The space was surrounded by a high-security fence, which separated the preschool from a park.

Table 1.1 shows the range of methods used when working with the Mosaic approach in this study. Starting with observation, the researcher worked with groups of children to find out their views and experiences of this existing play space in order to form the basis for any changes to the provision. Children took photographs of the space and made these into individual books. Others took the researcher on a tour of the site, recording the event with a camera and by making an audiotape. Working in pairs or small groups, the children made maps of the outdoors using their photographs and drawings.

The researcher interviewed children individually or in groups outside or on the move. Four practitioners and four parents were also interviewed for their perspectives on how the children used the outdoor space.

A new tool was added to the Mosaic approach for this study: the magic carpet. This was designed to open up new conversations with the children about their wider environment. What local spaces were the children aware of, what were their experiences of these places and what additional insights could these give to the current and future uses of their outdoor space? A slide show was made using images of the local town centre, local landmarks and the park (all taken from a child's height). The researcher added images of her local park as well as images

Table 1.1 Methodological 'pieces' of the Mosaic approach

Method	Comments
Observation	Qualitative observation accounts
Child interviewing	A short structured interview conducted one to one or in a group
Photography and book making	Children's photographs of 'important things' and books
Tours	Tours of the site directed and recorded by the children
Map making	2D representations of the site using children's own photographs and drawings
Interviews	Informal interviews with practitioners and parents
Magic carpet	Slide show of familiar and different places

taken during the study of the preschool's outdoor space. The home corner was converted into a darkened tent and children sat on a 'magic carpet' to watch the slides in groups. Christine Parker (2001) had tried this idea after her trip to Reggio Emilia as a way of talking to young children about different places.

There were two stages in the original study: first gathering material, then reflection and interpretation. The practical focus of: the *Spaces to play* study led to the articulation of a third stage to the Mosaic approach, in order to emphasise the decision-making element of the listening:

- Stage One: gathering children's and adults' perspectives;
- Stage Two: discussing (reviewing) the material;
- Stage Three: deciding on areas of continuity and change.

Although this describes the gathering and reviewing as two distinct phases, in reality these stages become to some [extent] blurred. For example, practitioners began to review the children's use of the outdoor space when the researcher placed photographs from the observation in the cloakroom area during the first weeks of the study. Reflecting on meanings and reassessing understandings is implicit throughout the whole approach, but this second stage allows a concentrated period of reflection.

Reviews were held with children, practitioners and with Learning through Landscapes. The aim was to make the review as focused as possible on the children's perspectives. The researcher made a book of the children's comments and photographs to centre the review on the children. This was designed in story form with Barney the dog as the main character together with a cartoon caterpillar. Barney, a toy dog, had been introduced by the researcher and was used as an intermediary in many of the conversations with the children. Children discussed the book with the researcher and this piece of documentation became the focus of two sessions to review the material with practitioners during staff meetings.

The researcher and Learning through Landscapes' Development Officer reviewed the visual and verbal material. Each of the tools was discussed in turn in order to reveal emerging themes. Discussions centred around two main questions:

- Which places do children see as important in this outdoor space?
- How do the children use these places?

The results of these discussions were mapped out on a large plan. Similar ideas were linked and conflicting meanings noted. This led to Stage Three: deciding areas of continuity and change.

Four categories of place in the outdoor space were identified through the review process.

Places to keep: the caterpillar

A large plastic caterpillar tunnel was regularly placed outside. It had been apparent from the first visit that the children enjoyed this strange shape. However, the use of the different research tools had emphasised just how important this piece of equipment was for the children. This was a play space not to try to change.

Places to expand: the house

Observing the children revealed the house to be a key resource for them. The children confirmed this through their photographs, the tour and their interviews. Parents also mentioned the house as an important space in the preschool. However, the interviews with practitioners showed that the house was a source of tension. They felt it was too small. The review with children, practitioners and Learning through Landscapes recognised these opposing views and raised some possible solutions. The preschool has now turfed a new area for children to use to build their own temporary structures.

Places to change: the fence

The children's photographs and maps emphasised how the security fence dominated the outdoor space. Close observation revealed another dimension. The gaps in the security fence were wide enough for the children to see through. Solutions needed to bear in mind the importance of leaving these gaps, so the people spotting and dog watching could continue. The parents have designed and made paint and chalking boards in the shapes of caterpillars and butterflies to attach to the fence. This distracts from the steel but still gives room for children to spy through.

Places to add: new seating and digging areas

The research process identified places chat could be added to the outdoor space to enhance the children's enjoyment. The first was more places for adults and children to sit together. Parents have added seating so children and adults can now sit together by a fountain or on a brightly painted bench.

The second was places to dig. Observation had shown the popularity of the inside sandpit: one child included a photograph of the inside sand tray in his book of important outdoor spaces! The preschool has now added an outdoor sandpit.

The pedagogy of listening and the Mosaic approach

[...] Rinaldi [2005] describes the multifaceted nature of the pedagogy of listening, which has been one of the cornerstones of practice in Reggio Emilia. The elements include:

- internal listening or self-reflection;
- multiple listening or openness to other 'voices';
- visible listening, which includes documentation and interpretation.

Each of these features relate to the listening processes, which have emerged from working with the Mosaic approach. The following section will examine these elements in turn with the help of case studies taken from the *Spaces to play* study.

Internal listening

Internal listening acknowledges the importance of listening as a strategy for children to make sense of their world. Listening is, therefore, not just an avenue for other people receiving information but a reflective process for children to consider meanings, make discoveries and new connections and express understandings. [...] Rinaldi [2005] describes one of the first questions the educators in Reggio ask themselves: 'How can we help children find the meaning of what they do, what they encounter, what they experience?'.

The question at the centre of the Mosaic approach has been: 'What does it mean to be in this place?'. The question can be interpreted in many ways but at one level it is asking children: 'What does it mean *to be you* in this place now in this present moment, in the past and in the future?'. There is a physical dimension to this question. It has directed children to reflect on the specific environment of their early childhood institution, whether inside or outside. However, the place could be a city, a park or a bedroom. [...] The important ingredient here is that children are given the opportunity to reflect on their lived experiences rather than an abstract concept. This is in keeping with constructivist models of learning in which the environment is a key factor in children's search for meanings (MacNaughton, 2003).

It is a question with no 'wrong' answer. Children can explore their understandings without the fear that they have to second-guess the intended response. This helps to make the internal listening a creative process in which there is the freedom to express an idea for the first time or in a new way. This dimension of listening is in contrast to the understanding of listening as 'extracting the truth', a viewpoint encountered during the development phase of the Mosaic approach when discussions with some children's rights officers implied that children should be enabled to say what they thought, without the interference of adult interpretation. The Mosaic approach is more in keeping with the view that 'it's not so much a matter of eliciting children's preformed ideas and opinions, it's much more a question of enabling them to explore the ways in which they perceive the world and communicate their ideas in a way that is meaningful to them' (Tolfree and Woodhead, 1999, p. 21).

Developing a multimethod framework has helped the Mosaic approach to promote internal listening. This was one of the reasons for including more than one research tool. The greater the diversity of methods with different learning styles used then the more opportunity children will have to find new ways of thinking, of looking at the same question in a variety of ways. Taking photographs, leading a tour or watching slides provide different mirrors for reflecting on the central question: 'What does it mean to be in this place?'.

Some young children would be barred from answering this question if they were only offered one traditional research tool, such as interviewing. This might include children with limited verbal skills. The multimethod approach is necessary if as many children as possible are to be allowed opportunities for internal listening.

So using different methods is designed to be beneficial to the children who participate. It has another advantage for adults by enabling different understandings to be compared and for common themes and areas of disagreement to emerge. This theme of multiple listening will be examined later.

The following case study will illustrate different dimensions of internal listening through the use of the Mosaic approach in the *Spaces to play* study.

CASE STUDY

Internal listening and inclusive practice

Rees was four years old, and about to start school. He was an affectionate child who appeared to be thoroughly enjoying preschool.

However, his verbal language skills seemed limited, in the context of the preschool. He was, however, fascinated with cameras. He took great interest in the researcher's camera and was keen to volunteer to take his own photographs. He was delighted with the results and concentrated for an extended period on making a book of his images (see Table 1.2). Rees insisted on 'writing' his own captions. The practitioners were surprised when they saw his book as he had shown little interest in experimenting with writing in the preschool.

Rees's photographs were taken in a great hurry. They covered a range of subjects including other children and members of staff, but there was only one shot of just one other child. Rees did not appear to have a particular friend at the preschool.

He chose a photograph of the playhouse for the cover. The house was not the obvious focus of the photograph but Rees's naming of the photograph clarified its subject. This prioritising of the house tallied with the responses of many of the children who indicated the significance of this play space.

His choice of the pram was interesting. He filled the pram with pebbles from the edge of the play space before taking his photograph. This indicated his awareness of detail and interest in natural objects. Observation had revealed that Rees was one of the boys who enjoyed playing with the pram and pushchairs.

Rees was invited to take part in the child interview. This was designed to be as flexible as possible with some children choosing to answer the questions on the move. However, when the researcher started the interview Rees copied the questions but made no other response.

Table 1.2   Description of the photograph book compiled by Rees

Rees's photographs	Captions	Researcher's description
Cover	The house	Close-up of girl by the side of the climbing frame (house to the side)
Page One	The pram	Close-up of pram with pebbles
Page Two		Small barrier with cartoon figures
Page Three	[name of staff member]	Two members of staff on the edge of the play surface
Page Four		Close-up of girl, fence in background
Page Five		Close-up of inside of the house, boy in the corner

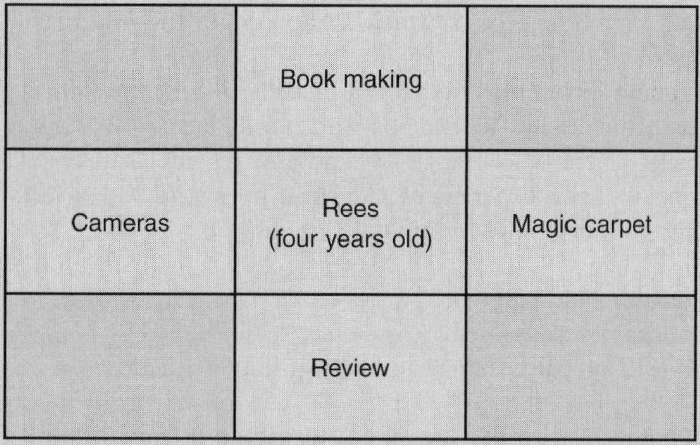

	Book making	
Cameras	Rees (four years old)	Magic carpet
	Review	

Figure 1.1   Diagram to show Rees's participation in the study

Rees enjoyed taking part in the magic carpet slide show. He was captivated by the mechanics of the slide projector and expressed his delight at learning how to operate the buttons to produce a new image: 'I've got that one', he explained. When a slide appeared showing Barney, he picked up the toy dog and matched him to the image on the screen.

Rees chose to hold Barney as he took part in the review of the study and listened attentively as the researcher read the book of the children's words.

Rees had been able to convey important features of his experience at the preschool. These included the pleasure of being with other children but with no particular friend, his liking for the playhouse and the pram and an interest in mechanical objects. Rees had conveyed these 'ways of seeing' through the Mosaic approach, using a range of languages and learning styles (see Figure 1.1). This in turn led to Rees displaying an interest in communicating through developing graphic skills as well as entering into more conversations with the researcher.

However, had the study relied solely on the interview he would have been another invisible child and Rees would not have had the opportunity to engage with the question 'what does it mean to be in this place?' and perhaps more importantly 'what does it mean *to be me* here?'. One concern is that Rees will not be offered the same range of languages and learning styles in order for him to make sense of the transition to school.

This section has focused on the links between the Mosaic approach and internal listening. The emphasis will now move to examine the role of multiple listening in the Mosaic approach.

Multiple listening

[...] Rinaldi [2005] describes multiple listening as the opportunities for practitioners, groups of children and individual children to listen to each other and to themselves. This conveys the multifaceted nature of listening: it is not limited to one exchange between two individuals but is a complex web of interactions, continually moving from the micro to the macro level. This is in keeping with an interpretivist model of learning (Carr, 2000; MacNaughton, 2003), which acknowledges the importance of multiple perspectives.

Multiple listening recognises the need to make space for the 'other', emphasising listening as an ethical issue. Researchers and practitioners who promote multiple listening acknowledge the importance of time and resources to enable children to reflect on their ideas and experiences with their peers and with adults. The Mosaic approach creates opportunities for multiple listening:

- with practitioners and parents;
- with the researcher and other professionals;
- through individual, paired, small and large group interaction.

The Mosaic approach acknowledges the importance of a framework for listening, which does not exclude the perspectives of practitioners and parents; a culture of listening should extend to all involved with an early childhood institution (Clark et al, 2003). There are opportunities in the Mosaic approach for listening to practitioners and parents through interviews and through the second-stage review process. Listening to practitioners' perspectives in the *Spaces to play* study focused on their general perceptions of children's interests and priorities outdoors, rather than focusing on individual children. It was important to interview the manager as well as a range of new and more experienced practitioners. This acknowledged that there was not a hierarchy of listening that privileged senior practitioners at the expense of the views of younger members of the team. The review process provided other opportunities for multiple listening with practitioners. The staff meetings led by the researcher to review the children's material provided a formal opportunity for reflecting on different perspectives (see the case study below).

Many parents have an in-depth understanding about the details of their children's lives that represent their current concerns, passions and interests. [...] Interviewing parents, in the Mosaic approach, is a formal way of acknowledging the different 'ways of seeing' parents can offer. One of the disadvantages of working within the confines of a research study is the limited time available for such listening. While the numbers of opportunities to listen to parents' perspectives have been small, the insights have added an important element to the overall picture of 'what does it mean to be in this place?'. Several parents, for example, mentioned that their children enjoyed having opportunities at home to dig and this reinforced the practitioners' desire to expand the outside digging spaces at the preschool.

What is the researcher's role in the Mosaic approach in relation to multiple listening? The researcher is at times 'architect': a creator of spaces and opportunities where multiple listening can take place and at other times more of an intermediary relaying different perspectives between different groups and individuals. An example of the 'architect's' role is the book-making activity. The children in the *Spaces to play* study worked on their books of their own photographs. This opened up discussions with other children who gathered round the table, watched with interest and discussed the images. Practitioners were interested in what was happening and talked to the children about the images they had taken.

The intermediary role relates to the researcher facilitating listening between the children and other professionals with an interest in children's perspectives. This is a way of extending the process of listening beyond the bounds of adults who are in daily contact with young children. This may involve professionals working in a range of disciplines, for example social workers (see Clark and Statham, 2005). However, in the *Spaces to play* study these conversations have been with professionals concerned with redesigning play spaces. The researcher led the review with the Development Officer from Learning through Landscapes, which focused on the documentation of the children's perspectives. Reflection on the role of documentation or visible listening will be discussed later.

The following case study will illustrate the opportunities for multiple listening for adults and children by focusing on the playhouse in the *Spaces to play* study.

📁 **CASE STUDY**

Multiple listening – the playhouse

The playhouse was a small wooden shed given to the preschool by a local business. It had a door, which opened out onto decking, and two windows, which had clear views of the play surface, the decking and muddy ground. There was a plastic barbeque set, table and chair in the house. Four children or more could squeeze inside. Observation showed that the house was in use most of the time. It was regularly used for group role play and at different times of day for a 'time out' space.

Interviewing children about the playhouse revealed more details about the imaginative play that took place in this space, but also the noise level. The following are excerpts from child interviews:

Researcher:	'Tell Barney about the house.'
Henry:	'This is where we play and talk and cook.'
Bob:	'… and sit on the chair. Henry and I can whistle.'
Milly, Alice and Bill:	'He can play doctors … There is a seat to sit on, and a table to sit on but you're not all allowed to sit on the tables.'
Julie:	'Play. We play doctors, we play vets. See this you put the chair there and you lay down on it [then Jessica stops to play vets with the 'dogs'].'
Jim:	'When it's night-time it gets dark. Bats are hanging on the window-sills. I love staying there, all there.'
Robert:	'I don't like playing doggies in here – it's too noisy too many in here some of the teachers gets one of them out.'

Children's photographs emphasised the importance of the house by the number of images, which showed close-ups of the inside of the house or games happening outside. Children took the researcher to the house on their tours and chose photographs and drawings of the house for the maps.

Listening to practitioners' views highlighted some differences of opinion between the children and the adults. The practitioners were aware of how popular the house was but they each had reservations about its current use:

Heather:	'Children use the house; they tend to use it as a buffer. Some think it's a wonderful activity in there … then it can become a fight, [they] lob things

(Continued)

(Continued)

Table 1.3 Multiple listening using the Mosaic approach to focus on the playhouse

Research tool	Playhouse
Observation	Children used the house as a social place. It is a space for being noisy, talking together and for imaginative play.
Cameras and book making	The house was in 12 of the 60 photographs taken by the children and chosen for inclusion in their books. These included inside and outside shots. This was a place in which to hide, talk to friends and watch what was happening outside.
Tours and map making	Children took inside and out photographs on their tours and included these photographs on their maps.
Practitioners' interviews	Practitioners recognised the children used the house for multiple purposes. Three out of the four practitioners interviewed named the house as the item they would like to give away.
Parents' interviews	One parent identified the house as somewhere she thought her child enjoyed [playing] outside at the preschool: 'Role play is a key thing here'. Another parent described how her child had a playhouse at home.
Child interviews	The children gave detailed descriptions of what happens in the house. Several identified the house as their favourite place while others recognised that it could get too noisy.

	out of the window or shout. But I don't think it's used successfully, even if three [children are there]. They like taking toys in but … the main problem is it's too small.'
Louise [the manager]:	'The house originally faced the shed. It was absolutely hopeless. They belted from one side to the other so we moved it round so it is part of the quiet area. It's all right for two children but it isn't big enough to put things in. We are trying to make use of it … I wish it was twice as large.'

While practitioners were aware of the popularity of the house, they were concerned that it had become overcrowded, encouraged aggressive play and as a result needed constant supervision.

Parents indicated the importance of role play in the house and how one child had his own playhouse at home, which acted as a retreat: 'He loves his little house. He puts pictures up in his house of trains' (Jim's mother).

As noted earlier, the multiple listening made the differences of opinion about the house visible (as summarised in Table 1.3). These different ways of seeing formed the basis for discussions, which led to the creation of a newly turfed outdoor space for the children to build temporary structures where they can 'sit, talk and cook'.

Visible listening

Moving on from examining the links between internal listening and multiple listening and the Mosaic approach, this next section will examine the role of documentation or visible listening. Rinaldi [2005] describes the process of documentation as visible listening through the construction of traces. She describes how these traces, through note taking, photographs, slides and other means, not only record the learning process but make the learning possible by bringing it into being – making it visible. There is a connection here with multiple listening because documentation allows listening to take place at different levels and with a range of individuals and groups. […] This section will focus on the role of documentation within the Mosaic approach, led by a researcher.

The Mosaic approach creates opportunities for visible listening by promoting platforms for communication at an individual, group, organisational and wider community level. Children's book making is one example of visible listening at an individual level. The process of map making is visible listening at a group level, which opens out into listening at an organisational level by displaying the maps for practitioners, parents, other children and visitors to engage with.

Further opportunities for promoting visible listening were added in the *Spaces to play* study during the review and evaluation phase. The review focused on a book made by the researcher, which was a collective record of the children's responses and photographs (in contrast to the children's own individual book making). This *Spaces to play* book provided a platform for communication at an organisational level with practitioners and children. These discussions led to the subsequent changes to the outdoor environment.

Documentation was a key part of the discussions with Learning through Landscapes. The chart assembled by the researcher provided the focus for discussions about the children's use of the play space, drawing on the researcher's notes, the children's photographs and maps and the interviews. This illustrates how the Mosaic approach provided a platform for communication with the wider community, in this instance with an external organisation interested in working with the preschool but not engaged with the children on a daily basis.

Traces of the study were drawn together for the evaluation. This collection of photographs acted as a platform for children to discuss together what they remembered and had enjoyed about participating in the study.

One question arises from this process: who is the documenter? The Mosaic approach enables both researcher and children to be co-documenters. The participatory methods have emphasised the children's role as documenters of their experiences of 'being in this place'. The researcher has in turn documented her observations and reflections on the process, which include both a visual and verbal contribution to the process. One possibility would be to extend the documenting role to the practitioners, thus strengthening the platform for communication and encouraging future visible listening.

The following case study illustrates how one of the tools, map making, provided several opportunities for visible listening at a number of levels, from the individual to the community.

📁   **CASE STUDY**

Visible listening – map making

Ruth and Jim (both three-year-olds) met with the researcher to make a map of the outdoor space. This was based on the photographs they had taken on a tour of the site and copies of photographs chosen for their books. The children added their own drawings to these images. The map became both an individual and a joint record.

Both children were keen to see themselves depicted on the map and Ruth added her name. Jim ensured that there were traces of his love of trains on the map, with close-ups of his mobilo train and of the shed 'where the toys sleep' Ruth chose the photograph she had asked Jim to take of the close-up of the pebbles, and Jim and Ruth added drawings of the trees, which surround the play space, beyond the fence.

During the map-making session, Gina, a visitor from Learning through Landscapes, came to see the study in action. The map provided the basis for 'visible listening' and one in which the children played a central role.

Ruth:	'This is a very pretty map.'
Researcher:	'It's a very pretty map. You know, it tells me such a lot about outside. Shall we see what Gina can see on our map? Gina, what do you think about our outside …'
Gina:	'I can see that Ruth and Jim have very special things outside. I can see that you chose the prams and the buggies, and I can even see you in the picture so 1 know you like playing with those things, maybe. And, Jim, your favourite thing … I think your favourite thing outside might be the train. Yes? And can we have a picture of you outside with the train?'
Ruth:	'What do I like?'
Gina:	'You tell me what you like. Do you like Heather [member of staff] with the climbing frame?'
Child:	'No, I like going on.'
Gina:	'Oh, you like going on the climbing frame'.

This extract illustrates how the map making enabled Ruth to take control of the meaning making. Ruth asked the visitor to interpret her priorities and then enjoyed contradicting this interpretation.

Practitioners, parents and other children became part of this meaning making and exchange through the display of the maps in the cloakroom area. Display space was at a premium in the crowded building but the cloakroom provided one space where parents and children visited daily. Visitors to the preschool were another group to interpret meanings.

This section has illustrated different aspects of listening facilitated through using the Mosaic approach. However, there is a considerable time commitment involved in such a way of working. While efforts were made to include every child in the sample in more than one of the tools, this was not always possible. A detailed impression was gained of some of the children's understandings of being 'in this place', but for others their part-time attendance or the limits imposed by the preschool's or the researcher's timetable meant that a more cursory impression was gained.

Discussion

This final section will raise three questions emerging from the development of the Mosaic approach in relation to listening to young children. These questions have arisen after many discussions with practitioners, researchers and policy makers arising from training days and conference talks:

- the question of power;
- the question of 'the hundred languages';
- the question of visibility.

A question of power

Communicating with young children involves questions of power: whether this is adults imparting 'knowledge' to children or children communicating their ideas to adults. Whichever way round the exchanges happen, there are differences in status, which are difficult to address. These differences are, perhaps, most noticeable when adults are working with young children. Many factors contribute to this imbalance, but expectations are one element. Adults' expectations of young children influence how they communicate with children and how they enable children to communicate with them. Viewing young children as weak, powerless and vulnerable may lead to high expectations of the adults' role in terms of protection and nurture but low expectations of children in terms of how they can express their perspectives, priorities and interests.

Viewing young children as competent communicators requires researchers and practitioners to readdress their relationship with young children and therefore their roles. The Mosaic approach includes an element of *role reversal* for the adults involved. Children participate as documenters, photographers, initiators and commentators. Children play an active role, taking the lead in which ideas, people, places and objects are given significance.

An early years trainer who had been using the Mosaic approach in a research study discussed the following example of these shifting relationships. The trainer was talking to a practitioner about a child. The practitioner commented: 'She listens if she thinks she is getting what she wants. She would like to reverse roles'. The trainer remarked that this was exactly what the Mosaic approach allowed this child to do. The roles were reversed and she was able to lead the process. She particularly enjoyed giving her commentary to the visiting adult on the tour.

This example perhaps highlights the contrast between the role that children are enabled to play in using the Mosaic approach and the day-to-day position that many young children experience where adults expect to take the lead, whether in delivering a curriculum or creating an appropriate environment. One of the challenges in allowing a shift in relationships is accepting the place of the unexpected. In research terms, this may mean being relaxed about the focus of the study and not worrying if children lead the study into unplanned areas. This occurred in the *Spaces to play* study where children sensibly blurred the distinction between indoor and outdoor play. One child, for example, took photographs of the toilets and the indoor sandpit and included them in his book about the outdoor space. The advantages of accepting a shifting in power are a release from the need for adults to 'know all the answers'. Listening in the ways discussed in this chapter releases adults from this burden.

A question of 'the hundred languages'

Language has an important part to play in debates about power. If exchanges between adults and young children are focused on the written and spoken word, then it is difficult for young children to have the 'upper hand'. The case studies have illustrated how children of different abilities can be supported in sharing their perspectives if they are given a range of multisensory means to communicate. These visual, spatial and physical tools should not be seen as a 'creative extra' but offer a challenge to the dominant learning styles that value verbal/linguistic skills at the expense of other means of communication. It is interesting to note that the verbal/linguistic skills are often the languages adults feel most secure in using. The Mosaic approach requires adults to relearn other languages they may be unfamiliar with using in an educational context or to acquire new skills.

Digital technology offers many possibilities for developing new shared languages between adults and children. Future studies using the Mosaic approach will incorporate young children's use of digital cameras. There was an initial reluctance on the part of the researcher to include digital cameras partly due to the cost, but also due to a lack of personal competency with the technology. It is a good example of how adults may need to take the leap to be co-learners with children in order to listen more effectively.

A question of visibility

Documentation is a powerful advocate for the competencies of young children. This was illustrated in 'The Hundred Languages of Children' exhibition, which was on tour in England in 2004. One of the opening panels showed photographs of two sculptures made from ready-made objects. One was by a two-year-old and one was by Picasso. This was not a glib gesture but a serious contribution to debates about the artistic process. The sculpture could have remained a personal delight for the child but not reached a wider audience. The documentation enabled this individual child's achievement to help a wider audience possibly rethink their views and expectations of young children.

The *Spaces to play* study has raised the possibility of using the Mosaic approach to create a platform for communication between young children, early years practitioners, architects and designers. The Focus in this study has been on outdoor spaces but this same approach could facilitate exchanges between adults and children concerning the built environment. A three-year study beginning in July 2004, called Living Space[3], uses the Mosaic approach in the planning, designing and changing of indoor and outdoor provision. Starting with a case study of a project to build a new early childhood centre, the researcher will work with three- and four-year-olds to document their experiences of their existing space in order to inform future spaces. The young children's photographs and maps will form a visible hub for conversations involving the whole school community about 'what we want it to mean to be in this place'. This platform for communication will then extend to architects who will feed these insights into the final building.

   This is one example where visible listening could have wide applications not only within a learning environment but also in altering the expectations and the role that young children can play in the wider community.

Conclusion

This chapter has examined a particular framework for listening to young children, which plays to children's strengths rather than to adults'. Listening using the Mosaic approach has been shown to encourage listening at different levels and in different contexts, whether this is children 'listening' to their own reflections, enabling multiple listening to take place between children, their peers and adults or creating possibilities for visible listening. This is an important endeavour to continue because 'unless adults are alert to children's own ways of seeing and understanding and representing the world to themselves, it is unlikely that the child will ever manage to identify with the school's and teacher's ways of seeing' (Brooker, 2002, p. 171).

Notes

1. Since 1981, the Reggio exhibition – 'The Hundred Languages of Children' – has travelled the world, accompanied by speakers from Reggio: in this time, it has had well over a hundred showings in more than 20 countries.
2. 'Preschools' (previously called 'playgroups') are a widespread form of early childhood service in the UK, mostly attended by three- and four-year-olds on a part-time basis (that is, most children attend three to five morning or afternoon sessions per week during term time). Community groups or other non-profit organisations mostly run them, and many today are funded by government, to deliver early education, following the Foundation Stage curriculum.
   [...]
3. Funded by the Bernard van Leer Foundation.

   [...]

References

Brooker, L. (2002) *Starting school: Young children's learning cultures*, Buckingham: Open University Press, p. 171.

Carr, M. (2000) 'Seeking children's perspectives about their learning', in A. Smith, N.J. Taylor and M. Gollop (eds) *Children's voices: Research, policy and practice*, Auckland, New Zealand: Pearson Education, pp. 37–55.

Christensen, P. and James, A. (eds) (2000) *Research with children*, London: Falmer Press.

Clark, A. (2003) 'The Mosaic approach and research with young children', in V. Lewis, M. Kellet, C. Robinson, S. Fruser and S. Ding (eds) *The reality of research with children and young people*, London: Sage Publications, pp. 157–61.

Clark, A. and Moss, P. (2001) *Listening to young children: The Mosaic approach*, London: National Children's Bureau for the Joseph Rowntree Foundation.

Clark, A. and Moss, P. (2005) *Spaces to play, More listening to young children using the Mosaic approach*, London: National Children's Bureau.

Clark, A. and Statham, J. (2005) 'Listening to young children: experts in their own lives', *Adoption and Fostering*, vol. 29, no.1, pp. 45–56.

Clark, A., McQuail, S. and Moss, P. (2003) *Exploring the field of listening to and consulting with young children*, Research Report 445, London: DfES.

Cooke, B. and Kothari, U. (eds) (2001) *Participation: The new tyranny?*, London: Zed Books.

Edwards, C., Gandini, L. and Foreman, G. (eds) (1998) *The hundred language of children: The Reggio Emilia approach to early childhood education* (2nd edn), New Jersey, NJ: Ablex Publishing Corporation.

Hart, R. (1997) *Children's participation*, London: Earthscan/UNICEF.

Johnson, V., Gordon, G., Pridmore, P. and Scott, P. (eds) (1998) *Stepping forward: Children and young people's participation in the development process*, London: Intermediate Technology.

MacNaughton, G. (2003) *Shaping early childhood: Learners, curriculum and contexts*, Maidenhead: Open University Press.

Mayall, B. (2002) *Towards a sociology for childhood: Thinking from children's lives*, Buckingham: Open University Press.

Parker, C. (2001) 'When is she coming back?', in L. Abbott and C. Nutbrown (eds) *Experiencing Reggio Emilia: Implications for pre-school provision*, Buckingham: Open University Press, pp. 80–92.

Qvortrup, J., Bardy, M., Sgritta, G. and Wintersberger, H. (eds) (1994) *Childhood matters*, Vienna: European Centre.

Rinaldi, C. (2005) 'Documentation and assessment: What is the relationship?', in A. Clark, A. Kjørholt and P. Moss (eds) *Beyond listening: Children's perspectives on early childhood services*, Bristol: Policy Press. pp. 17–28.

Rinaldi, C. (2006) *In dialogue with Reggio Emilia*, London: Routledge.

Seidel, S. (2001) 'Perspectives on research in education', in C. Giudici, C. Rinaldi and M. Krechevsky (eds) *Making learning visible: Children as individual and group learners*, Reggio Emilia: Reggio Children, pp. 330–5.

Tolfree, D. and Woodhead, M. (1999) 'Tapping a key resource', *Early Childhood Matters*, no. 91, pp. 19–23.

2

Is my city or community child-friendly?

Dora Giusti, Roger Hart and Selim Iltus

Overview

This chapter summarizes how the Child Friendly Cities (CPC) approach may effectively contribute to the fulfillment of the rights of children, and particularly of the youngest ones at the local level. It describes innovative action research supporting cities and communities to engage in a participatory process of self assessment and monitoring that may contribute to better policies and programmes for children.

[...]

For the first time in history, in 2007, the urban population in the world exceeded the number of rural inhabitants (Cities Alliance 2007). In 2002, it had already been estimated that approximately half of the world's children lived in urban areas, mostly in low- and middle-income countries in Africa, Asia and Latin America (UNICEF 2002). Besides providing a range of opportunities and services, urban settings expose children to risks that may hinder their healthy development. Pollution, contamination, and inadequate drainage and sanitation systems have significant impacts on the incidence of respiratory and gastrointestinal diseases that are among the most common causes of death amongst children under 5 years of age. Services like secure housing, caregiving facilities and access to education are often inadequate in low-income urban settlements. Traffic, noise and pollution may prevent children from playing and interacting. In

Guisti, D., Hart, R. and Iltus, S. (2009) 'Is my city or community child-friendly?', *Early Childhood Matters*, November, pp. 29–35.

some neighbourhoods, crime and violence may threaten children's safety and freedom (Bartlett 2002.)

In the early 1900s, in response to the high pace of urbanisation and the living conditions of many children in urban areas, cities of different sizes began to develop initiatives aimed at implementing the newly approved United Nations Convention on the Rights of the Child (UNCRC). The trend toward decentralised government contributed to interest in enhanced local responsibility. Policy development at the local level started to be seen as a key strategy for the realisation of children's rights. In 1996, UN Habitat and UNICEF launched the Child Friendly City Initiative (CFCI) at the UN Habitat Conference on Urban Settlements (Habitat 11). For the first time, the well-being of children was acknowledged as the ultimate indicator of a healthy habitat, a democratic society and good governance (CFC website).[1] The CFCI took the shape of a movement, gathering a wide range of partners, and flourished alongside other experiences such as UNESCO's Growing up in Cities and UN Habitat's Safer Cities. A CFC Secretariat was created in 2000 at the UNICEF Innocent Research Centre in Italy, to serve as a focal point, document practices, identify lessons learned and provide a common reference as well as guidance for the CFC Initiative and movement.

Towards the realisation of child rights at the local level

A CFC refers to a city or system of local governance that is committed to fulfilling the rights of children. Gradually, the term has been extended to include communities in different settings. In a CFC, the idea is that all children, without discrimination, participate in decision-making processes; have access to basic services, such as education, health and water and sanitation facilities; enjoy a pollution-free environment in which to play and interact; and are protected from abuse and exploitation. In a CFC child well-being is pursued by all policies and programmes. Becoming child-friendly is a process which unfolds through a number of steps, defined in the CFC Framework as nine key components (commonly known as building blocks): the development of a plan of action/strategy; the existence of a suitable legal framework; the establishment of a coordinating mechanism overseeing progress; the creation of a monitoring system; the production of a regular report on children; the promotion of awareness-raising efforts; the presence of an independent voice for children; and the allocation of resources for children. Child participation is the ninth element and is cross-cutting in a CFC (UNICEF IRC 2004).

Early childhood and Child Friendly Cities communities

Early childhood development entails integrated access to education, health and nutrition, as well as care-giving services so children may have a good start in life. At least 200 million children under five around the world are not fulfilling their potential for development because of poverty, malnutrition and the lack of stimulating, nurturing environments (UNICEF 2006). Policy development and good governance at local level help to realise the rights of the youngest children through integrated strategies for early childhood development, building on national level plans and policies.

Experiences of CFCs worldwide have proven the effectiveness of the approach for the realisation of children's rights. Indicators for health, schooling, and protection have showed significant improvements in cities and communities committed to becoming child-friendly. Impact on indicators, particularly relevant to children under five, is documented from the CFC experience implemented by UNICEF Brazil, in coordination with municipal authorities of the semi-arid region and the central government. The Seal of Approval rewards local governments for action supporting the fulfilment of children's rights and the Millennium Development Goals. Positive competition is triggered among cities to obtain the prestigious UNICEF Seal, which is granted upon good performance in the area of social impact, public policy management and civic participation. In 2005, municipalities participating in the 'Seal' competition were found to perform better than non-participating municipalities. During the two year timeframe of evaluation, the infant mortality rate in towns registered in the competition had decreased by 16.4% compared to 12.1% in non-participating towns; and late neonatal mortality had decreased by 8.5% against 1.6%. In addition, malnutrition rates among children aged 0–2 declined from 9.2% to 6.8% and access to early childhood education went up from 56 out of 100 children aged 0–6 to 63.5 out of 100 children (Buvinich et al. 2008). Evidence from the Philippines concluded that in child friendly *barangays* (local administrations), children and women had greater access to basic services than in other neighbourhoods (Racelis and Aguirrre 2005).

Central to the CFC approach to planning is the perspective of children. This is difficult with children except when redesigning small-scale spaces with which they are already familiar. But the parents of these children can contribute greatly to planning for this age group and their perspective is also usually missing.

A renewed vision for research on CFC and child rights

The CFC Secretariat promotes knowledge brokering on the issue by documenting good practices and a wide range of initiatives, identifying and disseminating lessons learned. One of the products of these efforts is the CFC Framework, which reflects the richness of a wide variety of initiatives in different regions and settings (UNICEF IRC 2004). The framework has been further developed based on experiences in journal articles and other publications, and websites. Insights into child participation in city planning, the relationship between children and the environment and other topics have been identified and shared (Children Youth and Environments website).[2]

Analysis of a variety of experiences has led to a focus on existing monitoring mechanisms used within CFC initiatives. Monitoring is a key component of certification systems established as part of CFC strategies in different countries. A certification approach grants the 'child friendly' recognition/label to cities and communities that have met minimum requirements, based on a city or community's performance attained in relation to pre-defined indicators of child well-being. These are generally grouped into domains that correspond to specific rights: health, education, play and recreation, protection and safety, environment, participation, etc. Other components include rights awareness, policy management, cooperation, etc. In France, Spain and Switzerland, tools such as questionnaires, quizzes and scoreboards, containing the set of well-being indicators, have been developed by evaluation committees to guide the monitoring and assessment process. Although the monitoring process involves a cross-sectoral effort by the city's administration to complete the questionnaire or collect the data according to the indicators, very little room is left for the city and the community to engage in a process of self-criticism and analysis. In addition, it mainly consists of top down assessment methods, with very little involvement of parents and children. Finally these processes tend to rely on quantitative indicators, taken from available statistics, which may be limited at the small area level and are usually applicable to the nationwide context without being representative of local settings.

Through a review of current tools and methods used, practitioners and researchers have acknowledged the need for instruments that enable communities and cities to assess their child friendliness and to monitor their progress in improving the situation of children. The needed tools should allow for a participatory approach involving children, including the most marginalised and excluded ones. In addition, experts agreed that a universal set of template tools was required; these would have to be easily adapted to different settings (UNICEF IRC/CERG 2008).

To help bridge these gaps, Child Friendly Cities and Communities Research was initiated in mid-2008 by UNICEF IRC, in partnership with Childwatch International, a network of research institutions focusing on children's rights, and with other offices of UNICEF, including the Adolescent Development and Participation Section in UNICEF Headquarters (IRC/Childwatch-CERG 2009). The research is being coordinated jointly by IRC and the Children's Environments Research Group (CERG)[3] based at the City University of New York, and with the support of the Bernard van Leer Foundation and other partners (Childwatch, UNICEF IRC and CFC websites).[4]

The goal of the research initiative is to improve the conditions of children living in cities and communities of different types, by increasing capacity of cities and communities to monitor and assess the situation of children and the level of progress towards realisation of children's rights. In terms of direct objectives, the research will sensitise stakeholders and communities to children's rights; generate a breadth of data on children in selected cities/communities, particularly qualitative data often neglected by official sources; and engage the community, including children, in the assessment and monitoring of performance. Concretely, universal template tools assessing the fulfilment of children's rights and the relevance of the governance structures and services, will be produced for adaptation to local settings.

The research process scheduled to end in the second half of 2010, started with a review of existing monitoring and assessment tools to ensure an innovative product. The tools were designed in a draft format and developed with input from a consultative group of experts. The tools were adjusted during a pilot phase to the specific needs of two countries (Brazil and The Philippines) before being tested to enrich the templates.

Selected cities and communities in 11 countries were invited to participate in the research after the completion of the pilot phase. The countries represent a variety of contexts in terms of location, setting and size: Brazil, the Dominican Republic, France, India, Italy, Jordan, The Philippines, Russia, South Africa, Spain and Sudan.

Based on the use of the assessment tools the aim is to generate: (a) a toolkit including a set of indicators, for communities and cities to self assess their degree of child friendliness, and a related guidebook; (b) a description of mechanisms used by local governance structures in the self-assessment process; and (c) data on the situation of children, based on a range of children's rights indicators, and the availability and quality of services in participating cities.

Enhancing local governments' capacities

This research relies on a highly participatory approach that is promoted through:

- Child-friendly community assessment tools that measure the degree of a city's or community's child-friendliness, by measuring the degree of fulfilment of children's rights, through the perspective of parents, professionals and children themselves.
- Governance assessment tools for assessing the capacity of local government structures and processes to promote the fulfilment of children's rights, by involving city officials, parents and children.

Through the instruments, detailed qualitative local data on the conditions of children in the selected cities and communities may be collected to supplement the existing quantitative statistics from censuses and surveys that are available to local governments. In this way, good governance with regard to the fulfilment of children's rights may be fostered through civic participation as well as through a better understanding of the real needs of children, which may shape planning and policy development.

The CFC assessment tools are simple and may be used by a community facilitator with limited experience. The approach aims to ensure that the perspectives of all children, including the marginalised and vulnerable, are taken into account without discrimination. The tool consists of a chart listing key indicators of a community's fulfilment of children's rights such as 'children can walk to a safe place in which to play' which children then fill in using graphic symbols. These can be completed by children aged 8 to 18 as well as by parents. It is important to highlight that the involvement of parents is also an innovative aspect in CFC-related monitoring tools. Their inclusion is particularly important to ensure that the rights of younger children are taken into account. The overall community is also invited to participate in the review and discussion of the data.

The tools, designed from a rights-based perspective, attempt to reflect the full breadth of the UNCRC by focusing on its four key domains: survival, development, protection and participation.

The community tools assess the degree of fulfilment of children's rights, looking into equal access to basic services (health, water and sanitation, education, social services), the right to protection, to leisure, to live in a family, to have the highest standards of living, and to participate in community life. More specifically, they aim to collect data on the following key aspects:

- Families and parenting – life in the biological family (safety, resources, parents' time for care, child rights knowledge) and existence of alternative care options;
- Home environments – adequate living conditions at home (water, sanitation, electricity, garbage disposal), secure housing, and a safe environment;
- Health and social services – including specialised, mental and emergency services;
- Early childhood and educational services – equal access to primary and preschool, including for children with disabilities, and excluded and minority children; the school environment and facilities in terms of health, quality of education, safety, protection, nutrition, recreation, respect for cultures and involvement of parents;
- Safety and protection – both safety from hazards, such as pollution and traffic, and protection from abuse and exploitation;
- Work, play and recreation – play facilities and spaces, as well as time dedicated to work and play;
- Community solidarity and social inclusion – community buffers, cultural life, opportunities for participation in the everyday community's life;
- Community governance – children's participation in planning, decision-making and implementation of initiatives.

The second participatory set of tools, on governance, complements the community assessment tools and is designed to measure the adequacy of structures and processes of local governance for children. The governance tools engage municipal officers, NGO staff, parents and city and community officers in assessing the availability and relevance of structures and processes for responding to and interacting with children. These tools are designed to maximise participation of community members, parents and city officials.

Together, these instruments are intended to serve as a general, valid universal framework that may be modified and made relevant to cities in different cultures. They will be applicable beyond the scope of the IRC/Childwatch-CERG (2009) research and will contribute to a new way of building 'child friendliness'.

Conclusions and the way forward

Child-friendly cities and communities can contribute to the realisation of children's rights at the local level. Locally collected data shows the impact of the CFC approach on the realisation of children's rights. A key challenge is assessing and monitoring the progress and performance of CFCs. As has been discussed, a new research initiative, through a partnership between UNICEF IRC and Childwatch International, aims to bridge a gap in the tools available for assessment and monitoring. It further aims to increase the capacity of cities and communities to self-assess their degree of child friendliness. Central to this process is the child rights approach, with the provisions of the UNCRC as the benchmark for assessing child friendliness. Also key is a bottom-up approach that fosters civic participation.

The research will allow data to be gathered on the real needs of children in selected cities and communities and will trigger the involvement of children and parents, as well as government and NGO professionals in the process. However, expectations for the research go beyond this. Once refined and enriched by the research process, the assessment tools will be available for all cities and communities around the globe interested in improving the living conditions of children. This may be the beginning of a new generation of child-friendly cities and communities.

CASE STUDIES

The Philippines

In the Philippines, the CFC approach promoted by the Child Friendly Movement – a nationwide intersectorial partnership – has brought the national plan of action on children, the *National Framework for Plan Development for Children – Agenda 21*, down to the local level. Child-friendly municipalities have to fulfil 24 goals and indicators in the areas of survival, development, protection and participation in addition to ensuring four 'gifts' to the children : a local development plan, an investment plan, a code on children and a state of the children report. Those cities that have promoted the four 'gifts' and have performed well in terms of the indicators are granted the child-friendly label through a 'Presidential Award'. Cities of different sizes, including urban communities, may participate in the competition. Thanks to the Award, an increasing number of municipalities have ensured the four 'gifts' are delivered. Furthermore, a 2006 UNICEF study showed that CFCs provide more attention to excluded groups compared to non-child-friendly municipalities.

Source: UNICEF IRC and Institute of Philippine Culture 2005

The Dominican Republic

The Child Friendly Municipalities initiative envisions a process of self-declaration by municipalities committed to becoming child-friendly. Essential requirements for the CFC label are: the establishment of legal mechanisms; the formulation of a municipal programme on children's rights; the development of a strategic plan of action on municipal development; the creation of mechanisms for effective participation of citizens and particularly children; the establishment of a specific department or unit dealing with child protection; and a minimum investment of 5% on children. So far, 115

(Continued)

(Continued)

municipal settings (94 municipalities and 21 municipal districts) have joined the initiative and have declared themselves child-friendly.

The strengths of the initiative were highlighted by a 2006 assessment and include the establishment of governance structures recognising children's rights, the role of youth participation councils, capacity building efforts and participatory planning processes as well as participatory budget revisions.

Source: www.unicef.org/republicadominicana

The Greater Amman Municipality

The Greater Amman Municipality started implementing a CFC approach in 2004 when, based on the Mayor's recommendation, the Municipal Council established an Executive Agency for a CFC that oversees the implementation of programmes for children and ensures intersectorial coordination at the local level. In the following year, a policy document – Policy and Priorities for Children – was developed through a participatory approach with the aim of making Amman child-friendly. The strategy outlined actions to enhance the quality of life for children, especially excluded ones, particularly by focusing on the areas of health, protection and safety, culture, informal education/school drop-outs and child-built environments. Child participation has been one of the strengths of the initiative, culminating with the election of four municipal councils for children, a process that has mobilised approximately 29,000 children.

Source: Speech by UNICEF Jordan at the Consultation on Child Friendly Cities Initiative: Proposed research and future directions for UNICEF, Geneva 21–23 January 2008.

Notes

1. Child Friendly Cities Website, www.childfriendlycities.org
2. Children Youth and Environment, www.colorado.edu/journals/cye
3. Children's Environments Research Group, http://web.gc.cuny.edu/CHE/CERG/about_cerg/index.htm
4. Childwatch International, www.childwatch.uio.no.,UNICEF IRC, www.unicef-irc.org

References

Bartlett, S. (2002). *Urban Children and the Physical Environment*. Paper presented at the Children in the City conference, Amman, 11–13 December.

Buvinich, M., Carvalho, M., Diechtiareff, B. and Gonçalves, L. (2008). *Achieving Policy Change: The UNICEF Municipal Seal of Approval in the Brazilian Semi-Arid Region as a Strategy to Reduce Poverty and Inequality*. Paper presented at the Fourth International Conference: Rethinking Poverty: Making Policies that Work for Children, New York, 21–23 April.

Cities Alliance. (2007). *Liveable Cities: The Benefits of Urban Environmental Planning*. Washington, DC: The Cities Alliance, United Nations Environment Programme (UNEP), and ICLEI – Local Governments for Sustainability.

IRC/Childwatch-CERG. (2009). *Child Friendly Cities and Communities Assessment Tools.* Draft, August.

Racelis, M. and Aguirre, A.D.M. (2005). *Child Rights for Urban Children in Child-friendly Philippines Cities: Views from the Community.* Children, Youth and Environment 15(2): 117–137.

UNICEF. (2002). *Poverty and Exclusion Amongst Urban Children.* Innocenti Digest No. 10. Florence: UNICEF.

UNICEF. (2006). *Programming Experiences in Early Childhood Development.* New York: UNICEF.

UNICEF IRC. (2004). *Building Child Friendly Cities: a Framework for Action.* Florence: UNICEF.

UNICEF IRC and CERG. (2008). *The Child Friendly City Research Program: Summary and Update.* Geneva, December. http://www.childfriendlycities.org/pdf/hague_report_summary_final.pdf

UNICEF IRC and Institute of Philippine Culture. (2005). *Making Philippine Cities Child Friendly: Voices of Children in Poor Communities.* Innocenti Insight.

3

Horses in the sandpit: photography, prolonged involvement and 'stepping back' as strategies for listening to children's voices

Alison Stephenson

Overview

What factors contribute to gathering deeper understandings of children's perspectives? In this chapter, Alison Stephenson begins by describing the use of photographs taken by adults and children to support young children (aged from 2 to 4 years) in exploring their experiences of an early childhood centre in New Zealand. She identifies the importance of the prolonged and sustained data-collection period and the process of 'stepping back' from the research agenda which allowed other, less overt messages to be heard.

[…]

Stephenson, A. (2009) 'Horses in the sandpit: photography, prolonged involvement and "stepping back" as strategies for listening to children's voices', *Early Child Development and Care*, vol. 179, no. 2, pp. 131–41.

Introduction

The problem of finding ways that will allow young children to share their thoughts about their lives is well documented (Clark, 2007; Formosinho and Araujo, 2006; Graue and Walsh, 1998; Lewis, 2001; MacNaughton et al., 2001; Te One, 2007), This [chapter] reports on strategies that emerged from research with children who were between two and four years old in a New Zealand early childhood education centre. The use of photographs and photography, the prolonged period of data collection and the intellectual process of 'stepping back' from the data to listen for other possible meanings were all found to contribute significantly to hearing unanticipated and more nuanced aspects of children's responses.

The context for the use of these strategies was a wider ethnographic study which explored the scope of curriculum as children experienced it, and enacted it, within an early childhood education centre. The genesis for this research lay in the breadth of the definition of curriculum used in the New Zealand early childhood curriculum, *Te Whāriki*. In that document 'curriculum' is used to describe: '… the sum total of the experiences, activities, and events, whether direct or indirect, which occur within an environment designed to foster children's learning and development (Ministry of Education, 1996, p. 10).

For teachers and teacher educators, the focus is primarily on the 'direct' aspects; on the content arising from responding to children's interests and planning for children; and on teaching strategies. However, as the definition acknowledges, alongside these 'direct' experiences, children have other significant experiences of which adults may be only marginally aware. The focus of the wider research was to explore these less overt aspects of curriculum in one early childhood centre. The centre selected, which was rated very favourably by the government review agency, was an all-day centre open from 8 am to 6 pm, which catered for children from zero to five years. The data were gathered during 50 visits, spread over a period of five months beginning in mid-winter and continuing through to summer. In the first weeks, visits were made four or five days a week but later visits were less frequent. Data-gathering covered all periods of the day, with visits lasting on average 2–3 hours and the longest visit 9.5 hours.

Foregrounding the children's voices

[…]

The re-conceptualisation of children as powerful social agents provides a challenge not only for educators, but also for researchers. As Woodrow (1999) points out, the image of the 'child as innocent' has been implicit in much of early childhood research. In recognition of this repositioning, for more than a decade there has been a ground swell of research which has experimented with a variety of approaches to include the perspectives of children (e.g. Christensen and James, 2000; Einarsdottir, 2005, 2007;

Graue and Walsh, 1998). However, in many research studies, the relationship between researcher and child is relatively brief. The work of Paley (e.g. 1984, 1986, 1995) and Gallas (1994, 1998) showed how the depth and length of relationship between teacher and their group of children allowed for more sensitive and nuanced understanding of what children might be conveying. It seemed likely that this was particularly important when working with very young children, and so the commitment was made to spend a prolonged time in the setting in this research.

[...]

Strategies explored and developed

Many children were keen to spend time with an adult who wanted to listen to them, and so the challenge was to search for ways of talking with them that they would find engaging, and that would allow them to articulate their ideas. Experience in this study reinforced the effectiveness of using a range of approaches (Clark, 2004, 2007; Clark and Moss, 2001); the approaches that used photographs and/or photography seemed particularly appealing to the children.

While the use of disposable cameras was considered, the expense of providing sufficient cameras capable of indoor/outdoor use for all the children who wanted to be involved, and the necessary restrictions on the number of photographs to be taken were factors that contributed to the decision to use a digital camera. Children enjoyed the immediacy of seeing the image using the 'quick view', and often this seemed sufficient gratification. However, printed versions of many of the photographs were given to children to keep and this provided a chance to revisit their experience.

There were four ways in which photographs and photography evolved to form a significant part of the data collection with the children: identifying photographs of places in the centre, using photographs to explore activities children liked and disliked, taking photographs of favourite places, and taking photographs of pages in their learning portfolios. Before these strategies were introduced, the research began with the camera being used to take photographs of the indoor/outdoor environments. This procedure had the advantage that children were familiar with me and the presence of the camera, before it was used with and by them.

The first strategy consisted of an A4 folder of 11 of my colour photographs of different rooms and spaces in the centre environment and this was used as a focus for conversations with children. The images included indoor and outdoor play spaces, as well as adult spaces like the office and the kitchen. Even quite young children with little language were drawn into this activity, and seemed to enjoy discovering familiar places. While the initial intention was to find the names children used for places in the centre, children's conversations around these photographs revealed more than this.

The labels children gave to places indicated their concept of the purpose of that space. Some rooms had a widely accepted name – for example, the term 'quiet room' was used frequently by adults, and most children also used this name. However, another of the side rooms, where the dress-ups and the family play equipment were kept, was less frequently named. Jeff, aged two, called it 'the girl room', but then after thought amended this to 'the girl room and the boy room and the pretend babies'. He knew the laundry as 'where they make the dough'. The washing and drying of the laundry in this environment was an adult task with which he had no connection.

One of the things that became apparent was that many children could not identify the adult spaces in the centre. The kitchen opened off the main play room, and there was a door with a plastic weave pattern through which children could and did look, and yet not all children recognised it as a photo of the kitchen. Fewer recognised the picture of the office as familiar and even fewer could name it. Yet, children passed its glass-panelled door every day as they arrived and departed. Children's inability to recognise the adult spaces also suggested they were likely to be unfamiliar with the tasks adults carried out in those spaces. [...]

The second strategy, based on descriptions by Cremin and Slatter (2004) and Wiltz and Klein (2001), focused on a set of photographs of activities and events within the centre (such as water play, dough play, collage, mat-time, rest-time and meals) which was used to initiate conversations with children and as a focus for exploring what aspects of centre life they liked, or disliked. As with all the strategies, the process evolved. At first these were a set of 30 photos which needed to be spread out, and children were given a limited number of coloured dots (yellow and black) to stick on the photographs of activities they liked or disliked. Children inevitably requested more dots, and the act of sticking on dots often seemed to surpass any decision-making about likes and dislikes. Spreading out this number of photographs also proved cumbersome, and so the experience was converted into a single chart of small photos, and coloured counters – 20 with happy faces, and five with sad faces (Ring, 2000) so that children were required to make some choices. New photographs were included to cover additional experiences at this stage. While the choices children made were interesting, the fact that children who chose to repeat the task invariably altered their choices suggested the fragility of basing assumptions on quantitative data gathered in a single episode. Often it was the shared interaction with the child as they engaged in the process that provided the most significant insights. The responses of Cassidy (aged 2) showed, for example, the irrelevance to him of the conventional categories of activities, and he had to add a plastic horse in order to show me what he liked to do at the centre. We will return to Cassidy and his horse later.

The third strategy involved children being invited to photograph their favourite places, the places they liked around the centre, as a form of the photo tour developed by Clark and Moss (2001) and subsequently used by others (Cremin and Slatter, 2004; DeMarie and Ethridge, 2006; Einarsdottir, 2005, 2007; Greenfield, 2004). Over the months of data collection, any child who expressed an interest had a chance to take a photo tour. Children were given the option of taking the photographs, or of being in the photos in places and with people that they nominated. The youngest children who did this were 2-year-olds, and they all chose to have themselves in the photographs. Einarsdottir (2007) reports using this strategy with children as young as 2, but does not describe the response of those youngest children. Returning prints of the child's photographs on my next visit provided a further chance for conversation, as Einarsdottir (2005, 2007) and Clark and Moss (2001) found, but here it often seemed that the tour and the conversation that took place during it provided the richest data. Interestingly, almost every child chose to take photographs outside initially, and many only moved inside when it was suggested to them that there might be inside places as well. Within the centre building, the child's own locker where their bag and spare clothes were kept was very often selected as a special place.

In the fourth strategy, photographs were used when children were showing me their learning portfolios. Portfolios are records of children's learning recorded in words and photographs and with pieces of children's work included. They are compiled during the child's time in the centre, and given to the family when the child leaves. Each teacher in the centre had responsibility for maintaining the portfolios for a small group of children. Some of the older children who had been at the centre since they were babies had three folders. Looking at learning portfolios with children was envisaged as a useful context for engaging in conversations about learning. The strategy of photographing favourite pages in the portfolios was not one described in the research literature and was introduced because the first children approached were not particularly keen to spend time looking at their portfolios. Once the option of taking photographs was introduced, their reluctance evaporated. As with the earlier strategies, while the children's choice of pages to photograph was interesting, the wider interaction of sharing the portfolio provided even more valuable insights. What children particularly valued were the photographs of others, of those who had left, and of themselves when they were younger – the portfolios provided a wonderful record of their time as a part of this evolving community of children and teachers in the centre. More surprising was how rarely children commented on what they might have been learning, although this was typically the focus of the teacher-written captions. [...] Their comments, the pages they chose to focus on, and their fascination with the photographs of themselves and others all suggested that for them the value of the portfolios was as a pictorial record of their time as part of the centre community.

In addition to these four specific strategies, there were a number of other ways in which photographs contributed to the data collection. For example, the camera was used to record settings as an adjunct to field notes and/or audio-taping of children's play. [...] [A]t times there were challenges in using a camera in research with young children. Children perceived it as very desirable, and when one was using it, there were usually a number more who wanted to have a turn. While I tried to avoid allocating each child a specific number of shots, at times children did need to be encouraged to pass it on. Once the camera was in use by children, this tended to drive the research agenda for that day and so there were days when I deliberately did not bring the camera to the centre. On balance, however, the camera was an attractive tool to a wide range of children and it provided an avenue through which they could express their thoughts in a way that they enjoyed.

A prolonged period of data collection

However, as well as reaffirming the value of photography in research with young children, it seemed there were two other, and perhaps more significant lessons to learn from this research experience. The first was the value of a lengthy period of data collection. Being in the centre for several hours a day, often for four or even five days a week, meant there was the opportunity for prolonged and sustained interactions with children. Some children approached me readily on my first visit, but others were initially wary and chose to approach me in their own time. During the first two weeks I was aware of a small fair-haired boy named Cassidy who circled around me but never came too close; later he was to become one of the keenest participants. The prolonged period also meant that there was the chance for all the children to engage in the research process, rather than a small pre-selected group, which broadened my understanding of the complexity of the centre community. It also resolved equity issues which have troubled me as a researcher, when only a small proportion of children are offered the chance to be part of what may be perceived to be a novel and interesting experience.

Being in the context for a long time meant there were opportunities for children to choose to engage in strategies, and to repeat them again and again over the months. While only the photographic strategies have been described above, other strategies used included unfinished story books (an approach mentioned by Carr [2000]) and a picture questionnaire (from a suggestion by Wiltz and Klein [2001]). As Clark and Moss (2001) had found with the 'mosaic approach', using a range of strategies was effective because not only did it allow for triangulation of data, but it meant that children could select the activity they preferred and so, to use their image, for each child a quite different mosaic pattern might be created. Here, Cassidy (aged 2) repeated the activity with the stickers/counters and photographs several times on different occasions but was less keen on taking photographs, while Sina (aged 4) was always keen to participate in any research activity where she could use the camera. As children became familiar with me, they would ask 'Have you brought your book [the photographs]?', 'Have you got the camera?'. And whenever a child repeated a process, there were inevitably changes in their responses which I believe contributed additional depth and complexity to their original response. It helped me to recognise just how much the immediate 'here' and 'now' influences a child's (or an adult's) response. I became increasingly aware of how precarious it might be to base conclusions on single research interactions.

There were also implications in what children said and did that would have been missed if relationships had not been built up over this extended time in the setting. It was only with this deeper contextual knowledge that possible implications of what the children said were recognised. Cassidy said, while he was putting stickers on photographs of centre activities, that he hated 'monsters', and got up to look out the window. Having seen him the day before run to a teacher saying 'there's a monster' when an older child came towards him dressed in a cape and a mask, suggested what he might be describing. However, I was also aware of just how many nuances I must still have missed. Even with five months on site, I was always aware that the data captured only a tiny portion of life at the centre. Even in the hours when I was present, children and teachers were often spread through several rooms and across the playground.

Finally, my prolonged presence helped to resolve another ethical issue that has troubled me – how to reciprocate children for their involvement in my process. Intellectually, I could argue that my research was focused on increasing understanding of young children's experience in early childhood education, and therefore of potential benefit to all New Zealand children. Emotionally, I was aware there was no reciprocity for these children here and now. Having the luxury of being in the centre for a prolonged period meant that I felt able to respond to requests to 'play with me', and I made a point of visibly setting aside my audio-visual equipment and my notebook (although I confess to never turning off my brain) at some stage every time I visited the centre. This seemed the most authentic act of reciprocity that I could offer them.

Learning to 'step back' from the interaction and the data

The second lesson that was learnt from this research experience, and one which arose from the prolonged involvement, was the importance of learning to 'step back' from the data, which is aligned to Clark and Moss's (2001) emphasis on reflexive listening. While the photographs the children took provided interesting data, 'stepping back' and considering the interactions with a wider lens allowed other, more nuanced, messages to be heard. At times, the message conveyed by the children's responses was relatively straightforward – the fact that almost every child chose to take the camera outside to photograph their favourite places seemed significant. However, very early the importance of slowing down and thinking outside the framework of the research activities was recognised. I came to call this mental process 'stepping back'. Being prepared to do this, and to relinquish the narrow framework of the research agenda, allowed other messages to be 'heard', messages that were not answers to the questions that were being asked. For example, children were very keen to use the camera, indeed their enthusiasm often seemed to take priority over thoughtful selection of favourite places. Was this just the novelty of the camera? Or was it partly that they were able to be in charge of what they perceived to be an 'adult' tool? I recognised more clearly how rare it was for a child to have access to an 'adult' tool in this environment which was filled with equipment that was defined as 'for children'. Other 'adult' equipment – the computers, the photocopier, the microwave, the oven and the dishwasher – were all in the adult-only spaces. Only the tape recorder was kept in the playroom, but it was up on a shelf and defined as being for adult use only. Stepping back in this instance reaffirmed how strong the demarcation was between children and adults.

To return to Cassidy and his horse – as the episode below will show, stepping back from my agenda allowed me to hear what he said within the wider context of the interactions we had already shared, which in turn led to my own assumptions being challenged. When Cassidy first did the activity in which he chose his favourite places, I was still using the photographs and the coloured stickers. Cassidy, looking at the top picture of the books, with the soft toys stowed in open shelves underneath, said:

Cassidy: The animals went out of the way, the animals went out, went out of the way.

1 had seen this as a photograph of the books; he focused on the animals. I took the rubber band off the photographs and we began to go through them. He asked:

Cassidy: Where's me?
Researcher: Where's you? These ones, most of them, haven't got any people in.

I mentally noted this as a reminder of the significance of seeing yourself, and began to spread them out so he could see them, describing them as I did to engage him in the process.

Researcher: That one's all the books – and this one's in here isn't it – all the dress-ups.
Cassidy: I'm trying to find the ... (long pause, looking through them as I am spreading them out on the floor).

I commented on the lack of people in them, as he continued to search through them. I wondered if he might be looking for a horse, and pointed out what might be a plastic horse in one of the photographs.

Researcher: ... Oh look, is that a horse?
Cassidy: No (answers very quickly – he can tell at a glance whether the little animal in the photo is, or is not a horse).

I realised that I had not included a single photograph of a horse, and so we agreed he [could] put the little plastic horse which he had in his pocket on a photograph. He chose to lay it on the photo of the sandpit, and in response to the suggestion that he put a sticker on something he liked doing at the centre, he pressed one down beside the horse. Over the next few minutes he stuck on four more stickers:

Researcher: Right five on the sandpit.
Cassidy: There's five, five.
Researcher: Are there any *other* things you like to do, like do you like to have lunch, or dress up, or play with the dough?
Cassidy: I play with the horses.
Researcher: Play with the horses, yeah (Pause). Great, Cassidy.

Finally, I relinquished my research agenda which was discovering the variety of activities a child enjoyed, and heard his message that playing with horses was what he liked to do. However, this interaction also challenged my assumptions in a more fundamental way. I recognised, with hindsight, that my activity was based around the familiar categories of equipment and experiences that I had long used as a teacher and a teacher educator. In his reactions to my photographs, Cassidy showed me how a child might categorise centre life in a quite different way. For him the defining feature was horses. It was only from my previous interactions with him that I was able to recognise the depth of his interest in them. From those episodes, many of them momentary, I was aware he knew where he could find horses – horse books, pictures of horses, horse puzzles, plastic horses, soft toy horses – in every area of the centre. It seemed that the fundamental categories that Cassidy might be using were 'horse' and 'not-horse'. Would I have recognised how thoughtfully Cassidy was engaging with my process without this contextual knowledge? Or would I have decided that he was not interested in the photographs and drawn the interaction to a close?

This interaction again reinforced the value of the combination of visual images and verbal language in research with young children. Children are experts in their own lives; here Cassidy was an expert about what he liked to do, but had limited language with which to express himself. There is a danger of equating verbal facility with competence, and so excluding younger or non-verbal children from research. By using the photographs and the plastic horse, as well as his words, Cassidy was able to convey his answer to my question. Without those prompts would he have found a way to tell me, and would I have understood him if he had?

Final thoughts

My time with the children in this centre reinforced the image of research as stepping out into the unknown. If this process had been a shorter, tighter one – using pre-developed research strategies with a small group of children over a brief period – and less of a step into the unknown – I suspect the results would have been very different. While using photographs and photography proved to be strategies that children enjoyed, the fact that I was in the centre for a prolonged period meant that I was more sensitive to the nuances in their responses. For the children, it had the advantage that they could choose when and how they interacted with me, and they could select whether they wanted to engage (and re-engage) in particular research activities. The luxury of being able to spend a sustained period of time with the children, to develop relationships, to introduce a range of research strategies and use them flexibly and responsively, contributed to the complexity of the data gathered. My growing familiarity with the children through the myriad of interactions I shared with them each day helped me to step back from the immediacy of an interaction and 'hear' other possible layers of meanings. Graue and Walsh have written that 'Doing research with young children is as complex, rewarding, and messy as living and working with them' (1998, p. 13). This research experience suggested that living and working with children for sustained periods might be the route to understanding a little more of the complex reality of their lives within the centre.

References

Carr, M. (2000). Seeking children's perspectives about their learning. In A.B. Smith, N.J. Taylor, & M.M. Gollop (Eds.), *Children's voices: Research, policy and practice* (pp. 37–55). Auckland: Pearson Educational.

Christensen, P., & James, A. (Eds.). (2000). *Research with children: Perspectives and practices.* London: Falmer Press.

Clark, A. (2004). The mosaic approach and research with young children. In V. Lewis, M. Kellett, C. Robinson, S. Fraser, & S. Ding (Eds.), *The reality of research with children and young people* (pp. 142–156). London: Sage.

Clark, A. (2007). A hundred ways of listening: Gathering children's perspectives of their early childhood environment. *Young Children, 62*(3), 76–81.

Clark, A., & Moss, P. (2001). *Listening to young children: The mosaic approach.* London: National Children's Bureau & Joseph Rowntree Foundation.

Cremin, H., & Slatter, B. (2004). Is it possible to access the 'voice' of pre–school children? Results of a research project in a pre-school setting. *Educational Studies, 30*(4), 457–470.

DeMarie, D., & Ethridge, E.A. (2006). Children's images of preschool: The power of photography. *Young Children, 61*(1), 101–104.

Einarsdottir, J. (2005). Playschool in pictures: Children's photographs as a research method. *Early Child Development and Care, 175*(6), 523–541.

Einarsdottir, J. (2007). Research with children: Methodological and ethical challenges. *European Early Childhood Education Research Journal 15*(2), 197–211.

Formosinho, J., & Araujo, S.B. (2006). Listening to children as a way to reconstruct knowledge about children: Some methodological implications. *European Early Childhood Education Research Journal, 14*(1), 21–31.

Gallas, K. (1994). *The languages of learning. How children talk, write, dance, draw and sing their understanding of the world.* New York: Teachers College Press.

Gallas, K. (1998). *'Sometimes I can be anything': Power, gender and identity in a primary classroom.* New York: Teachers College Press.

Graue, M.E., & Walsh, D.J. (1998). *Studying children in context: Theories, methods, and ethics.* Thousand Oaks, CA: Sage.

Greenfield, C. (2004). Transcript: 'Can run, play on bikes, jump on the zoom slide, and play on the swings': Exploring the value of outdoor play, *Australian Journal of Early Childhood, 29*(2), 1–5.

Lewis, A. (2001). Research involving young children. In T. David (Ed.), *Promoting evidence-based practice in early childhood education: Research and its implications* (pp. 253–271). Oxford: Elsevier Science.

MacNaughton, G., Rolfe, SA. & Siraj-Blatchford, I. (2001). *Doing early childhood research: International perspectives on theory and practice.* Buckingham: Oxford University Press.

Ministry of Education. (1996). *Te Whāriki: Early childhood curriculum. He Whāriki mātauranga mo nga mokopuna o Aotearoa.* Wellington: Learning Media.

Paley, V.G. (1984). *Boys and girls: Superheroes in the doll corner.* Chicago: University of Chicago Press.

Paley, V.G. (1986). *Mollie is three: Growing up in school.* Chicago: University of Chicago Press.

Paley, V.G. (1995). *Kwanzaa and me: A teacher's story.* Cambridge, MA: Harvard University Press.

Ring, K. (2000, September 7–10). *Young children talking about their drawings: Methodological dilemmas.* Paper presented at the British Educational Research Association Annual Conference, Cardiff University. (Retrieved 10 April 2008, from www.leeds.ac.uk/educol/documents/00001926.htm).

Te One, S. (2007). Participatory-research methods with young children: Experiences from the field. *Early Childhood Folio, 11,* 21–25.

Wiltz, N.W., & Klein, E.L. (2001). 'What do you do in child care?' Children's perceptions of high and low quality classrooms. *Early Childhood Research Quarterly, 16,* 209–236.

Woodrow, C. (1999). Revisiting images of the child in early childhood education: Reflections and considerations. *Australian Journal of Early Childhood, 24*(4), 7–12.

4

Conducting research with young children: some ethical considerations

Rosie Flewitt

Overview

How can young children's participation in research be approached in an ethical way? In this chapter, Rosie Flewitt draws on her own experiences of conducting ESRC-funded ethnographic video case studies on how four 3-year-old children express their understandings at home and in a pre-school playgroup during their first year of early years education. The chapter reflects on the processes of negotiating initial and ongoing consent, discusses the notions of 'informed' consent in exploratory research with young children and explores the specific issues raised by using visual data. This flexible, reflective stance can reveal understandings about children's perspectives and also how to include children in the research process.

[…]

Introduction

Ethical issues arise in all aspects of research, and are particularly salient when studying vulnerable members of society, such as in the study reported here that followed the

Flewitt, R. (2005) 'Conducting research with young children: some ethical considerations', *Early Child Development and Care*, vol. 175, no. 6, pp. 553–65.

lives of young children experiencing change as they entered preschool and in the privacy of their homes. Denzin (1989, p. 83) suggests:

> … our primary obligation is always to the people we study, not to our project or to a larger discipline. The lives and stories that we hear and study are given to us under a promise, that promise being that we protect those who have shared them with us.

Denzin highlights the sharing nature of the research process, an approach that can serve as an ethical anchor throughout any social research. Here I report on how the notion of 'sharing' informed the myriad ethical decisions taken in response to issues as they emerged in the field, including the negotiation of initial and ongoing consent, participant consultation during data analysis, issues of anonymity when re-presenting visual data in research write-ups and keeping participants of all ages informed about the possible outcomes and disseminations of the study. Sharing decisions in this way in no sense absolves the researcher of ultimate responsibility for decisions taken, but by listening to and respecting *all* participants' wishes, it can at the very least help to balance the unequal power balance between researcher and researched.

Negotiating initial consent and gatekeepers

I began the process of negotiating initial consent for my year-long study by contacting the leader of the preschool selected as the site of study and subsequently arranging a group consultation with all paid staff. During this consultation, I outlined the broad aims and scope of the research, including criteria for the selection of case-study children; that is, all case-study children should be 3 years old and have only recently started or be due to start preschool. I was also aiming for an equal number of girls and boys from diverse social backgrounds. The staff responded by considering individual children, proposing some who spoke very little in the setting and others who they perceived as communicatively confident and competent. They gave thoughtful consideration to the circumstances of individual family groups, the stability of their lives and potential benefits and harm for the children and their families of being included in a longitudinal study. This resulted in a list of eight children due to begin preschool during the period of research. From the outset therefore, the staff acted as gatekeepers to the parents and children who attended their setting, and in so doing, began to shape the research outcomes by proposing particular children as central figures in the study.

There are ethical concerns when accessing research participants through a gatekeeper as the researcher risks exploiting the relationship between the gatekeeper and the person they are introducing. For example, preschool parents may feel a certain obligation to agree to participate in the research in order to 'get off to a good start' with staff in the setting, fearing that refusing to take part could damage either their relationship with the staff or the services their child receives. It is essential, therefore, to build in both formal and informal opportunities for participants to say no in a safe environment.

In my own research, the staff and I decided that staff should make initial contact with parents of potential case-study children and make clear to parents their rights to decline to participate, to reassure parents that there would be no negative outcomes if they chose not to participate and to answer any questions they were able to. If the parents were interested, staff then introduced me to the mother at the end of a preschool session, and I made an appointment to visit the family at home. During the home meetings, the mothers,[1] children and I jointly agreed 'working boundaries' for the research. For example, we discussed the frequency and length of recording sessions, the most convenient times for home visits, the need for parents, staff and researcher to respond sensitively to any indications of discomfort a child might show whilst being filmed, and the need to develop open, dialogical lines of communication between researcher, parents and staff throughout the process of research. I also chatted with the children, who by then had met me in preschool, showed them the recording equipment, let them handle it and use it if they so wished, and stressed that they could make their own films. I emphasised to the children that they could choose whether to take part or not, and that if they decided to participate they were always free to change their minds – for a few minutes, for a whole session or forever. Although this flexibility might appear unnecessary to many experienced researchers, it enabled the children, parents and staff to become increasingly familiar with the technical equipment, and this in turn helped to demystify the research process, empowering the participants rather than making them the objects of research. Some of the children made short films and these texts gave valuable insights into their perceptions of home and preschool settings.

In addition, I asked parents to talk about the research with their child without the researcher or staff present, and to inform staff and researcher of the child's responses. This second process of consultation revealed some clear child parameters. For example, one boy asked if the research would interfere with his outside playtime, and one girl expressed concern that the study might restrict her playing with her best friend.

As a result of consultation with children, parents and staff, three girls and three boys from varying social backgrounds were identified for case study. I sent a letter to all other parents informing them of the nature, duration and broad topic of my study, giving them the opportunity to opt out of the research. A more detailed letter outlining the agreed parameters of the research was sent to the parents of the case-study children, again giving parents and children the opportunity to choose whether to participate or not.

With regard to child consent, Article 12 of the United Nations *Convention on the rights of the child* (United Nations, 1989) clearly states children's rights to express their views on all matters that affect them. Some researchers prefer to use the term 'assent' rather than 'consent', arguing that minors are unable to give legal consent. However, as Alderson and Morrow point out (2004, pp. 98–99) in English law, 'competent minors' under 16 can give valid consent, with 'competence' defined as having sufficient understanding and intelligence to understand what is proposed. When I talked with the case-study children about the processes of their involvement, and as the children handled the equipment, they asked many highly appropriate questions, such as whether their voices would be on the audio and video recordings, whether they could watch/listen to them, who else would watch/listen to them. These responses indicated strongly that although only 3 years old, they were 'competent' and confident enough to grant or withdraw consent – with some more outspoken and enquiring than their parents.

As a result of all staff, parent and child comments, it was agreed to restrict recording time to 1 hour only during each 2.5 hour preschool session, outside play would not be included and no child movements or activities would be restricted as a result of being recorded. Given that the aim of the study was to collect naturalistic data, the latter condition merely served to reinforce to all involved in the research process the need to allow children to go about their lives without consideration for the study.

The process of negotiating initial consent for the study stretched over several weeks, running concurrently with a period of initial observation in the preschool setting. Although such a protracted timescale may sound unnecessary and impracticable for short-term studies, in all interpretive research the strength of relationships established at the outset can have a profound impact on the progress and outcomes of the study. A period of negotiation for initial consent gives participants time to reflect upon the information the researcher gives them, to ask questions, express doubts and to iron out any differences in researcher and researched perceptions of potential harm.

'Provisional' consent

The negotiation of consent at the outset of research is often referred to as 'informed consent', yet in exploratory or investigative research the notion of 'informed' is problematic, as the precise course to be taken by the research is unpredictable. Explaining to young children the nature and consequences of research can make the term 'informed' seem even more inappropriate. A more fitting description used in this study was 'provisional consent'. That is, the participants' agreement was understood to be provisional upon the research being conducted within a negotiated, broadly outlined framework and continuing to develop within the participants' expectations. 'Provisional consent' is therefore ongoing and dependent on the network of researcher/researched relationships built upon sensitivity, reciprocal trust and collaboration.

Negotiating ongoing consent

Once initial 'provisional' consent has been established, ongoing consent cannot be assumed, but is negotiated in situated contexts on a minute-by-minute basis (Simons and Usher, 2000). Negotiating ongoing consent is difficult to regulate for, but during the process of gaining initial consent for my study, I voiced a commitment to being sensitive and responsive to any negative reactions the children might have to being observed and recorded. However, I was dependent upon the staff and parents' more intimate knowledge of the children to identify their often subtle signs of discomfort at being filmed. Therefore, in addition to my own growing sensitivity towards individual children's behaviours, the trust established through my developing relationships with the staff and parents acted as a pivot for gauging the children's ongoing consent during periods of observation. [...]

After a few weeks of recording, it became apparent that the children found wearing the small tape recorder cumbersome. To reduce this physical discomfort, I researched alternative lighter weight audio-recording equipment,[2] which resulted not only in a more comfortable solution for the children, but also in better quality, digital recordings for the researcher. The choice of a hand-held compact digital video recorder with an easily viewable side-opening screen also allowed maximum movement for myself to follow the children as they moved from area to area and from room to room. I frequently stood with the video camera at some distance from the children, using the zoom to capture the detail of their interactions. Although the children knew they were being filmed, by standing at a distance my presence was not intrusive and did not appear to interfere with the natural progression and development of their play.

At the beginning of each recording session, I asked each case-study child if they would mind wearing the small, lapel microphone and audio recorder, which slipped into the tiniest of pockets. Very occasionally, children preferred not to wear the recorder, particularly if 'dressing up', where the wires became problematic, but said they did not mind if I filmed them. However, making video recordings with no audio back-up did not always result in good data! The following extract, written in field notes immediately after an abandoned recording session, illustrates one of many hundreds of large and small ethical dilemmas encountered:

> This morning's session was frustrating. Tallulah was talking much more than usual, mostly to her mother and brother, but also a lot of self-directed speech. However, because she didn't want to wear the recorder … I couldn't record what she was saying, and she speaks so quietly I couldn't hear most of it. She didn't mind me videoing her though, and watched bits afterwards. Maybe I could get someone to lip-read that!

On other occasions, children approached me and asked to wear the audio equipment, and then incorporated it in their play as a 'mobile phone' or a 'walkie talkie'. In such instances, I was mindful of the kudos a child gained from being the holder of relatively high-tech equipment, so to avoid exploiting the children's enthusiasm, I always asked if I should leave the equipment switched on to record their play or if they would prefer me to switch it off. Sometimes, children not in the case study would also ask if they could wear the recorder or if I could film them. Although I was frequently unable to do this immediately, I tried to ensure I always had an extra tape and battery available to fulfil their wish during the same preschool session, and when possible took time to view these short recordings with them.

Eventually, I collected detailed data on just four of the six identified children: one boy moved away and one girl consistently agreed to wear the audio recorder, but then equally consistently went to play with a friend in a concealed area, such as inside the climbing tubes or under blankets. Clearly, the presence of the video was not permitted. Occasionally, the case-study children asked to watch particular sections of the video, which we did together once I had completed the filming session, and I made field notes on the children's reactions to the film. These moments gave rich insights into the children's perspectives.

This open, responsive approach led to an increasingly collaborative framework for data collection, with staff and children sometimes assuming responsibility for the video recordings. Although the practicalities of staff:child ratios and the general 'busyness' and learning agenda of the preschool setting meant that the majority of video data was collected by the researcher rather than by the participants, the rare insights gained from participant recordings were data 'gems'. Being flexible in this way is potentially time-wasting for the researcher, and occasionally, after travelling to the setting, I would be unable to collect data on a particular child. However, such instances were comparatively rare, and the benefits of increasingly trusting researcher– researched relationships far outweighed the drawbacks of loss of time as children, staff and parents came to know that they did indeed have the right to refuse.

Anonymity and visual data

As Price (1996, p. 207) argues, it is better to 'compromise the research rather than compromise the participants' and this includes protecting anonymity. Official British education research guidelines (British Educational Research Association, 2004) suggest that participants' identity should not be revealed, unless individuals choose to be identified; that is, participants' names should be changed, and precise details that could make a setting or participant identifiable should not be given.

However, visual methods of data collection in education research do not have a history of established ethical practice (Prosser, 2000). The main corpus of observational data collected for this study was video footage, and as the analysis focused on how children used combinations of words, body movements, manipulation of objects, gaze and facial expression to express meanings in the settings of home and preschool, the use of visual images was sometimes imperative for the construction of a convincing argument. This resulted in a long personal journey through a minefield of ethical predicaments. Although participants' names may be changed in written accounts and erased from audio recordings, visual images make them easily recognisable not only whilst in the public sphere of work but also in the privacy of their homes. This puts children at particular risk and renders parents and practitioners vulnerable to criticism, anxiety and self-doubt.

Even if adult participants give signed consent for visual images of their children to be reproduced at the outset of a research project, participants' life circumstances and attitudes to consent may change over time. As young children grow, physical changes in their appearance make them less recognisable, but this does not negate the researcher's responsibility to protect the privacy of their younger selves. Children may give verbal consent, or, as Harcourt and Conroy (2004) suggest, young children can also express their consent through drawings and mark-making. Furthermore, even if the researcher makes positive comments on the data, readers or viewers of texts interpret or 'judge' participants from their own inevitably diverse standpoints. In my research I have attempted to find solutions to these contradictory interests.

Talking to staff and parents informally during the study revealed that participant anxiety about being filmed and about visual images being reproduced was associated with a loss of control. All adult and child participants were therefore encouraged to choose their own pseudonyms, to view and comment on the video data and to make their own recordings – backed up by an all-risks insurance policy for the camera. Adult and child participants have also been shown and have approved the visual images used in research presentations. This more transparent approach to data collection and analysis helped to overcome participant concerns and to reinforce the trusting, cooperative relations that were essential for the success of this study.

With regard to the use of visual images in the public domain, the researcher should reflect on the degree of visual detail that is relevant to a research claim. If precise detail is not essential, then digital technology has made possible the obscuring of on-screen images, such as 'fuzzing' participants' faces to protect identity, or using a relatively simple technique to obscure on-screen images by reducing pixel count, as illustrated in Figure 4.1.

[…] Alternatively, sketches of video stills can be drawn to indicate body positioning and directionality of movement.

Occasionally, I have used extracts of video in research presentations where adult and child participants are clearly identifiable. For each section used, I have gained prior permission from all participants present in the extracts, including all staff, children and parents of the children. For future projects, I plan to collate key video data extracts, circulate them to all participants and seek permission to use those extracts as still or moving images for stated and agreed purposes.

Figure 4.1   Video still of reduced pixel count image

One further danger of displaying visual data where participants are identifiable is that the data is extracted from the richly situated context in which it occurred. Researchers working with visual data therefore have a responsibility to reconstruct contextual details that situate data extracts in the complex particularity of their original settings.

Each research project creates its own sets of compromises, but in education research there is a developing awareness of ethical issues in the use of visual data and new technologies. Approaching ethical issues in visual research in the manner described in this [chapter] builds on the principles underpinning British Educational Research Association (BERA) ethical guidelines suggesting that 'all educational research should be conducted within an ethic of respect for persons, respect for knowledge, respect for democratic values, and respect for the quality of educational research' (BERA, 2004).

Confidentiality: deciding what to leave out

Just as researchers must protect participant privacy, so they must also respect participant rights to confidentiality and avoid intrusion into participants' personal affairs. In the UK, formal guidance on issues of confidentiality is given in the Data Protection Act (1998), which clearly states that data about individuals must only be used for agreed, specified purposes, and that data should be relevant, adequate and not excessive to the purpose for which it was gathered. However, in the busy field of data collection and analysis, decisions about when to stop observing participants, or about when not to transcribe data also relate to a researcher's personal understandings of privacy and respect. The trusting relationships built up during longitudinal ethnographic research can result in the researcher being privy to details of private lives that should not be disclosed. The following extract from the research diary kept during the course of the study is one example:

> My role as researcher is blurred in the homes, where the mothers and I seem to be in a new kind of social 'bubble' somewhere between an acquaintance and a friend. The recording equipment and prepared questions for interview bring formality, but this seems to disappear as the interviews develop. I'm often treated more as a 'fellow' mother, and a confidante, sometimes playing the listening role of a counsellor, hearing deeply personal details of the participants' lives that have a place in our 'bubble' but no place in my research.

During data collection for this study, if mothers or children began to talk about issues that were clearly outside the research aims, I turned off any recording equipment, or, if this action appeared intrusive, I later erased sections of personal details. In other cases, where borderlines of confidentiality were more blurred, I kept the original recorded data, but did not transcribe it – leaving any data available for future use if later deemed to be of direct relevance to the overall research findings. Leaving data out can have strong implications for shaping research findings, so to give some systematicity to data exclusions, I made a note of all these subjective decisions in a confidential section of the research diary, and was therefore able to track trails of both included and excluded data.

Including participants in respondent validation

During data collection and analysis, a researcher's interpretation of events may be significantly different from the perspectives of participants, and it is possible that 'what researchers consider innocent is perceived by participants as misleading or even betrayal. What appears neutral on paper is often conflictual in practice' (Christians, 2000, p. 139).

In an attempt to insure against any such potential harm, and to avoid the 'thwarting biases' of researcher subjectivity (Peshkin, 1988, p. 20) that can mar interpretive research, I had many informal conversations and more formal meetings with participants to gain their insights into the recorded data. This process revealed the multiplicity of realities and meanings attributed to any single act by different participants and by the researcher. However, the timing of these consultation sessions was problematic. [...] As mentioned, the children sometimes asked to watch the videos during data collection, and sometimes viewed short sections whilst in preschool. The children's views on their activities were often very clear, and were recorded in field notes, but the agenda of preschool activities tended to dictate how much time was free for this. There was more flexibility of time during home visits, where parents could also voice their interpretations of the data.

All participant comments fed into the field notes and research diary, where trails of ideas could be traced as they developed over time and embryonic themes began to shape data collection and analysis. For example, I began the study by observing one child for set periods of time at each activity. The data seemed to imply that different types of interaction occurred at different activities, dependent on the degree of control a child had over the activity. After consultation with staff, I began to categorise activities accordingly, gradually sharpening the research focus. Thus the processes of data collection, early analysis and respondent validation developed as intertwining spirals.

After completion of data collection, I returned to the preschool setting with video extracts for consultation with staff regarding key analytic themes. For each theme, I proposed different possible interpretations that gave rise to debate, again feeding back into the interpretive process. Similar discussions were held with the mothers and children as we watched short clips of the video together in the children's homes. Although the children's recall was sometimes sharp and they enjoyed watching the videos, these sessions were less successful than I had hoped, but have enabled me to plan future possible methods of consulting children, including shorter periods of time between video recording and video viewing, and making video recordings of the children watching the original videos of themselves.

With the benefit of hindsight, I realised that building in more time for joint viewings of selected passages of video could have enhanced the collaborative nature of the study, but respondent validation is very time-consuming and could become onerous for the participants. Furthermore, it could lead to tensions between participants as they observed each other's behaviours, thus risking potentially harmful outcomes for participants. The balance between these considerations can only be judged on a project-by-project basis, but if anticipated, the format and ethos of participant consultation could be negotiated with participants at the outset.

Informing participants of research outcomes and dissemination

As discussed, interviews and consultations with participants, and the subsequent representation of their views in the research text all combine to provide a platform for their voices and give participants a sense of ownership over the data. However, participants should also be informed about the outcomes and dissemination of research texts. At the outset and even during a study, potential outcomes can only be partially known, and a general sentence written in a permissions agreement can do no more than outline unconfirmed plans for dissemination. In the case of short-term research, where relationships with participants are more fleeting, this may be the only indicator for longer-term outcomes. However, when conducting longitudinal research, meaningful relationships are built up and these enable the researcher to recontact participants. I have continued to visit the site of the study reported here, for example to attend the preschool setting's fundraising events. These informal occasions have provided a platform to discuss with staff further outcomes from the study. Similarly, I have met informally with all the mothers, kept them informed of new uses for the data and in return have learnt how their children continue to fare in preschool and in primary school.

Concluding thoughts

This [chapter] has argued that researchers have a responsibility towards participants of all ages not only to establish a robust and negotiated ethical framework for their research, but also to ensure that these ethical principles are applied throughout all stages of the research process.

As Alderson and Morrow (2004) point out, one purpose of ethical reflection is to balance the potential risks of research against the likely benefits, yet this calculation is far from straightforward, and short-and long-term risks are hard to predict. During the process of conducting this study on and with 3-year-old children, their parents and preschool practitioners, I began by reflecting on my general ethical stance, encapsulated in the Denzin quote given in the introduction, which [laid] the foundations for guiding principles that informed the countless ethical dilemmas I encountered. However, reconciling those general principles with the particular ethical considerations that arose during research was inevitably problematic, and I found little practical support in formal ethical guidelines. My daily ethical practices underpinned the relationships of trust that built up between myself and the participants, and those relationships in turn shaped the nature and quality of data collected. The ethical solutions I found often resulted from sharing my reservations and fears with the research participants, and it is my firm belief that this sharing approach significantly enhanced the quality of the overall study.

Guidelines for ethical reflection

Negotiation of initial consent

- Have all parents and children who attend the preschool setting been made aware of the planned research project?
- Have the researchers and/or gatekeepers made it clear to participants of all ages that they are under no obligation to participate in the research?
- Have all participants been reassured that there will be no negative outcomes if they choose not to participate?
- Have participants been given both informal and formal opportunities over a period of time, to accept or decline to participate in the research, e.g. through informal discussions and opt-out/opt-in written agreements?
- Have participants been given the opportunity to ask the researcher/research team questions about the research?
- Have the participants had occasion to view/handle the recording equipment before the onset of data collection?
- Have parents talked privately with their child(ren) about the research and reported back any child concerns?
- Have all participants been given researcher contact details, e.g. phone number and address?
- Have all of the above negotiations been conducted in the participants' first language/via an interpreter if necessary?

Negotiation of ongoing consent

- Is the research being conducted within a negotiated, broadly outlined framework?
- Is the research continuing to develop within the participants' expectations?
- Have staff and parents been encouraged to report any ongoing concerns or adverse effects of the research on individual children?
- Has the researcher responded appropriately to any child indications of discomfort at being observed?
- Are researcher/researched relationships being built upon sensitivity, reciprocal trust and collaboration?

Anonymity, confidentiality and visual data

- Have participants of all ages been asked for prior, outline permission for the use of visual images for specific purposes, e.g. 'for research reports, presentations and education training'?
- Is any visual data presented relevant, adequate and not excessive to the purpose for which it was gathered, e.g. would fuzzed faces, drawn images or similar be sufficient?
- Have all selected visual data extracts been shown to all visible participants? Have all participants given written consent to the use of agreed still and moving visual images?

(Continued)

(Continued)

Participant consultation and research outcomes

- Have participants of all ages had the opportunity to view and comment on data extracts to gain their perspectives on what is happening?
- Have participants of all ages been informed about the possible outcomes and disseminations of the study, including web-based formats (if applicable)?
- Have the participants been given copies of recorded data of themselves and a short report on the final research findings?

Notes

1. Two of the case-study children's fathers/male guardians were sometimes present during home visits and also contributed, but most home visits were conducted with only mothers present.
2. Sony Memory Stick 1C Recorder ICD-MSl.

References

Alderson, P. & Morrow, V. (2004) *Ethics, social research and consulting with children and young people* (Ilford, Barnardo's).

British Educational Research Association (BERA) (2004) *Revised guidelines.* Available online at: www.bera.ac.uk/guidelines.html (accessed 7 February 2005).

Christians, C. G. (2000) Ethics and politics in qualitative research, in: N. K. Denzin & Y. S. Lincoln (Eds) *Handbook of qualitative research* (Thousand Oaks, CA, Sage).

Denzin, N. K. (1989) *Interpretive biography* (London, Sage).

Harcourt, D. & Conroy, H. (2004) Informed consent: ethics and processes when researching with young children as a basis for classroom pedagogy, paper presented to *European Early Childhood Education Research Association 14th Annual Conference.* Malta, 1–4 September.

Peshkin, A. (1988) In search of subjectivity – one's own. *Educational Research,* 7, 17–22.

Price, J. (1996) Snakes in the swamp: ethical issues in qualitative research, in: R. Josselson (Ed.) *Ethics and process in the narrative study of lives* (vol. 4) (London, Sage).

Prosser, J. (2000) The moral maze of image ethics, in: H. Simons & R. Usher (2000) *Situated ethics in educational research* (London, Routledge/Falmer).

Simons, H. & Usher, R. (2000) *Situated ethics in educational research* (London, Routledge/Falmer).

United Nations (1989) *Convention on the rights of the child* (New York, UN).

5

Promoting young children's development: implications of the UN Convention on the Rights of the Child

Martin Woodhead

Overview

The focus of this chapter is on the implications of one of the most significant documents shaping research, policies and practices for all children, globally. The chapter explores the significance of the United Nations Convention on the Rights of the Child, 1989 (abbreviated as UNCRC), especially as it applies to professional work with young children; the implications of the UNCRC for recent developments in policy and services in England; and one of the key principles of the UNCRC, 'the development of the child', which is also one of the six elements of the Common Core of Skills and Knowledge for the Children's Workforce (DfES 2005).

[…]

This chapter is a revised version of 'Early childhood development: a question of rights', *International Journal of Early Childhood*, 37(3), 79–98.

Woodhead, M. (2008) 'Promoting young children's development: implications of the UN Convention on the Rights of the Child', in Miller, L. and Cable, C. (eds) *Professionalism in the Early Years*, London: Hodder/Arnold Publishers, pp. 154–66.

Children's rights and children's services

Building early childhood services on respect for the rights of the child is one of many kinds of rationale currently available to the professional. Other kinds of rationale include:

- scientific evidence about early childhood programmes improving outcomes in later stages of education;
- social welfare concerns that children's services protect children while at the same time enabling families, especially mothers, to combine working with caring;
- economic arguments that the long-term benefits to society can outweigh the costs of providing services for children and families;
- and political priorities for early childhood services to serve as a powerful tool for intervention in social inequalities (based on Myers 1992).

In many ways, a human rights argument for early childhood services is the most compelling case of all. It does not rest on the availability of scientific evidence, cost-benefit analyses, nor even a political context valuing social justice, even though each of these is important to implementing rights in practice. The significance of the UNCRC is that the child is placed at centre stage. Survival, health, development, education, etc., are recognised as each child's entitlement, irrespective of their linkage to wider policy goals, and that feelings and views of the child must be respected in decision-making, from birth onwards.

Over the past two decades, the UNCRC has become a powerful catalyst for action on behalf of young children, with ratification virtually universal (192 countries, all except USA and Somalia). [...] The UNCRC requires all children to be respected as persons in their own right, including the very youngest children. National governments ('States Parties') make regular reports on progress in meeting their obligations to the UN Committee on the Rights of the Child. This committee comprises 18 independent experts elected by UN States and representing major world regions, providing a highly significant mechanism of international accountability. But the influence of the UNCRC is arguably much more pervasive, as fundamental children's rights principles gradually become embedded within the policies and practices of all who work with and on behalf of young children.

[...]

For the early childhood professional, adopting a rights-based perspective can require a radical shift from some more traditional ways of working with young children. [For] members of the UN Committee [...] a fundamental goal is 'to emphasize that the young child is not merely a fit object of benevolence, but, rather, that the young child is a right-holder as is the older child and, indeed, every human being' (Doek et al. 2006: 32). To achieve this goal, it is not sufficient to think of young children as in need of care and teaching, as developing through a pre-planned curriculum, or as objects of social intervention. Of course, these perspectives have a place in professional work, but the foundation principle is respect for each young child in their own right. Ensuring quality of life for and with young children now and in the future is valued as an end in itself, and not just as the means to achieve broader goals of protecting and promoting human potential and preventing social ills. The UN Committee summed up this shift towards a positive agenda for early childhood:

> A shift away from traditional beliefs that regard early childhood mainly as a period for the socialization of the immature human being towards mature adult status is required ... Young children should be recognized as active members of families, communities and societies with their own concerns, interests and points of view. For the exercise of their rights, young children have particular requirements for physical nurturance, emotional care and sensitive guidance, as well as for time and space for social play, exploration and learning. These requirements can best be planned for within a framework of laws, policies and programmes for early childhood. (General Comment 7, para 5)

Note how the young child is re-positioned in the extract above, as the rights-bearer, who 'for the exercise of their rights' requires the protection, support and guidance of peers, parents, professionals, etc., in order to realise their rights. In this way, a rights perspective sets new challenges for all who claim to be 'child-centred'.

[...]

The Every Child Matters agenda has prompted radical overhaul of professional training for early years, notably through specification of a Common Core of Skills and Knowledge for the Children's Workforce (DfES 2005). Interestingly, the introduction to the guidance document does include 'the rights of children and young people' as part of the rationale for the Common Core, even if not as its central justification:

> The Common Core reflects a set of common values for practitioners that promote equality, respect diversity and challenge stereotypes, helping to improve the life chances of all children and young people and to provide more effective and integrated services. It also acknowledges the rights of children and young people, and the role parents, carers and families play in helping children and young people achieve the outcomes identified in Every Child Matters. (DfES 2005: 4)

The six areas of professional expertise set out in the Common Core are: effective communication and engagement; child and young person development; safeguarding and promoting the welfare of the child; supporting transitions; multi-agency working; and sharing information. The first three of these areas most obviously connect with articles of UNCRC, and with the guidance given on implementing child rights in early childhood within General Comment 7. The rest of this chapter explores these connections, taking just one element of the Common Core as a starting point, the 'development of the child'. Numerous textbooks are available to professionals, summarising the most up-to-date knowledge about children's development. My aim is to step back from the particularities of research findings, and summarise some key debates surrounding what 'promoting development' entails within a framework of rights.

The young child's right to development

The UN Committee emphasises that rights to development are to be understood in a holistic way and that all rights are interrelated, interdependent and indivisible. To this end, the UN Committee has identified four articles which – when taken together – can be seen as offering general principles. These, briefly, are:

- Article 6 ensures to the maximum extent possible the survival and development of the child;
- Article 2 assures rights to every child without discrimination;
- Article 3 sets out that the best interests of the child are a primary consideration;
- Article 12 states that children have a right to express views in all matters that affect them.

The reason for highlighting these general principles is that – when taken together – they begin to point to some of the challenges in interpreting children's right to development. For example: how far should professional frameworks build on assumptions that child development is a universal process; and how far is it more appropriate to be thinking in terms of respect for a range of developmental pathways, according to children's individuality, their economic and social circumstances, and their parents' cultural beliefs and aspirations? How can a balance be achieved between respecting diversities in children's development (in terms of expectations, treatment, styles of care and approaches to education) and guaranteeing all children's entitlements, without discrimination, for example related to their gender? How should 'best interests' be applied in practice – and by whom – especially when there is dispute amongst parents, professionals and others? How far can, or should, children's voices be listened to in these circumstances? How can they be enabled to express their views, and what are the roles and responsibilities of adults in (individually and collectively) guiding children's effective participation?

As a vehicle for exploring these dilemmas in greater detail, I will concentrate on three key debates: about the universality of child development processes; about what drives and shapes development; and about the status of the child in these processes. I will pose these as a set of competing perspectives, which I call the three 'Ns' and the three 'Cs'. The three 'Ns' involve thinking about what is 'Normal' and 'Natural' as well as about children's 'Needs'. The three 'Cs' involve thinking about development in ways that are 'Contextual', 'Cultural', and based on respect for children's 'Competencies' (see Table 5.1).

Summarising diverse views on early childhood into three Ns and three Cs is of course an oversimplification. Neither the 'Ns' nor the 'Cs' offer a complete picture, nor are they necessarily in opposition, as will become clear if we look at each in turn.

Table 5.1 Debating early childhood three Ns or three Cs

Major theme	'Ns'	'Cs'
Universality and diversity	Normal development	Contexts for development
Influences on development	Natural processes	Cultural processes
Status of the child	Needs of children	Competencies of children

Normal development or contexts for development?

Identifying 'normal' patterns of development – as well as the extent and causes of variations – has been a major feature of child development research. The singular 'child' has been the starting point and a major goal has been to identify universal features of growth and change, for example through detailed accounts of stages of physical, mental, social and moral development associated with the names of Piaget, Kohlberg, Erikson and other leading theorists. While identifying universal features of development as an attractive starting point for realising rights for all children, this approach also has serious limitations. Despite claims to universality, developmental accounts are often very closely tied to quite specific cultural contexts and expectations about what makes for a normal early childhood.

[...]

Dominant expectations of what is 'normal' child development are not about normality in the statistical sense; on the contrary, conventional understandings of what makes for a normal childhood are in global terms often quite unusual, highlighted, for example, by studies of children's early initiation into work, which is still 'normal' for millions of the world's children (Woodhead 2002). Normal childhoods defined by professionals in one society are similarly likely to reflect a range of features of a very particular developmental niche (Super and Harkness 1986). They risk overlooking the diversities in children's developmental contexts and experiences, even within a community or region, including differences in the ways children learn, play and communicate, develop personal identity and social understanding, as well as the diversities in the ways they are treated according to parents' cultural goals for their development. Any particular account of young children's development is always partial, and can never encompass the varieties of childhood. The risk is when specific cultural patterns of early development and care become normalised and universalised. For early childhood professionals, the practical implication is that looking beyond dominant, textbook accounts of development is essential, especially for those working in multi-ethnic settings, as illustrated in Brooker (2002). This requires recognising that a range of pathways through early childhood can be consistent with promoting children's well-being, and that the challenge is to negotiate what is in each child's best interests (Woodhead 1996).

Child development as natural or cultural?

Ideas about 'normal' development have been closely linked to beliefs that development is underpinned by 'natural' processes of maturation. In the same way the importance of 'context' goes hand in hand with recognising that children's development is fundamentally a social and a 'cultural' process. Respecting young children's nature has roots in Rousseau's philosophical writing and found strongest expression in Jean Piaget's account of the child's progress through sensori-motor, pre-operational, concrete-operational and formal-operational stages (Donaldson 1978). Piaget's developmental stage model was coupled with a vision of individual children's exploratory play as the process through which they construct an increasingly sophisticated understanding of the world. These theories became the underpinning rationale for child-centred curricula and play-based pedagogy, as well as being reflected in guidelines on Developmentally Appropriate Practice issued by the US National Association for the Education of Young Children (Bredekamp and Copple 1987; see also Mallory and New 1994).

Piaget's universal stages in cognitive development offers a persuasive framework for interpreting children's development which strongly resonates with Western images of young children – innocence, playfulness and learning. But the scientific evidence for the theory is much less robust than has generally been assumed (Donaldson 1978). Since the 1970s, increasing numbers of developmental psychologists turned to a different theoretical framework which seems to account much more adequately for the social and cultural dimensions of the developmental process, informed by the work of Lev Vygotsky and his followers. In this view, developmental stages are embedded in institutional and social practices and relationships as much as in processes of maturation. In fact, children's development might most accurately be described as 'naturally cultural' (Trevarthen 1998: Rogoff 2003).

There is nothing fundamentally natural about modern environments for childcare, either at home or within a pre-school setting. The early childhood settings and practices that foster early development are culturally constructed, the product of generations of human activity and creativity, mediated by complex belief systems, including about the 'proper' way for children to develop. The most significant features of any child's environment are the humans with whom they establish close relationships, parents, siblings and peers, care workers, teachers, etc. These individuals are themselves shaped by their cultural history, circumstances and training, and in the case of professionals, by the laws and policies that guide their work. These structures, relationships and belief systems translate into the everyday interactions that give meaning and direction to the experiences of young children, as adults scaffold their acquisition of skills and ways of communicating. For example, comparing mother–child dyads in India, Guatemala, Turkey and the USA, Rogoff et al. (1993) found that 'guided participation' was a feature in all these settings, but that the goals and processes of learning and teaching varied. These in turn were linked to the extent to which children's lives were segregated from the adult world of work. For example, while US mothers were often observed to create teaching situations, the Guatemalan mothers relied on a child's engagement with activities of the community.

Acceptance of this view – that children's behaviour, thinking, social relationships and adaptation, are culturally as much as biologically constituted – has profound implications for the way children's right to development is understood. The 'developmental appropriateness' of children's experiences, the 'harmfulness' or 'benefits' of their environment cannot be separated from the social and cultural processes through which they develop, the values and goals that inform the ways they are treated and understood. Unlike frameworks that emphasise normal and natural criteria for judging the quality of children's development, as well as the appropriateness of a particular environment or professional practices, cultural approaches argue that these criteria are culturally constructed and embedded in the particularities of child development contexts. In due course, human societies may come to share beliefs about what is 'normal' and 'natural' for young children. Indeed, in some ways, the UNCRC is a step in that direction. But universal consensus about the rights of the child does not make the beliefs and principles, or the arrangements for their implementation, any less cultural. The implication of accepting that child development has to be understood as a cultural process is that benchmarks are not intrinsic to the child, fixed and pre-scribed by nature in a simplistic sense. They are, to a large extent, also relational, historically specific and negotiable within a framework of promoting respect for young children's rights, as understood now, and in the future.

Needs or competencies?

Making a claim for children (or any other minority, low status group – the poor, the disabled, etc.) in terms of 'meeting needs' emphasises their dependencies. While children's right to protection from neglect, ill-treatment, exploitation and abuse is an important principle within the UNCRC, the underlying image of the needy child has been criticised, as underestimating children's actual and potential agency, in terms of their capacities to contribute to their development and well-being. While children's innocence, immaturity and vulnerability is emphasised, the role of adult society is disguised, through the projection of society's judgements onto children, as 'the child's needs' (Woodhead 1997). Framing children's development and welfare in terms of safeguarding their needs continues to be influential (Thomas 2005). [...]

Other theorists have emphasised respect for children's competencies as a more positive starting point for policy and for professional work. This is very much more in the spirit of the UNCRC and General Comment 7. It involves recognising the young child as a social actor, engaged with their social environment from the beginning of life. Moss et al. (2000) compare traditional discourses of the 'child in need' within British policies on early childhood with discourses of 'the rich child' associated with early childhood services in Reggio Emilia, inspired by the work of Loris Malaguzzi:

> Our image of children no longer considers them as isolated and egocentric ... does not belittle feelings or what is not logical ... instead our image of the child is rich in potential, strong, powerful, competent and most of all, connected to adults and other children. (Malaguzzi 1993:10)

While an image of the child in need can be linked to protection rights, an image of the competent child is more consistent with participatory rights, summed up in Article 12 of the UNCRC.

> States parties shall assure to the child who is capable of forming his or her own views the right to express those views freely in all matters affecting the child, the views of the child being given due weight in accordance with the age and maturity of the child. (UN Convention on the Rights of the Child, 1989, Article 12)

Article 12 sets one of the strongest challenges for early childhood professionals, and is linked to Articles 13, 14, 15 and 16 on freedom of expression, thought, conscience and religion and the right to privacy and freedom of association, according to children's evolving capacity. These articles of the UNCRC demand a reappraisal of children's role in shaping their development, in influencing those with responsibilities for their care and education and being listened to in all matters that affect them. Article 12 reminds us that children have their own perspective on the issues that concern parents, teachers, psychologists and child rights' workers. To put it bluntly, respect for children's rights to participation demands that children be viewed not just as 'subjects of study and concern', but also as 'subjects with concerns' (Prout 2000). Article 12 demands that children's views be respected, not as evidence of their relative competence, but as evidence of their unique experiences of the world they inhabit (Woodhead and Faulkner 2008). 'Effective communication with children, young people and families' is of course one of the areas of expertise within the Common Core of Skills and Knowledge for the Children's Workforce (DfES 2005). This area of expertise builds strongly on respect for children's capacities, concerns and preferred ways of communicating ideas and feelings.

During the past decade, numerous initiatives have translated participatory principles into practice, including in early childhood (Alderson 2000). For example, Lancaster (2006) proposes five principles for listening to children: recognising children's many languages; allocating communication spaces; making time; providing choice; and subscribing to a reflective practice. Other initiatives have been about effective consultation with young children, and increasing opportunities for contributing meaningfully to decision-making about issues that affect them (Einarsdottir 2007; MacNaughton et al. 2007). Amongst the most influential has been the Mosaic study that has developed techniques to listen to the perspectives of 3- and 4-year-old children on their nursery provision, for example based around children's drawings, their photographs and tape recordings (Clark and Moss 2001).

Respecting children's competence is not an alternative to safeguarding their welfare, especially for very young children. It is important to emphasise the qualifier in Article 12 that the views of the child should be given 'due weight in accordance with the age and maturity of the child'. Achieving balance between respecting the competent child and acknowledging their need for guidance is crucial to the practical implementation of participatory principles. How the balance is struck, in turn, depends on which theories about developing competence are given strongest weight. In earlier sections of this chapter, I contrasted two very different views of development.

One view drawing on Piagetian theory might argue as follows:

> Stage theories of intellectual development can be used to predict when children have sufficient capacities for understanding, such that their views should be listened to and taken seriously. Stage theories can also guide judgements about when children's capacities have evolved sufficiently that they no longer require so much direction and guidance from parents. According to this line of thought, the key question would be: 'At what stage does the child become competent to participate?' The role of adults would be to monitor children's growing capacities and make judgements about whether they are ready to participate.

An alternative view drawing on Vygotskian ideas would be:

> The stage theorists are asking the wrong question! Respecting children's growing competence isn't about measuring the progress of their development, like you might measure the height of a growing tree in order to decide when it should be felled. The more useful question is, 'How do children's competencies develop through appropriate levels of participation?' This way of posing the question draws attention to principles of guided participation. It highlights the ways children's competence can be guided and supported, or 'scaffolded' by adults and more competent peers in ways that are sensitive to their 'zone of proximal development'.

Different views on developing competencies are not exhaustive, nor necessarily in opposition. Lansdown (2005) suggests three interpretations: a developmental concept – fulfilling children's rights to the development of their optimum capacities; an emancipatory concept recognising and respecting the evolving capacities of children; and a protective concept – protecting children from experiences beyond their capacities. (For further discussion of theoretical perspectives that support participatory rights, see also Smith 2002; and Woodhead 2006.)

Summary

This discussion began by asking about the meanings attached to the concept of development, when viewed as one of children's fundamental rights. I have offered two contrasting paradigms for understanding development, summarised as three Ns versus three Cs. Polarising these paradigms is, of course, an oversimplification designed to draw attention to the diversity of ways that a 'right to development' can be interpreted in practice. Recognising the interdependencies between children and adults sets a further challenge. Realising children's rights requires close attention, not only to children, but also to the status and role of the adults children are destined to become. Conventional images of childhood view individual, adult maturity as a developmental endpoint; of having achieved independence, autonomy, competence, etc. Against this standard, children are marked off as dependent, needy and incompetent, as 'human becomings' rather than 'human beings' (Uprichard 2008). Promotion of children's participatory rights would be better served by recognising that the process of 'growing-up' is relative, not absolute. Adults can also be dependent, albeit in more subtle and sophisticated ways, surrounded by elaborate systems of biological, social, emotional and informational support. These patterns of interdependency are prerequisites for 'mature' psychological functioning and social adjustment, enabling adults (most of the time) to convey the impression of competence and autonomy that Western societies have so much valued as a 'developed status'. Arguably, a lifespan perspective (addressing the shifting patterns of participation and dependency from birth to old age) is a more appropriate basis for addressing these issues (Hockey and James 1993; Greene 1998). In short, implementing the UNCRC does not just alter the status of children. It also alters the status of adults, professionals, parents and others. Respecting the rights of young children changes the way we think about ourselves!

[...]

References

Alderson, P. (2000) *Young Children's Rights: Exploring Beliefs, Principles and Practices.* London: Jessica Kingsley Publishers

Bredekamp, S. and Copple, C. (eds) (1987) *Developmentally Appropriate Practice in Early Childhood Programs.* Washington: National Association for the Education of Young Children

Brooker, L. (2002) *Starting School: Young Children Learning Cultures.* Buckingham: Open University Press

Clark, A. and Moss, P. (2001) *Listening to Young Children: the Mosaic Approach.* London: National Children's Bureau

Department for Education and Skills (2005) *Common Core of Skills and Knowledge for the Children's Workforce.* London: DfES

Doek, J.E., Krappman, L. and Lee, Y. (2006) *Introduction to the General Comment, in Implementing Child Rights in Early Childhood: a Guide to General Comment 7.* The Hague: Bernard van Leer Foundation

Donaldson, M. (1978) *Children's Minds.* London: Fontana

Einarsdottir, J. (2007) 'Children's voices on the transition from preschool to primary school'. In A. Dunlop and H. Fabian (eds) *Informing Transitions in the Early Years: Research, Policy and Practice.* London: McGraw-Hill

Greene, S. (1998) 'Child development: old themes and new directions'. In M. Woodhead, D. Faulkner and K. Littleton (eds) *Making Sense of Social Development.* London: Routledge

Hockey, J. and James, A. (1993) *Growing Up and Growing Old.* London, Sage

Lancaster, Y. J. (2006) *RAMPS: a Framework for Listening to Children.* London: Day Care Trust

Lansdown, G. (2005) *The Evolving Capacities of Children: Implications for the Exercise of Rights.* Florence: UNICEF Innocenti Research Centre

MacNaughton, G., Hughes, P. and Smith, K. (2007) 'Young children's rights and public policy: practices and possibilities for citizenship in the early years'. *Children & Society, 21(6)*, 458–469

Malaguzzi, L. (1993) 'History, ideas and basic philosophy'. In C. Edwards, L. Gandini and G. Forman (eds) *The Hundred Languages of Children.* Norwood, NJ: Ablex

Mallory, B.L. and New, R. (1994) *Diversity and Developmentally Appropriate Practices: Challenges for Early Childhood Education.* New York: Teachers College Press

Moss, P., Dillon, J. and Siatham, J. (2000) 'The "child in need" and "the rich child": discourses, constructions and practice', *Critical Social Policy, 20(2)*, 233–254

Myers, R. (1992) *The Twelve who Survive.* London: Routledge

Prout, A. (2000) 'Children's participation: control and self-realisation in British late modernity', *Children & Society*, 14, 304–15

Rogoff, B. (2003) *The Cultural Nature of Child Development.* New York: Oxford University Press

Rogoff, B., Mosier, C., Mistry, J. and Goncu, A. (1993) 'Toddlers' guided participation with their caregivers in cultural activity'. In *Contexts for Learning: Socio-Cultural Dynamics in Children's Development.* New York: Oxford University Press

Smith, A.B. (2002) 'Interpreting and supporting participation rights: contributions from socio-cultural theory', *International Journal of Children's Rights, 10,* 73–88

Super, C. and Harkness, S. (1986) 'The developmental niche: a conceptualisation at the interface of child and culture', *International Journal of Behavioral Development*, 9, 545–69

Thomas, N. (2005) 'Interpreting children's needs: contested assumptions in the provision of welfare'. In J. Goddard, S. McNamee, A. James, and A. James (eds) *The Politics of Childhood. International Perspectives, Contemporary Developments.* Basingstoke: Palgrave Macmillan

Trevarthen, C. (1998) 'Children's need to learn a culture'. In M. Woodhead, D. Faulkner and K. Littleton (eds) *Cultural Worlds of Early Childhood.* London: Routledge

UNCRC (1989) *United Nations Convention on the Rights of the Child.* Geneva: Office of the United Nations High Commissioner for Human Rights

Uprichard, E. (2008) 'Children as "being and becomings": Children, childhood and temporality', *Children & Society, 22(4)*, 303–13

Woodhead, M. (1996) *In Search of the Rainbow: Pathways to Quality in Large Scale Programmes for Young Disadvantaged Children.* The Hague: Bernard van Leer Foundation

Woodhead, M. (1997) 'Psychology and the cultural construction of children's needs'. In A. Prout and A. James (eds) *Construction and Reconstruction of Childhood* (2nd Edition). London: Falmer

Woodhead, M. (2002) 'Work, play and learning in the lives of young children'. In L. Miller, R. Drury and R. Campbell (eds) *Exploring Early Years Education and Care.* London: David Fulton

Woodhead, M. (2006) 'Changing perspectives on early childhood theory, research and policy' (Background paper to UNESCO EFA Global Monitoring Report 2007), *International Journal of Equity and Innovation in Early Childhood, 4(2)*, 5–48

Woodhead, M. and Faulkner, D. (2008) 'Subjects, objects or participants? Dilemmas of psychological research with children'. In A. James and P. Christensen (eds) *Research with Children: Perspectives and Practices* (2nd Edition). London: Falmer Routledge

Part 2
Diversity and transitions

Introduction

Rose Drury

The chapters in this part of the book will, we hope, challenge readers to explore and reflect upon their understandings of familiar terms and concepts re-framed as critical issues. In all the chapters, many commonly held 'truths' about our understandings of children and how they develop and learn, the curriculum and pedagogical approaches are re-examined. The themes which emerge include: diversities, inclusion, parents' perspectives and early intervention, rural poverty, constructing relationships with key workers and friends, and postmodern perspectives on early childhood education.

In Chapter 6, diversity is considered as a critical issue within early childhood education. Jeanette Rhedding-Jones argues powerfully that diversity as a concept should be embedded in contemporary society and education systems, rather than treated in a tokenistic manner. Drawing on observations and recordings made of children aged 2 to 5 years in day care centres in North America and Europe, and presenting scenarios from practice, she problematizes 'mainstream diversity' and interrogates practical manifestations of diversity. She makes the case for looking critically at definitions of difference in relation to diversity and suggests actions which might lead to the construction of 'critical diversities'.

In Chapter 7, Christine Hickman and Kyffin Jones raise important questions about the issues surrounding the inclusion of children with special educational needs in the early years. They discuss the historical and legislative context of the term inclusion, and highlight the need to view inclusive education in a wider societal context. Of particular significance are the debates they present relating to the medical model of SEN and segregated specialist education and also the issues of equality and human rights enshrined in the social model. The authors use case studies to illustrate the range of challenges facing practitioners and to promote the notion that inclusion is a process which is highly individualized and wider than the current debate in the UK regarding specialist versus mainstream provision.

Concepts of professionalism in general, and of reflective and reflexive professionalism in particular, are discussed in Jan Peeters' and Michel Vandenbroeck's chapter on childcare practitioners and the process of professionalization. An analysis of narratives of professionals during 30 years of action research puts the agentic voice of practitioners in focus. In Chapter 8, the authors draw upon a large-scale action research project on respect for diversity in childcare in which the ethnic minority course members and their Flemish mentors speak about a paradigm shift in relation to diversity in early childhood and about the difficulties of constructing an inclusive professionalism. The narratives show that open discussion of complex problems is required as they ask for interpretations of professionalism which move beyond reflection and develop the ability to be reflexive. The authors formulate the hypothesis that practice, enabling reflection on 'doing things right' as well as 'doing the right things', asks for four categories of basic and generic competencies, including 'the ability to focus on the meeting of the Other, the one we do not know'.

The context for early intervention programmes, in particular the Early Support Programme (DfES, 2004) in England, is critiqued in Chapter 9, where Alice Paige-Smith, Jonathan Rix and Anna Craft explore the relationship between parents, professionals and children with learning difficulties or disabilities in the early intervention process. They argue that such programmes, which are based on a deficit developmental view of the child, may have an effect on parents' and children's experiences. They offer an alternative 'family-centred' approach, in which parents engage in a process of reflecting on their own child's learning, thus transforming their role into one of reflective collaboration between parents and professionals.

The challenge of rural poverty in Wales is the focus of Chapter 10, where Siân Wyn Siencyn presents a definition for child poverty and sets the historical, political and social context for the Welsh Assembly Government of Wales' commitment to ensure that children are not disadvantaged by poverty. The case studies in the chapter of children living in rural poverty in Wales illustrate the challenges faced by many children and families. In order to improve the life chances of such children and meet the 2020 target of eradicating child poverty (WAG, 2005), the chapter ends with recommendations from a 2009 Joseph Rowntree Foundation report (Winkler, 2009), including improving childcare provision and the skills and qualifications of adults.

Liz Brooker presents an 'ethical pedagogy' in Chapter 11 in which the relationship of care is constructed by children under 3 and the adults who look after them. Brooker considers the 'contested' nature of care and the caring relationship and emphasizes the agency shown by very young children and the ways in which adults respect their responses. The observations of children aged between 7 and 18 months in a Children's Centre suggest a range of contributions to the new relationships and to the child's identity and well-being in the setting.

Friendship as a key factor in young children's transitional experiences is explored in Chapter 12. Sally Peters examines the complex nature of the 'transition to school' through a study of children's experiences of friendships in a large urban school and three kindergartens in New Zealand. She reveals that friends play an important role in facilitating learning, as well as supporting children's transition to formal schooling. The author suggests a range of strategies to empower children and to facilitate friendships, including the need to examine the classroom climate and the way children are positioned within it.

The final chapter in this part of the book presents an overview of a postmodern theoretical position, together with associated theories – post-Fordism, post-structuralism and post-colonialism. In Chapter 13, Deborah Albon demonstrates how such theorizing can be applied to practice and she deconstructs some commonly held 'truths' about early years practice, such as what is meant by a 'child' and how children develop and learn. Postmodern thinking troubles the idea that the world is 'knowable'; this is a viewpoint that embraces diversity and recognizes that all knowledge is socially constructed. Most significantly, she argues that postmodernist thinking is valuable in helping practitioners maintain a critical stance to what they do and why; this is a theme which has permeated all the chapters in this part of the book.

References

Department for Education and Skills (DfES) (2004) *Early Support Family Pack*. Nottingham: DfES.

Welsh Assembly Government (WAG) (2005) *A Fair Future for our Children*. Cardiff: Welsh Assembly Government.

Winkler, V. (2009) *What is Needed to End Child Poverty in Wales?* York: Joseph Rowntree Foundation.

6

Questioning diversity

Jeanette Rhedding-Jones

Overview

The concept of diversity is interrogated in this chapter as an important aspect of the postmodern condition. Rhedding Jones argues that diversity as a concept should not be treated superficially or in a tokenistic manner in education systems in contemporary society. Observations and recordings made in day care centres in North America and Europe provide examples to illustrate the ways in which diversity is enacted and encountered in early childhood education. The implications for professionals in early childhood education are considered.

[...]

This chapter interrogates the concept of *diversity,* an important aspect of the post-modern condition. It argues that diversity, as a concept, should matter in contemporary society and the education systems that are embedded in them, and it should *not* be treated *superficially*, or in a tokenistic manner. Diversity is understood in various ways within early childhood education. We need to carefully consider how early childhood educators perceive diversity since it can have far-reaching implications for the ways in which we enact our professional lives. In this chapter the concept of diversity is made problematic. Various observations and recordings made in day care centers in North America and Europe are critically questioned in relation to the current issues. These contexts were observed when visiting children aged 2 to 5 years of age in care settings. The examples are chosen to create focal points for interrogation and to

Rhedding-Jones, J. (2005) 'Questioning diversity', in Yelland, N. (ed.) *Critical Issues in Early Childhood*, Buckingham: Open University Press, pp. 130–45. © 2005. Reproduced with the kind permission of Open University Press. All rights reserved.

illustrate the ways in which diversity is enacted. The field notes and the references that are analyzed within this chapter have been arranged so that diversity is considered from a variety of perspectives within management discourses, to see how diversity may be encountered in early childhood education contexts. The chapter considers the ramifications of this and asks if the term diversity is still a term that is relevant in contemporary times. At the end of the chapter the implications for professionals in early childhood education are drawn together. The aims of the chapter are to do the following:

- to show that diversity is a critical issue and, as such, the term needs to be carefully considered;
- to assist readers to consider the ways they might deal with 'diversity' in early childhood education practice;
- to question the practical and discursive positioning of early childhood education in relation to the wider discourses of diversity.

A political agenda for change is built into the chapter. For example, one critical issue is related to the integration of ethnic and linguistic 'minorities' in early childhood contexts. This becomes problematic when it operates in practice as assimilation, rather than as transformation of the monoculture and the monolingual through a critical and anti-racist multiculturalism (May, 1999), and through strategies of anti-bias in early childhood education and care (Creaser and Dau, 1996; Derman-Sparkes, 1991; Makin et al., 1995). In focusing on diversity, the chapter deals with this issue as something that is able to be seen and heard; and also as a set of discursive constructions.

The *seeing* and the *hearing* that happens in the following scenarios can be through words, silences, actions and non-actions of the adults and the children. The first scenario is presented here for your critical interrogation. Here, I as the narrator, have juxtaposed my notes from everyday events from early childhood education and care settings. In New York, I was behind glass to 'observe' young children in a center. In Oslo, I spent two days with a group of visiting international people also observing early childhood education and care practices. We were invited into the Norwegian day care centers and the explanations were given in English. The scenarios I present in this chapter are framed by my note-taking at these centers. This was informed by my critical questioning, including issues such as: What is happening and not happening here in terms of diversity and language(s)? Who are the adults here? What are they saying and writing and why? As the narrator of the scenarios I was mindful not to be exempt from the critique.

Scenario 1

It is 11.30 a.m. and we're in the language room in the *barnehagen* [a day care centre in Norway, for children aged 3 to 5 years]. It has '*språk rom*' (language room) written on the door. There are lots of testing and teaching objects visible, cards with pictures on them for example, and small toys. The *barnehagelærer* (day care teacher-carer) calls what happens in here 'mapping'. They map what each child can do with language.

Teacher-carer:	I use this book from Sweden and I can see how many words they know. I use [the book and the objects] to find out what they know [in Norwegian language]. To the parents, I tell them 'speak your mother tongue'.
Women in observation group:	At home. [not expressed as a question]
Teacher-carer:	At home. [expressed as an answer]
Second woman observer:	What about the father's language? [The teacher doesn't understand. She is, after all, trained in special pedagogy not in critical theory.]

From my reading, the issues here appear to be that:

1. This day care centre does provide for children speaking another language at home, but it does so by locating the explicit teaching and testing of the national language behind a closed door, specifically for those children not from the nationally dominant ethnicity. By doing so the children's home languages are perhaps not seen as 'language' at all.
2. The English words here may not 'mean' what speakers of English at home might think. Similarly, the Norwegian language used by the children learning to speak it as a second or third language in this pre-school may not 'mean' what the Norwegians think it does.
3. The professionals in this scenario assume that they are able to 'map' what the children can do with language and that language is able to be rated and evaluated by people listening to it. By trusting the writers of the 'Swedish book', as experts from another country, the Norwegian teacher-carers are not trusting their own professional experience and knowledge.
4. The so-called 'mother tongue' is not valued in the day care center because that is where the normalized and colonizing language of Norwegian rules. If the children hear and speak their home languages only at home they soon learn that home is not the place that matters, at least that will be how they think Norwegians see non-Norwegians.
5. 'Special' pedagogy has a lot to do with setting up pedagogical events like the one in this scenario. If 'critical' pedagogues decided what happened, then the events might be otherwise.
6. The questions asked by the two women observing in this scenario show that they are being critical: of gender matters (the 'mother tongue' and the 'father tongue') and of the split between the private home and the public pre-school (the implication that children must not speak their home language when not at home).

These narratives might benefit from postmodern readings, where readers resolve the split between narrative and exposition, and where there are many unfixed possibilities and implications for practice. The aim is to show that the creation of a critical diversity is crucial for early childhood education for a number of reasons. These include:

- being able to better understand objections or resistance to the concept of 'diversity', particularly in its present use in early childhood education;
- a desire to focus on the political justice aspects of equity rather than simply on the rhetoric of superficial aspects;
- a consideration of resisting 'diversity' strategies favoring individuals, groups and cultures that are already well supported.

It is anticipated that people will have multiple interpretations of the concept(s) of diversity, and these may actually be what help us to create contexts for discussions which will have important implications for practices. What this chapter cautions against are situations in which a term or word is adopted without awareness of its discursive histories and effects. Meanings have to be considered in context and related to practice. A problem with normalized understandings of diversity is that they appear to require an 'add-on multi-culturalism that "celebrates" exotic otherness' (Laubscher and Powell, 2003, p. 221). […] Early childhood education should aim to go beyond an 'add-on multiculturalism' simply celebrating the exotic. What we are doing about the national constructions of 'diversity' is not so clear.

Definitions and discourses

This section deals with diversity definitions in operation, that is, how usage of the term diversity shows what people think diversity is, and then how this might translate into practice. Discourses are about sets of practices that are not always understood. They include describing and knowing what people do, and what they say, and realizing the impact of values, life histories and socio-cultural contexts on behaviors. Because diversity exemplifies what happens with discourses and power, the term itself serves to show what discourses exist and how they operate.

In early childhood education the term 'diversity' has been used in connection to support identity, difference and complexity (e.g. Grieshaber and Cannella, 2001; Siraj-Blatchford and Clarke, 1998). These issues need to be further explored in critical ways related to everyday practices in learning environments with young children. In the scenario that follows, there is a description of what was happening in practice, at a particular place and time. It is relevant to consider what ideologies here are supporting identity, complexity and difference. What is managing diversity in the face of difference? Is it pedagogy that normalizes the management of space, time and children? Further, what definitions and discourses of diversity have allowed me as a privileged White woman to here become a passive observer and critic?

Scenario 2

Through the New York observation glass I view a young man sounding sounds, a young woman psychology student that I was introduced to earlier, a mother and an assistant to the teacher-carers. The children are all in a circle. [cut] Now the children are lining up for the adults and going out the door. Don't know where to. The empty room has the usual pale wood midget furniture. Tokenly compartmentalized for child action of assorted kinds. The PhD student of psychology is now planning her dinner on the mobile phone … Outside the playroom the Parent Bulletin Board is up high above the lockers. Says 'For sale: car seat, baby swing, electronic'. The next notice is in Spanish. The third says 'Admission into session for prospective parents at … school'. On the far wall are 'Our Family Books'. These are published by four men I've not heard of: Don, Bill Jnr., Jo and Pete. In the corridor is information about bilingualism. A poster says something in an Asian script that I cannot understand.

The issues embedded here are many and include:

- Diversity is obvious in the parent notice board but not in what these 5-year-olds are actually doing, which is a normalized circle activity based around English-language phonics, followed by all lining up and going together to another room at the same time.
- Here the psychology student's phone calling appears to demonstrate a disengagement from early childhood practice and its critical issues.
- The men-as-experts who have published the books for the parents to read have very White and American names. Despite the Hispanic and 'Asian' languages of the families of these children, there appear to be no 'experts' from them. Further, there are no women 'experts' writing the books, despite the large numbers of women professionals in early childhood education, and the fact that the 'parents' I am seeing today are all mothers.
- By placing observers behind one-way glass, the notion of childhood is perhaps quite close to animal-hood. If the children are not free to spy on adults, and to move among adults as they might wish, then what is in this scenario as a discourse of adult control and surveillance of the young? Because this is a day care center with most children speaking languages other than English at home, they are subjected to the observation glass in ways that 'majority' children are not, because visitors like me come to look at them.
- Although this institution is recognized as 'multicultural', the multiculturalism is not made critical, as the catering for diverse language and cultures appears to be tokenistic. Effects of the diversity discourses and definitions here are that the languages other than English are visible or audible only on the parents' notice board, where Euro-American men appear as experts and 'Asian' and Hispanic parents communicate with each other.
- Managing diversity appears to be happening through the normalizations of psychology, the teaching of Anglo-American phonics, and the children all doing the same thing at the same time. By being with the children and the

man who is their teacher-carer, the mother and the assistant and the psychology student are validating a non-critical pedagogy regarding diversity. Management via pedagogy thus eliminates bilingualism, despite the notice board's proclamation of it.

What follows links these diversity issues to general usage and then to management discourses more explicitly. In general usage, people in the Western world are likely to understand diversity as being about difference or variety. [...] For example, in Australia a 1998 public service document says:

> Diversity relates to gender, age, language, ethnicity, cultural background, sexual orientation, religious belief and family responsibilities. Diversity also refers to the ways we are different in other respects such as educational level, work experience, socio-economic background, personality profile, geographic location, marital status and whether or not one has a carer. (Bacchi, 2000, pp. 75–6)

Here new diversities, such as family responsibilities, have crept in, but race and disability are left out. [...] As ways into studying a problematized term or word then, what the chapter does next is consider diversity as it is used in differing discourses. For early childhood education professionals, what are the implications of the political positionings that follow as discourses?

[...]

Mainstream diversity

With mainstream diversity the focus is on the 'other': on individuals seen as 'different'. Here [...] the social justice of diversity may be only rhetoric, and not actual. Bacchi says that the effect of a mainstream approach is to totalize and individualize. This means that 'qualitative differences among employees are equalized or averaged and translated into workplace norms governing behavior and performance' (2000, p. 71). The problem with mainstream diversity is that it simplistically ignores the groups and the cultures, in its focus on ways that individuals are different from each other, and its attempts to make them the same. With this approach the focus is on who is 'different' or 'other' from yourself. Here difference and otherness are *not* seen as a normal part of everyday life, but as something to be got rid of, reduced or glossed over. Mainstream diversity [...] aims to make everyone appear as similar as possible. So what is done in the workplace, the play-places and the classrooms is the same everywhere, regardless of who the children and their families are. Following this, how children and staff are judged is in relation to some expected 'average' which is constructed after the dominant culture's values. Here 'competence' and 'quality' are critical issues. What tends to dominate is conformity.

[...] In scenario three, the children as individuals are taught and tested in a special room, as 'others' to normalized Norwegians. Without this practice though, would the 'others' still learn the Norwegian language before going to school? [...] What are the national responsibilities of immigrants to become assimilated? Why are there no 'ethnic minority' professionals in this pre-school? Here is a third scenario which might provide some answers.

Scenario 3

While she works with the children, the Pakistani Norwegian who is an assistant tells me without my asking, and in our only common language, which is Norwegian, that she only has *grunnskole*. [Primary schooling, which might have been until she was 16, but she could have been as young as 12. She has had no formal, institutionalized education since then.] So she can't go further, she says. She means she can't do a course, because she doesn't have the schooling prerequisites to get in.

She has the children in a circle, and is singing Norwegian songs to them. Not one of these children is of Norwegian background. All are here as children whose parents have recently migrated. They need to know the songs for when they go to school next year. The woman assistant wears the *salwar kamij* [traditional Pakistani women's clothes: matching loose long and all-covering tunic, loose long trousers and long scarf]. I have my *salwar kamij* at home, from when I worked in Bangladesh. I wear the *salwar kamij* to the formal dinner that night.

In considering this scene it is useful to raise some questions. For example:

- How is the assistant positioned as 'other'?
- How do she and I decide to position ourselves?
- Was my subsequent wearing of the *salwar kamij* a token gesture to make me feel better about my education and wealth?
- Was it to differentiate myself from the others at the dinner?
- Why are these children not learning Pakistani songs?
- What are the effects of the assistant singing in Norwegian while embodying the non-Norwegian?
- How are we to understand the desire for difference and the desire for non-difference happening at the same time?

Some of the problems associated with mainstream diversity are that 'this insistence upon "individual differences" can mean simply bypassing groups' (Bacchi, 2000, p. 71). So my scenario-writing risks an emphasis on the assistant and myself as individuals, without acknowledging the groups and cultures we represent. These include not only ethnicity, race and language but age, socio-economic class, gender, sexuality, religion and ability. Here what appeared as a scenario showing something of 'multiculturalism' becomes by the agency of this pre-school assistant, a focus on her socio-economic positioning in relation to mine. This shows at the level of personal contact, which is where early childhood education always is, and must be, that we *cannot* get rid of our own subjective positioning in relation to 'others'. [...]

Productive diversity

A newer 'productive diversity … emphasizes the need for … members of organizations to change, to learn new languages, for example, and to learn to assess the value of different ways of doing things, instead of insisting that there is only one way' (Bacchi, 2000, p. 68). Here a productive diversity in institutions will be *against* 'shared vision and corporate culture, teams, win–win conflict situations, benchmarking, setting standards, quality management'. Its underlying discourses, says Bacchi, are social justice, understanding and individual differences. Productive diversity then (Cope and Kalantzis, 1997) might move an institution beyond assimilation and the prevailing practice of organizational monoculturalism. For early childhood education this seems preferable to managing diversity.

Cope and Kalantzis' model of 'productive diversity' is based on the concept of culture as cohesion through diversity and focuses on 'the dynamic relationship of differences in the establishment of common ground' (1997, p. 16). Diversity, they say, is a critical issue to be negotiated, with qualitative differences in value systems, ways of thinking and ways of communicating (p. 144). Further, it 'is not just a matter of hiring a few people of minority background … Productive Diversity changes everything we do in organizations because it changes the fundamentals of organizational life' (p. 209).
 […]

Scenario 4

It's very very hot. The children are all inside the *barnehage,* in Norway. There is no water play. Outside there is fenced land around the (day care) building but no-one has mown the lawn so it's just long weeds. This is cultural difference. Here there seems to be no pedagogical use of the earth. There could be a gently running hose, shady trees for outdoor play, growing vegetables for children to eat, flowers not from a florist shop. What could these mothers from African countries, Turkey and Pakistan (or any mothers from anywhere else) do with this day care centre's land? Are they unlearning their relationship to seasonal growth? Or just trying to be as Norwegian as possible after their migration? Inside the water-less *barnehage* one of the children is trying on my sunhat. As I don't stop him the hat turns into *everybody's* dress-up prop, with sideways glances from the mirror to see what I will do. Here they don't wear hats.

As a *productive diversity*, the scenario might demonstrate a cohesion through diversity because the children and the mothers appear to be acting as one group. Yet this is not a *productive diversity* because what is being produced is more of the same Norwegian monoculture. So diversity, at least at that moment […] has not been negotiated as a critical issue, with changes to practice-as-usual. Here the practices regard the exceptionally hot weather and the uses of the land and the play areas, and the non-use of water. […] For the children and the mothers from African countries, Turkey and Pakistan, this may be their only experience of a pre-school. So how could they, or others without experience of doing things differently, imagine it otherwise?

How could we, without experience of the home nations of the mothers imagine what their 'diversities' might request, desire or construct?

Critical discourses

What has become increasingly evident is that diversity is a political term and may be used in a variety of contexts in order to appease and placate. For example, Chandra Mohanty (1990) wrote of the challenges for education, regarding race and voice. [...] Calling for reconceptualization she says:

> The challenge of race resides in a fundamental reconceptualization of our categories of analysis so that differences can be historically specified and understood as part of larger political processes and systems. The central issue, then, is not one of merely *acknowledging* difference; rather, the more difficult question concerns the kind of difference that is acknowledged and engaged. Difference seen as a benign variation, for instance, rather than as conflict, struggle, or the threat of disruption, bypasses power as well as history to suggest a harmonious and empty pluralism. (p. 181)

[...]

Early childhood education discourses

This section very briefly presents some key writings within early childhood education. First, we look at text by Viruru (2002) whose research focused on fieldwork with young children in her homeland of India. She says: 'the concept of Relation is that it is opposed to the idea of "essence" ... To exist in Relation, is to be part of an ever-changing and diversifying process, whereas to be reduced to an essence is to be fixed with permanent attributes' (p. 37). Here then are no expected categories, no unchangeable values, no core personalities and no predictability. Viruru's diversifying is a process: a verb and not a noun. An 'ever-changing and diversifying process' exists because of our relations with other people, other discourses, other positionings. Here is not a diversity with people as its objects. Rather this is about the subjective and fluid processes of not being the same, and of changing according to who you are with, or where you are at a particular point in time (e.g. Rhedding-Jones, 2001, 2002a, 2002b, 2003a, 2003b). It might be contended from postmodern readings that Viruru aligns herself with critical theorists such as Bhabha (e.g. 1994, 1996) and Mohanty (1990), by resisting the noun 'diversity'.

From professional literature for early childhood practitioners, the practical advice about what should be done about *linguistic diversity* is: make sure that families are key participants and learn from them; maintain and develop the languages the children bring from home; make the programs culturally and linguistically relevant; have all children explore other languages; cater for bilingual children and see bilingualism's advantages (after Makin et al., 1995, pp. 69–104). Related strategies for working with *anti-bias* are: plan for change; change policy and procedures; develop the staff's professionalisms; have more information and communication between families and staff; record keep about children's sense of identity, languages and self-esteem (adapted from Khoshkhesal, 1998). Also closely related are *anti-discriminatory* approaches that: shape policies and practices by reviewing and revising organizations; acknowledge discriminations; understand and accept anti-discriminatory principles; change procedures of recruitment, selection and promotion of staff; examine and learn to understand oppression; implement culturally appropriate curricula not mono-cultural curricula; intervene in children's processes of learning if this is discriminatory. In the UK these approaches specifically target inequality and 'diversity' regarding black children, refugees, children as girls and boys, traveller children (Gypsies), children with disabilities, and children from homosexual families (Brown, 1998, pp. 45–6).

As what-to-do advice for teachers and carers, this is focusing on the children and staff themselves, rather than on the management matters of how to manage, how to make diversity productive, how to appear to be catering for it. However, given economic rationalism, such curricula and institutional strategies are constantly at risk. Further, unless we develop critical perspectives around diversity and take up matters of social justice, the term 'diversity' (with its management connotations) could actually displace the anti-bias, anti-discriminatory approaches, the equity work and the critical multicultural work currently being developed and conducted. I am therefore asking people to be conscious of any shift towards a 'new term', and its political implications and possible negative consequences. This is not just about fashion and the comings and goings of 'hot words'. It is about the dangers of being politically manipulated into something you did not know about. In this case, if we follow some of the management approaches, the 'something' could be the future of ethnic and racial minorities in early childhood education.

Conclusion

Throughout this chapter, I have posed questions and interrogated practical manifestations of diversity. We now have to ask whether diversity, with all the problems here interrogated, is still a term we want. If we say we are working for a critical diversity, then this would differentiate the reconceptualizing of diversity from that which is non-critical, such as those in the management approaches, and perhaps some of the early childhood education approaches also. The chapter has presented various scenarios and critiqued and problematized the notions of diversity to show that, from critical perspectives, diversity is not a word to be adopted and used without thought. Seen as a critical issue, diversity is 'loaded' with complexities, innuendoes and omissions. Thus, I have tried to offer, via the scenarios from practice with children, critical insights on the problematization of difference and inclusion: of integration, assimilation and transformation of cultures, institutions and people. What is evident is that we need to make problematic our definitions of difference in relation to diversity. This means looking critically at what is happening as practice in the name of 'diversity', so that difference becomes usual, and what becomes problematic is normalization. Further, we need to ask critical questions about socio-economic diversity, and the structural inequities that cause it. For example, we might:

- make diversity plural, as *diversities*;
- see that culture is not fixed;
- not categorize people into homogenous groupings;
- focus on equity and social justice in our everyday actions and words;
- prepare both children and adults to become change agents via challenging stereotypes and norms of behavior;
- raise our own awareness of what middle-class *whiteness* entails;
- be wary of management discourses and programs and their applicability to early childhood education;
- critique and transform the relations of power in early childhood settings.

Through these actions we might then facilitate and construct *critical diversities*.

References

Bacchi, C. (2000) The seesaw effect: down goes affirmative action, up comes workplace diversity, *Journal of Interdisciplinary Gender Studies*, 5(2): 64–83.

Bhabha, H. (1994) *The Location of Culture*. London and New York: Routledge.

Bhabha, H. (1996) Culture's in-between, in S. Hall and P. Du Gay (eds) *Questions of Cultural Identities*. London: Sage.

Brown, B. (1998) *Unlearning Discrimination in the Early Years*. London: Trentham Books.

Cope, B. and Kalantzis, M. (1997) *Productive Diversity: A New, Australian Model for Work and Management*. Annandale, NSW: Pluto Press.

Creaser, B. and Dau, E. (1996) *The Anti-Bias Approach in Early Childhood*. Woden: Australian Early Childhood Association, Harper Education, Australia.

Derman-Sparkes, L. and the ABC Task Force (1991) *The Anti-Bias Curriculum. Tools for Empowering Young Children*. Washington DC: National Association for Early Years Curriculum.

Grieshaber, S. and Cannella, G.S. (eds) (2001) *Embracing Identities in Early Childhood Education: Diversity and Possibilities*. New York: Teachers College Press.

Khoshkhesal, V. (1998) *Realising the Potential: Cultural and Linguistic Diversity in Family Day Care*. Sydney: Lady Gowrie Child Centre.

Laubscher, L. and Powell, S. (2003) Skinning the drum; teaching about diversity as 'other', *Harvard Educational Review*, 73(2): 203–24.

Makin, L., Campbell, J. and Jones Diaz, C. (1995) *One Childhood, Many Languages: Guidelines for Early Childhood Education in Australia*. Pymble, NSW: Harper Educational.

May, S. (ed.) (1999) *Critical Multiculturalism: Rethinking Multicultural and Anti-Racist Education*. London: Falmer Press.

Mohanty, C.T. (1990) On race and voice: challenges for liberal education in the 1990s, *Cultural Critique*, Winter 1989–1990: 179–208.

Rhedding-Jones, J. (2001) Shifting ethnicities: 'native informants' and other theories from/for early childhood education, *Contemporary Issues in Early Childhood*, 2(2): 135–56.

Rhedding-Jones, J. (2002a) An undoing of documents and other texts: towards a critical multicultural early childhood education, *Contemporary Issues in Early Childhood,* 3(1): 90–116.

Rhedding-Jones, J. (2002b) Doing diversity: dealing with complexity, difference and multiplicity in practice, theory and research methodology. Invited plenary presented at the International Education Symposium, 'Quality, Culture and Diversity in Education', Oslo University College, Norway, 7 May.

Rhedding-Jones, J. (2003a) Feminist methodologies and research for early childhood literacies, in N. Hall, J. Larson and J. Marsh (eds) *Handbook of Early Childhood Literacy* (pp. 399–410). London: Sage.

Rhedding-Jones, J. (2003b) Questioning play and work, early childhood and pedagogy, in D. Lytle, *Play and Educational Theory and Practice* (pp. 243–54). Westport, CT: Praeger.

Siraj-Blatchford, I. and Clarke, P. (1998) *Supporting Identity, Diversity and Language in the Early Years*. Philadelphia, PA: Open University Press.

Viruru, R. (2002) Colonized through language: the case of early childhood education, *Contemporary Issues in Early Childhood*, 2(1): 31–47.

7

Inclusive practice for children with special educational needs

Christine Hickman and Kyffin Jones

Overview

This chapter discusses the issues surrounding the inclusion of children with special educational needs in the early years. Inclusion as a term and philosophy is defined and discussed within a historical and legislative context. Case studies are used to demonstrate a range of provision for a range of need. While the importance of a multi-agency approach is commented upon, the main focus is on educational perspective.

[…]

'I had a really great time. Nobody talked to me all night!' (Michael, aged 7)

Michael illustrates one of the underlying principles of the education of children with Special Educational Needs (SEN) – the notion that how they see the world and what is important to them is individual and might differ from adults' reality. Michael has Asperger Syndrome which is characterized by impairment in social interaction, and for him an enjoyable night at his local youth club entailed being completely ignored

Hickman, C. and Jones, K. (2009) 'Inclusive practice for children with Special Educational Needs (SEN)', in Waller, T. (ed.) *An Introduction to Early Childhood*, London: Sage, pp. 26–38.

by his peers. This gave him the space to read his favourite science textbooks uninterrupted. What is clear, however, is that without a firm understanding of Michael's identity, both our assumptions and our interventions will not be accurate and might even be detrimental. This chapter will introduce a range of themes relating to the field of SEN while emphasizing the need to adopt a highly individual and sensitive response, one which pays heed to the child's own identity and perspective. While this chapter will recognize that specific disorders and conditions can be linked to general strategies and good practice, it will also urge the reader to look more widely than simply labels and categories in order to optimize interventions.

It is true that an understanding of the principles of conditions such as Asperger Syndrome might in some way aid the practitioner, but they are worth nothing without a clear understanding of the individual's perspective. If Michael is to be a fully functioning and included member of society, his inclusion is in some way dependent on our skills to understand him as much as his skills to fit in with us.

Inclusion, therefore, is not simply the debate about pupils with SEN being educated in mainstream schools, it is about the role society has in including all children equally.

The legislative framework

It is clear from the wealth of literature on the subject that the movement towards inclusive education has been part of the educational scene in Britain for many years (Booth and Ainscow, 1998; Drifte, 2001; Dyson and Millward, 2000; Jones, 2004; Norwich, 1997; O'Brien, 2001; Roffey, 2001; Wilson, 1998; Wolfendale, 2000). Some maintain it can be mapped back to the Education Act 1944 which extended the right to education to most (but not all) of Britain's children, as Stakes and Hornby (1997: 24) highlight:

> Children with SEN were to be placed in one of eleven categories of handicap: blind, partially sighted, deaf, partially deaf, epileptic, educationally subnormal, maladjusted, physically handicapped, speech defective, delicate and diabetic. The 1944 Act required that LEAs had to ascertain the needs of children in their area for special educational treatment. It indicated that this should be undertaken in mainstream schools wherever possible.

It is important to note that, at this time, disability was firmly categorized into medical subgroups and that the remit of education was to treat rather than educate. Subsequent reports such as that by the Warnock Committee (1978) highlighted the principle of integrating children with disabilities and developed the process of obtaining a statement of special educational need. In effect, a contract between pupil and educational provider based on careful assessment. The findings of Baroness Warnock and her team helped inform the subsequent 1981 Education Act.

A greater emphasis was given to the education of children with special needs during the 1980s and early 1990s and this culminated in the implementation of the Code of Practice for Special Educational Needs in 1994, updated in 2001. At the time, this was the most prescriptive guidance on special needs to have been issued by the UK government. It aimed to expand the roles and responsibilities of schools and local education authorities (LEAs) highlighted in the 1981 Education Act. This trend of redefining SEN provision has continued and during the past decade has gained momentum and evolved considerably. The Code of Practice (2001) stresses that 'provider' means all settings which early years children may attend, therefore adherence to such guidelines impacts upon a wide range of professional practice. The early years have specified strands in the Code: *Early Years Action* and *Early Years Action Plus*. According to Drifte (2001: 4), 'both stages involve individualised ways of working with the child, including the implementation of IEPs (Individual Education Plans), on a gradually increasing level of involvement'.

Early years provision has always crossed over fields, i.e. health and education, therefore previous legislation such as the 1981, 1993 and 1996 Education Acts may not have enabled a more cohesive approach to SEN in the early years (Wolfendale, 2000: 147). However, more recent legislation appears to be addressing this (Roffey, 2001: 14). *Curriculum 2000* contains an inclusive statement concerning the provision of effective learning opportunities for all pupils. It sets out three principles that are essential to developing a more inclusive curriculum:

1. Setting suitable learning challenges.
2. Responding to pupils' diverse learning needs.
3. Overcoming potential barriers to learning and assessment for individuals and groups of pupils (QCA, 2000).

The global and national perspective

Inclusive policies have been found increasingly higher up the agenda of the UK government, local education authorities and individual schools. This is due in some part to the United Nations Educational, Scientific and Cultural Organisation (UNESCO) Salamanca statement on principles, policy and practice in special needs education published in 1994. This statement urged national governments to pursue inclusive educational practices for all children.

It is the consensus of many educationalists (for example, Booth and Ainscow, 1998) that the goal of inclusive education is a worthy one but it leads us to ask two questions. First, what do we mean by inclusive education or 'inclusion', and second, why do we need it? Finding a concrete definition of inclusion can be difficult and it is clear that confusion abounds, affecting providers, parents and the pupils themselves.

The Centre for Studies on Inclusive Education (CSIE) is an independent educational charity set up in 1982. In their literature they define inclusion as, 'disabled and non-disabled children and young people learning together in ordinary pre-school provision, schools, colleges and universities, with appropriate networks of support' (CSIE, 2000: 1).

Such a short definition belies the incredibly far-reaching, controversial and challenging task of the inclusion movement. Essentially the CSIE is advocating the end of segregated education and with it the traditional model of special education in this country. It follows that there must be a compelling argument behind this radical approach if one is to answer the second of the above questions. Why do we need inclusion? Again the CSIE (2000) answers this in a succinct and direct way, 'Because children – whatever their disability or learning difficulty – have a part to play in society after school, an early start in mainstream playgroups or nursery schools, followed by education in ordinary schools and colleges is the best preparation for an integrated life' (CSIE, 2000: 2).

Early intervention is an essential component to any debate on early years and inclusion (Mortimer, 2002). In this respect the UK government's agenda includes healthy living, community support, multi-agency working and a focus on families. Initiatives such as Education and Health Action Zones and Sure Start are examples of these ideals (Wolfendale, 2000: 149).

Inclusion: a human right?

It is clear therefore that issues of equality and human rights are central to such a rationale, and as the above quote highlights, education is only one part of the picture. The drive towards inclusive education has to be seen in a wider societal context if it is to be meaningful and successful. In other words, inclusion should be less about teachers and pupils and more about the responsibilities of all citizens. As Huskins (1998: 10) makes clear, 'communities have responsibility for providing the social, health and educational services necessary to complement the role of families in promoting the development of the "whole" child and for addressing social inequalities'.

As mentioned previously, there has been a need to bring together the differing areas in the field of early years. Inclusion is promoted by careful, joint planning, utilizing a broad range of expertise from a range of professionals in a cohesive manner.

Soon after gaining power in May 1997, the Labour government published the White Paper *Excellence in Schools* in June 1997. This was followed by the Green Paper, *Excellence for all Children*, published in September of the same year. These documents highlighted a clear shift in traditional policy towards children with disabilities. The educational landscape has changed considerably since the Education Act of 1944. Merely providing a school place for children with special needs is no longer acceptable; the quality of that education has to be second to none.

Models of disability and the role of special schools

If large numbers of children with SEN are in specialist provision, we need to ask why. This has resonance for the very young child with a disability, whose future may seem to be firmly placed in a specialist setting. The answer to this question might lie in the dominant position of the medical model. In this model, the child's needs are defined in medical terms and the idea that these children have different and exclusive needs is perpetuated. Also implicit in the medical model is the notion of impairment and that problems are predominantly found within the child. Inclusion is aided by the use of educational terminology, e.g. 'learning difficulty', rather than reliance on categories ('autistic child') or medical labels. However, there is often a strong desire for a diagnosis and its subsequent 'label' as that is seen to be the route to support and funding for the child. It is here we see the areas of health and education both involved with a child, and where we would aim to see multi-agency working and partnership. [...] Hall (1997: 74) describes the causal link between the medical model and segregated specialist education thus:

> The medical model is only able to see the child and his impairments as the problem, with the solution being to adapt the child and his circumstances to the requirements of the world as it is. All of the adjustments must be made to the lifestyle and functionality of the child. Hence a range of prosthetic devices will be offered, along with a separate educational environment and transport to facilitate attendance. The notion that the world might need to change hardly arises because the child *has* and *is* the problem.

The final sentence of the above quote is important and outlines the argument of the Disability Movement, which has gained momentum in both the global and national arena. This argument advocates the use of the social model of disablement. Such a model is concerned with environmental barriers, and the notion that it is these barriers that disable people. The Disability Movement makes it clear that the effective removal of impairments is rare, but a great deal more can be achieved by removing those barriers, which include not only the physical environment, but also associated policies and attitudes.

This sentiment was made law within the provisions of the Special Educational Needs and Disability Act (2001) and this has wide implications for the inclusion of children who were excluded from mainstream institutions for reasons of accessibility. Accessibility mirrors our interpretation of inclusion as a varied and individual concept. What is required is a broadening of the concept of access to include whatever barriers to learning impact on the individual child.

Sainsbury (2000), an adult with autism, is aware of the debates regarding identity, inclusion and disability rights and advocates a wide interpretation of these factors to meet the particular needs of those on the autistic spectrum. This is demonstrated by her definition of access and what constitutes an optimum learning environment for pupils with Asperger Syndrome: 'we don't need ramps or expensive equipment to make a difference for us; all we need is understanding' (Sainsbury, 2000: 9).

Although the social model is now favoured above that of the medical model by many disabled people and their advocates, it is also true that for a great number of educationalists, parents and children the segregated model has a lot of defenders. Jenkinson (1997: 10) categorizes the perceived advantages, which are broken down into practical and economic factors, together with specific effects on disabled and non-disabled children. She highlights the efficiency of necessary aids and equipment, specialist teachers and ancillary services [being] located in one place. This complements the perceived benefits to the students found in smaller classes with more one-to-one attention and a curriculum pitched at an appropriate level.

It is also fair to say that the majority of professionals in specialist provision feel they are working in the best interests of the children they teach. In many respects 'special education' is seen as a worthy profession with established models of good practice and pedagogy. Any suggestion that they are helping to deny disabled children basic human rights or perpetuating institutional discrimination would be denied by many. A more cynical observation would be that it is in the interests of the two branches of education to remain distinctive to preserve the status quo and consolidate their expertise and influence.

Hindrances to inclusion

Current UK government policy seems to be increasing scrutiny of student attainment and performance related indicators with the publication of school league tables (Gabriel, 2004). To some teachers, inclusion is perceived as a hindrance to these factors as it is often felt that inclusion is merely the opposite of exclusion. As a result many teachers see the acceptance of children with emotional and behavioural problems into their class as synonymous with inclusion and to the detriment of their mainstream peers.

Social inclusion can therefore cause a great deal of anxiety in schools, as staff might be reluctant to consider issues of behaviour within the context of special needs: 'Teachers in normal schools may be willing to accommodate the "ideal" child with special needs in their classroom – the bright, brave child in a wheelchair – they will still want to be rid of the actual "average" child with special needs – the dull, disruptive child' (Tomlinson, 1982: 80).

Fortunately the concept of education for *all* is a right that is enshrined in law at local, national and international levels. Issues regarding the inclusion of children with SEN are ongoing and often controversial, highlighting the evolutionary nature of this debate. However, we must not lose sight of the fact that in the recent past, many of the children at the centre of this agenda were deemed ineducable. Scholars must recognize the nature of these advances and place the current arguments into this wider historical perspective.

Case studies

The following case studies demonstrate the experiences of a range of children in the early years and the varied nature of SEN and support. They show the difficulties facing practitioners involved in setting up appropriate interventions together with an indication of the areas that require targeting.

CASE STUDY

Chantelle is 3 years and 2 months old. Her nursery teacher was concerned about her overall development which appeared to be delayed in all areas. Chantelle's speech is particularly problematic. She is difficult to understand and salivates excessively when speaking, resulting in constant 'dribble' on her chin and chest. Her social behaviour is immature and she is becoming increasingly ostracized by her peers.

This visibly upsets her; staff feel she is becoming more 'naughty' in an attempt to gain favour and attention from the others. However, her nursery teacher's opinion is 'she doesn't help herself ... and she is so smelly, would you want to be friends with her?'

The LEA support service pre-school team became involved as part of 'Early Years Action' (Code of Practice, 2001). Chantelle was tested for developmental verbal dyspraxia. This affects the muscles in the throat which control all movement for speech, and swallowing. She was found to have difficulties in this area as well as general learning difficulties. Staff were given details of a range of exercises to do with Chantelle in order to strengthen and help co-ordinate these muscles.

A referral was also made to the Speech and Language Therapy service. The LEA support service teacher made a number of recommendations. Social inclusion was prioritized on Chantelle's IEP.

The need for an advocate for Chantelle was stressed to the teacher. There were concerns about the standard of care at home but this was clearly not Chantelle's fault. A Support Assistant who primarily worked with another child was particularly sensitive to the situation and she began to include Chantelle in small group activities. Positive modelling of behaviour towards Chantelle from the Assistant began to positively affect the behaviour of her peers. Chantelle was also introduced to a visual timetable using photographs of the day's activities. Photographs were also used to help her make choices, for example between different play equipment. This had the effect of slowing her speech down and enabling her to focus upon pronunciation.

CASE STUDY

Ashlyn was born prematurely and has a diagnosis of cerebral palsy. She is 18 months old. Her parents were devastated when they were given the diagnosis, and had no idea what the future may hold for them and their daughter.

A referral was made to the Local Portage service. This was funded by the LEA. Fortnightly visits were set up by the Portage home visitor, whose background was in physiotherapy. In the first visit Ashlyn was observed and the Portage worker played with her. The Portage checklist was introduced to her parents and they were encouraged to set aside a regular time each day to work with Ashlyn. Written weekly teaching activities were agreed with Ashlyn's parents, based on her priority areas of need. In Ashlyn's case these were gross motor skills, fine motor skills, self-help and communication/socialization. The parents then did daily activities with their daughter. This made

(Continued)

(Continued)

them feel totally involved in her progress, and they said they felt their knowledge about Ashlyn's condition was greatly enhanced.

New teaching targets were developed over time; each stage was evaluated taking into account the views of the parents. Ashlyn has made considerable progress. Ashlyn's mother has joined a parent support group which has a toy library. Both parents feel more positive about the years ahead.

CASE STUDY

Shaun is 4 years and 8 months old and attends the nursery department of his local primary school. He is described as an energetic and boisterous child. Staff find him to be happy and sociable, actively seeking contact with peers and adults, Shaun's parents, however, have been worried about him for some time as they feel he is developing at a slower rate than his siblings did. This view is supported by the nursery teacher who has confirmed that Shaun's language is significantly less developed than his peers and he only has a repertoire of a few key words. Shaun also has a problem with understanding and rarely responds to instructions given verbally unless they are broken down into short words and phrases.

Shaun spends a lot of time playing in the water tray and he gets very excited repeating the same kind of activities, often getting wet and pouring water over himself and others. Recently he has become anxious when told to move on to another activity and has, on occasion, demonstrated defiance.

At table-top activities, Shaun enjoys playing with a variety of objects, but has poor fine motor control. He does not seem to notice his difficulties.

He will play alongside peers, but will not attempt to converse with them, or respond to their questions. The family GP has suggested that Shaun might have general learning difficulties. There has been no contact with the authority's Educational Psychologist as yet. Following advice from the GP, staff have started showing Shaun photographs of activities in an attempt to help with transitions. This has been successful.

A variety of photographs have been made available to Shaun, including favourite toys, family and objects. He has started to bring the photograph to an adult and say the associated word, e.g. 'crisps', in an attempt to communicate his wishes.

CASE STUDY

John is 7 years and 10 months old. He has recently been given a diagnosis of autistic spectrum disorder. John attends a large inner-city mainstream primary school and has brothers in the school.

John has odd and idiosyncratic speech, which often has a maturity beyond his years, e.g. 'I find this work tedious in the extreme'. Both peers and staff find it difficult to

(Continued)

(Continued)

understand what he is saying as he often mumbles or whispers his words and makes little use of eye contact or gesture. He seems to 'switch off' if adults address him directly.

John is an avid reader of books, particularly non-fiction books relating to football statistics. As a consequence of his communication difficulties, John is ostracized and bullied by his peers who find him odd.

John has begun to go up to groups of boys at lunchtime and forcefully push them, causing them to chase and abuse him. Staff have repeatedly told him not to, but this has no effect and John gives the impression he enjoys the chase and insists that he is *playing* with the boys.

Recently a volunteer has come in at playtime and has introduced some playground games, some with a football theme. He wrote a simple set of rules to accompany each game for the children to refer to. John was excited to read the rules and became animated when the games were played. He tried to direct his peers, and it was noticeable that they were far more accepting of him in this context.

Staff have followed on from this approach in the classroom and have started to write down information for John to refer to. He has responded well to this and staff have noticed that he is far more willing to communicate with them. They have also made attempts to use his knowledge of football-related statistics to lift his profile within the class. His peers are very impressed with his knowledge, and while they still regard him as odd, they respect his abilities and tolerate his differences.

Summary

These case studies serve to illustrate the notion that there are aspects of good practice that are generic with regard to the support of these children and work across the board. These include:

- the use of structure and routine
- practitioner language
- visual systems
- individualized motivators
- practitioner awareness and knowledge
- appropriate and creative use of support staff
- knowledge of the individual child's perspective and sensibilities
- a recognition of the role of other children and peer relationships
- a recognition of the role of parents
- a commitment to an inclusive philosophy

It is equally important, however, that strategies are optimized to take account of those individual factors particular to the child. These include the sensitive use of John's football interests and Shaun's highly visual learning style. It is not the purpose of this chapter to provide a 'one size fits all' definition of inclusion, but rather to promote the notion that it is a process which is highly individualized and wider than the issue regarding specialist versus mainstream provision. Effective early years practitioners will be those professionals who are able to look beyond labels, diagnoses and particular settings and look to individual factors to ensure the child with SEN is both prepared for and accepted within society.

References

Booth, T. and Ainscow, M. (eds) (1998) *From Them to Us: An International Study of Inclusion in Education*. London: Routledge.

CSIE (2000) *Index for Inclusion*. Bristol: Centre for Studies on Inclusion.

Drifte, C. (2001) *Special Needs in Early Years Settings: A Guide for Practitioners*. London: David Fulton.

Dyson, A. and Millward, A. (2000) *Schools and Special Needs: Issues of Innovation and Inclusion*. London: Paul Chapman.

Gabriel, N. (2004) 'Being a child today', in J. Willan, R. Parker-Rees and J. Savage (eds) *Early Childhood Studies*. Exeter: Learning Matters.

Hall, J. (1997) *Social Devaluation and Special Education*. London: Jessica Kingsley Publishers.

Huskins, J. (1998) *From Disaffection to Social Inclusion*. Bristol: John Huskins.

Jenkinson, J. (1997) *Mainstream or Special: Educating Students with Disabilities*. London: Routledge.

Jones, C. (2004) *Supporting Inclusion in the Early Years*. Maidenhead: Oxford University Press.

Mortimer, H. (2002) *Special Needs Handbook: Meeting Special Needs in Early Years Settings*. Leamington Spa: Scholastic.

Norwich, B. (1997) *Inclusion or Exclusion: Future Policy for Emotional and Behavioural Difficulties Education. SEN Policy Options Steering Group*. Tamworth: NASEN.

O'Brien, T. (ed.) (2001) *Enabling Inclusion: Blue Skies ... Dark Clouds?* London: Stationery Office.

QCA (2000) *The National Curriculum Inclusion Statement*. Available online at: www.qca.org.uk/qca _6757.aspx

Roffey, S. (2001) *Special Needs in the Early Years*. London: David Fulton.

Sainsbury, C. (2000) *Martian in the Playground: Understanding the Schoolchild with Asperger's Syndrome*. Bristol: Lucky Duck Publishing.

Stakes, R. and Hornby, G. (1997) *Meeting Special Needs in Mainstream Schools*. London: David Fulton.

Tomlinson, S. (1982) *A Sociology of Special Education*. London: R.K.P.

Wilson, R. (1998) *Special Educational Needs in the Early Years*. London: Routledge.

Wolfendale, S. (2000) 'Special needs in the early years: prospects for policy and practice', *Support for Learning*, 15 (4): 147–149.

8

Childcare practitioners and the process of professionalization

Jan Peeters and Michel Vandenbroeck

Overview

In this chapter, concepts of professionalism in general, and of reflective and reflexive professionalism in particular, are discussed in relation to an analysis of the narratives of professionals during 30 years of action research. It shows how professionals who engage with pedagogic guidance can become actors of change and develop new pedagogic practices. The research arising from a large-scale project on respect for diversity in childcare played an important role in changing practitioners' conceptions of the profession.

[...]

Introduction

Academic attention to the professionalization of the early years workforce is relatively new and is dominated by studies in the United States of America, Australia and the United Kingdom. As a result, the academic discussion on professionalism in early childhood is dominated by contexts, marked by a history of significant differences

---

Peeters, J. and Vandenbroeck, M. (2010) 'Childcare practitioners and the process of professionalization', in Miller, L. and Cable, C. (eds) *Professionalization, Leadership and Management in the Early Years*, London: Sage, pp. 62–76.

in staff qualifications, large shares of care work provided by private providers, and little government regulation regarding staff qualifications, though in the case of the UK this has recently changed (OECD, 2006; Unicef, 2008). Notwithstanding this bias in published research, some consensus emerges from the literature regarding the relationship between quality and professionalization. Higher levels of qualifications correlate positively with better childcare quality as well as with better developmental outcomes for children (e.g. Cameron and Moss, 2007; Fukkink and Lont, 2007; Sylva et al., 2004). Research also shows that in-service training (on the job) may be as important as pre-service (initial) qualifications, provided it is of sufficient length and intensity (e.g. Fukkink and Lont, 2007). However, this does not mean that qualifications can be considered in isolation, nor that the professionalization of the workforce is in itself sufficient to predict the quality of provision. First, it is important to note that educators with higher levels of qualification tend to choose to work in higher quality provision. Second, more highly qualified practitioners can bring about quality results only when the staff is supported in implementing the insights gained through training in their practice and when the working conditions (including salaries) do not jeopardize the continuity of the workforce (Early et al., 2007).

In addition, there is also a considerable degree of consensus on how this professionalism may be understood. There is general agreement that a specific body of knowledge, as well as a series of skills, are necessary but that these do not suffice. Indeed, reflection is considered by many writers to be the most important part of professionalism (Dunn et al., 2008; Urban, 2008). However, the concept of the 'reflective practitioner', although frequently mentioned in the literature, remains rather underdeveloped and the apparent consensus on the need for reflection may very well disguise a lack of consensus on what it actually means. We can distinguish between reflection-for-action (what will I do?); reflection-in-action (what am I doing?) and reflection-on-action (what have I done?) (Cheng, 2001). Overall, however, the concept of reflection that is most dominant in academic literature is about 'doing things right'. As Coussée, Bradt, Roose and Bouverne-De Bie (2008) rightly argue, this is quite different in nature to reflection on 'doing the right things'. The reflective practitioner moves towards becoming reflexive by questioning taken-for-granted beliefs and by understanding that knowledge is contestable (Kuisma and Sandberg, 2008; Kunneman, 2005; Miller, 2008; Urban and Dalli, 2008). While the first approach focuses on documenting and evaluating one's practice within a fixed paradigm, the second approach questions the very paradigms in which one is operating. A recent thematic monograph published by the *European Early Childhood Education Research Journal* (Urban and Dalli, 2008), is one of the few international publications exploring this second approach. A second observation is that practitioners are virtually absent from the discussion about their reflexive professionalism. The result is that – paradoxically – the literature on reflexive practitioners risks reducing the practitioners to objects, rather than including them as reflexive and agentic subjects. According to Sorel and Wittorski (2005), it is essential that the individuals who are 'professionalizing' themselves are not reduced to the role of a 'consumer' of the knowledge that is presented to them. Yet, little is known about the practitioner's views on this emerging role transformation, with its new emphasis on negotiating and networking competencies (Oberhuemer, 2000). As a result, important questions of how individuals develop their professionalism, remain. This may imply a need for participative action research in this field. Leitch and Day (2000) have argued that action research can play an important role in increasing professionalism providing that it is oriented towards change, critical reflection and participation. Action research, as opposed to pragmatic research, raises the possibility of questioning the social position of research. According to Roose and De Bie (2003), participative research may be a driving force for cultural action, a process of searching for new definitions of reality, leading to a commitment to critical thinking.

Three decades of action research

Since the late 1970s, action research projects have been set up with early years workers by the Faculty of Psychology and Educational Sciences of Ghent University. Initially, these projects were theoretically inspired by social constructivism and by the notion of the 'teacher-as-researcher' (Stenhouse, 1975) and the Freirian notion of 'cultural action'. These frameworks were put into practice in adult education through democratic, participative and experiential training methods (as developed for instance in the Friedrich Ebert Stiftung) and theorized in the Frankfurter Schule. Some of the guiding principles included: avoiding the hierarchical dichotomy between researchers and practitioners; involving practitioners in debates on their everyday work; and documenting their experiences as actors of change. These action research projects may be viewed as 'communicative spaces' for practitioners and researchers (Dahlberg and Moss, 2005). Rinaldi (2005) argues from the rich experiences of the children's centres in Reggio Emilia, where a high level of professionalism has been developed since the 1960s, that the participation of the practitioners is an important factor in the process of professionalization: 'The staff member should be the first to nurture the pleasure of participation, to draw meaning from meetings, and find the opportunity to qualify and enrich his/her professionalism through participation' (Rinaldi, 2005: 51).

In this vein, 11 action research projects were set up within Ghent University, between 1979 and 2008, with the aim of increasing the level of professionalism of the childcare workforce. In each project, video documentaries were made to document the processes of participation that enriched the professionalism of the practitioners. All recordings from 1979 until 2006 were produced in the same way. The researchers used typical research methods (observations, interviews and questionnaires) to identify an issue (e.g. multiple conflicts between toddlers) and subsequently did a literature search in order to investigate possible framings of the issue. In addition, the researchers looked for parents, children and/or practitioners, willing and able to describe the problem concretely from their own experiences in the childcare centres.

Then the researchers looked for practitioners who had reflected on the problematic situation and had experimented successfully with the problem. These practitioners were interviewed and their practice was documented on video. This sample of practitioners has therefore no claim whatsoever to represent the population or to be 'average' practitioners. On the contrary, they may be identified as 'actors of social change' (Urban, 2006) as they, together with the researchers, played an active role in a process of change that aimed to increase the level of professionalization over the past 30 years.

The last film, made in 2007, had a different framing. Three practitioners who participated in several of the projects (and thus have a long-standing career in childcare) and were still active in the field, were confronted with a video showing interviews from 1981. They were asked to comment on continuity and change over the last three decades, drawing on 'video-elicitation' methodology (Declercq, 2002), in which the videos themselves do not serve as data, but as triggers for the interview. Their interviews were again video-taped, transcribed and analysed.

In total, 30 documentaries, featuring 84 practitioners, 23 parents and six children were analysed by the researchers. The selected fragments focus on how childcare workers have interpreted their work from the 1970s to the present. The focus of the analysis is therefore on the 'little narratives' (Lyotard, 1979) of the actors of change themselves and may, therefore, convey multiple, even contradictory meanings. These contradictions, however, may be very useful, since it is dissensus, rather than consensus, that has the potential to create emancipation and greater equity (Dahlberg and Moss, 2005; Hughes and MacNaughton, 2000; Vandenbroeck, 2009). The analysis of these narratives formed part of a larger PhD study on evolutions in professionalism, both in practice and in policy, in Flanders, Denmark, France, New Zealand and England (Peeters, 2008).

Agentic practitioners looking for new possibilities

Thirty years ago, the childcare sector in Belgium was entirely dominated by a discursive medical-hygienic regime. It was common practice that parents were forbidden to enter the premises; childcare workers were seldom allowed to talk to parents, as this was the monopoly of their head, a hospital nurse; children were undressed, bathed and dressed in clothes provided by the centres upon their arrival; the staff wore white clinical uniforms; play materials were stacked out of the reach of children; a strict hierarchy was observed, with the doctor at the top, the nurse next and the childcare worker at the bottom; (team meetings were scarce and it was most uncommon to discuss educational matters with the staff (Mozère, 1992; Peeters, 1993; Vandenbroeck, 2004).

The statements of the staff members talking in 2007 about the late 1970s illustrate the dominance of specific discursive regimes and how they influenced the image of the self. In this case, the testimonies give explicit examples of how their view of their profession was influenced by the medical-hygienic regime.

My training during the 1970s consisted exclusively of providing care and the nurseries paid an excessive amount of attention to what was 'healthy'. Children were dressed too warmly, so that their freedom of movement was severely curtailed. The children spent all of their waking and sleeping hours in the same room. For that reason, the room had to be aired and we would put on the hats and sweaters and open the window for 10 minutes. We then closed the window and waited until the room get back up to the correct temperature. Only then did we take off the hats and coats. Thus, the child was never given the chance to relax and could not sleep when tired. No one ever asked what that meant for the child. That is something that they would now never be able to have me do. But at that time, you are young, you don't have any experience, this is the way you learned it and you go along with it without question – until your eyes are opened. (Childcare worker, 2007)

Narratives by parents from 1980 make it clear how negatively this cool and distant way of dealing with children and parents was experienced:

One is not allowed to enter the playroom, they call the name of the child and the parent must wait in the hall until they give him to you. (Father, 1980)

You are not introduced to the childcare workers and you do not know their names. (Father, 1980)

I would like to have received information about what my child did during the day, but you never got that spontaneously. You had to ask explicitly and the reaction was generally very short. 'He has eaten and slept well'. Other than that, you didn't get any information. (Mother, 1980)

The 1980s were a period of major changes within the sector (Vandenbroeck, 2003). The medical-hygienic discourse was to a large extent abandoned and committed staff members (actors of change) engaged in action research experimented with more pedagogic interpretations of professionalism. The video images show how the childcare workers in this period expanded their interpretation of professionalism by becoming themselves actors in the innovations that were being implemented. Rinaldi summarized this participatory process succinctly: 'Participation nurtures professionalism' (Rinaldi, 2005: 51). The following short fragments from the narratives illustrate the positive impact of the participatory process.

I have experienced the change as extremely positive. We were given more space to determine for ourselves how to develop our activities.

In the past, if you had an idea about how to improve the activities, it was difficult to implement it. Now, we have a team meeting in which this is discussed, so that you get support from your colleagues and can achieve better results when improving the activity. (Childcare workers, 1981/1982)

The staff members' narratives demonstrate that being involved in a process of change, in which they are agentic actors, gives them hope and self-confidence, and increases their job satisfaction. These participative action research projects provoked a major change in professional attitudes towards the parents. From the exclusion of parents in the 1970s, they gradually moved towards inviting parents to get to know the way the centre worked in order to increase the wellbeing of the children.

> If the parents stay a little bit longer in the playroom before they go to work, the children cry less. (Childcare worker, 1981)

> After seeing the video of a day in the life of the centre, parents are astonished about the many things their child is doing at the centre. They ask a lot of questions and they give information about how their child is at home. (Childcare worker, 1982)

> I do not replace the parents, but I take over as much as possible the habits of the parents, the way they interact with their child. I ask how they put their child to bed, how they feed their child, what their child likes and how they comfort it at home, in order to make the children feel as good here in the day care centre as at home. (Childcare worker, 1985)

These actors were very concerned with increasing the wellbeing and involvement of the children, by making the playroom into a more stimulating environment and by introducing activities that enhanced meaningful adult–child and peer interactions. They also developed a researching attitude. They reflected on pedagogic practice and constructed new pedagogic knowledge.

> Now we can choose the furniture of the play room ourselves and we have bought a second-hand lounge suite. I find it much more cosy. We are now reading a book together in the chair and the children like it. (Childcare worker, 1981)

> We have started to make play corners, and we position the play materials so that the children can take the toys they want to play with by themselves; and the children are now able to put away the toys themselves. (Childcare worker, 1981)

> In the beginning we have to work things out, such as: 'Is the baby tired?' or 'What is the matter with him?' But once he's been here a while we know that the baby has a certain rhythm that is repeated. And then the rhythm of the baby changes around 6–7 months. (Childcare worker, 1987)

The childcare workers emphasize that their initial training was inappropriate to reflect on these day-to-day problems and that they consequently had to look for answers themselves to the new complex problems they were facing.

> I think far too much is expected of nursery nurses, given their training. For some people, expectations are too high for us to be able to meet them. (Childcare worker, 1981)

> We have to learn on our own how to interact with children in the daily experience. (Childcare worker, 1985)

Respect for diversity: a paradigm shift

Our analysis of the narratives on continuity and change show that the discussions on respect for diversity in the 1990s played an important role in changing practitioners' conceptions of the profession. In 1995, with the support of the governmental organization Kind en Gezin (Child and Family), a large-scale action research project on respect for diversity in childcare was set up. This project was aimed at diversifying the work-force as well as adapting the pedagogy of childcare centres to the multicultural society (Somers and Peeters, 1998). The numerous narratives collected in this proj-ect show how it confronted the practitioners with a paradigm shift. Both ethnic minority and ethnic majority trainees testified about the difficulties in addressing diversity issues.

> Female Moroccan graduates like me have to be assertive at work and make eye contact with others, but in my home situation this is unheard of.

> I used to think that the purpose of criticism was to put you down. I now know that you can also learn from criticism, that criticism can also be constructive. Subjects also came up that were taboo for us, such as, for example, homosexuality.

> We used to do things simply because that was the way they were done. Now, however, we continually ask ourselves why we did this or that. In the beginning, we therefore had conflicts with our family and friends. They saw us change and we confronted them with their own norms and values.

> (Ethnic minority trainees, 1997)

Both the ethnic minority course members and their Flemish mentors spoke about this paradigm shift and about the difficulties of constructing an inclusive professionalism. Working with respect for diversity in early childhood presupposes a focus on respect for the uniqueness of the Other (Moss, 2007b). Dahlberg and Moss (2008: 64) state 'Putting everything one encounters into pre-made categories implies we make the Other into the Same … To think another whom I cannot grasp is an important shift and it chal-lenges the whole scene of Pedagogy'. This implies that in contexts of diversity, the focus may be on dealing with what we cannot understand, rather than on trying to under-stand or trying to 'grasp' the Other into our own frames of reference. This requires openness and flexibility and the recognition of multiple perspectives and paradigms, acknowledging and welcoming that there is more than one answer to most questions.

The narratives show that during the project, open discussions were held in the childcare centres on these issues, for example through discussions on practical mat-ters such as whether or not a headscarf was an impediment to a professional approach. This search for the other appeared to be extremely successful in develop-ing, together with the parents, new practical knowledge.

> A baby [whose parents were from Zaire] had trouble sleeping in a bed and often wept. We talked to the parents and they said that they first rock their child before they put her in bed. We tried that in a hammock and it worked well.

> We ask the parents for pet words or nicknames that they use with their child. We try to say these words in the child's native language so that they hear familiar sounds when they are with us. We search for things that are recognizable for the child, such as music from their native country. This is extremely important if the child is still adjusting.

> (Flemish childcare workers, 1997)

The testimonies suggest that dealing with diversity presents the early years practitioners with complex problems that cannot be solved with a technical body of knowledge, since they ask for interpretations of professionalism based on continuous
reflection on their practice as well as the need to move beyond reflection and develop
the ability to be reflexive.

At the beginning of the new millennium, another aspect of diversity creates new
possibilities for reflection and change. Fierce discussions emerge on the gender-
specific interpretation of childcare professionalism. Our study suggests that, as in
many other European countries, the childcare professions in Flanders are based on a
female-oriented construction of professionalism and that this 'mother-like practice'
excludes both male staff and fathers (Peeters, 2003). When more men are part of the
staff, new questions emerge that challenge traditional constructions of the early years
professional as female, mother-like and 'naturally' caring (Cameron, 2006). However,
in order to be able to realize a gender-neutral construction of professionalism, the
atmosphere in the training courses and in the centres also needs to change
(Vandenbroeck and Peeters, 2008). The focus on a narrow care concept needs to be
abandoned as broader interpretations of professionalism are realized (Hauglund,
2005; Wohlgemuth, 2003), making a place for more social functions of childcare
(Meleady and Broadhead, 2002; Vandenbroeck, 2004). By the social functions of childcare, we mean the multiple ways in which childcare is contributing to social justice, as
part of the welfare system. This may include issues of tackling unequal access, but also
issues of how professionals relate to parents in reciprocal ways and how parents, children
and local communities are involved in the decisions that affect their lives.

Children as active citizens

Since the end of the 1990s, the practitioners have become more interested in the way
parents educate their young children at home and in questioning how the childcare
centre could take on some of the practices of the parents. In this evolution, children
are increasingly considered as active citizens who can decide upon important aspects
of daily life in the childcare centre.

> I find it very important that the parents can stay for a while in the morning; that they have
> the time and the opportunity to talk about their child. Did he sleep well, what did he eat,
> what else happened in the family; for us all those things are important when we take over
> the [care of the] child. (Childcare educator, 2001)

> To say goodbye is not easy for the child or for the parent. When the parents are on the
> street they give their child a hand through the mailbox; the child sees the parent and
> touches their hand through the mailbox; this ritual makes saying goodbye easier for the
> parent and for the child. (Childcare educator, 2001)

> Children can decide themselves if they want to participate in the play and when they
> want to stop playing. How long and how frequently they want to participate in activities
> is up to the children to decide. (Childcare educator, 2001)

Possibilities of a close collaboration between research and practice

Several authors argue that there are no universal answers for the problems facing childcare workers and teachers in early childhood education (e.g. Cameron, 2008; Moss, 2007a; Urban, 2008). They therefore advocate for professionals who are able to continually reflect on their practice and who can, time and again, find new solutions for the complex situations they face. This raises timely questions on how to facilitate this process. The analysis of praxis in day-to-day working situations contributes, according to Favre (2008), to the construction of a professional identity that is focused on change. From his perspective, professionalism can only evolve if the institution allows it a discretionary space to do so. Early years practitioners should take up the challenge to question their work and be focused on the continual adjustment of their pedagogic practices on the basis of reflection. Annalia Galardina (2008) documents how, in Pistoia, the introduction of reflexivity to the work of the institution is developed by the *pedagogistas*. The task of these pedagogic counsellors consists of instigating a mutual dialogue between the centres and encouraging the professionals' ongoing reflection on their approach and their beliefs. In the action research projects from Ghent University, the childcare workers were also supported by researchers or pedagogic counsellors who fulfilled a similar role to the pedagogistas of Pistoia. Their task is to assist the early childhood workers in 'discovering what is possible' (Dalli, 2008: 17).

Pedagogic counsellors/researchers or pedagogistas can play an important role in the construction of new pedagogic knowledge by supporting the practitioners in the analysis of their practice. From our study of the narratives of the Flemish actors of change, we would argue that it is important that the childcare workers and staff members are given sufficient autonomy by the counsellors in their search for what is possible: practitioners must remain the main 'actors of change'. In this sense, a close collaboration of researchers and practitioners, blurring the boundaries between both, may be very useful.

Competencies for change

The action-oriented competencies that educators acquire through the process of engagement with action research and pedagogic counsellors, provide the staff with the possibility of changing existing pedagogic practices, and allow them to deal reflexively with complex situations and to construct practical knowledge in interaction with children, parents and colleagues.

> The intense collaboration with parents starts with the intake procedure when the parents show us how they deal with important things about their child. In the past we were explaining to the parents how we are working, now we ask the parents: how do you want us to care for your children? (Pedagogic counsellor, 2003)

There was a transition period, where we as parents showed the childcare workers how we dealt with Zoë; it was good to feel that they were interested in how we were dealing with our child, they do not see themselves as the experts. I expect that they will continue what we are doing at home. (Father, 2006)

We have a mother from Somalia here who is a political refugee, and her child cries a lot. We asked the mother to show us how she comforted her baby: she was singing for her child. The childcare worker recorded the song of the mother and now when the child is crying she plays the tape of the mother singing, and it helps a lot, the child calms down hearing the voice of his mother. (Pedagogic counsellor, 2003)

Discussion

As we have said, literature that unveils what is meant by reflective and reflexive professionalism is rather scarce and the voice of practitioners is often missing. The analysis of the narratives of professional actors of change in Flemish childcare settings, shows different evolutions over the last 30 years. Most importantly, there has been a notable evolution in the way childcare workers have viewed children since the 1980s: from the child as an object that needed to be cared for, to a child as subject and actor in the process of development. Interestingly, this shift coincides with a second evolution: a shift in how these professionals themselves are treated. The rigid hierarchy of the settings until the late 1970s prohibited professionals from speaking up (and prohibited parents or 'experts' from addressing the professionals directly). When professionals were observed by researchers, they were constructed as objects of study, rather than as agentic subjects. The narratives of these professionals document how a shift in the hierarchical view enabled them to reflect upon their practice and to reconstruct what it may be to 'do things right'.

A third shift – during the late 1990s – seems to be of another nature and occurred in the diversity projects that encouraged the professionals to also take parental opinions and views into account. The agentic childcare workers gradually conceptualized the education of the child in the centre as a shared responsibility between parents and childcare workers. In addition, they were confronted with questions of inclusion and exclusion and traditional power relations were challenged. These projects questioned taken-for-granted opinions in a much deeper way and invited the professionals to not only think about 'doing things right' but also about 'doing the right things'.

In a provisional attempt to further unravel and concretize this concept of reflexive professionalism, we formulate the hypothesis that practice, enabling reflection on 'doing things right' as well as 'doing the right things', asks for four categories of basic and generic competencies:

1. *The ability to look for (always provisional) solutions in contexts of dissensus.* The most significant results have been achieved in teams who displayed the ability to discuss different opinions intensively and where on the basis of these debates concrete decisions were taken and put into practice.

2. *The ability to focus on the meeting of the Other, the one we do not know.* The 'little' narratives in this study document that the orientation to try to understand the parent who is 'different' is a basic competence of working in childcare (Dahlberg and Moss, 2008).
3. *The ability to co-construct knowledge with others (colleagues, parents, children).* This study has given several examples of how the childcare workers developed, in collaboration with the researchers or the pedagogic counsellor, the competence of being able to construct new practical knowledge, new ways of working with children, parents and colleagues.
4. *The ability to act with a focus on change.* The participation in action research projects has created a belief in the possibilities of experimentation. The 'little' narratives document how the 'actors of change' have developed competences that help them to discover what is possible in working in early childhood education.

Ongoing research by the European DECET network (Diversity in Early Childhood Education and Training) will further elaborate this hypothesis.

Taking into account the experiences and the meaning making of the professionals, may also shed some light on the conditions that are necessary to let reflexive professionalism flourish. One of the more salient conditions is the creation of communicative spaces. Dahlberg and Moss (2005) advocate these 'communicative spaces' or 'islands of democracy' where researchers, policy-makers and staff work together to develop new knowledge. They use the concepts of minor and major politics, referring to Deleuze and Guattari (1980) and argue that:

> The two forms of politics should not be seen as in opposition. Each can provoke the other into creativity; minor politics may, for example, connect up with a whole series of other circuits and cause them to fluctuate, waver and reconfigure in wholly unexpected ways. (Dahlberg and Moss, 2008: 56)

Final thoughts

Action research projects combine some features of these communicative spaces, where minor and major politics meet. During the past 30 years, the most significant evolutions occurred when representatives of the sector, the academia and policy-makers collaborated in democratic ways to develop new types of professionalism. The most interesting project from this perspective was the action research on respect for diversity in the late 1990s. In the diversity project, representatives of childcare centres and community organizations working with ethnic minorities, together with researchers and policy-makers, discussed what professionalism was about and this brought about lasting and creative results. The professionalization process needs to be considered as a social practice and as a result of complex interactions between social evolutions (e.g. the growing diversity of families), policy measures (e.g. new legislation) and new scientific insights (e.g. the importance of men in the development of young children), interacting in turn with researchers or pedagogic counsellors, staff members and users (parents as well as children). These insights also point at the crucial role of pedagogic counselling. Many authors have already pointed to the fact that some pedagogic guidance is necessary to allow professionals to implement the knowledge, skills and attitudes from the initial training (e.g. Early et al., 2007). In addition, we argue that examples from practice show that this counselling, be it by action researchers or by pedagogistas (Galardina, 2008) may also help construct professionalism, in the case of insufficient initial training. This is not to say that initial training should be dismissed. Indeed, one needs to acknowledge that the projects presented here and the evolutions described are about a small sample of 'actors of change' and need to be considered as the fruition of long periods of sustained, intensive guidance and collaboration, rather than as 'products' of eclectic short-term interventions.

References

Cameron, C. (2006) 'Male workers and professionalism', *Contemporary Issues in Early Childhood*, 7(1): 68–79.

Cameron, C. (2008) 'What do we mean by "competence"?' *Children in Europe*, 15: 12–13.

Cameron, C. and Moss, P. (2007) *Care Work in Europe: Current Understandings and Future Directions*. London: Routledge.

Cheng, D.P.W. (2001) 'Difficulties of Hong Kong teachers' understanding and implementation of play in the curriculum', *Teaching and Teacher Education*, 17(7): 857–69.

Coussée, F., Bradt, L., Roose, R. and Bouverne-De Bie, M. (2008) 'The emerging social pedagogical paradigm in UK child and youth care: deus ex machina or walking the beaten path?', *British Journal of Social Work*, 40(3): 789–805.

Dahlberg, G. and Moss, P. (2005) *Ethics and Politics in Early Childhood Education*. London: Routledge.

Dahlberg, G. and Moss, P. (2008) 'Au-delà de la qualité, vers l'éthique et le politique en matière d'education préscolaire', in G. Brougère and M. Vandenbroeck (eds) *Repenser l'éducation des jeunes enfants*. Brussels: Peter Lang. pp. 53–78.

Dalli, C. (2008) 'Early childhood teachers in New Zealand', *Children in Europe*, 15: 16–17.

Declercq, A. (2002) 'Visuele sociologie: het gebruik van video, film en foto's als onderzoeksmateriaal'. Ongepubliceerde cursus. Universiteit Gent.

Deleuze, G. and Guattari, F. (1980) *Mille plateaux*. Paris: Editions de Minuit.

Dunn, M., Harrison, L.J. and Coombe, K. (2008) 'In good hands: preparing research-skilled graduates for the early childhood professional', *Teaching and Teacher Education*, 24(3): 703–14.

Early, D., Maxwell, K., Burchinal, M., Bender, R., Ebanks, C., Henry, G., et al. (2007) 'Teachers' education, classroom quality, and young children's academic skills: results from seven studies of preschool programs', *Child Development*, 78(2): 558–80.

Favre, D. (2008) 'Educateur de jeunes enfants in France', *Children in Europe*, 15: 20–1.

Fukkink, R.G. and Lont, A. (2007) 'Does training matter? A meta-analysis and review of caregiver training studies', *Early Childhood Research Quarterly*, 22: 294–311.

Galardina, A. (2008) 'Pedagogistas in Italy', *Children in Europe*, 15: 20.

Hauglund, E. (2005) 'Men in childcare in Norway', paper presented at the Men in Childcare Conference, National Children's Bureau, London, 20 September.

Hughes, P. and MacNaughton, G. (2000) 'Consensus, dissensus or community: the politics of parent involvement in early childhood education', *Contemporary Issues in Early Childhood*, 1(13): 241–57.

Kuisma, M. and Sandberg, A. (2008) 'Preschool teachers' and students preschool teachers' thoughts about professionalism in Sweden', *European Early Childhood Education Research Journal*, 16(2): 186–95.

Kunneman, H. (2005) 'Social work as a laboratory for normative professionalisation', *Social Work & Society*, 3(2): 191–200.

Leitch, R. and Day, C. (2000) 'Action research and reflective practice: towards a holistic view', *Educational Action Research*, 8(1): 173–93.

Lyotard, F. (1979) *La condition post-moderne*. Paris: Editions de Minuit.

Meleady, C. and Broadhead, P. (2002) 'Diversity: the norm, not the exception', *Children in Europe*, 2(2): 11–15.

Miller, L. (2008) 'Developing professionalism with a regulatory framework in England: challenges and possibilities', *European Early Childhood Education Research Journal*, 16(2): 255–68.

Moss, P. (2007a) 'Bringing politics into the nursery: early childhood education as a democratic practice', *European Early Childhood Education Research Journal*, 15(1): 5–20.

Moss, P. (2007b) 'Meetings across the paradigmatic divide', *Educational Philosophy and Theory*, 39(3): 229–45.

Mozère, L. (1992) *Le printemps des crèches: Histoire et analyse d'un movement*. Paris: L'Harmattan.

Oberhuemer, P. (2000) 'Conceptualizing the professional role in early childhood centres: emerging profiles in four countries', *Early Childhood Research & Practice*, 2(2). Available from: http://ecrp.uiuc.edu/v2n2/oberhuemer.html (accessed 14 January 2008).

Organisation for Economic Co-operation and Development (OECD) (2006) *Starting Strong II: Early Childhood Education and Care*. Paris: OECD.

Peeters, J. (1993) 'Quality improvement in the childcare centres with the support of the Bernard van Leer Foundation', in J. Peeters and M. Vandenbroeck (eds) *Working Towards Better Childcare: Report over Thirteen Years of Research and Training*. Gent: RUG, VBJK. pp. 39–79.

Peeters, J. (2003) 'Men in childcare: an action-research in Flanders', *International Journal of Equality and Innovation in Early Childhood*, 1(1): 72–83.

Peeters, J. (2008) *The Construction of a New Profession: A European Perspective on Professionalism in Early Childhood Education and Care*. Amsterdam: SWP.

Rinaldi, C. (2005) *In Dialogue with Reggio Emilia*. London: RoutledgeFalmer.

Roose, R. and De Bie, M. (2003) 'From participative research to participative practice: a study in youth care', *Journal of Community & Applied Social Psychology*, 13: 475–85.

Somers, A. and Peeters, J. (1998) *Diversiteit in de Kinderopvang*. Gent: VBJK.

Sorel, M. and Wittorski, R. (2005) *La Professionalisation en Actes et en Questions*. Paris: L'Harmattan.

Stenhouse, L. (1975) *An Introduction to Curriculum Research and Development*. London: Heinemann.

Sylva, K., Melhuish, E., Sammons, P., Siraj-Blatchford, I. and Taggart, B. (2004) *The Effective Provision of Preschool Education (EPPE) Project: Final Report*. Notingham: DfES Publications – The Institute of Education.

Unicef Innocenti Research Centre (2008) *Report Card 8: The Child Care Transition*. Florence: Unicef.

Urban, M. (2006) *Strategies for Change. Gesellschafts- und fachpolitische Strategien zur Reform des Systems frühkindlicher Bildung*. Halle: Bertelsmans Stiftung.

Urban, M. (2008) 'Dealing with uncertainty: challenges and possibilities for the early childhood profession', *European Early Childhood Education Research Journal*, 16(2): 135–52.

Urban, M. and Dalli, C. (2008) 'Editorial', *European Early Childhood Education Research Journal*, 16(2): 131–3.

Vandenbroeck, M. (2003) 'From crèches to childcare: constructions of motherhood and inclusion/exclusion in the history of Belgian infant care', *Contemporary Issues in Early Childhood*, 4(2): 137–48.

Vandenbroeck, M. (2004) *In verzekerde bewaring. Honderdvijftig jaar kinderen, ouders en kinderopvang*. Amsterdam: SWP.

Vandenbroeck, M. (2009) 'Let's disagree', *European Early Childhood Education Research Journal*, 17(2): 165–70.

Vandenbroeck, M. and Peeters, J. (2008) 'Gender and professionalism: a critical analysis of overt and covert curricula', *Early Child Development and Care*, 178(7–8): 703–15.

Wohlgemuth, U. (2003) 'One for all: men on the pedagogue course', *Children in Europe*, 3(5): 22–3.

9

Reflective family-centred practices: parents' perspectives and early intervention

Alice Paige-Smith, Jonathan Rix and Anna Craft

Overview

This chapter considers the context for early intervention programmes (i.e. a variety of therapeutic and support services for pre-school children with disabilities or difficulties in learning and their families) and in particular, the Early Support Programme (DfES 2004b). The experiences of ten parents of young children with Down syndrome, and the implementation of early intervention programmes are explored through a study that brought parents into a reflective relationship with their practice.

[...]

Introduction

This chapter first considers the context for early intervention programmes (i.e. a variety of therapeutic and support services for pre-school children with disabilities or difficulties in learning and their families). In particular, the Early Support Programme (DfES 2004b), an early intervention initiative implemented in England, is considered, through an evaluation of parents' experiences of this service. We then consider how early intervention programmes based on a developmental view of the child can deeply shape and affect parents' and children's experiences. As the programme is implemented, the child's home becomes, in effect, the early years setting. The family can be seen as experiencing 'transition' from one set of identities, roles and purposes to another, overlapping set. We explore the experiences and perspectives of ten parents of young children with Down syndrome, and the implementation of early intervention programmes through considering a study that brought parents into a reflective relationship with their practice, through interview and reflective diaries. We explore issues in recognizing parents as reflective practitioners involved in a team of multiple perspectives and shared responsibility, in the support of children with learning difficulties or disabilities.

The context of early intervention and approaches to children's learning

Within the English context of early intervention policy and practice, the Department for Education and Skills (DfES) has placed an increasing emphasis on the education of children with learning difficulties and disabilities in relation to inclusive practice, improving partnership with parents and early intervention (DfES 2004a). This increased government commitment included the launch of a £13 million initiative in the form of the Early Support Pilot Programme in September 2002, as a part of the wider initiative of the Sure Start programme for supporting children and families (Paige-Smith and Rix 2006).

The Sure Start programme started in 1997 in order to support families, to integrate family support such as health and early learning services, and to provide high-quality integrated care. One of the main programmes for families of children with learning difficulties or disabilities supported by Sure Start has been the Portage service, which provides a home-visiting educational service for pre-school children who experience difficulties in learning or have disabilities. Portage is named after the town of Portage in Wisconsin, USA, and was developed to support parents and their children in their own homes. The service developed there because parents found it difficult to get to centre-based services within that rural area (National Portage Association 2007). In 2004/5, there were 152 NPA-registered Portage services in England, with a total of 1194 Portage home visitors providing support for 5370 families through home visits and other related activities. There were at that time also 31 local authorities in England that did not offer Portage provision, and in four local authorities the Portage service was not offered to all families because of geographical restrictions. In addition, 1437 families were identified as waiting at their homes to be referred for regular visits from the Portage service (Russell 2005). By September 2006 provision for children with learning difficulties or disabilities had expanded to be encompassed within the work of 1000 children's centres comprising about 500 Sure Start Local Programmes, 430 former Neighbourhood Nurseries and 70 Early Excellence Centres (National Audit Office 2006: 3, *Value for Money Report, Executive Summary*). The expansion of early intervention services for children and parents within this context of expanding children's services, is documented in the report *Removing Barriers to Achievement* (DfES 2004a). This government document relates to the education and the inclusion of disabled children and other children with difficulties in learning. In 2006 the Early Support (ES) programme was evaluated by a team of multi-disciplinary professionals (DfES 2006). The report indicates that despite efforts to improve provision, the attempt to provide seamless support was far from borne out in practice.

- Many of the families had a disjointed experience with professionals from different services; some of these professionals were directly involved in ES and others had come into the home from other services.
- Multi-agency meetings happened in an ad hoc way. This should have been better coordinated by the Child Development Centre, which coordinates locally organized child health professionals (an example being given in the report of a parent having to coordinate a multi-agency meeting despite the presence of an Early Support programme).

The report also notes that:

> Another parent [23] told us about being part of ES but feeling that not everyone else who was involved with her child knew they were. She described the paediatrician involved as being 'on an island' and whilst the mother herself thought she had been allocated a key worker and thought she might know who it [the key worker] was, nobody had actually said as much to her. (DfES 2006: 192)

Other studies also document how within early intervention programmes parents experience anxiety about their own roles (Bridle and Mann 2000; Paige-Smith and Rix 2006). Such perspectives are considered to be affected by the type of contact parents have had with professionals and to what extent they feel listened to by them (Russell 2003). In particular, target-led, task-based programmes can result in tension and conflict between parents and their children (Rix and Paige-Smith 2005). However, parents 'teaching' their children more informally in the early years has been associated with progress in attainment in language, pre-reading and early number concepts (Sammons et al. 2004: 698). Woodhead (2005) refers to how Rogoff's (2003) framework of 'guided participation' provides a means to understanding how children are inducted into communities of learners through such informal methods. Development in such a context is seen as naturally social and cultural, as much as biologically constituted – a view of the child's development that contrasts with Piaget's (Donaldson 1986).

Recognizing the significance of social and cultural contexts in development in this way places parents at the heart of early intervention and underpins family-centred practice. Such a stance acknowledges the important role of parents in their children's well-being, health and education through partnership with professionals and their involvement with their child. Careful consideration of parental involvement within early intervention is perhaps particularly important for children with learning difficulties or disabilities, whose needs can heighten the demands made of their parents, as Beveridge notes:

> Parents vary in the personal resources they bring to their role. For example, their knowledge and understanding of child development, their communicative skills and their educational aspirations for their children are all likely to influence not only the nature of their parent–child interactions, but also their relationships with schools and other services. (Beveridge 2005: 42)

Families experiencing transition of role

Families that go through the process of implementing early intervention programmes could be considered to go through a process of 'transition' in so far as there is an expectation on the roles of the parents to provide a structured education programme for their child. Supporting this transition process during early intervention entails effective management and a variety of communications systems 'to make the transition meaningful to everyone' (Fabian 2007). Fabian writes about the importance of certain activities that enable children's adjustment, not only in terms of their environment, but in the sense that there is a need to 'build a transition in children's thinking which supports the crossing between philosophical learning boundaries – from play to formal learning' (Fabian 2007: 12).

She suggests professionals need to co-construct such transitions with parents in a positive climate, sharing goals, values and expectations. At the same time she notes that it is important for children to be given some control and ownership of their transition so that they can have 'transition capital'. As Dunlop (2007) suggests, all of childhood represents a 'transitional territory between infancy and adulthood in which families have a part and can be social actors and agents' (Dunlop 2007: 157).

Transitions can be 'managed for and by children' (Dunlop 2007) through using a 'listening to children' approach. For instance, Clark (2004) has reflected on 'children's experience of place', which led her to develop the 'listening to children' approach that draws on three theoretical starting points:

1. children as having their own time, activities and space
2. participatory appraisal – the giving of 'voice' to children
3. the notion of the competent child within the pedagogic framework of Loris Malaguzzi, which sees learning as a collaborative process between adults and children.

An approach that recognizes the needs of individual children and their families could be seen as family-centred.

Family-centred practice

Effective family-centred practice within early intervention could, then, include the principles of listening to children, as well as parents, alongside the coordination of coherent services. Carpenter et al. (2004) consider that equal partnership with parents and professionals provides an inclusive model of family-centred training that does not involve the transplanting of teachers' skills onto parents. He suggests the professional's role is to 'nurture the family, restoring for and with them their aspirations for their child' (Carpenter 2005: 181) in contrast to traditional parent education programmes traditionally based on a deficit model (Carpenter et al. 2004), which may not recognize adequately what Woodhead (2005) calls a child's 'right to development'. Woodhead argues that government should promote children's optimal development, recognizing that early childhood settings and practices are culturally constructed, which includes the promulgations of belief systems about the 'proper' way for children to develop (Woodhead 2005: 90), through the practices of the family: 'The way parents care for their children [is] shaped in part by their cultural beliefs (or ethno-theories) about what is appropriate and desirable, in terms both of the goals of child development and the means to achieve those goals' (Woodhead 2005: 50).

Counteracting negative assumptions and expectations within programmes that may be based on a deficit model should be a primary aim between parents and professionals, a process of engagement that requires reflective communication – effectively, the development of collaborative reflective practice.

Russell (2003) suggests that partnership between parents and professionals requires them to negotiate different and new ways of thinking about situations and future events in order to reconsider expectations and plan accordingly. Parents' perspectives in the evaluation of the ES programme indicate that the family has to engage with professionals in order to access services and learn how to support their child's development. Early intervention programmes may be considered to be based on a developmental model of the child. Implementation prompts a transition for families who then need to work closely with other professionals accessing services and learning how to support their child's development, as part of a team encompassing multiple perspectives and sources of expertise.

A close-up look at reflective practice in early intervention

The role of reflective practice in early intervention can be illustrated through a small-scale study undertaken by the first two authors (Rix and Paige-Smith 2005;

Paige-Smith and Rix 2006), which involved two stages of interviews with parents of children with Down syndrome in England. It explored the following questions.

- How do parents, professionals and the 'child' collaborate and instigate pedagogy?
- What is parental knowledge of the child and how is this linked to the developmental perspective?
- How do parents use their knowledge with their children?

In the first stage of the study, informal interviews were carried out with three families, the parents of three children, including three mothers and one father; and in the second stage, six parents of six children were interviewed, one father and five mothers. The first set of interviews focused on the parents' views of their experiences of early intervention. The findings from the first set of interviews (Paige-Smith and Rix 2006) informed the second (Rix and Paige-Smith 2005). In the first set, with four parents, it became clear that parents considered early intervention to consist of a variety of activities such as yoga and play. They also said that they found it difficult to implement structured educational early intervention activities in the home and that at times this led to tensions between themselves and their children. Further questions were then considered, in relation to the pedagogy of early intervention programmes and activities, and looking at whether parents found that different approaches towards their children affected their experiences of 'being' with their children, in the context of early years education and care, which places an emphasis on the importance of play and creativity (Miller and Paige-Smith 2004).

As one of the researchers was himself also implementing early intervention activities in his own home, this added an extra dimension to our insight into the research process of interviewing. He was himself interviewed, reflecting on his own data alongside views and perspectives of other parents in the study. Analysis of the interview data was informed by this ongoing in-depth reflection, which occurred throughout the data collection process. Parents in the study were aware that we were conducting this research with one of the researchers being an 'insider', in the sense of both researcher and researched. Other parents in the study engaged in the reflection of their role with their child and reflective diaries were collated by two of the parents in the second stage of the research, which included the personal details and thoughts that the mothers had about being with their children. This data, alongside the interview material, was analysed according to grounded theory (Strauss and Corbin 1998).

Learning together

Emergent from our analysis was a set of findings around how parents viewed their child when they were involved together in early intervention. The following discussion of the findings indicates parents' experiences when implementing early intervention programmes; some of these experiences relate directly to the early intervention activities. The parents' accounts also indicate how they perceived themselves and their role as a parent due to their early intervention experiences.

The view of the child

During implementation of early intervention, parents and their children were expected to carry out activities that were identified after discussion with professionals. These activities were intended to move the child towards an agreed developmental target, and commonly involved some sort of teaching. One parent reported that she was offered 'tools' to learn how to play with her child, by a professional. The parents in this study were pleased when their child reached developmental milestones such as walking, talking, singing and drinking from a cup. Parental perspectives included a developmental view of their child through which they framed their child's behaviour and learning. Examples of this included one parent who said that, because she had read a book that explained the developmental stages of 'ordinary' children, she was able to predict what her child would be like when she [was] older. The following comments indicate further how they framed the view of the child in relation to a developmental perspective:

> I'm always looking at what he'll be like when he's 3 rather than worry what he's like when he's 1 and a half

> Eva's gross motor skills have always been age appropriate ... Eva has always been cognitively age appropriate and remains so now at age 5

> As a parent, I think I compare him. I think what I do, sort of day to day, I sort of assess where he's at by looking at what the other children are doing. And sometimes I'm doing that with other children with disability and sometimes I'm doing it with typically developed children

Ensuring that the child 'fits in with other children' was considered to be important by one parent; another pointed out how she was pleased when her child 'gets the hang of things'. However, one parent also noted how difficult it was for her when other people judge her child:

> I think professionals sometimes forget that they are dealing with first and foremost a child, and then secondly that child has Down's syndrome, so that then affects that child's mother, they don't do it deliberately, they don't you know, most of them are really good, they're very good at what they do, but you know, they do it so often, day in, day out that they forget, which is very understandable.

This view of the child could have a significant impact on the child's identity and self-esteem within a learning situation, especially if the child is viewed 'first and foremost' within developmental milestones. In this case, the label of Down syndrome seems to limit the perspective of the professionals so that they see the 'Down syndrome' rather than a 'child'.

The following perceptions of the child's experiences represent parents' perspectives about their child's learning at home and through early intervention activities. The parents considered the child would be:

- 'ready' to do activities – enjoys certain activities
- sometimes allowed to 'just play'
- instigating a song or a story, and the parent may respond

- getting cross if others want certain activities carried out
- in a position that they would have goals set by parents and professionals.

The parents' perspectives on their experiences with their children perhaps demonstrate how they perceive their child. Their description of these experiences provides an insight into what it may be like for a child to participate in the early intervention process.

Doing activities

Some of the parents described how they would carry out activities with their child:

> I would spend every morning with Richard for half an hour, 20 minutes, carrying out activities with him. And throughout the day, whenever 1 would do things, we'd try and interweave those activities into whatever it was that I was doing with him.

These activities would be measured within timescales, and were considered to be an important part of the day:

> I try to give her an hour every evening when we sit down together and we do various activities together. And then in the morning when she wakes up early I give her another hour then ...

Providing this type of support was considered to be an essential part of supporting the child's learning experience:

> She has a lot of input at home, we simply don't waste an opportunity.

The home is considered by this parent as a place for the child to learn, and where her role is to support the child's learning. In the above examples the families go through a time of transition in terms of their activities relating to the child's learning and development. The child's experiences, according to these findings, indicate that the parents spend significant amounts of time supporting their children's learning through structured activities provided by professionals. Rix and Paige-Smith (2005) and Bridle and Mann (2000) have noted how there can be a perpetual 'tension' surrounding the expectation that there should be perpetual learning through activities. However, parental responses indicated that learning was not always through structured activities and that there were times that spontaneous play occurred, though often this was within play initiated by the adult.

Playing

One parent noted how she was encouraged by professionals to play with her child:

> Just seeing the way she was interested in whatever the Portage visitor brought, she always wanted to know what was in the box, and had very definite ideas about what she would or wouldn't play with ...

Another parent noticed how her son enjoyed his play and had progressed to imaginative play with encouragement:

> Richard fed the baby [doll], gave it a bottle of milk and then self-initiated putting the baby to bed wrapped in my cardigan!

The importance of letting the child play was recognized, but the concept of play was interwoven with ideas around developmental progress and learning through play:

> She needed from me the ability to be able to play and she would often, she'd quite often, I think she needs time to rest as well, time to use what she's learning everywhere and time to just express it herself. So quite often I would find the easiest way to get somewhere with Katy was just to let her play …

The child in these accounts seems to know or be empowered to choose to play or not to play; the parent's response was also to respond to the child's lead, which in some cases occurred spontaneously.

Parents' participation with their child

This parent wrote about how she interweaves support for her child's learning into his everyday life:

> We walk down to the school to pick the girls up. We point at cars, trees, birds, cats and dogs and talk about them on the way there and the girls join in on the way back as well as chat about their day at school.

The opportunity to just 'be with' a child may also take place in the morning, a time of the day when the parent may be with the child on a one-to-one basis while getting dressed:

> On the bed the other day, a few mornings ago, he just sat there and he started doing the frog sign and he wanted me to tell the frog story, which he hadn't heard in six months, which was brilliant. He only let me get two-thirds of it, and as soon as I got close to the end, he hopped off, because he hates the end of stories, he wants the story to go on for ever I think …

Parents reflected on their interpretations of and responses to children's lived experiences in learning – for example, anger. One parent interpreted her son's anger as deriving from frustration, in being unable to do what was expected:

> We have to do a lot of sound activities and they have been an absolute unmitigated failure. He won't do the sound cards, [saying] 'sod off, go away, I'm an angry young boy, I hate you, I don't want to do this'.

Children's anger may [be] rooted in a number of possible factors, including anxiety about failure, the experience of frustration, the desire to take power and even enjoyment

[in] the 'destructive' act (for example, throwing). Parents reflected on their own responses to children's feelings, as they implemented early support practices:

> He can concentrate for short periods of time so looking at books needs to be kept brief or he will end up throwing the book across the room.

> Now she gets cross with her school writing because I wanted her to form her letters properly, and she just wants to put them down as she feels like, and obviously she can't do that ...

The methodology within the 'listening to children' approach (Clark 2004) could be considered to be appropriate, in order to provide more insight into the child's experiences and how these could be understood.

Goal-setting

Most of the parents reported in some way that they felt their child should be achieving certain milestones, and that they felt as though these were expected of their child. There were many examples of how the developmental expectations on their child's learning and behaviour were provided by professionals through goal-setting within the early intervention programmes. For example:

> the pre-school advisory teacher came round to our house to do, give us some developmental play stuff to do in the home ... what she'd do is she'd come with a bag of toys and say 'try these toys with her and try this and try this'.

Discussion: learning together

The parents' perspectives documented in our study provide examples of how, through close engagement with professionals and through reflecting on experience and practice, their own behaviour changed over time, including their relationship with their child and their understanding of how their child learns. Contextualizing early support in a developmental framework prompted family transition into a partial educator role entwined with the carer one. This transitional process led some parents to interpret their own behaviour in terms of 'how effective' they considered themselves to be in relation to 'teaching' and playing with their child: a shift of role due to clear expectations and closer collaborative reflective practice.

It is important for professionals to consider such shifting dynamics in the expectation on the parents and, in addition, on the child, during early intervention. From the parents' accounts, it appears that the children's experiences of goal setting have been driven by professionals who inform parents about 'how to play' with their child. One parent expressed concern about how her child is perceived in terms of the label rather than as a child, because of being located within the context of a developmental model of their learning – a difficulty of using such a model. The progress of children with special educational needs is framed uncomfortably in relation to a developmental framework of learning, as McDermott notes about children's experiences in the classroom:

> Failure and success define each other into separate corners, and the children are evenly divided as if by a normal curve, into successful and failing. Among those who fail are those who fail in ways that the system knows how to identify with tests, and these children are called special names. Learning Difficulty acquires its share of the children. (McDermott 2003: 295)

Parents focus, then, on the evaluation of their child's progress in the context of both family and relationship with services, in relation to goal-setting. Whether the *child* engages with goal-setting could be a consideration of further research in order to establish whether and how the children are active participatory agents in the home setting when they engage in early intervention. Laevers' (1997) signals of engagement/ involvement may provide appropriate and fertile indicators of the child's learning with the parent and professional (Arnold 2003).

Conclusion

This chapter has highlighted how the relationship between children and parents in the early intervention process offers a 'window' on particular issues in reflective practice associated with parental involvement. We have sought to illustrate ways in which, in family-centred early intervention practices, parents too are early years practitioners, reflecting on their own child's learning, perhaps exquisitely aware of their own pedagogy. We have suggested that an alternative to the 'special needs family' that Bridle and Mann (2000) suggest can be created by early intervention experiences, might be practice that is more 'family-centred'. Such a family-centred approach should recognize partnership with parents, by professionals supporting and listening to parents and their children. As Carpenter (2005) notes, the notion of partnership within family-centred practice is in a state of flux, with high expectations being placed on parental knowledge and empowerment, or the creation of a 'professional parent' within a transdisciplinary team.

The process of early intervention consists of parents, professionals and the child collaborating and instigating pedagogy in the home setting. As Wenger (2005) notes, there could be considered to be a profound connection between identity and practice:

> Practice entails the negotiation of ways of being a person in that context ... inevitably, our practices deal with the profound issue of how to be a human being. In this sense, the formation of a community of practice is also the negotiation of identities. (Wenger 2005: 149)

We have considered how a 'family-centred approach' should include not only a focus on the family but also on increased and consciously reflective *collaboration* between parents and professionals in order to support the child's learning experiences.

Parents' experiences of 'family-centred practice' within early intervention have been considered to be about the development of 'professional parents' (empowered with knowledge and information). The transformation the child and parent go through includes understanding more about the developmental view of the child, yet the challenge inherent in the developmental model is the implication of deficit in relation to the child who has 'special needs'.

[…]

References

Arnold, C. (2003) Sharing ideas with parents about key child development concepts, in M. Whalley (ed.) *Involving Parents in their Children's Learning*. London: Paul Chapman.

Beveridge, S. (2005) *Children, Families and Schools, Developing Partnerships for Inclusive Education*. Oxford: Routledge Falmer.

Bridle, L. and Mann, G. (2000) Mixed feelings – a parental perspective on early intervention, originally published in *Supporting Not Controlling: Strategies for the New Millennium: Proceedings of the Early Childhood Intervention Australia National Conference*, 1–23 July: 59–72, at www.altonweb.com/cs/downsyndrome/eibridle.html (accessed 21 December 2004).

Carpenter, B. (2005) Early childhood intervention: possibilities and prospects for professionals, families and children, *British Journal of Special Education*, 32(4): 176–183.

Carpenter, B., Addenbrooke, M., Attfield, E. and Conway, S. (2004) 'Celebrating Families': an inclusive model of family-centred training, *British Journal of Special Education*, 31(2): 75–80.

Clark, A. (2004) The Mosaic approach and research with young children, in V. Lewis, M. Kellett, C. Robinson, S. Fraser, and S. Ding, (eds) *The Reality of Research with Children and Young People*. London: Sage.

Department for Education and Skills (DfES) (2004a) *Removing Barriers to Achievement: The Government's Strategy for SEN*. Nottingham: DfES.

Department for Education and Skills (DfES) (2004b) *Early Support Family Pack*. Nottingham: DfES.

Department for Education and Skills (DfES) (2006) *Early Support: An Evaluation of Phase 3 of Early Support*, Brief no: RB798, September. Nottingham: DfES.

Donaldson, M. (1986) *Children's Minds*. London: HarperCollins.

Dunlop, A.-W. (2007) Bridging research, policy and practice, in A.-W. Dunlop and H. Fabian (eds) *Informing Transitions in the Early Years*. Berkshire: Open University Press.

Fabian, H. (2007) Informing transitions, in A.-W. Dunlop and H. Fabian (eds) *Informing Transitions in the Early Years*. Berkshire: Open University Press.

Laevers, F. (1997) *A Process-Oriented Child Follow Up System for Young Children*. Leuven: Centre for Experiential Education.

McDermott, R. (2003) The acquisition of a child by a learning disability, in S. Chaiklin and J. Lave (eds) *Understanding Practice: Perspectives on Activity and Context*. Cambridge: Cambridge University Press.

Miller, L. and Paige-Smith, A. (2004) Literacy in four early years settings, in L. Miller and J. Devereux (eds) *Supporting Children's Learning in the Early Years*. London: David Fulton: 124–136.

National Audit Office (2006) *Value for Money Report, Executive Summary – Sure Start*. DfES, at www.nao.org.uk/publications/nao_reports/06-07/0607104es.htm (accessed 28 February 2007).

National Portage Association (2007) www.portage.org.uk/gen-Faq.html (accessed 30 April 2007).

Paige-Smith, A. and Rix, J. (2006) Parents' perceptions and children's experiences of early intervention – inclusive practice? *Journal of Research in Special Educational Needs, NASEN,* 6(6): 92–98.

Rix, J. and Paige-Smith, A. (2005) The best chance? Parents' perspectives on the early years learning of their children with Down syndrome and the impact of early intervention activities. Paper presented at the International Conference on Early Intervention and Developmental Issues in Down Syndrome, University of Portsmouth, September.

Rogoff, B. (2003) *The Cultural Nature of Child Development.* New York: Oxford University Press.

Russell, F. (2003) The expectations of patents of disabled children, *British Journal of Special Education,* 30(3): 144–148.

Russell, F. (2005) *The Extent of Portage Provision in England,* Final Report of the NPA Survey 2005. National Portage Association, DfES.

Sammons, P., Elliot, K., Sylva, K., Melhuish, E., Siraj-Blatchford, I. and Taggart, B. (2004) The impact of pre-school on young children's cognitive attainments at entry to reception, *British Educational Research Journal,* 30(5), October: 691–712.

Strauss, A. and Corbin, J. (1998) *Basics of Qualitative Research: Techniques and Procedures for Developing Grounded Theory.* Newbury Park, CA: Sage.

Wenger, E. (2005) *Communities of Practice, Learning Meaning, and Identity.* New York: Cambridge University Press.

Woodhead, M. (2005) Early childhood development: a question of rights, *International Journal of Early Childhood,* 37(3): 97–98.

Paige-Smith, A., Rix, J. and Craft, A. (2008) 'Reflective family-centred practices: parents' perspectives and early intervention', in Paige-Smith, A. and Craft, A. (eds) *Developing Reflective Practice in the Early Years,* Maidenhead: McGraw Hill/Open University Press, pp. 145–59. © 2007. Reproduced with the kind permission of Open University Press. All rights reserved.

10

The challenges for children experiencing rural poverty in Wales

Siân Wyn Siencyn

Overview

In this chapter, Siân Wyn Siencyn addresses rural poverty in Wales. She defines poverty and makes the distinction between poverty and rural poverty which has particular characteristics. The chapter considers the reality of child poverty; its immediate and long-term consequences for children's life chances; and the opportunities and challenges that living in a rural setting brings. She also considers, through two case studies, how the Welsh Assembly Government is tackling poverty and what this means for children.

[...]

Introduction

It is generally accepted that there is little to be gained from a discussion of childhood, as if childhood were one universally agreed, chronologically delineated experience. The

---

Wyn Siencyn, S. (2010) 'The challenges for children experiencing rural poverty in Wales', in Clark, M.M. and Tucker, S. (eds) *Early Childhoods in a Changing World*, Stoke-on-Trent: Trentham Books, pp. 45–55.

terms 'multiple childhoods' and 'multiplicity of childhoods' have become common (Dalhberg and Moss, 2005), reflecting the differences in children's experiences. These differences are individual, social, linguistic and economic and are governed by the complex political and cultural forces which impact on children's lives.

As elsewhere, children's lives in Wales have changed and are changing. The impact of the establishment of the Welsh Assembly in 1999 has driven many of those changes. The Foundation Phase 3–7 years, the early years curriculum in Wales, is a radical departure from the previous approaches to early learning. Children's well-being is at its core and learning through play for all children [aged] 3–7 years is its underpinning principle. Another important entitlement in the Foundation Phase is the role of the Welsh language. Welsh language development is now an area of learning for all children, giving them the right to become bilingual in the official languages of Wales, Welsh and English.

Wales is a small country in the west of the British Isles with a population of just under three million. Of the total population, some 19 per cent is under the age of 19 years. The population of Wales is mainly located around the urban centres of *Caerdydd* (Cardiff) in the south-east and *Wrecsam* (Wrexham) in the north-east.

As in other areas of the United Kingdom, the population profile is shifting and these demographic changes have important messages for planners. The child population of Wales is falling: for example, the age group 0–4 years has seen a decline from almost 191,750 in 1991 to 163,680 in 2007 whilst the age group 5–9 years has seen a similar decline of some 20,000 (www.statistics.gov.uk).

A consistent downfall in the number of children, particularly in the groups under 10 years, has implications for a range of services. There will, for example, be a smaller school population and this is already resulting, in Wales, in the training of fewer teachers and in teacher unemployment or re-deployment. Some areas of Wales are already seeing a decrease in private daycare due, in the main, to fewer takers. What is perceived as expensive provision, not easily accessible [and] less well paid work are all factors that impact on the viability of childcare.

Many of the Welsh Assembly Government (WAG) initiatives relating to children share the same underpinning principles as those of other countries of the UK. The same challenges face all: safeguarding and protecting children, ensuring good learning experiences for all children, eliminating poverty and its dire consequences for children. The WAG *National Service Framework for Children, Young People and Maternity Service* (NSF) was launched in 2005 with the aim of improving quality and equity of services, in a partnership between health, social care, education, housing, leisure, the voluntary sector, together with parents, carers, children and young people. In line with almost all the WAG's initiatives for children, the NSF is rooted in the 42 Articles of the UN Convention on the Rights of the Child (United Nations, 1989) and the Assembly's seven core aims for children and young people all relating to a 'flying start', access to learning, to play, to leisure and culture, physical, mental, social and emotional health (including the right to respect and a voice, and to be safe).

This chapter will focus on one major area of policy commitment which has challenged the Government of Wales and one of its core aims which is to ensure that children are not disadvantaged by poverty.

Child poverty in Wales

The Welsh Assembly Government (WAG) has, from its establishment, committed itself to the UN Convention on the Rights of the Child. Indeed, Wales was the first country in the UK to appoint a Children's Commissioner, in March 2001. It is in the spirit of that commitment to children's rights that, for the first time, in the UK, comprehensive statistics on expenditure on children has been released. In 2006–7 the WAG allocated some £4.4 billion of its budget to children in Wales, which is something in the region of 28 per cent of its total expenditure. Furthermore, annual public expenditure per child is increasing. In 2005–6 some £5,600 was spent on every child in Wales and the projected expenditure per child in Wales in 2010–11 is £7,100 (source: http://wales. gov.uk – for current update, see http://wales.gov.uk/newsroom/).

In her statement, releasing these statistics, Jane Hutt, the Children's Minister said:

> We have made it our goal to eradicate child poverty by 2020. By making significant financial investments in children's lives, ensuring they have the rights which they deserve, we can help make this goal a reality. (from above web reference, no page given)

There are major threats to this ambitious goal, not least amongst them is the impact of the economic recession. Higher levels of unemployment are leading to rises in the benefits budget and will inevitably make huge demands on the public purse. It is a concern that, when governments face economic crises, children are in danger of bearing the brunt of stringent belt tightening.

The eradication of child poverty is a major challenge in Wales. Although Wales has seen a reduction in child poverty, indeed, the fastest reduction in any country of the UK, over the past few years, that rate of reduction seems to have halted. It is increasingly difficult for policies and services to attack the deeply entrenched poverty in some areas that some families face. The link between child poverty and low educational achievement is long established. Egan (2007) outlines a number of innovative education policies the WAG has developed in order to combat the discriminatory impact of poverty on children's learning prospects, including *Flying Start* and *Free Breakfast Clubs.*

A Fair Future for our Children (WAG, 2005), launched in February 2005, outlined the WAG's programme for meeting its commitment to halve child poverty by 2010 and eradicate it by 2020.

In February 2008, Save the Children and the Bevan Foundation published *Children in Severe Poverty in Wales: an agenda for action* (Save the Children, 2008) presenting the findings of an investigation into the lives of children living in the most severe poverty in Wales. The report states that whilst the WAG has 'demonstrated a commitment to tackling child poverty with a child poverty strategy (2005), an implementation plan (2006) …' (Save the Children, 2008: 4) the challenges are daunting. The report itself makes sobering reading:

- over one in ten children in Wales live in severe poverty where household incomes are below 50 per cent median;

- there is a strong link between severe child poverty and living in a household where no adult works;
- a third of children in severe poverty have a disabled parent;
- there is a strong association between severe child poverty and living in a lone parent household;
- factors associated with severe child poverty include: living in a large family; living in an Asian or Asian British family; living in a family where mothers do not have any educational qualifications.

The report states clearly that:

> the links between household characteristics and severe child poverty are complex with many of the factors overlapping, making it especially hard for such families to leave poverty. (Save the Children, 2008: 2)

This kind of research has provided the WAG with compelling evidence on which to act further. On 2 March 2009, the Children and Families (Wales) Measure, which aims to tackle child poverty and strengthen support for families in need, was laid before the National Assembly for Wales. This places a duty on Welsh Ministers to develop a new Child Poverty Strategy for Wales, which will be reviewed regularly with the goal of eradicating child poverty by 2020. In June 2009, the Joseph Rowntree Foundation published *What is Needed to End Child Poverty in Wales?* reiterating the figure of approximately 32 per cent of children in Wales living in poverty (Winkler, 2009).

Defining poverty

One traditional way of defining poverty, prevalent in the early twentieth century, was in terms of physical needs that were either not met or were inadequate: food, shelter, clothing and so on. As standards of living improved and the welfare state became more established, this absolutist approach became, over time, less relevant. By the 1970s, Townsend (1979) proposed a concept of 'relative poverty'. He argued that poverty was:

> the lack of resources to obtain the types of diet, participate in the activities and have the living conditions and amenities which are customary ... in societies to which (people) belong. (Townsend, 1979: 87)

Current thinking on definitions of poverty, as proposed by New Labour governments, the European Commission and anti-poverty organisations, use methodologies based on official statistics on income levels. Families living in poverty are defined as those with incomes of less than 60 per cent of the national median income level (Milbourne and Hughes, 2005: 4).

Contemporary discourses on poverty are often complex and relate to philosophical and political debates around social exclusion and the more practical challenges of promoting social inclusion. Walker and Walker (1997) describe social exclusion as:

a dynamic process of being shut out, fully or partially, from any of the social, economic, political or cultural systems which determine the social integration of a person in society. (1997: 8)

Whatever approach is taken, there is general consensus that poverty excludes people, and children in particular, from accessing services, resources, income, from power, and from choices in their own lives.

Rural poverty

The WAG's public policies and services for young children and families are provided through a number of key initiatives such as *Flying Start* and *Integrated Children's Centres.* These initiatives target the most disadvantaged communities in specific geographical areas, areas with high concentrations of communities and people living with complex disadvantages. This results in services being increasingly centralised. This can, in many ways, lead to more effective services: cost effectiveness and resource effectiveness. But this can be disadvantageous for people living in rural communities. There is evidence, disturbing but not surprising, that families with children with disabilities have difficulty in accessing appropriate services and this is made even more challenging when they are families with low incomes (Sharpe, 2003).

Children living in rural areas can have particularly difficult experiences. Rural poverty is not, of course, new and it is often not as evident as urban poverty. In a government enquiry into women and children in agricultural employment in *Ceredigion* (Cardiganshire) in 1865, the following evidence was given by one David Jenkins:

> I am an agricultural labourer and can speak only a little English. My wages are 1s 6d a day all the year round … I have six children … None of them can read or write. There is no school in the parish where I live, and if there was I could not afford to send my children to it. I never get meat except now and then a bit of bacon. I live upon potatoes, bread and cheese. The labour of children becomes valuable after 10 … Children are useful in tending cattle, weeding, etc. Education is a good thing, but bread is better *(Report of the Commissioners on the Employment of Children, Young Persons and Women in Agriculture*, 1870: 130)

Although rural and urban poverty share many common experiences such as stigma and social exclusion, there are other unique features experienced by children living in poverty in rural areas. Akhtar (2008) outlines some of them such as: access, transport, employment and education, social networks and clubs, and housing.

Access to facilities, services and goods

As well as the financial barriers to accessing services, there are also the physical factors in reaching out to services – services that may not, of course, even exist. It can often be difficult, for example, to access play, leisure and sport facilities. Additional challenges include being able to access a range of health services, including health centres, dentists and clinics. There are also limited community Internet facilities, libraries and access to home entertainment, such as digital television. Broadband and mobile phone connections are often very restricted.

Accessing goods is also a challenge, not only financially but also physically. Small rural shops are closing and when they are accessible, they are often more expensive and offer limited choice. Affordable clothes shops are located in towns or in out-of-town shopping centres.

Transport

The lack of public transport remains a key concern for children and young people in rural areas, with infrequent and costly bus services the sole option, particularly for those without a family car. The cost and time involved in catching two buses to make an appointment or to access a short break service for a disabled child can prove particularly challenging. It is important to remember, also, that families do not necessarily live in villages. Many will live on isolated farms and smallholdings some miles from the nearest village. Children and young people regularly report that transport, or lack of it, is important to them as it restricts both their social and learning opportunities.

Employment and higher education opportunities

There are specific challenges in maintaining rural communities where there is a large emigration from rural to urban areas of young people seeking job or education opportunities, which may not be accessible locally. Transport issues are again key.

After-school activities

Many children rely on school transport to and from school and this raises particular challenges in terms of attending after-school clubs and activities arranged by the school.

Travelling to school

Many children travel significant distances each day to and from school, and this can be a particular concern for infant school age children and children who attend special schools. Travelling long distances for long periods of time daily can impact on the health and well-being of a child.

Sustaining friendships

Children may live some distance from each other, given the large catchment areas for many rural schools, and this makes it difficult to meet outside school hours.

Housing and homelessness

It has been well documented that there is an acute lack of affordable housing, private rented stock and social housing in many rural areas, which is forcing many young people to leave their area of birth.

Positive impact of rural living

There are, of course, positive benefits for children who live in rural communities. *Children in Wales* reports that children in rural areas feel safer; [and that] there is space for play outdoors with no adult interference (Children in Wales, 2008). Even with all the social and economic pressures, there are still strong feelings of community and there are informal networks of community support. Small rural schools often act as a community focus and parents can become involved in organising fund-raising events which can be powerful promoters of social cohesion. These small schools can also be democratic in nature as all children in the community attend. There is not always an evident social hierarchy. The duality of the leafy suburb versus the inner-city schools is not usually prevalent in a rural community. Furthermore, in many areas, these small schools are important learning centres, offering the wider community use, for example, of up-to-date computer suites. Young farmers' clubs are often vibrant and inclusive places and there are opportunities for promoting Welsh cultural and language activities such as the Urdd and its sports and other activities (www.urdd.org).

Initiatives and projects

There are examples, throughout Wales, of new initiatives and longer-term services that work well in rural communities. *Mudiad Ysgolion Meithrin* (www.mym.org) has a well established network of *cylchoedd meithrin and cylchoedd Ti a Fi* (Welsh medium playgroups and parent and carer toddler groups) serving rural communities. They will often have informal transport arrangements whereby parents or carers will pick up other users. Most counties have mobile services such as toy libraries and play services which are often delivered in specifically adapted buses.

Conwy County in the rural north has established a bilingual telephone support line for parents of young children who may be facing difficulties with parenting. It is particularly suited to rural areas as it is accessible and free. Parents can talk at a time that suits them; there is no need to travel or make childcare arrangements. Users of this service are primarily from low-income and rurally isolated areas. Three Action for Children *(Gweithredu dros Blant Cymru)* social care practitioners deliver the service and, after an initial assessment, an action plan is drawn up and weekly calls are made for around 12 weeks. The *Ynys Môn* Rural Family Service, which is run by Barnardo's, targets services, people and communities who may not show up in deprivation profiles as the numbers are so small. The Family Service brings together a multi-disciplinary team, working as outreach services in rural communities.

In rural Carmarthenshire, a network of family centres has been developed and a mobile service is provided by a specially adapted bus. There is a dedicated rural worker who provides parenting education through the medium of Welsh. She makes home visits and runs groups in small, isolated villages. However, she reports a common challenge – parents living in poverty will often not take up a service as it is perceived as being stigmatising.

The following two case studies outline some of the challenges facing children experiencing rural poverty. Llinos and Josh's stories are uniquely their own but they are also, in many ways, common experiences. They demonstrate the challenges faced by many children and their families living in rural areas.

📁   **CASE STUDY**

Llinos (4 years)

Llinos lives with her older brother Aled (7 years) and younger brother Sion (2 years) in a local housing association house in west Wales. Her father used to work in the local cheese factory until it closed a year ago. He was offered another job, with the same company, in the north of England. He tried it for four months but the cost of travelling and lodging away from home made it difficult. Llinos's mother works during the holidays, cleaning in a holiday caravan complex which is 10 miles away. She has not worked much since Sion was born. She is feeling a little down and has seen the doctor who has given her anti-depressants. Aled has a language delay and some speech difficulties which require him to attend a Speech and Language Therapy Clinic in a town some 16 miles away. The clinic is open there on the first Wednesday of every month. There is a bus on Thursday mornings through the village where Llinos and her family live. Llinos started part-time in the local village school, the term after her third birthday. Her mother has to take the three children to school by 9 am and then return to pick Llinos up by 12.00, back again by 3.30 pm to pick up Aled.

After Sion was born, the health visitor suggested that the family receive support from the local Home Start group. A Home Start volunteer came once a week for a couple of months. Llinos's mother enjoyed that; someone to talk to, to take Aled to school, to help play with Llinos. But Home Start has been in financial trouble since its core funding was cut. The local paper said it was something to do with National Lottery money going to the London Olympics.

The village post office closed last year, which has put a strain on the viability of the village shop. Although there is a supply of fruit and vegetables, these are not always very fresh. Family meals are not regularly set at [the] table and the children snack on crisps in front of the television. Aled has been to the dentist once, Llinos has never been.

CASE STUDY

Josh (9 years)

Josh lives with his mother and sister Lauren (7 years) in a private rented house in a small village in mid Wales. The house is not in good condition and two of the bedrooms are damp. Josh and Lauren share a room and their mother sleeps in the living room. She is a single parent on income support. Josh's grandmother bought him a second-hand computer for his birthday but they cannot get broadband in the village. The landline phone was disconnected as the rental was expensive. You have to walk half a mile, up a country road, to get a mobile phone signal.

Josh enjoys taking part in the school *eisteddfod* activities. He is in the *band taro* (percussion band) and his modern dance group won second prize throughout Wales in the *Urdd Eisteddfod*. His teacher thinks he has a real talent and has suggested that he joins a dance and theatre club but that is held on Thursday evenings at the theatre which is almost 15 miles away. She has offered to give him a lift there but there will be no way for him to come back home.

A new after-school club has just opened in the school and Josh's mother volunteers there and is enjoying it. Josh is giving his mother ICT lessons on the school computers.

Conclusion

Developing and funding services for children and families, by the Welsh Assembly Government are often targeted by indicators of deprivation and driven by numbers. This is neither an easy nor often an appropriate model for rural areas. Children living in poverty in rural areas are not counted and, too often, not seen. They can be hidden in affluent areas.

Services in rural areas, often delivered through the voluntary sector and funded through specific streams such as *Flying Start* and *Communities First,* can take longer to set up and to staff. The pressure of time for short-term funding projects is great. The costs are, of course, greater. Transport, travel, staff time and so on strain project and service budgets. Mobile services make an important contribution, but buses are expensive to buy and to maintain.

In June 2009, the Joseph Rowntree Foundation published a report on child poverty in Wales, outlining complex and integrated steps the WAG needs to take in order to reach the 2020 target of eradicating child poverty (Winkler, 2009). The report's recommendations include: improving childcare provision, promoting flexible and good quality employment, [and] improving the skills and qualifications of adults. The Welsh Assembly Government has much to do by 2020.

[...]

References

Akhtar, L. (2008) Response to Welsh Assembly Government Rural Development Sub-Committee RDC (3): 5. Cardiff: 6 March.

Children in Wales (2008) *Families not Areas Suffer Rural Disadvantage: support for rural families in Wales*. Cardiff: Children in Wales.

Dahlberg, G. and Moss, P. (2005) *Ethics and Politics in Early Childhood Education*. London: RoutledgeFalmer.

Egan, D. (2007) *Combating Child Poverty in Wales: are effective education strategies in place?* York: Joseph Rowntree Foundation.

Milbourne, P. and Hughes, R. (2005) *Poverty and Social Exclusion in Rural Wales*. Research Report 6. Aberystwyth: Wales Rural Observatory.

Report of the Commissioners on the Employment of Children, Young Persons and Women in Agriculture (1870) Parliamentary Papers, XII: 130.

Save the Children (2008) *Children in Severe Poverty in Wales: an agenda for action*. Cardiff: Save the Children.

Sharpe, T. (2003) *The Good Life? The impact of rural poverty on family life in Wales*. Cardiff: NCH.

Townsend, P. (1979) *Poverty in the United Kingdom*. London: Penguin.

United Nations (1989) *Convention on the Rights of the Child*. Geneva: United Nations.

Walker, A. and Walker, C. (1997) *Britain Divided: the growth of social exclusion in the 1980s and 1990s*. London: CPAG.

Welsh Assembly Government (WAG) (2005) *A Fair Future for our Children*. Cardiff: Welsh Assembly Government.

Winkler, V. (2009) *What is Needed to End Child Poverty in Wales?* York: Joseph Rowntree Foundation.

11

'Just like having a best friend': how babies and toddlers construct relationships with their key workers in nurseries

Liz Brooker

Overview

Building positive relationships is significant in supporting children to feel secure in an early years environment. In this chapter, Liz Brooker explores the issue of transitions and considers how key workers view building relationships with children. The chapter is based on study of an inner-city children's centre where children aged between 7 and 18 months were making a transition into extended daycare. It examines how children make relationships and show their individual preferences and how practitioners respond to individual children.

[...]

Brooker, L. (2009) 'Just like having a best friend: how babies and toddlers construct relationships with their key workers in nurseries', in Papatheodorou, T. and Moyles, J. (eds) *Learning Together in the Early Years*, London: Routledge, pp. 98–108.

Introduction

The description 'I would say it's just like having a best friend' was offered to me in an interview with a key worker in a babies' room in response to the question, 'How would you describe the relationship you have with your key child?' The response surprised me – I had anticipated something, if not more 'motherly', then more 'adult', suggesting a responsibility of care for the child, rather than a relationship of equality and reciprocity. However, as I continued my research in this children's centre, it began to make sense. This chapter describes the ways in which relationships of care and friendship were constructed by the young children in the study and the adults who looked after them. It emphasises both the agency shown by very young children in this matter and the ways adults found to respect the children's wishes.

The chapter first discusses some key issues to be considered when children under age 3 enter group care. The impact on children's sense of identity as they encounter a new environment and new relationships, at a time when their sense of self is still evolving, needs careful consideration if positive rather than negative outcomes are to be ensured. These 'outcomes' concern the child's feelings of well-being and belonging, and inform all the supportive structures that professionals aim to provide as young children move into new settings. Meanwhile, the nature of 'care' and the caring relationship remains a contested issue (Dahlberg and Moss 2005; Tronto 1993).

The chapter goes on to discuss findings from this small-scale study of the ways in which children aged from birth to 3 establish relationships with their key worker that suit their own needs and the ways in which practitioners' expertise supports and enables this process.

Key issues in early transitions

Early relationships: early identities

Young children's construction of a personal, social and cultural identity begins at birth or earlier, and the nature and outcomes of their early interactions with caregivers have been extensively documented (Schaffer 1996; Trevarthen 1998; Woodhead 2007). The sense of self which evolves through reciprocal engagements with their caregivers enables children to understand their own separate nature and their own agency in relation to others and to the inanimate world of objects. Some infants may enter a rapidly widening circle of acquaintances during their early days and weeks of life, while others remain within a small family nucleus, but the infant's experience provides her with her earliest understanding of the world she inhabits and with continually developing hypotheses and expectations about its nature and stability (Cole and Cole 1989; Schieffelin and Ochs 1986). All children, except those in exceptionally adverse circumstances, will develop a sense of belonging within their own family environment, which is fashioned to accommodate them and which, in turn, accommodates itself to them as they grow and acquire mastery of their surroundings.

Early moves into group care

Despite cultural variations in caregiving (Rogoff 1990), children in both pre-industrial and post-industrial societies have typically spent their early years in the care of family members and, for the most part, in family homes or in the local community. Only in the past half-century has out-of-home care been offered to children from an early age and only in the past decade has it become the norm in many societies, including in the UK, where public policy now encourages mothers to enter or re-enter the workforce before their children are 3 years old. The impact of these early transitions into group care has only recently engaged researchers, although the long-term effectiveness of educational provision from the age of 3 is now demonstrated (Sylva et al. 2004). Public policy in this field appears to derive its rationale as much from the benefits which will flow to parents and the economy, as from the demonstrable benefits to young children. It is for this reason and in order to assure the most desirable outcomes for babies and young children, that a focus on the quality of early relationships in group care is needed.

Care as a concept

There has been a struggle in recent years to describe the relationship between 'care' and 'education' for preschool children: grounds for the debate are still shifting. Most practitioners as well as policy-makers will agree that care and education are insepa-rable but that the 'caring' aspect of the provision leads the 'educating' aspect in the case of children under 3. At the same time, the whole concept of 'care' as an instru-mental or technical service, in which one individual (generally older, more experi-enced or more competent) has responsibility for the physical needs of another, has been challenged by feminist writers such as Tronto (1993) and by those who have reconceptualised early childhood services (Dahlberg and Moss 2005). Early childhood professionals 'care' for their children in more senses than this and the relationships they construct with children are based on mutual feelings of affection and pleasure, as well as on custodial responsibilities.

The 'care' relationship, it is increasingly recognised, is a triangular one con-structed for the mutual benefit of the child, the parent and the practitioner. It may include a strong emphasis on nappy-changing, feeding and sleep routines but it will also describe the ways in which the child communicates her wishes, interests and feelings – and these feelings will almost certainly include 'caring' for her main care-givers. Identifying the contributions of children to this 'triangle of care' (Hohmann 2007) allows us to move away from the idea of a service provided *by* adults *for* babies and young children towards an understanding of a co-constructed social environment.

The nature of transitions

Transitions, as Bronfenbrenner (1979: 26) has argued, involve not simply a change of location or environment but also a change of role and identity. For a young child, new roles and relationships may radically challenge some aspects of her emergent identity. The outcomes may be positive, in the form of a more multifaceted and conscious 'self' who can reflect on her existence in more than one environment and with more than one array of relationships, but such a successful outcome requires strong links and continuities to be created and sustained during the transition period. For the youngest children, the most important of these links will be the relationships established with their new caregivers.

Research on children's transitions has contributed some helpful descriptors for the outcomes which demonstrate children's *well-being*, which is understood both as a short-term goal and as a vital precursor to their longer-term development. Two phrases continually recurred during the fieldwork for this study: that of Laevers et al. (1997), who adopt Bourdieu's and Wacquant's (1992: 127) image of children who 'belong' being like a 'fish in water'; and that of Brostrom (2002: 52), who describes the well-integrated child as 'feeling suitable' in her setting. These evocative phrases aptly describe the babies and toddlers who established successful caring relationships with the adults in the nursery environment.

Relationships and friendships

A number of empirical studies have demonstrated the key role of relationships in early transitions into educational settings. Transitions of this kind (such as that from pre-school to school) have been described as essentially a process of relationship formation (Pianta and Cox 1999) and the links between systems, which underpin Bronfenbrenner's ecological systems theory (1979), consist in the main of human links between micro-systems. For young children, whose principal micro-systems may be home, preschool and school, these links take several forms, including visits to and from homes and settings by each of the parties involved. Research (Brostrom 2002; Entwisle and Alexander 1998) indicates that most nurseries, preschools and schools employ at least some of these strategies for scaffolding the transition process. With very young children, such as those in this study, a 'settling period' of two weeks or more is common, during which the child can access both her familiar and her 'new' caregivers simultaneously.

A smaller number of studies have focused specifically on the role of friendships in supporting children's transitions. With few exceptions, these studies indicate that children who make a move along with existing friends settle more easily in their new environment, suffer fewer negative feelings and 'recover' from the transition and pick up the threads of their development more quickly (Brooker 2002; Corsaro et al. 2003; Peters 2000). Friendship, however, is understood in these studies as an existing relationship between peers, rather than a new relationship with an adult: hence my initial surprise at the idea of an adult who aspires to be the 'best friend' of an infant who has made the transition into her care.

The study

The fieldwork for this study was conducted in an inner-city children's centre which offers extended-day childcare for children from 6 months to 5 years. Childcare is organised in three age ranges: 'babies' for children from 6 to 24 months, 'toddlers' for children aged 24 to 36 months, and 'kindergarten' for children aged 36 to 60 months.

Children who were making a transition into each of the three phases were selected for the study. Three children aged 7 to 18 months, three aged 24 to 27 months, and six aged 36 to 39 months were identified by the staff, and the parents of all the children gave written consent to their participation (the children's own consent to participation had to be judged on a daily basis by the researcher). The 'babies' moved into a suite of spaces catering for up to 12 children, where each key worker was responsible for up to three key infants and the 'toddlers' into a parallel set of spaces catering for up to 24 children, where each key worker looked after up to six key children. 'Kindergarten' children were in key groups of ten children within larger classrooms.

Ethnographic observations, with the purpose of building a picture of the everyday life and culture of the nursery, were interspersed with more focused observations. Each of the children was observed repeatedly for periods of 15 to 20 minutes, usually by means of an unstructured narrative but sometimes using the Leuven observational format (Laevers 1994). Semi-structured interviews were conducted with the children's parents and key workers.

After all the data had been transcribed, a series of categories emerging from the observations was developed and then refined by reference to the interview transcripts. The emergent categories described a range of contributions to the children's adaptation and their construction of new relationships and a new identity in the setting. These contributory factors included the child's own actions, the behaviours of key workers and family members, and the actions of peers.

Making relationships

Observations of the children, and interviews with the adults in their lives, suggested the wide range of key worker relationships available to the child; the similarities to, and differences from, parental relationships; the contributions made to the relationship by all three participants in this triangular relationship of care; and the contribution of this relationship to the child's sense of belonging and well-being in the new setting.

'Not like a parent'

None of the key workers in this centre felt that their own *relationship* with their key children in any way resembled a parent's, although they acknowledged that their *roles* – feeding, changing, comforting, playing, getting to sleep – were often essentially similar to those of parents. Although the key workers (KW) acknowledged the intimacy of the tasks they undertook with the child, and even referred to the fact that the child might spend more of her waking hours in their care than in parental care, they still felt that there were significant differences in the relationships they formed.

> We are definitely not a parent; they are there for them 24 hours a day but we are just providing a service ... They see us as a friend, as educators, as another human being who is helping them and whom they can play with. (KW: Kindergarten)

This particular (male) key worker expresses, like many of his colleagues, what we might call the 'view from the child': key workers' responsibilities are to be available when the child needs a playmate, a comforter, a help-mate or an emotional support, rather than to be either a constant presence, or someone who can demand reciprocal attention:

> He just comes to me for comfort, if he gets upset; and sometimes if he's coming in from the garden, he'll just call my name and just check that I'm there, so I suppose it's just that bit of security ... he doesn't spend much time with me during the day but he'll always call my name when he comes in and, if I pop my head round, I'll say 'You OK?' and he'll say 'Yeah' and he might go back off out again; but I do feel we've built up a good kind of relationship. (KW: Toddlers)

> I'd like to think I'm their friend, I use this quite a lot, if they're upset, I say 'Would you like a little cuddle? I know my cuddle's not as good as mummy's cuddle but I can give you my cuddle now and then we'll wait and mummy will come and she'll give you a nice big cuddle'. (KW: Toddlers)

> I think if you had to put a name to it I would say it's just like having a best friend. Somebody that you can go to, somebody that you know is always going to be there for you. (KW: Babies)

All the key workers' accounts suggested that the nature of the relationships was shaped by the child's own wishes: that some children wish for more explicit and visible shows of affection, and attention whereas others prefer to maintain their independence. In this respect, it is clear that the adults' professional role requires them to be less demanding of the children themselves than a parent might be, though several acknowledged how devastating it can be to say goodbye to a child when it is time for the next transition.

Children's individual preferences

However young the children are, their key workers describe them as individuals with strong personal preferences rather than as generic 'children' for whom particular professional strategies are required. These impressions are often formed during the home visit which precedes the child's first visit to the nursery, as these extracts suggest:

> He was quite interested with what I brought, because we take a bag of toys and he was quite happy playing with the musical instruments and things like that, so that's something he appeared very keen on, so I thought if I needed anything that would be my key for Billy, that he is interested in sounds and music. (KW: Babies)

> We had quite a bit of interaction: he was interested and curious about what I had in the bag ... So I sat on the floor and just did some play-partnering, just to get to know him, and I had the opportunity then to talk to him as well, just about the routine of the day. (KW: Toddlers)

> He knew I was coming to talk to him about going to nursery, so he seemed quite happy to have us there and to share his toys, and he showed me his bedroom. I was interested in just seeing what Jack wanted to show me during the home visit, his kind of favourite things. (KW: Toddlers)

In the settling-in period too, respondents emphasised the importance of following, rather than leading, the child's interests. An additional member of staff is drafted into each room at this time so that the new child's key worker can observe her continuously and offer one-to-one attention as needed:

> Obviously I was with her on those days and there was more one to one, I was play-partnering her and most of the time we played in the home corner. We play-partner them for the first week. (KW: Kindergarten)

This close attention is a means to discover the child's preferences, both for activities and for personal relationships:

> He showed a lot of confidence: he quite happily explored different areas of the room, and actually he loved being outdoors ... he was showing lots of interest in the environment.

> I suppose I see myself as a security, a sort of emotional security. Davey is not a very tactile child whereas other children are, they want to be on your lap. (KW: Toddlers)

In each case the key worker, in conjunction with the child's parents, has tried to interpret their wishes and respond with the kind of relationship that meets their needs. To some extent these differences are age-related, with older children relying more on peer friendships and less on their key adult. To some extent, they reflect family and cultural experiences (as in the case of a Chinese child from a large family who was used, as her mother confirmed, to seeing to her own needs) and to some extent they reflect the child's own strategies for adaptation. As one key worker pointed out, 'They have different uses for you'. She went on:

> I think you do have different relationships, because someone like Liam especially is quite independent ... then Hana I had to work very hard at, so that was a very different relationship. (KW: Babies)

These different 'uses' may follow different patterns: some of the children begin with a close attachment to their key worker and only gradually relinquish it, while others take time to request and construct an overtly affectionate bond. In the case of the Chinese child, her key worker reports:

> If you tried to pat her, she would push your hand away: she didn't want it. But now, if you go up to her and touch her – a little rub on her cheek or a little tickle – it really brings a smile to her face. She's got this smile, so that's a really big thing that's moved on and she'll often come and lean against my leg, or she'll bring a chair to sit beside me, and the conversation is starting to build as well. (KW: Toddlers)

Similarly for Davey who was 'not very tactile' when he started settling in:

> Davey doesn't come for that kind of attention, but just recently he has started to. He just runs up, puts his arm round my leg, and then just runs off again. I do enjoy picking children up and having a cuddle but it has to be very much on their terms … it's just reading the situation. (KW: Toddlers)

Children's initiatives: adults' responses

Observations undertaken over the three-month period reveal many instances of young children making overtures to adults in the setting and taking the initiative in choosing activities and pursuing relationships. Staff are adept at waiting for the child to show intentions in this way and responding to these intentions, as Liam's encounter with his key worker demonstrates:

> Liam picks up a Bob-the-builder doll as he enters the room and approaches Lillian to show her. Lillian responds with interest and he collects more soft toys, presenting them to her and awaiting her comments (e.g. 'This one looks like an owl, doesn't he?'). He attends carefully to these responses and continues until they have examined several soft toys together. He continues to lead the activity and interaction for the next few minutes, jiggling up and down so that Lillian will copy him, which she does, and they end up jiggling together. (Observation: Babies)

At 8 months old, Billy can initiate a satisfying activity with another member of staff:

> Billy is sitting in a little chair sucking his toast while adults talk. Suddenly he notices Jacintha's nails (which are very long, sparkly, orange, and plastic) and starts to play with them. Jacintha offers her hand and he plays with each finger and all fingers with noisy amusement, pulling at each nail and giggling, separating each finger for a separate attempt. (Observation: Babies)

A few days later, this staff member is observed, still slightly behind and to the side of the child, unobtrusively accompanying his play without seeking to influence it:

Jacintha deposits Billy gently on the mat by the sounds baskets. He immediately selects a long plastic-coated chain and sucks it. Jacintha sits alongside him and slightly behind; he sometimes leans towards her, otherwise is obviously aware of her presence at his side, but is independent. (Observation: Babies)

CASE STUDY

Hana has a Danish father and a Greek mother and has travelled all over Europe visiting members of her extended family during her short life. She was abroad when her home visit was booked, so her 'induction' took place on the first day of the settling-in period. On that day, in Lillian's words, 'she didn't depend on her mum, and mum said she'd been left before and she's very happy, and mum didn't foresee any problems with her'.

This did not prove to be the case once the separation process began. Lillian reported that 'Mum stayed with her for the first few days but was quite keen to go ... but I did say we need to judge this by Hana'. In the event, Hana became increasingly distressed on parting every morning and periodically throughout the day. Lillian and her colleagues had recourse to a number of strategies for helping her to link home and nursery and providing her with resources which would comfort and reassure her, but many of these strategies required close cooperation with her family, which was not always forthcoming. One of the first problems was with the actual 'goodbyes': the nursery insists that parents always say goodbye to their child but both Hana's mother and father sometimes 'snuck out' as the staff described it, denying the child any opportunity to come to terms with their departure.

Among the transitional objects the staff find effective are favourite toys from home and family photos, and both of these were helpful to Hana, so long as her parents remembered them:

> She started asking for Bear quite a bit, which we asked mum to bring in but, unfortunately, she kept forgetting, so we ended up having to phone her, and mum would bring it in and leave it at reception, and that seemed to ease her a little bit. We'd phone her up and say she's distressed, could you bring the bear in, but you'd be going all morning, without the bear, and it just appeared at lunchtime.

There was a long delay too before the family photos were produced, but when they were, 'It was literally just like a magic button!'

> She carried them around – she's very close to Dad – she carried his photograph around with her that day, and literally she went to sleep with the photograph in her hand; so what I did, I actually had it scanned so it was always accessible for her ... and from then she seemed to settle in.

Once reconciled to the separation, and reassured by the routines, Hana transformed herself into one of the most active, engaging and sociable children in the babies' area. Her relationship with Billy brought pleasure to them both – this observed moment is typical:

> Hana is passing Billy, who has a basket of sound objects, and decides to stop and sit down with him She squats and then kneels a short distance from him, and

(Continued)

(Continued)

picks up two metal jar-lids, which she bangs together experimentally. She then repeats the action with more intention and pleasure and begins to interact teasingly with Billy, who looks at her with interest She continues to bang, pause, look, tease and turn-take with Billy and both giggle. (Observation: Babies)

On another occasion Billy reaches out for her from the safety of his cushioned support in the garden and strokes her hair, while she obediently bows her head to allow him; and it was not uncommon to see the two of them simply grinning and giggling at each other – as Lillian reported, 'He seems to find Hana hysterically funny!'

After five weeks, Hana appeared fully settled and demonstrated her confidence daily in exploring all the areas, all the activities and all the resources the environment offered her. As Lillian pointed out, she had even begun to 'escape' from the babies' area: 'She also ventures over into Toddlers occasionally which is good, it shows she's not relying on the familiar adults she's got here.'

Conclusion: an ethic of care

As Dahlberg and Moss (2005: 1) affirm, pedagogy must be understood as 'a relation, a network of obligation', and the pedagogical relationship is one which requires 'infinite attention to the other'. This attention should not have the aim of making the 'other' like ourselves but should allow the other – even the small child – to develop independently as an individual with rights and desires of their own. Genuine 'ethics of care' for young children require adults to take their cue from the children: to watch and wait and respond to their preferences, rather than to 'know what they need'. When this ethical pedagogy is offered, children like Hana, Billy and Davey are able to show their caregivers the kind of care, and education, they require. We can learn from them.

References

Bourdieu, P. and Wacquant, L. (1992) *Invitation to Reflexive Sociology.* Bristol: Polity Press.

Bronfenbrenner, U. (1979) *The Ecology of Human Development*. Cambridge, MA: Harvard University Press.

Brooker, L. (2002) *Starting School: Young Children Learning Cultures*. Buckingham: Open University Press.

Brostrom, S. (2002) Communication and continuity in the transition from kindergarten to school. In H. Fabian and A-W. Dunlop (eds) *Transitions in the Early Years.* London: RoutledgeFalmer.

Cole, M. and Cole, S. (1989) *The Development of Children.* New York: Scientific American Books.

Corsaro, W., Molinari, L., Hadley, K. and Sugioka, H. (2003) Keeping and making friends: Italian children's transition from preschool to elementary school. *Social Psychology Quarterly*, 66(3): 271–291.

Dahlberg, G. and Moss, P. (2005) *Ethics and Politics in Early Childhood Education.* London: RoutledgeFalmer.

Entwisle, D. and Alexander, K. (1998) Facilitating the transition to first grade: the nature of transition and research on factors affecting it. *Elementary School Journal*, 98(4): 351–364.

Hohmann, U. (2007) Rights, expertise and negotiations in care and education. *Early Years*, 27(1): 33–46.

Laevers, F. (1994) *The Leuven Involvement Scale for Young Children*. Leuven (Belgium): Centre for Experiential Education.

Laevers, F., Vandenbussche, E., Kog, M. and Depondt, L. (1997) *A Process-oriented Child Monitoring System for Young Children*. Leuven: Katholieke Universiteit.

Peters, S. (2000) *Multiple Perspectives on Continuity in Early Learning and the Transition to School*. Unpublished paper, EECERA, London.

Pianta, R. and Cox, M. (eds) (1999) *The Transition to Kindergarten*. Baltimore, MD: Paul Brookes.

Rogoff, B. (1990) *Apprenticeship to Learning*. Oxford: Blackwell.

Schaffer, H.R. (1996) *Social Development*. Oxford: Blackwell.

Schieffelin, B. and Ochs, E. (1986) *Language Socialization Across Cultures*. New York: Cambridge University Press.

Sylva, K., Melhuish, E.C., Sammons, P., Siraj-Blatchford, I. and Taggart, B. (2004) *The Effective Provision of Pre-school Education (EPPE) Project: Technical Paper 12 – The Final Report: Effective Pre-school Education*. London: DfES/Institute of Education, University of London.

Trevarthen, C. (1998) The child's need to learn a culture. In M. Woodhead, D. Faulkner and K. Littleton (eds) *Cultural Worlds of Early Childhood*. London: RoutledgeFalmer.

Tronto, J. (1993) *Moral Boundaries: A Political Argument for the Ethics of Care*. London: Routledge.

Woodhead, M. (2007) *Changing Perspectives on Early Childhood: Theory, Research and Policy*. Paper commissioned for the EFA Global Monitoring Report 2007, Strong Foundations.

12

'I didn't expect that I would get tons of friends ... more each day': children's experiences of friendship during the transition to school

Sally Peters

Overview

There is an increasing acknowledgement of the important role that friends play in supporting very young children during transitional experiences. In this chapter, Peters examines how friends can ease children's transitions into formal schooling and also suggests how parents and teachers can be proactive in supporting children in making and maintaining friendships.

[...]

Peters, S. (2003) "'I didn't expect that I would get tons of friends ... more each day": children's experiences of friendship during the transition to school', *Early Years: An International Journal of Research and Development*, vol. 23, no. 1, pp. 45–53.

Introduction

For many children around the world, attending some form of schooling outside the home is a dominant feature of their lives. Their initial contact with the school system is often labelled 'the transition to school' and in recent years this event has received increasing attention in the education literature. The impact of this transition experience is believed to have consequences for children's later success at school. Margetts (1997) notes that children who adjust adequately to the first year of school are likely to be 'more successful in their future progress than children who have difficulty adjusting to the new situation' (p. 54). Likewise, Dockett and Perry (1999) claim that the way in which the transition is managed 'sets the stage not only for children's success at school, but also their response to future transitions' (p. 1). Such claims have been supported by longitudinal studies that indicate stable trajectories of performance relating to the nature of a child's early experience at school (see, for example, Early et al., 1999). However, a New Zealand study of the transition to school by the author suggested that the long-term impact of transition related more to the ongoing nature of the children's experiences. One important factor influencing the nature of these experiences appeared to be the patterns of social interactions that developed, especially in relation to their families and friends (Peters, 2000).

The relationship between having friends and other measures of children's adjustment during the transition to school has been identified in correlational studies in Australia (Margetts, 1997, 2000) and the USA (Ladd, 1990; Ladd and Price, 1987). Margetts (2000) found that 'Children who commenced school with a familiar playmate in the same class were rated as having more social skills, less problem behaviour and greater academic competence than children who commenced school without a familiar playmate in the same class' (p. 4). Ladd (1990) suggests that prior friendships provide a context for immediate companionship, conversation and play and that having access to close friends during school entrance may be especially important in the establishment of positive school perceptions.

Developing new friendships, as well as maintaining old ones, was also found to be important. Making new friendships at school was related to gains in school performance and Ladd (1990) proposes that this might, in part, be due to the more supportive learning environment provided by having a number of friends in the classroom. In contrast, the child without friends was likely to have less favourable school attitudes, increasing school avoidance and lower levels of performance. However, as with all correlations, the nature of the relationship between friends, attitudes and performance is not clear. While it is proposed that lack of friendships may lead to negative attitudes, Ladd (1990) also suggests that poor attitudes towards school may reduce children's opportunities to nurture and maintain relationships with peers, or that other factors may be at work.

In their detailed case studies of English children, Pollard and Filer (1999) provide further insights into the complex relationship between academic performance and peer relationships. They revealed the important connection between teachers' actions and perceptions of a child and his/her role, acceptance and status within the peer group. Where a teacher's actions facilitated and promoted a positive image of a child, this supported the child's peer relationships and a positive cycle of learning and development was likely to develop. In contrast, if a child's approach to learning and identity was not accommodated or valued, this could become part of a negative cycle of deteriorating relationships and loss of motivation, often accompanied by unhappiness and a lack of enthusiasm for school.

Cullingford's (1991) interviews with older children indicated that they were aware of the impact of their relationships with peers on their school experiences. He found that children spent much of their time subconsciously reflecting on how to make a friendship or how to avoid being isolated or teased, suggesting, 'A school's virtues derive from the pleasures of friendship; its terrors from loneliness and isolation' (p. 48).

The New Zealand study referred to earlier, explored the complex nature of the transition to school, where friends appeared to play an important role (Peters, 2000). This [chapter] considers the issue of friendship in more detail. Observation and interview data are used to explore 23 children's experiences of friendship and the way in which this impacted on their early experiences of school. The data also provide insights into how friendships might be facilitated before, during and after transition, while also drawing attention to practices that could make the consequences of not having a friend less detrimental.

The study

This study was carried out in Kowhai School, a large (500 + pupils) urban primary school in the North Island of New Zealand, and three contributing kindergartens; Azure, Blue and Cobalt.[1]

The data for this [chapter] were gathered from seven case study children and their families, 16 other new entrant children and their families, and the teachers of the 23 children. Seventeen of the 23 children were Pakeha (European). The backgrounds of the other children were Asian, Polynesian and Arabic. Three children had English as their second language. All the children started school on or near their fifth birthday.[2]

The researcher spent 76 hours observing in three new entrant classrooms at Kowhai School and 21 hours observing the case study children in the three kindergartens. The data presented here are drawn from these observations and from 44 semi-structured interviews conducted with the adult participants, seven semi-structured interviews with the case study children and a number of informal conversations with both adults and children throughout the study.

The case study parents were interviewed three times: before the children started school, when the children had been at school for about 2 months and again 18 months later. The 16 other parents were interviewed once or twice during the child's transition to school. The new entrant and kindergarten teachers were interviewed once. Later, in order to learn more of the children's perspectives, the seven case study children were interviewed during their third year of school (when they were 8 years old) to obtain their reflections on the transition process.

Friendship as a factor in transition to school

During the initial phase of the study, the observations, parent and teacher interviews and informal conversations with the children, established friendships as an important factor influencing the nature of the children's transition to school. Later, when the seven case study children reflected on their experiences of starting school, friendship was again a dominant theme in the data. The predominant reason for the importance of friendship was because of the support friends provided during the transition, both in and out of the classroom, and in particular in dealing with the lunch break.

Coping with lunchtimes

When the children first started school, one of the most common causes of distress was the hour-long lunch break. Eight of the 23 parents commented that their child really hated lunchtime because they had no one to play with. In many cases this led to otherwise happy children not wanting to go to school:

> He said to me 'I like Mrs Knight and my classroom but I don't like lunchtimes' ... He knew this boy from kindy ... The boy would run off and leave him. One time the duty teacher found him crying and he said 'I want my mummy, when does lunchtime finish?' And that really tugs. And in the end he actually hated lunchtimes.

> I think she found lunchtimes at school really hard, and I think she still does [after several weeks]. I think her only concerns were the lunchtime thing, I think, just the playing. I think she handled everything in the classroom all right.

For those children who were not included in games with other children, the lunchtime represented a long boring time with almost nothing to do, feeling 'alone and out of place' (Mother), or 'Lonely ... Bored, 'cos you have got no idea what to do' (Steve). Negative attention from other children sometimes contributed to their distress.

The observations were consistent with the children's and parents' comments and showed a great many new children wandering around by themselves at lunchtime. The teachers were aware of the problems many children experienced and usually made an effort to pair a new child up with a classmate who was supposed to play with them during the lunch break. Some children were very responsible in the care they provided for peers but the observations showed that in practice these pairings seemed to work best if the children were already friends.

Even when children did have some friends they were sometimes deserted when their friends ran off and left them. Given the size of the school grounds most new children found it impossible to locate the children they knew once they moved away from the lunch area. Kathy apparently told her mother one day. 'I couldn't find any of my friends so I sat under a tree and cried where no one could see me'. A number of children were too frightened to eat their lunch because they worried they would be left by themselves, and probably wouldn't be able to find their friends when they had finished.

Conversely, pleasure in having friends was often an important motivation that got children to school: 'That's why he goes to school really' (Mother). For three of the new entrants, the opportunity to play with friends made lunchtime one of the best parts of the day.

Supporting each other in the classroom

As well as being a source of pleasure and companionship, friends could also provide important support for children's learning. The careful scaffolding that Jenny, who had been at school for a few months, provided for her friend Heather when Heather arrived at school, has been described in detail (Peters, 1999). This included locating materials and resources, modelling the work they were supposed to be doing, defending Heather from interruptions or criticism from other children, and providing a willing partner for cooperative activities. This is a potential benefit of the New Zealand system, whereby children join the class throughout the year. However, it doesn't necessarily happen for all children. Anna, who joined the same class in the same week, received very little peer support and often floundered during activities, unsure of what she should be doing. Very quickly Heather was established as a successful member of the class while Anna was perceived by her teacher to be having problems, and within 3 weeks Anna concluded that she 'hated' school. Heather went on to forge more friendships, confiding to the researcher that she didn't expect to get 'tons of friends … more each day', while Anna complained that she 'didn't know anybody' even though she was familiar with several of the children in her class because they had been to kindergarten together.

As Pollard and Filer (1999) suggest, teachers need to consider the way that they position children within the class and the impact this has on their peer relationships. Anna struggled to become involved in classroom activities without the support of friends, and even when she was successful this was often overlooked. Her resulting status within the class may then have worked against her achieving the acceptance she clearly desired.

A conclusion from the study is that it is important to reflect on the nature of the classroom climate that children experience and to consider ways in which friendships can be promoted, while also evaluating practices that draw attention to children who do not have friends. For example, simple organisational routines like asking children to line up in pairs, when repeated several times a day, seemed to highlight some children's isolation, whilst confirming the popularity of others. While friends vied for each other's hands to hold, other children were often not selected and were sometimes actively rebuffed when they tried to find a partner. For a child like Anna, who was already disappointed at not having a special friend, alternative methods of organisation might have been preferable.

As the case study children looked back on their experiences, some talked explicitly about the role that friends had played in their learning. Given that friends appear to play such an important role, not just in the transition to school, but throughout children's school careers, it is helpful to look at some of the factors that were associated with making friends.

Making friends

When they talked about the transition to school, many parents of 5-year-olds raised the issue of their child's personality as it impacted on their relationships with other children.

Personality

Parents clearly viewed the sociable child as having an advantage in the school situation:

> I don't worry about the new school because it is no problem for her. She is easy to play with other children. No problem.

> I didn't have any concerns because he gets on well with other children and he is a fairly pleasant sort of little chap.

> She loves school. She is very sociable. She likes people.

On the other hand, parents were concerned about more reserved children:

> He mixes well with other children and he plays well but sometimes he can hang back a little and not move himself forward. I hope that's not going to be a disadvantage when he goes to school.

> She hated it [school]. She cried all the time. She is a very shy person.

One parent found a language barrier could create difficulties for even a normally sociable child:

> In Japan she was socialised. She was more positive and she likes to play with friends … [In New Zealand] we didn't realise that [she] had a problem to contact people. She was very frightened. She realised English is very different from her language, and she was not able to communicate enough.

However, a parent's assessment of a child's personality was not always predictive of how the child would experience friendships at school. Anna's mother's description of her as an outgoing person who fitted into any situation was only partially borne out in the classroom, where Anna did 'fit in' but was unhappy that she did not have a special friend. Clearly the ability to make friends is not simply a characteristic that is located within individual children. As Pollard and Filer (1999) showed, it is also shaped and framed by the context. It seems then that the development of friendship should not just be left to chance, and a number of strategies were identified by participants in this New Zealand study as useful means of supporting children's friendships.

Strategies to support friendships

Contact with other children in the class

A number of parents commented on how helpful it would be if early childhood centres could provide information about which children were going to which school so that they would know who was likely to be going to the same school as their child. With this information parents/caregivers and teachers could facilitate the development of friendships amongst children who would be going to the same school, in the months before school started. This is important, because as Anna's story showed, simply being acquainted with children through attending the same kindergarten did not automatically lead to friendship. Kathy's mother also commented on this: 'I look at all the girls in her class and I think "Oh I wish she'd played a bit more with her at kindy [kindergarten] and got to know them a bit more"'.

When a child was the only one moving from a particular early childhood centre to a school, allowing parents to visit the school along with their children gave parents the chance to see who was in their child's class and to perhaps initiate some out-of-school contact with class members before the child started. Even though Nicola didn't know anyone at her school, her mother was able to arrange for a couple of children to play with Nicola in the weeks between her first school visit and her first day at school. These new friends proved useful during Nicola's transition.

Whilst establishing contact out of school appeared to be an important strategy, the teachers noted that not all families were able to do this. It is therefore also important to consider ways in which friendships can be facilitated in school.

Resources

Out-of-school contacts with potential friends were perhaps useful because they provided contexts where resources could support the move from proximity to friendship. In the school playground the lack of resources seemed to influence the nature of the interactions that took place. For example, observations showed that some boys initiated play by punching or kicking another child, then running away, inviting the recipient to chase them. Carl indicated ambivalence to this type of interaction, joining in frequently in the school setting but later complaining to his parents about the blows he had received. His mother advised him to avoid the boys who did this and was puzzled that he persisted in this type of play. However, it seems that perhaps for Carl the social contact this afforded was important. Rough and tumble play may serve social affiliation and social cognitive functions, including initiating and sustaining play (see Wood, 2000, p. 3). While this may have been due to the personalities of particular boys, it also appeared to be a feature of the school context where, during lunchtimes and playtimes when such behaviour occurred, there was ample outdoor space but few resources to play with. In the kindergarten setting, where there were many resources, boys appeared to initiate social contact through shared activity.

Including more resources to play with at school, particularly at the new entrant level, might benefit both boys and girls, and could be particularly helpful in facilitating entry to social groups for children who do not share the dominant language of the school setting. One day, when a Japanese girl who could speak almost no English at all when she started school, brought a doll from home, she became engaged in sustained family play with a number of other girls in her class over the lunchtime period. From then on she often took her dolls to school. Her mother noted: 'Once she realised that she could bring her dolls and she could play with other children with dolls she was very happy'. Even for children who share a common first language, materials can afford social strategies. In her study of 4-year-olds at kindergarten, Carr (1997) suggests that when *being a friend* was taken out of those contexts that supported it with plenty of physical affordance and mediation, many four-year-olds may have been at a loss as to how to play by the rules' (p. 231). The same seems equally true for the just turned 5-year-olds in this study.

After the first phase of this study, staff at Kowhai School painted some games onto the concrete playgrounds. Other schools have created outdoor play areas for new entrants that resemble those found in early childhood centres. As well as supporting children's social interaction, with appropriate resources, children's learning could be enhanced through their play, regardless of whether they were alone or with others, instead of those who had no one to play with spending an hour or more each day aimlessly wandering around.

Support from older children

Several of the children who had older siblings at school played largely with their siblings and their siblings' friends during their early weeks at school. Generally teachers preferred children to play within their own age groups. 'Brothers and sisters can be a bit protective and that can be a bit of a nuisance because it stops them from making their own friends' (Teacher). In contrast, most parents were pleased that their children were involved in these mixed-aged friendship groups, where role models and a degree of protection were provided.

> She [older daughter] said that the teacher said that I shouldn't play with my sisters. I said that I'd rather you did. I want you all to stay together. I don't see anything wrong with playing with your little sisters. (Mother)

A number of parents believed that for children without an older sibling a buddy system would be useful, where older children could be paired with new entrant children, to sit with them while they ate their lunches and then help them to find someone to play with afterwards.

Teaching social strategies

As an 8-year-old, Anna said that the best thing adults could do to make school a better place would be to 'make sure everyone's got a friend'. While teachers and parents/caregivers cannot make friendships happen, they can put in place strategies that support children's social relationships. For some children direct teaching of social strategies proved beneficial. Based on advice in a book on preventing bullying, Nicola's mother encouraged Nicola to invite a child who was bullying her to join in and play with her and her friends. Other examples were given, and it seemed that a deliberate focus on the development of social skills as part of the programme at Blue Kindergarten could have contributed to the smooth transitions to school of two of the case study children (see Peters, 2000).

Parents and teachers need to be fully aware of the influence of the wider context on children's social interactions. At the same time, the views and experiences of the participants suggested that more direct attention to the development of social skills could be a useful addition to early childhood and beginning school programmes. An example of this is the work of Fabian in the UK. Fabian (2000) has been developing discussion scenarios, with a view to empowering children by helping them to think through the strategies that could be helpful in situations that they might meet during the transition to school (such as having no one to play with at lunchtime). This idea could be adapted to a range of settings.

Conclusion

The precise nature of the support friends can supply, both at lunchtimes and in the classroom, helps to explain the relationship identified in previous studies between having a friend and the nature of children's transition to school (Ladd, 1990; Ladd and Price, 1987; Margetts, 1997, 2000). Although the nature of children's transition to school is complex, and influenced by many factors, the absence of a friend was found to be problematic for many children, while the presence of friendships appeared to go a long way towards establishing a positive experience of school.

It appears that this aspect of transition is worthy of parental/caregiver and teacher attention. Clearly a key step is to examine the classroom climate and the way children are positioned within it (Pollard and Filer, 1999). The participants also suggested a number of strategies to facilitate friendships, through contact between children going to the same school, providing resources to support the establishment of friendships in the context of play, allowing mixed-aged friendships (which provided modelling and protection) and the direct teaching of social strategies. The data also suggest that school practices could be adapted to make the consequences of not having a friend less devastating. In a context where there is less 'terror' associated with 'loneliness and isolation' (Cullingford, 1991, p. 48), children may be more able to engage in the learning opportunities provided.

Notes

1. Pseudonyms have been used for the name of the school, the kindergartens and the participants.

2. In New Zealand, although not compulsory until age 6, most children start school on or near their 5th birthday, and new entrant classes grow in size throughout the year.

References

Carr, M. A. (1997) *Technological Practice in Early Childhood as a Dispositional Milieu.* Unpublished D.Phil. thesis, University of Waikato.

Cullingford, C. (1991) *The Inner World of the School: children's ideas about schools* (London, Cassell).

Dockett, S. and Perry, B. (1999) Starting school, *AECA Research in Practice Series,* 6 (3) (Watson, ACT, Australian Early Childhood Association).

Early, D. M., Pianta, R. C. and Cox, M. J. (1999) Kindergarten teachers and classrooms: a transition context, *Early Education and Development.* 10 (1), pp. 25–46.

Fabian, H. (2000) Empowering children for transitions, paper presented at the *10th European Conference on Quality in Early Childhood Education,* University of London, August/ September.

Ladd, G. W. (1990) Having friends, keeping friends, making friends, and being liked by peers in the classroom: predictors of children's early school adjustment? *Child Development,* 61, pp. 1081–1100.

Ladd, G. W. and Price, J. M. (1987) Predicting children's social and school adjustment following the transition from preschool to kindergarten, *Child Development,* 58, pp. 1168–1189.

Margetts, K. (1997) Factors impacting on children's adjustment to the first year of school, *Early Childhood Folio,* 3, pp. 53–56.

Margetts, K. (2000) The transition to school: complexity and diversity, summary of a paper presented at the *10th European Conference on Quality in Early Childhood Education.* University of London, August/September.

Peters, S. (1999) Continuity and discontinuity: issues for parents and teachers seeking to enhance children's transition to school, paper presented at *Sharing Research in Early Childhood Education. The Third Warwick International Early Years Conference,* University of Warwick. Coventry, April.

Peters, S. (2000) Multiple perspectives on continuity in early learning and the transition to school, paper presented at the *10th European Early Childhood Education Research Association Conference,* University of London, August/September.

Pollard, A. and Filer, A. (1999) *The Social World of Pupil Career: strategic biographies through primary school* (London, Cassell).

Wood, E. (2000) 'I don't want to stereotype but …': the roots of underachievement in the early years, paper presented to the *British Educational Research Associations,* University of Cardiff, September.

13

Postmodern and post-structuralist perspectives on early childhood education

Deborah Albon

Overview

This chapter offers an understanding of a postmodern theoretical perspective and associated theories – post-Fordism, post-structuralism and post-colonialism – and explores how such theorizing might be applied to the field of early childhood. Whilst not a theory about learning or an approach to learning in itself, Deborah Albon argues that the key contribution postmodernist thinking has made to early childhood education and care is in disrupting commonly held 'truths' about our understandings of children and how they develop and learn and, consequently, the curricula and pedagogical approaches practitioners employ in early childhood settings.

[…]

What is meant by 'postmodernism'?

The prefix 'post' indicates that there is a theoretical position known as modernism prior to the development of postmodern theorizing. This section of the chapter,

Albon, D. (2010) 'Postmodern and post-structuralist perspectives on early childhood education', in Miller, L. and Pound, L. (eds) *Theories and Approaches to Learning in the Early Years*, London: Sage, pp. 38–52.

then, aims to provide some discussion of this. In addition, it aims to interweave some related terms which are similar in their theoretical stance: post-Fordism, post-structuralism and post-colonialism.

Modernism as a set of ideas, or modernity as the period it encompasses, developed and pervaded thinking during and from the 17th to the 18th century in Western Europe (Bauman, 1993). This period is also commonly known as the 'Age of Enlightenment'. This period was characterized by a belief that the world is knowable and that science and technological advancement can make the pursuit of such 'truths' and the progress they promise possible. Further to this, the quest for these 'truths' can be linked to the modernist desire for certainty, order, rationality, standardization and universality (Dahlberg et al., 1999).

In the scientific world, this can be seen in positivist thinking: the search for objective and value-free 'truths' free from the relativist confines of place, culture and time (Mukherji and Albon, 2010). Associated theorizing can also be seen in the economic world, with the term 'Fordism' sometimes applied to the late modern period of industrialization, with 'post-Fordism' applied to arrangements made after this period. In brief, Fordist ideas are akin to the manufacturing practice of the Ford car industry. Fordist modes of production can be likened to modernism as they emphasize standardization of product (as opposed to niche markets), order and certainty. In addition, Fordist modes of production can be related to large-scale organizations overseen by hierarchical management systems (Brown and Lauder, 1992).

But the modernist pursuit of certainty, order and universal 'truths' came in for criticism in the latter part of the 20th century. For Bauman, the quest of nation states for order, certainty and homogeneity has legitimated some of the horrors of 20th-century events such as the Holocaust (Dahlberg et al., 1999). Further criticisms of modernism relate to its inability to allow for diversity, subjectivity, uncertainty and complexity (Dahlberg et al., 1999). Indeed, Giroux (2005) notes the way that modernism constructs borders that do not allow for diversity.

Post-colonialist thinking, which shares much of the postmodern critique of modernism, furthers this criticism by identifying modernism with the way that the ideas of minority world countries have held powerful sway across the globe, silencing perspectives that are different, seeing them as 'Other'. Cannella and Viruru (2004) draw on Said's work, which makes the distinction between the orient and the occident. The East, or orient, is conceptualized as inferior and exotic, and the occident, or West, in terms of the belief in the primacy of Western (or minority world) thought and actions. In the pursuit of progress, modernist/colonialist thinking has viewed majority world countries in terms of what they might *become* as opposed to what they *are* now (Gandhi, 1998). This, as we will see in the next section, can be applied to the way children are viewed too.

So what is meant by postmodernism? A key difficulty in defining 'postmodernism' in a clear and concise way is that it resists such easy and 'scientific' classification. Indeed, it is characterized by complexity, fluidity and heterogeneity. Although postmodernist roots can be seen in a range of movements in the 1950s and 1960s, it was really in the late 1970s and 1980s that the term 'postmodernism' became pervasive – and primarily in the minority world (Malpas, 2005). We should also be mindful that, although it could be argued that we live in postmodern times, features of modernity still abound (Grieshaber, 2004). We will see this later in the chapter when postmodernist ideas are applied to early childhood education.

Lyotard (1979) sees the modernist position as one that aims at legitimating itself through the development of 'grand' narratives or 'metanarratives' or universally held truths. Thus, he states, 'I define *postmodern* as incredulity toward metanarratives' (p. xxiv). For Dahlberg et al.:

> From a postmodern perspective, there is no absolute knowledge, no absolute reality waiting 'out there' to be discovered. There is no external position of certainty, no universal understanding that exists outside history or society that can provide foundations for truth, knowledge and ethics. (1999: 23)

In other words, knowledge, from a postmodern perspective, is socially constructed; it is contingent on culture, time and space. In addition, knowledge is not seen as derived from a position of scientific neutrality but through our own interactions and relationships with the world. Thus, knowledge can never be value-free and objective. For Lyotard (1979), by distancing ourselves from 'metanarratives' it is possible for 'micro-narratives', or little narratives, to develop, which are reflective of the thinking of smaller communities and contingent on their particular socio-cultural understandings. Sarup (1993: 146) sees this as 'localised creativity' and Giroux (2005: 49) argues that this offers a promise of a 'cultural politics that focuses on the margins'.

Another term – post-structuralism – is often used synonymously with postmodernism (Brown and Jones, 2001). A key writer associated within this position is Foucault. For Foucault (1977), power is of key importance. Power is not understood as held by people for all time over others; rather, it operates on a far more fluid basis, making it possible for everyone to hold power, be governed by others and also police themselves in given situations. This last form of power – disciplinary power – is especially interesting because it relates to the way particular ideas or 'regimes of truth', which can be likened in part to Lyotard's metanarratives, hold sway at given times. The 'beauty' of disciplinary power is in the way that the ideas embodied in such regimes of truth are seen as so self-evidently 'true' that they are accepted uncritically. From a post-structuralist perspective, therefore, individuals take up such ideas or discourses in such a way that they embody those discourses. In other words, for Foucault, individuals become 'docile bodies' (Holligan, 2000) as these discourses govern their own behaviour and thinking. But more than this, disciplinary power operates in a way that ensures the governability of *groups* of people. This happens through the 'normalizing' of certain practices and concepts to such an extent that surveillance of groups of people for their 'well-being' is largely legitimated (Flax, 1990). I discuss how this applies to early childhood practice in the following section.

Another key aspect of postmodernism is the speed at which ideas, technologies and fashions are embraced, rejected and transformed (Malpas, 2005). This can be seen most clearly in the idea of globalization and the notion of the world as shrinking, not least due to technologies such as the internet, which make access to a wide array of knowledge possible. In returning to the idea of Fordism discussed earlier, one aspect of post-Fordist theorizing is the greater economic demand for a knowledgeable and skilled workforce as well as the development of flexible as opposed to hierarchical management systems (Brown and Lauder, 1992). When applied to education, the perceived need for *ongoing* professional development and the increased emphasis on leadership and management might be positioned within a post-Fordist conceptual framework. However, the *standardization* of curriculum imposed by the English National Curriculum can be linked to Fordist thinking. As noted earlier, we should not suppose that Fordist or modernist thinking has disappeared.

To sum up the postmodernist position discussed so far, it is a theory that embraces diversity, uncertainty and complexity. However, it is a theory (or rather a range of theories) that originated not within the early childhood tradition or the field of education, but within the wider milieu, and can be applied to almost all aspects of social, cultural and economic life. Although in this section I have outlined the key ideas behind modernist and postmodernist theorizing, it would be wrong to see these positions as exclusive and constantly at odds with each other in every detail. An example might be some of the advancements made in the field of medicine that have made a real difference to the life expectancy and quality of life of many people – advances borne from the application of strictly scientific (and modernist) principles. It is the supposed applicability of such thinking to *all* aspects of social, cultural and economic life that many postmodernists question.

The value of postmodern theorizing to early years education

So far in this chapter, I have discussed postmodernism in terms of understanding it in its broadest sense. In this section, I aim to show how such theorizing can be applied to early childhood practice. Like Alloway (1997), who takes the idea of Lyotard's (1979) 'metanarratives' or commonly held 'truths' and applies this to various aspects of early childhood practice in order to show its important contribution to practice, my aim here is to deconstruct a few commonly held 'truths' about early childhood practice.

1. There are universal understandings of 'children' and 'childhood'

One such 'truth' we might deconstruct is that there are universal understandings of 'children' and 'childhood'. Aries (1962) was one of the first writers to view childhood as multiple and perspectival and posit the idea that 'childhood' itself is a recent human construction. Gradually, human beings who are younger have come to be seen as a distinct group that can be categorized differently than older human beings. In the late 19th and 20th centuries, the work of developmental psychology has served to add further weight to this distinction. This can be seen most prominently in the criticisms of Piaget's work, which is seen as confining children to particular stages of development (Burman, 1994).

The understandings derived from developmental psychology about what is 'normal' and 'natural' in young children's behaviour and understanding have resulted in pedagogies designed with such understandings in mind, and thus are complicit in the production of understandings of children that categorize them as developing 'normally' or 'abnormally' (Walkerdine, 1986). We will see some examples of this later in this section. Because of this, Viruru (2001) asserts that young children have been 'colonized' by adults in a similar way that we might describe the colonizing of countries in the majority world by minority world countries. She maintains that: 'Colonised human beings (including those who are younger) are created as subjects who are lacking, not fully advanced and needing intervention' (Viruru, 2001: 141). This has similarities to Qvortrup's (1994) notion of children being viewed as human 'becomings' as opposed to human beings.

Crucially, by employing the idea of colonial power – something outlined earlier in this chapter – to children, we might envisage children, like those territories that were (and are) colonized, in terms of what they might *become* as opposed to what they *are* at present (Gandhi, 1998). Thus, the postmodern/post-colonialist task is for practitioners to 'rethink and reconceptualize what they think they know about the child and childhood' (Cannella and Viruru, 2004: 84).

But whilst *childhood* is viewed as a variable of analysis, a postmodernist perspective does not view children's experiences of their childhoods as homogenous. Variables such as gender, race, ability, class, as well as comparative research looking at childhoods in different parts of the world, show that it is differently experienced. Thus, when Piaget talks about 'the child', he is criticized for representing in the singular the supposed naturalness of *all* children's development (Prout and James, 1997). Postmodernist thinking embraces the idea that individuals can be located within a *range* of discursive positionings (Grieshaber, 2004), which has particular resonance for the way issues of diversity are conceptualized in early childhood practice. For example, in the area of gender, this means that being a male or female does not carry with it *fixed* traits because subjectivities are viewed as changeable (Robinson and Diaz, 2006).

2. Children need to be socialized into 'appropriate' behaviours

Another metanarrative that can be applied to early childhood practice is the way it is seen as important that children are socialized from birth into the gradual control of their emotional and bodily expressions (Leavitt and Power, 1997). Indeed, the distinction of 'child' from 'adult' is often described in terms of dualisms such as: body v. mind; dependence v. independence; savage v. civilized (Cannella and Viruru, 2004), with control of the body, for example, viewed as an essential part of becoming an adult. For Grosz (1994: 3), children's bodies are often conceptualized as 'unruly' and 'disruptive'. Therefore, managing the child's body – with all the implications of disciplinary power that this suggests – is often regarded as a crucial part of daily practice in early childhood settings (Leavitt and Power, 1997). Moreover, the construction of early childhood practitioners' professional identities is often intertwined with issues of *controlling* children in childcare settings (Phelan, 1997).

In practice, the 'disciplining' of children's bodies can be seen in the use of timetables and mechanistic routines in which time is demarcated to such an extent that the immediate lived needs of young children are subordinated to the imposed timetabling of practitioners. This impacts on the opportunities children have for periods of uninterrupted play (Polakow, 1992). Recent curricula developments such as the Primary Frameworks for Literacy and Mathematics (DCSF, 2009) are further examples of the way that time is demarcated into 'units', with learning compartmentalized and fragmented into segments. This can also be linked to the post-Fordist critique of standardized and bureaucratic Fordist education systems (Brown and Lauder, 1992).

The child who adheres compliantly to the temporal and spatial elements of a particular early childhood programme is viewed as 'normal' and the child who finds this more problematic is viewed as 'abnormal' (Polakow, 1992). Indeed, the categorization, measurement and labelling of children in such a way can be regarded as a further exemplar of Foucault's notion of 'docile bodies' produced discursively through practices deemed 'appropriate' for young children, as we will also see in the next section.

3. There is such a thing as a 'normal child'

The 'normalizing gaze' that Foucault discusses (Holligan, 2000) can also be seen in other areas of practice, such as assessment instruments used in early childhood practice – for instance, the Foundation Stage Profile, as well as a range of assessment instruments used in the identification of children deemed to have 'special educational needs'. As Holligan (2000: 137) notes, 'They [children] have to be kept under close surveillance to see how normal they are becoming'.

As I noted in the previous section, the 'beauty' of such a system is the way it is viewed as neutral and objective and thus goes unquestioned (Holligan, 2000). It is because of this supposed neutrality that discursive practices that result in the identification of the 'normal' and 'abnormal' child have developed. Furthermore, these are taken up regionally or nationally to assume greater uniformity and this uniformity (and the guidance produced to ensure this happens) begins to be accepted as a 'true' measure and is thus taken up by practitioners.

Parents too are caught up in this process, because developmental milestones serve to structure their observations of their children and also act as a seemingly 'neutral' baseline from which to compare their child's development with others (Burman, 1994). Thus, long before schooling even starts, the idea that there are 'norms' from which children can be measured has been taken up by parents; indeed, parents may be subject to a high degree of state intervention and stigmatization should their child's development be deemed to be 'behind' that considered 'normal' for their age, owing to a belief that parents may be to some degree responsible for optimizing their children's development (Burman, 1994).

This also impacts on schools. In schools with low baseline testing scores, the school's performance may be assessed according to the impact they have had in ameliorating the supposed 'defects' of the child's home and accelerating the child's development and learning towards that considered more 'normal' for their age – as measured through testing. The corollary of this is that parents and schools are judged against the 'normalcy' of the children in their care and become engaged in a competition – parent against parent; school against school – to see how 'advanced' the children in their care have become. A postmodern perspective encourages us to challenge the conception of the 'normal child' and the supposedly rational instruments that have been devised to measure this.

4. Play is important in the early childhood curriculum

Another metanarrative in early childhood is the primacy of play as a vehicle for learning (Alloway, 1997) and that the curriculum should be child-centred, based on what is 'known' about how young children develop. The belief in the importance of play cannot be overestimated in early childhood writings [...] Play is commonly viewed as vital in children's 'natural' growth and development and is seen as 'normal' behaviour for young children. This 'truth' has been accepted by many early childhood practitioners and taken up in their classroom pedagogies, with play seen as appropriate in the world of early childhood and work being the preserve of adults.

Yet Cannella and Viruru (2004) point out that many parents do not share this belief in the primacy of play in the early childhood curriculum. Furthermore, the separation of work from play seems to be a minority world construct, with the latter conceptualized as offering the possibility for pleasure and the former characterized by its seriousness. In majority world countries, such a distinction is often non-existent, or, at least, far more blurred than this suggests. It is also another example of the binary distinction made between 'child' and 'adult', with children seemingly confined to the romantic world of play and separated from the adult (and less innocent) world of work.

Further criticisms of child-centred, play-based pedagogies have also come from *within* the minority world. Alloway (1997) encourages us to consider the critique of Lisa Delpit [...] who argues that progressivist, child-centred approaches to education may privilege white, middle-class children as opposed to poor or black children. Whilst not advocating an overly didactic curriculum of 'drill and skill' (p. 3), Delpit suggests that pedagogies that make *explicit* the expected codes of behaviour in a setting and involve greater direct teaching, as opposed to a more child-centred, progressivist pedagogy, might serve the needs of poor and black children better.

We can see, then, that postmodern theorizing problematizes many long-held 'truths' about early childhood practice and there are many other examples that are worth exploration, but which could not be included in a short chapter such as this. This is further complicated as some of the discourses or 'truths' outlined above may also imply different forms of action (see Stainton-Rogers, 2001). An example might be that claim number 2 suggests that children need to be socialized into 'appropriate' behaviours, whereas claim number 4 suggests that play is key to young children's learning and development. The former 'truth' implies adult control and the latter implies a degree of freedom from adult control.

Limitations with postmodern theories

Whilst in this chapter I have outlined the value postmodern theorizing has had on our thinking about early childhood education and care, it can also be criticized. The critique offered here focuses on three main areas that relate to early childhood practice: the lack of recognition of very young children's vulnerability and dependence on adults and sometimes older children; the lack of recognition of embodiment in early childhood practice; and the reluctance to reconstruct a sense of what practitioners *should* do in providing education and care for young children. I also include a fourth criticism, which asks, more broadly, whether postmodernist theorizing is in danger of becoming yet another metanarrative; one that could be regarded as politically weak.

Critique 1: The young child as vulnerable and competent

In critiquing the positioning of children as dependent, less competent and vulnerable, which has long been the project of developmental psychology, there seems to be a dismissal of very young children's *vulnerability* in postmodern writings. In writing about early childhood research, Lahman (2008: 285) holds a view of the child as both vulnerable and competent at the same time, stating: 'I believe both the notions of competent and vulnerable, worded as *competent yet vulnerable child* may be held simultaneously as a way of considering the unique position of children'.

Babies and very young children are dependent to a great extent on adults or possibly older children for their physical and emotional care (Manning-Morton, 2006). This is a biological fact as opposed to social construction. *How* this care is provided and what is considered *appropriate* in this area is a social construction and this is an important distinction to make. But it is not just babies and very young children who are physically and emotionally dependent – levels of dependency are likely to fluctuate in all of us throughout the course of our lives. Lahman's 'competent but vulnerable child' perspective recognizes that alongside their vulnerability, young children are also able to participate and have a right to be listened to. This, I am sure, is something that postmodernists would agree with and the idea of a fluid and changing self fits in well with a postmodernist perspective. However, much postmodernist writing seems to ignore the dependence babies and young children have on those who care for them and this neglect appears to silence what for many early childhood practitioners are the *realities* of their daily practice.

Critique 2: The importance of an embodied and relational perspective in early childhood

Another criticism that can be levelled at postmodernist theorizing is that there appears to be a downplaying of the importance of the body. Whilst postmodern theorizing is important in encouraging a consideration of multiple and fluid identities, it emphasizes 'reading' the body 'at the expense of attention to the body's material locatedness in history, practice, culture' (Bordo, 2003: 38). Similarly, James et al. (1998: 147) argue that 'embodied action [is] performed not only by texts but by real, living corporeal persons'.

Other theoretical perspectives such as phenomenology see our bodily experiences as the *foundation* upon which we make meaning about the world. This alternative perspective might also elevate the body as a means through which we know the world that may not involve language and discourse – something postmodernists neglect (Burr, 2003). Similarly, Flax (1990) argues that postmodernism fails to recognize that the *self* of a person may not be rooted in socio-historical constructions alone. She maintains that there are other important sources of self-formation, such as early mother–child relations, which are highlighted by psycho-analytical writers especially. [...] Further criticism can also be made of the lack of attention postmodernist thinking pays to the desires and fantasies of a person and the role this plays in personal agency, such as why we do what we do (Burr, 2003).

In applying the ideas presented here to early childhood practice, these criticisms are especially appropriate. Much of young children's experience of the world appears to be immediate and physical, and positive, sustained relationships are of central importance to young children's all-round development and learning (see e.g. Elfer et al., 2003; Manning-Morton and Thorp, 2003). In addition, to suggest that young children are purely subject to discourse appears to assign them a passive rather than an active role. For early childhood, this may be a criticism that has particular resonance because the young child has often been conceptualized as a blank slate and passive receiver of knowledge rather than an active co-constructor of knowledge. To sum up critique 2, it would seem that there are some difficult issues relating to our physical and relational selves, which also relate to tensions between agency and structure, for postmodernist thinking to resolve (Burr, 2003).

Critique 3: Beyond deconstruction – what should practitioners actually do?

A key criticism that might be levelled at postmodernism when applied to early childhood practice is that in emphasizing deconstruction and encouraging the disruption to long-held 'truths' about early childhood practice, it rarely offers anything *concrete* in its place. Of course, to offer anything as certain as 'what early childhood practitioners might do to improve the quality of their practice' on a large scale begins to look suspiciously like a metanarrative. Yet, settings *do* need to engage with reconstructing a sense of good practice and how to achieve this on a *micro* level and on an *ongoing* basis in order to reflect diversity as well as changing ideas about young children and how they might be educated and cared for. Lyotard's (1979) notion of micro, or little, narratives is highly relevant here and at least offers the promise of *reconstruction* for practitioners and crucially for children and families. In sharing examples of practice from Reggio, for instance, writers from a postmodernist perspective such as Dahlberg et al. (1999) offer a vision of early childhood education that appears to recoil from proclaiming universal applicability and prides itself on localized 'dissensus' and a distinct lack of rigid, formalized standards to be adhered to by practitioners (Moss, 2001).

However, the development of localized micro-narratives such as this might be viewed as problematic in terms of monitoring practice. In critiquing the notion of universally held ideas about what constitutes 'good practice', how might we recognize good or poor practice? Are there *some* standards we would want in place on a regional or national scale to act as *safeguards* for young children and families? Is there a basic entitlement that *all* children in a region or nation should have access to? If there is, how prescriptive should it be and how should it be monitored? These are very real questions about early childhood practice. We might also ask, as Sarup (1993) does, why we would want to abandon *all* metanarratives, as writers such as Lyotard seem to ask us to do.

In thinking about this, I and many other practitioners and commentators on early childhood would not want to abandon the idea that play is a prime vehicle in young children's learning and development, for example. There is a wealth of research in this area too numerous to document in this short chapter. The postmodern critique of play and the child-centred curriculum is important in alerting us to alternative thinking and might argue that this wealth of evidence about the primacy of play has served to form its own 'regime of truth', a term noted earlier. However, it rarely offers something *concrete* in its place that is helpful to the majority of practitioners working in early childhood in a given context. Also, implicit in the postmodern critique is a suggestion that many practitioners are simply *subjects* of discourse, unable to stand outside and therefore criticize their everyday practices, unlike the academics that write about them (Burr, 2003).

Critique 4: Isn't postmodernism another metanarrative or set of metanarratives (albeit that it does not want to be)?

Finally here, in offering up a theory or rather a set of theories, postmodernism might also be described as yet another metanarrative or set of metanarratives in the same way that Marxism is a metanarrative (Sarup, 1993). Sarup (1993) draws upon the work of Rorty, who argues that the postmodern positions put forward by writers such as Foucault and Lyotard can be characterized by their 'dryness' and their reluctance to ally themselves to any group long enough to say 'we' or 'our'.

This could be seen as political weakness because the postmodern idea of the shifting nature of subject positions, that may (or may not) be taken up within a given context, makes it difficult for individuals to collectivize their experiences beyond the micro-level in order to struggle against oppression (Henriques et al., 1984). Given that issues of race and social class – to name two 'macro' subject positionings – are still dominant in terms of persistent inequalities in attainment in education, this would seem to be very important. Issues of racism and poverty are *real* and *lived* and surely require *action* at least as much as deconstruction.

Final thoughts

Perhaps postmodernist thinking is most valuable in making all of us concerned with early childhood education and care to 'look again' with a critical eye at how we view young children, how they develop and learn and how the early childhood curriculum and associated pedagogy should be developed. This is vital. At a time of increased government intervention into early childhood practice, for example the introduction of statutory frameworks such as the Early Years Foundation Stage in England (DfES, 2007), it is imperative that practitioners maintain a critical stance – the 'incredulity' Lyotard emphasizes (1979: xxiv, mentioned earlier) – towards what they do and why.
[…]

References

Alloway, N. (1997) 'Early childhood education encounters the postmodern: What do we know? What can we count as true?', *Australian Journal of Early Childhood*, 22(2): 1–5.

Aries, P. (1962) *Centuries of Childhood: A Social History of Family Life*. New York: Knopf.

Bauman, Z. (1993) *Postmodern Ethics*. Oxford: Blackwell.

Bordo, S. (2003) *Unbearable Weight: Feminism, Western Culture and the Body*. Berkeley: University of California Press.

Brown, P. and Lauder, H. (1992) 'Education, economy and society: an introduction to a new agenda', in P. Brown and H. Lauder (eds) *Education for Economic Survival: From Fordism to Post-Fordism?* London: Routledge.

Brown, T. and Jones, L. (2001) *Action Research and Postmodernism: Congruence and Critique*. Buckingham: Open University Press.

Burman, E. (1994) *Deconstructing Developmental Psychology*. London: Routledge.

Burr, V. (2003) *Social Constructionism* (2nd edn). London: Routledge.

Cannella, G.S. and Viruru, R. (2004) *Childhood and Postcolonialism*. London: Routledge/Falmer.

Dahlberg, G., Moss, P. and Pence, A. (1999) *Beyond Quality in Early Childhood Education and Care: Postmodern Perspectives*. London: Falmer.

Department for Education and Skills (DfES) (2007) *The Early Years Foundation Stage*. Nottingham: DfES.

Department of Children, Schools and Families (DCSF) (2009) *Primary Framework*. Available at: http://nationalstrategies.standards.dcsf.gov.uk/primary/ (accessed 5 July 2010).

Elfer, P., Goldschmeid, E. and Selleck, D. (2003) *Key Persons in the Nursery: Building Relationships for Quality Provision*. London: David Fulton.

Flax, J. (1990) *Thinking Fragments: Psychoanalysis, Feminism and Postmodernism in the Contemporary West*. Oxford: University of California Press.

Foucault, M. (1977) *Discipline and Punishment: The Birth of the Prison*. London: Penguin.

Gandhi, M.K. (1998) *Postcolonial Theory: A Critical Introduction*. New York: Columbia University Press.

Giroux, H. (2005) *Border Crossing: Cultural Workers and the Politics of Education* (2nd edn). London: Routledge.

Grieshaber, S. (2004) *Rethinking Parent and Child Conflict*. Abingdon: Routledge/Falmer.

Grosz, E. (1994) *Volatile Bodies: Toward a Corporeal Feminism*. Bloomington: Indiana University Press.

Henriques, J., Hollway, W., Urwin, C., Venn, C. and Walkerdine, V. (1984) 'Theorising subjectivity', in J. Henriques, W. Hollway, C. Urwin, C. Venn and V. Walkerdine (eds) *Changing the Subject: Psychology, Social Regulation and Subjectivity*. London: Methuen.

Holligan, C. (2000) 'Discipline and normalisation in the nursery: the Foucaultian gaze', in H. Penn (ed.) *Early Childhood Services: Theory, Policy and Practice*. Buckingham: Open University Press.

James, A., Jenks, C. and Prout, A. (1998) *Theorising Childhood*. Cambridge: Polity Press.

Lahman, M. (2008) 'Always othered: ethical research with children', *Journal of Early Childhood Research*, 6(3): 281–300.

Leavitt, R.L. and Power, M.B. (1997) 'Civilizing bodies: children in day care', in J. Tobin (ed.) *Making a Place for Pleasure in Early Childhood Education*. New Haven: Yale University Press.

Lyotard, J.F. (1979) *The Postmodern Condition: A Report on Knowledge* (translated by G. Bennington and B. Massumi). Manchester: Manchester University Press.

Malpas, S. (2005) *The Postmodern*. London: Routledge.

Manning-Morton, J. (2006) 'The personal is professional: professionalism and the birth to threes practitioner', *Contemporary Issues in Early Childhood*, 7(1): 42–52.

Manning-Morton, J. and Thorp, M. (2003) *Key Times for Play*. Maidenhead: Open University Press.

Moss, P. (2001) 'The otherness of Reggio', in L. Abbott and C. Nutbrown (eds) *Experiencing Reggio Emilia: Implications for Pre-School Provision*. Buckingham: Open University Press.

Mukherji, P. and Albon, D. (2010) *Research Methods in Early Childhood: An Introductory Guide*. London: Sage.

Phelan, A.M. (1997) 'Classroom management and the erasure of teacher desire', in J. Tobin (ed.) *Making a Place for Pleasure in Early Childhood Education*. New Haven: Yale University Press.

Polakow, V. (1992) *The Erosion of Childhood*. Chicago: University of Chicago Press.

Prout, A. and James, A. (1997) 'A new paradigm for the sociology of childhood? Provenance, promise and problems', in A. James and A. Prout (eds) *Constructing and Reconstructing Childhood*. London: Routledge/Falmer.

Qvortrup, J. (1994) 'Childhood matters: an introduction', in J. Qvortrup, M. Bardy, G. Sgritta and H. Wintersberger (eds) *Childhood Matters: Social Theory, Practice and Politics*. Aldershot: Avebury.

Robinson, K. and Diaz, C.J. (2006) *Diversity and Difference in Early Childhood Education: Issues for Theory and Practice*. Maidenhead: Open University Press.

Sarup, M. (1993) *An Introductory Guide to Post-Structuralism and Postmodernism* (2nd edn). London: Harvester Wheatsheaf.

Stainton-Rogers, W. (2001) 'Constructing childhood: constructing child concern', in P. Foley, J. Roche and S. Tucker (eds) *Children in Society: Contemporary Theory, Policy and Practice*. Houndmills: Palgrave.

Viruru, R. (2001) *Early Childhood Education: Postcolonial Perspectives from India*. New Delhi: Sage.

Walkerdine, V. (1986) 'Post-structuralist theory and everyday social practices: the family and the school', in S. Wilkinson (ed.) *Feminist Social Psychology: Developing Theory and Practice*. Milton Keynes: Open University Press.

Part 3
Pedagogy and practice

Introduction

Linda Miller

The chapters in this part of the book are concerned with pedagogy and practice, which are fundamental to the quality of early childhood provision (Sylva et al., 2003). A dictionary definition of pedagogy is 'the science of teaching' and professional practice is defined as 'action or execution as opposed to theory' but also as 'professional work' (Allen, 1991). We know, however, that in early years work, if practitioners are to be regarded as professionals, then theory must inform practice and good practice is dependent on the ability to reflect upon theory. Both pedagogy and practice take place in contexts affected by multi-layered influences, often referred to as macro, micro and meso influences (Bronfenbrenner, 1979). At the macro level, we see the influence of politics and policy on early childhood services and practitioners. Such influences ensure that the majority of the early years workforce remains feminized, of low status and poorly paid (OECD, 2006). At the micro level, the workplace community of practice and wider community of parents, carers and social structures influence the way early years practitioners carry out their work (Wenger, 1998). At the meso or individual level, practitioners use skills and knowledge on a daily basis which they may not readily articulate. For such practitioners, a considerable part of their professional development can take place in situations with colleagues in what Wenger (1998) describes as a 'community of practice', enabling participants to move beyond 'normative' practices which can become routine rather than questioning.

The chapters in this part of the book invite the reader to consider critical issues such as: the role of society and culture in constructing views of children; the roles of practitioners who work with them; the nature and practices of institutions which care for and educate young children; and how pre-schools capitalize on, or ignore, the often rich experiences that young children bring with them to early years settings and whether practice recognized as innovative in one geographical and cultural setting can successfully transfer to a different context. The final chapter in this part looks to Europe and considers more holistic approaches to working with young children. You are invited to consider these questions and issues in relation to your own situation.

In Chapter 14, Liz Jones, Rachel Holmes, Christina MacRae and Maggie MacLure enquire into what constitutes a 'good' or 'problem' pupil, drawing on research in four reception classes in England for children aged 4–5 years. The authors raise important questions about early years pedagogical practices and offer sometimes amusing, but often poignant examples of how the children are challenged to work out what constitutes behaviours such as 'good listening' or 'not being silly', in order to comply with requirements that relate to the teachers' views of what a young child is and can be. Using both an anthropological and psychoanalytic perspective, the authors pose and address the question of 'how things might be different'. The authors of Chapter 15, Christine Stephen, Joanna McPake and Lydia Plowman, examine young children's experiences with digital technologies, both in their homes and in pre-school settings, through a sample drawn from a wider survey of 346 3–4-year-olds in Scotland. The chapter draws on case studies of 19 families over a one-year period and describes how children engage with digital technologies at home regardless of socio-economic circumstances. The authors describe how the children's learning was driven by participating in everyday family practices around digital technologies. They contrast these experiences with the more prescribed learning that occurs in primary school and conclude that it is important for pre-school and primary school to build on the rich experiences children bring from home.

Mariane Hedegaard's chapter links to themes in Chapter 14 about the role of society and culture (both macro and meso) in constructing views of children and their development. In Chapter 16, she discusses how children develop through participation in institutional practices that are characterized by communication and shared activities but also how, even within the same institution, notions of 'good practice' can differ. She argues for the importance of taking the child's perspective (see also Part 1) and introduces a model for learning and development, and for framing research, that focuses on societal conditions, institutional practices and the motives and intentions of children in everyday activities; thus affording a more holistic approach to research with young children. Views of children and childhood are again considered in Chapter 17 by Trisha Maynard and Sarah Chicken, drawing on the vision of Reggio Emilia pre-schools in Italy where pedagogues, children, families and the community engage in a learning 'journey' through dialogue and the construction and re-construction of ideas, in the form of projects which stem from the children's interest and experiences. The importance of the social and cultural context of pedagogy and practice are foregrounded in this chapter as Maynard and Chicken explore the philosophy and practice of Reggio Emilia with seven early years teachers from five schools in Wales, working within the Foundation Phase for children aged 3–7 years. The aim of the project was not to 'transplant' the Reggio Emilia approach but to use it as a lens to enable the teachers to critically reflect upon their own professional practice in a Welsh context.

The challenge of transplanting ideas, roles and ways of working across cultural and geographical contexts is again considered in Chapter 18, where Pat Petrie, Janet Boddy, Claire Cameron, Ellen Heptinstall, Susan McQuail, Antonia Simon and Valerie Wigfall describe and discuss a holistic approach to working with children and young people across services through a social pedagogy approach. In developing the role of the Early Years Professional (EYP) in England, the social pedagogue model was considered and rejected by government and the EYP role was created as a status rather than a qualification linked to pay and conditions; thus perpetuating the view of early years workers, referred to above, as feminized, of low status and poorly paid (CWDC, 2006). Based on research carried out at the Thomas Coram Research Unit (TCRU) which included cross-national studies on service provision and its quality, the daily practice of staff, their training, education, qualifications, recruitment and retention in the workforce, the researchers conclude that the social pedagogue approach 'is well fitted to further English policy concerns'.

References

Allen, R.E. (ed.) (1991) *The Concise Oxford Dictionary of Current English*, 8th edition. London: BCA/Oxford University Press.

Bronfenbrenner, U. (1979) *The Ecology of Human Development*. Cambridge, MA: Harvard University Press.

Children's Workforce Development Council (CWDC) (2006) *Early Years Professional Prospectus*. Leeds: CWDC.

Organisation for Economic Co-operation and Development (OECD) (2006) *Starting Strong II: Early Childhood Education and Care*. Paris: Organisation for Economic Co-operation and Development.

Sylva, K., Melhuish, E., Sammons, P., Siraj-Blatchford, I., Taggart, B. and Elliot, K. (2003) *The Effective Provision of Pre-School Education (EPPE) Project: Findings from the Pre-School Period: Summary of Findings*. London: Institute of Education/Sure Start.

Wenger, E. (1998) *Communities of Practice: Learning and Meaning*. Cambridge: Cambridge University Press.

14

'Improper' children

Liz Jones, Rachel Holmes, Christina MacRae and Maggie MacLure

---

Overview

How children learn what counts as 'good' behaviour in a particular context is a complex process. In this chapter, Jones et al. draw on research in four reception classes to explore how children gain a reputation as a 'good' pupil or as a 'problem' pupil. The chapter considers how key discourses such as developmentally appropriate practice, a play-based curriculum and child development impact on this process.

[…]

Introduction

This chapter draws on research that is derived from a project whose principal aim was to investigate how children earn negative reputations such as being considered to be 'naughty'.[1] In particular it highlights how certain behaviours on the part of young people (4–6 years of age) become untenable to practitioners because they instil a form [of] ontological insecurity in terms of their own performances (Butler, 1997). By framing the data within notions of abjection (Douglas, 1966; Kristeva, 1982), we mark

---

Jones, L., Holmes, R., MacRae, S. and MacLure, M. (2010) '"Improper" children', in Yelland, N. (ed.) *Contemporary Perspectives on Early Childhood Education*, New York: McGraw Hill, pp. 177–91.

out how pedagogical mechanisms, including those ways in which 'the child' is conceptualized, become momentarily insecure, creating cognitive dissonance and leaving a severe sense of helplessness where everything that is of comfort in terms of what it means to be a teacher, disintegrates. In this space of abjection, meaning collapses and the 'clean and proper' becomes soiled, and is manifested in/as 'improper' children.

As a starting point we offer a brief résumé of the context in which the research was undertaken in order to provide context. We then move to present examples of data that attempt to capture what it might mean to be a 'proper' child within the context of early schooling. Our analysis at this point details some of the discursive practices which work at both summoning the 'proper' child and giving her substance, since without these insights it is difficult to appreciate what works at constituting the 'improper' child. Attention is then focused on some of the tensions, stresses and strains that swirl between 'improper' children and adults. [...] The chapter concludes by considering a number of complex/tricky 'so what' questions for further thinking and discussion.

Situating the chapter

This chapter emerges from an ethnographic research project which investigated the processes by which children become viewed as 'a problem' in their school lives. The research centred on children who were in their first 18 months of schooling. Hence we observed the children in their very initial stages of formal schooling when they were aged 4–5 years and we continued to track them as they moved from the first/reception classroom to Year I where UK children are 6 years of age. During the 18-month time span, a researcher spent a day a week in the classroom of four different schools in one of the large conurbations in the north of England. One was a Roman Catholic school in an area of the city with high levels of poverty. Another was located in a relatively affluent suburban district where the school population was mainly white. The third was in the heart of the city centre where over 30 different family languages were spoken by the children in the group; and the fourth was also a city school in an area of deprivation with children who were mainly of white heritage. Besides observing and tracking actions within the classroom, time was also spent watching and noting children's interactions in the playground, lunch queues and other settings within the schools in order to understand how children act and are perceived by others when outside the classroom. The data we draw on for this chapter are our written observations from the visits.

As previously stated, a key focus for our study was problematic behaviour as it emerged within and was shaped by the culture of the classroom. The research started from the premise that securing a successful reputation as a 'good' pupil, or acquiring a negative one as a 'problem' is never the sole responsibility of the individual child. In school contexts, children must not only act appropriately, but must be recognized as having done so. Reputation is therefore a public matter. A post-structuralist approach has been adopted when analysing the data. Such an approach conceptualizes subjectivity as an outcome of discursive practices that constitute and make sense of the world (Britzman, 1990; Gee, 1990; Brown and Jones, 2002; MacLure, 2003). Indeed, across the four sites it was possible to identify a number of discourses that within early years have gained considerable momentum and which would be immediately recognizable to those conversant with the field. These included: child development and developmentally appropriate practice (DAP) (Bredekcamp, 1987), play-based curriculum and humanist individuality.

Performing as a proper child

[...]

Schooling demands that children behave in ways that are regarded as normal, and what counts as normal is dictated by the discourses of the 'regular' classroom environment (Stormont-Spurgin, 1997). Both gaining access to and maintaining one's 'proper' place (Graham, 2006) within the regular classroom demands that children 'perform' their identities (Butler, 1997) within the discursive frames that regulate standardized or customary forms of participation (Popkewitz, 2004). Being a 'proper' child is not a straightforward matter for many young people, even though the rules and requirements are rehearsed many times a day, displayed on walls, endorsed in assemblies,[2] regulated by reward systems and so on. This is partly because *interpretive work* is required in order to understand what 'being good/proper' involves. Children need to learn what they are expected to do, or to refrain from doing, in order for their behaviour to be assigned to the category of 'good', or any of the various related categories that are used to regulate behaviour. These we noted would include 'sitting beautifully'; 'properly'; 'nicely'; 'good listening'; 'being sensible'; not being 'silly'; putting 'hands up'; and waiting to be chosen to speak while the teacher is speaking.

Some of the requirement imposed upon children were reasonably easy to trace back to particular behaviours (though not necessarily easy to comply with), such as putting hands up; but others needed quite sophisticated 'categorization work' (Baker, 2000). In one scenario, for example, the following observational notes were made:

> Olivia is sitting with her legs outstretched and is asked by Ms K to 'Sit properly in the classroom, Olivia, please'. (Chesterfield, 18 January 2007)

In this context, Olivia was required to examine her own posture and relate this to her knowledge of the rules for correct sitting in order to know she has offended and what she needs to do to 'sit properly'.

Being 'sensible' – a common term that was used in each of the four schools – may even be open to interpretation, as may be the range of behaviours that will be judged not to be sensible. In the following example, Ellie must inspect her own past behaviour and future intentions, and identify the nature of Ms F's dissatisfaction with her, in order to know what she has done to warrant the call to 'behave more sensibly':

Field note

Ms F starts a whole-group activity on the carpet.

Ms F: Ellie, come and sit by me.

Ellie: Why?

Ms F: Because you'll behave more sensibly, that's why. (Chesterfield, 20 April 2007)

Part of the problem with such interpretive requirements is that the evaluations are made *retrospectively:* children must read 'back' from the adult's assessment to the behaviour which has provoked it. At Chesterfield, weekly 'certificate assemblies' celebrated a wide range of behaviours and competences. For instance, certificates were awarded:

Field note

For always listening and being kind and helpful;
For always listening and working hard;
For fantastic joining in on the carpet;
For working really hard with his letter sounds;
For settling in so well (two new girls). (Dronsfield, 18 September 2007)

Interpretive work is needed if children are to identify what they have done in the past week that counted as 'fantastic joining in on the carpet', or 'being kind and help-ful'. And even when evaluations are made immediately after a particular action, children still need to do self-inspection to know what is specifically being referenced when they are commended for 'sitting beautifully' or for 'good listening'. Occasionally, children did not seem entirely sure what they had done in order to 'earn' an evaluation as good:

Field note

Christopher comes up to the researcher and says 'I've got a certificate'.

Researcher: Why?
Christopher: For being good.
Researcher: What did you do that was good?
Christopher: I was playing nicely.
Researcher: What were you playing with?
Christopher: I don't know. (Chesterfield, 29 September 2006)

The space between evaluations and the behaviours to which they retrospectively refer may be large enough for the evaluation to be *withdrawn.* For instance, Brent's teacher was angry with him (and his mother) when he came to school in wet clothes. As the class sat on the carpet before assembly, Ms M picked up a (blank) certificate:

Field note

'This certificate was for you Brent. It was for good listening. I can't give it to you now can I, 'cause you didn't listen to me yesterday when I told you not to get soaked again.' She tells the Teaching Assistant[3] in front of the assembled children that Brent's mum had been with him and hadn't done anything about it. (Martinsfield, 6 July 2007)

Brent's offending behaviour (coming to school 'soaked') is retrospectively identified as a breach of the 'good listening' for which he was prospectively to be commended, although he was not aware of the impending commendation until the point at which it was withdrawn. Evaluations and behaviour may exist in a strange 'future pluperfect' timescale in which the import of children's own actions will have been deferred, or even altered, by unforeseen events and unpredicted interpretations by others.

We identified that certain objects operated as materializations of power in the four project classrooms, aimed at rendering the children's bodies as docile. For example, carpeted areas where children would be gathered together were key sites for this regulation of the active body. The act of sitting on the carpet carried with it a set of implications where the contours of the child's body had to satisfy the requirement of 'sitting up straight, with arms folded and legs crossed'. Thus, matter such as carpeting becomes felt in the broadest sense – emotionally, physically and psychologically. [...] Children were sent to 'stand by the door' in one school when they had failed to comply with the requirements for sitting 'properly' (as regulated) on the carpet. However, these significant locales were also sites of resistance. For instance, while the intra-action between the 'spot' by the door and the child initially evoked obvious discomfort, the power of this spot had a limited life and was clearly affected by time. Children found other material items, such as the nearby Velcro name stickers, with which to distract themselves, and thus changed the discursive status of the act of 'standing by the door'. [...]

Breaching boundaries

As noted above, interesting boundaries and complex relations could be between inert objects and the constitution of the proper child, yet these boundaries were also open to various interferences. Such interferences were more marked when the margins that separated adult and child relations were trifled with. Take as an example the following extract of data where the children are sitting together on the carpeted area listening to a story about a postman who is struggling to deliver the mail on a particularly windy day. The teacher asks: *'Who likes to get a letter through the door?'*, whereupon Chloe responds, *'As long as you don't have to pay some money'*. *The teacher laughs* (field note, Dronsfield, 11 January 2007).

We laugh because something strikes us as funny. But there are moments when laughter is used as a cover. It conceals other emotions which while hard to explicate precisely, nod towards feelings of anxiety, nervousness and apprehension. Laughter in this instance is a symptom of an inner discomfort where what gives us comfort is destabilized. Given the occasion, we can hazard a guess that the expected response to the question: 'Who likes to get a letter through the door?' would be (should have been) unequivocally positive. The teacher's laughter can be understood as a response to finding something both funny and simultaneously rather 'peculiar'. In this case Chloe breaches what is 'properly' known about or associated with young people. It is because she has a knowingness that is un-childlike that she breaches a boundary, so while not a 'danger', in that the matter can be laughed off, she nevertheless threatens the social order (Butler, 1999). The familiar performance that is normally enacted at carpet time has been (in)significantly altered, and in so doing the line that lies between adult and child has momentarily faltered.

Similarly, the next example details similar infringements of 'the line':

Field note

In the art area, Ms S is trying to wind up a stick of glue. 'Why don't you wind it that way?' suggests Daniel to Ms S. 'Instead of telling me what to do, why don't you concentrate on your own work. Turn around and get on,' she replies. (Limefield, 7 March 2007)

Daniel, while showing initiative and clearly wanting to help, has nevertheless stepped out of a boundary or crossed a line. In this instance it seems that by making a suggestion, one moreover which could be understood as being kind and helpful, he has nevertheless destabilized Ms S. She appears displeased and it seems that it is this that prompts her to both ignore his suggestion while simultaneously implying he has erred. Her admonishment to 'turn around and get on' could be understood as a timely reminder to 'turn' in terms of 'revert': where he should turn back again to being a child – one moreover that does not tell adults what to do. Following Douglas (1966), we can perceive both Chloe and Daniel as unsettling 'patterns' and 'systems of ordering'. Douglas notes:

> from all possible materials, a limited selection has been made and from all possible relations a limited set has been used. So disorder by implication is unlimited, no pattern has been realised in it, but its potential for patterning is indefinite. This is why, though we seek to create order, we do not simply condemn disorder. We recognise that it is destructive to existing patterns; also that it has potentiality. It symbolises both danger and power. (Douglas, 1966: 94)

We would suggest that both Chloe and Daniel have gone against what is customarily sanctioned within early years education, of who the child can 'be'. Their utterances jar against those boundaries or framing mechanisms in which we situate children so as to 'know' them. The examples briefly allude to other possibilities, in which we could frame the children as examples of not being innocent; rather they have grasped some of the economic realities in which they find themselves situated. Nor do we normally credit them with having knowledge that stands outside that which we developmentally assign to them. Hence, the reiterative practice of adults asking children questions to which the adult already knows the answer. In the example of Daniel, we momentarily glimpse a child who understands both the problem and its solution and in so doing momentarily positions himself within the power/knowledge nexus where the adult is rendered as 'other'. It is possible, we think, to perceive of both instances as quick flashes of something akin to taboo, where children, by using their wits, make claims to subjectivities [to] which in the adults' minds they are not yet eligible, ready or, indeed, have no right to inhabit. They are in this sense 'dangerous'. Chloe's witticism and Daniel's suggestion tamper with those systems that circulate around what it means 'to be' an adult and a child within an early years classroom. Both the laugh and the admonishment of the adult can be understood as 'a crisis' where the ground for 'knowing' who one is, is threatened.

While Douglas's anthropological studies prompted her to examine the ways in which boundaries invoked social order, Kristeva's interest in boundaries followed a psychoanalytical perspective. She offers us an alternative way of perceiving both Chloe and Daniel, where they can be understood as being neither subject nor object within the (adults') terms in which they are situated. Thus, in speaking as he does, Daniel is seen as being out of order whereas Chloe is seen as being un-childlike. Both momentarily refuse the subjectivities that adults would prefer them to have and in so doing they are no longer known objects within the adult's gaze. They constitute a crisis because they are between two categories where they are neither subject nor object, and thus within Kristeva's terms are 'beset by abjection' (1982: 1). They have 'fallen' from what within the scope of the adult, is 'possible', 'tolerable' or 'thinkable' (Kristeva, 1982: 1). It is in the inability to 'see' the child as either subject or object that the self (the practitioner) who needs the other (child) in order 'to be', flounders, and it is in this floundering that abjection takes its place. Within Kristeva's psychoanalytical theories the laugh and the admonishment can be seen emerging from the unconscious so that 'it draws [the practitioner] toward the place where (traditional) meaning collapses' (1982: 2).

We found also that there were curious bonds, unions and attachments between imaginative worlds and children's positions/positioning within these. In the example that follows, it is apparent that there are some anxieties about how children re-enacted the story of Goldilocks and the three bears:

Field note

Teacher:	There is something I would like you [to] remember about Goldilocks' house.
Becky chips in:	Be sensible and play properly.
Teacher:	Yes, but you also need to talk to each other about who's being who and what words you will use to tell the story. (Limefield, 21 November 2007)

Within the child's response we can catch some of the rhetoric surrounding the rules and customary conventions of play, in that it should be both 'sensible and proper'. But it also illustrates some of the anxieties and pressures that teachers are under when, on the one hand, they might well have a commitment to children's 'free play' yet on the other they have to work within curriculum guidelines, where it is stipulated that children should be able to demonstrate various skills, including the ability to recall well-known fairytales/stories. While we might understand and perceive the teacher's promptings as relatively benign and sensible advice, it nevertheless foregrounds the ways in which the children must make an appeal to an external authority when deciding 'who will be who' and 'what words will be used'. It is within such moments that it becomes possible to see the injunctions of the 'hidden persuasion of an implicit pedagogy' (Bourdieu, 1977: 95) at work. So, while the teacher is not attempting to 'instil a whole cosmology', she is nevertheless trying to tie imaginative play to a particular set of parameters.

Interestingly, we had another encounter with *Goldilocks* in a different location.[4] At Chesterfield school the class teacher had gathered the children together onto the carpeted area so that, as a group, they could retell the story by acting it out. The teacher began by choosing six children who 'would be the woods'. These children were encouraged to stand up and to wave their arms about 'like branches'. Ms H then asked of the remaining seated children: '*Who would like to be Goldilocks?*' Samuel, an African Caribbean boy was the first to put his hand up. Ms H responded to him by saying: '*No Samuel. You can't be Goldilocks … for obvious reasons*' (field note, Chesterfield, 23 November 2007).

While we can be critical of Ms H's response on a number of fronts, and where, as a consequence, we could produce a typology of good/bad practice, we think that it is more fruitful to return to notions of taboo and abjection. By aligning Ms H's practice against these ideas, we want to foreground how she found herself within what we have come to think of as an 'intolerable' space. So while, on the one hand, the (im)possible is allowed, in that children can be trees, on the other hand, a black boy cannot be Goldilocks.

As a first step we need to refer to certain polarities in order to make evident just what sorts of work these perform on Ms H. We think that it is because Samuel is willing to perform as 'other' to him/self, that is, as white, blond and a girl, that he violently interrupts the smooth place (Deleuze and Guattari, 2002) that Ms H constructs in her mind's eye of what it means 'to be' within the classroom. […] To depart from or even tamper with signifiers, including those of 'white', 'blond' and 'girl', is clearly one 'line of flight' (Deleuze and Guattari, 1988: 506) that Ms H cannot permit herself, or indeed Samuel – *for obvious reasons* – to take. In volunteering to take on this (im)possible part it is as if the young boy pushes or violently ejects her from what is 'obvious' to the horror of incomprehension or abjection. Put a little differently, to let Samuel be Goldilocks would be like letting something healthy – maybe even life itself – become infected, and, as we know, infections can lead to death.

While we have included data that focus on the interplay between adults and children, the next extract focuses just on children.

> Outside in the home corner, children are role playing – bulldogs, puppy dogs and cats. There is a mum who is looking after the animals. Joshua, Olivia and Tyler are animals, all eating everyone else's food. 'That's the last of the dog food,' said Joshua. He takes a teapot and says to Olivia, 'I'm pouring boiling water all over you. 'Olivia responds, 'I'm telling my cousin, my BIG cousin of you.' Joshua stops pouring. 'I'm telling him,' says Olivia. (Chesterfield, 12 March 2007)

Despite the absence of a teacher there are, we think, moments within the data that cast interesting shadows across much that is assumed and privileged within early years pedagogical practices. Take, as an example, the way that the children-as-animals are eating 'everyone else's food'. While this could be considered a form of sharing, it prompted us to wonder whether it was the kind of sharing that we – including three of us (Jones, Holmes and MacRae, who were all previously early years teachers) – are accustomed to promoting within early years education. Here it is the discourse of liberal humanism that is central to practice (Walkerdine and Lucey, 1989), where, as a consequence, utterances such as '*It's so lovely seeing so many of you playing fairly in the house, especially you Ricky. You're playing properly …*' (field notes, Martinsfield, 14 October 2007), and others of this ilk, were relatively commonplace across the four sites. Joshua's threat to pour boiling water over Olivia serves to jolt us into a problematic space where our adult and teacher-like anxiety about violence and disrespect (and the felt imperative to stamp it out) comes up against our recognition that this is a play situation with pretend boiling water, regulated by children who want our interventions. Yet again, this does not prevent the pretence from also being a real threat, as Olivia clearly feels when she replies that she is going to get her 'BIG cousin' to sort Joshua out. One possible reading of Olivia's engagement with Joshua's 'excitable speech' (Butler, 1997) is that she herself resolves the situation, by abruptly terminating the status of the encounter as 'play' and returning it to a 'real' world of power and rivalry. But, of course, we do not know, and never will know, whether the big cousin was 'real' or another member of the imaginary family of dogs and humans conjured up by the children. The piece prompts questions that we will never be able to address with any certainty, but they nevertheless bring us face to face with those borders within which the integrity of identity is maintained. Joshua, when uttering, 'That's the last of the dog food', seems to locate himself within a place where order, including a lack of dog food, seems to matter. Unless these things are noted, dogs will go hungry. But in the next breath he seems to have crossed to some other location. The teapot, boiling water and his threat unhinge him from his previous persona and contribute towards making him a threat or what Kristeva terms 'an impossible' subject. Olivia, in order to safeguard herself from the ambiguity that Joshua threatens – where one minute he's knowable, the next a threat – summons the big cousin. It is the possibility of the violence that lurks within this figure that quells the potential violence lying within the pretend boiling water. The big cousin acts therefore 'as repression', which Kristeva visualizes as the 'constant watchman' who is necessary in order to maintain distinctions between a knowable Joshua and his untenable other.

[…]

Concluding remarks

By working within the anthropological frames of Mary Douglas and the psychoanalytical theories of Julie Kristeva, we have opened up some 'chinks' that could be possible starting points for discussions with teachers out of which different behaviours might emerge. One point of departure could centre on teacher/child interactions. Previously we have tried to illustrate how, at times, children threaten adults in ways that are not straightforward and hence are difficult to explain in normal, rational or common-sense ways. It is because such children confound us that we sometimes retreat to corrosive practices where we insist they conform to a mythical or stereotypical notion of what constitutes the child. In setting aside such myths, including that of the 'innocent' child, we might recognize that some young people have wisdom and experiences considerably in advance of either the innocent child or indeed the normative one that lingers within the trajectory of developmental psychology. Such recognition is the precursor for establishing different relations or interactions between adults and young people.

[…] In answer to the question 'how might things be different?', we recognize that any *major* changes in terms of pedagogical styles and behaviour are nigh on impossible because such innovations would have to be linked to, and occur within, powerful discursive and institutional forces. We would also have to offer solutions that were 'clear cut'. However, such an endeavour would ultimately fail because part of the problem that we are excavating is that the production of identity and behaviour in classrooms is regulated/constricted by both the structure and stricture of what Derrida (1998) referred to as a *double bind*. That is we are confronting a dilemma that within the terms of conventional logic would require us to settle for one thing over another. […] [A]nother step in considering how things might be different, would be to return to the 'politics of knowing and being known' (Lather, 1991: 83), a step which would have to be taken in the knowledge that it would not increase either out certainty or our authority about, for instance, 'best practice', but might prompt different questions leading to different imaginings, including those associated with childhood.

Notes

1. The research that underpins this chapter was supported by funding from the UK Economic and Social Research Council ('Becoming a Problem: How and Why Children Acquire a Reputation as Naughty in the Earliest Years at School', RES–062–23–0105).
2. Assemblies take place on a regular basis in English schools. It is a time when the whole school is gathered together in a large hall so as to participate in activities such as collective worship and/or rewarding children. Rewards might include certificates, stickers or in some instances prizes such as a set of coloured pencils.
3. Teaching Assistants are practitioners who, while taking on many of the duties associated with teaching, nevertheless do not have teaching status and all that that implies in terms of remuneration, cultural capital and so on. They are directed in their activities, and while they might contribute towards the planning of teaching programmes they do not have direct responsibilities for them.
4. It was not unusual to find the same stories being used in each of the four schools at similar points in time. This is because all four locations have to work within the Foundation Stage curriculum guidance set out by the Department for Education and Skills (2007).

References

Baker, C. (2000) Locating culture in action: membership categorisation in texts and talk. In A. Lee and C. Poyton (eds), *Culture and Text: Discourse and Methodology in Social Research and Cultural Studies.* Lanham, MD: Rowman & Littlefield.
Bourdieu, P. (1977) *Outline of a Theory of Practice.* Cambridge: Cambridge University Press.

Breadekamp, S. (ed.) (1987) *Developmentally Appropriate Practice in Early Childhood Programs Serving Children from Birth through Age 8.* Washington, DC: National Association for the Education of Young Children.

Britzman, D. (1990) The terrible problem of knowing thyself toward a post structural account of teacher identity. *Journal of Curriculum Theorizing,* 9(3): 23–46.

Brown, T. and Jones, L. (2002) *Action Research and Postmodrenism: Congruence and Critique,* Buckingham: Open University Press.

Butler, J. (1997) *Excitable Speech: A Politics of the Performative.* New York: Routledge.

Butler, J. (1999) *Gender Trouble: Feminism and the Subversion of Identity,* 2nd edition. London: Routledge.

Deleuze, G. and Guattari, F. (1988) *A Thousand Plateaus: Capitalism and Schizophrenia,* trans. B. Massumi. London: Athlone.

Deleuze, G. and Guattari, F. (2002) *A Thousand Plateaus: Capitalism and Schizophrenia,* trans. B. Massumi. London: Continuum.

Department for Education and Skills (2007) *Practice Guidance for the Early Years Foundation Stage.* London: HMSO.

Derrida, J. (1998) *Limited Inc.* Evanston, IL: Northwestern University Press.

Douglas, M. (1966) *Purity and Danger.* London: Routledge & Kegan Paul.

Gee, J.P. (1990) *Social Linguistics and Literacies: Ideology in Discourses.* London: Falmer Press.

Graham, L. (2006) Speaking of 'disorderly' objects: a poetics of pedagogical discourse. Paper presented to the American Educational Research Association Annual Conference, San Francisco, 6–11 April.

Kristeva, J. (1982) *Powers of Horror: An Essay on Abjection,* trans. L.S. Roudiez. New York: Columbia University Press.

Lather, P. (1991) *Getting Smart.* London: Routledge.

MacLure, M. (2003) *Discourse in Educational and Social Research.* Buckingham: Open University Press.

Popkewitz, T.S. (2004) The reason of reason: cosmopolitanism and the government of schooling. In B.M. Baker and K.E. Heyning (eds), *Dangerous Coagulations: The Use of Foucault in the Study of Education.* New York: Peter Lang.

Stormont-Spurgin, M. (1997) I lost my homework: strategies for improving organization in students with ADHD, *Intervention in School and Clinic,* 32(5): 270–274.

Walkerdine, V. and Lucey, H. (1989) *Democracy in the Kitchen: Regulating Mothers and Socialising Dauhters.* London: Virago.

Jones, L., Holmes, R., MacRae, S. and MacLure, M. (2010) '"Improper" children', in Yelland, N. (ed.) *Contemporary Perspectives on Early Childhood Education,* New York: McGraw Hill, pp. 177–91.

15

Digital technologies at home: the experiences of 3- and 4-year-olds in Scotland

Christine Stephen, Joanna McPake and Lydia Plowman

Overview

This chapter examines the debate on the use of digital technologies with young children through a survey of 346 3- and 4-year-olds' experiences with digital technologies, both in their homes and in pre-school settings. The chapter describes how children engage with digital technologies at home regardless of socio-economic circumstances. The authors discuss the role of the pre-school in enabling children to build on learning at home.

[...]

Introduction: digital technology – blessing or curse?

This chapter is about young children's experiences with digital technologies that are a now familiar part of their home life. In a survey of 346 families conducted in

Stephen, C., McPake, J. and Plowman, L. (2010) 'Digital technologies at home: the experiences of 3- and 4-years-olds in Scotland', in Clark, M.M. and Tucker, S. (eds) *Early Childhoods in a Changing World*, Stoke-on-Trent: Trentham Books, pp. 145–54.

Scotland by the authors in 2005, we found that most children aged 3 and 4 years were growing up in homes where a range of digital technologies was in use (Plowman et al., 2008a). Regardless of income levels, most of our survey respondents' children were living in households where there was access to a mobile phone (98%), interactive TV (75%) and a computer with internet access (69%). Two-thirds (64%) of the children living in homes with an internet connection made use of it for looking at websites, typically with adult supervision, although 10 per cent used websites on their own. About half the children (48%) used a mobile phone with adult help.

The advent of digital technologies has been heralded on the one hand as offering great potential for young children and on the other as a threat to their natural development or as another source of division and disadvantage. There is a debate between those who advocate the use of technology as a way of facilitating or enhancing learning and others who are concerned that using new technology is harmful for preschool children and who argue for the value of traditional toys. Those who argue that children need to be confident and competent users of new technologies claim that children will flourish and be prepared for the future through their interaction with computers, video games and hand-held games consoles (e.g. Prensky, 2006; Shaffer, 2007). On the other side of the argument, there are claims that new technologies can take over children's time for play, distracting them from other more active and positive traditional pursuits and threatening their cognitive, social and emotional development (e.g. Cordes and Miller, 2000; Palmer, 2006).

The policy environment in Scotland is supportive of children's use of digital technologies in preschool settings and at home. In 2003 the Scottish Executive launched a strategy aimed at developing the use of information and communication technologies (ICT) in preschool settings in the public, private and voluntary sectors. The policy was concerned with developing appropriate pedagogical practices, ensuring equal access for all children, encouraging providers to obtain resources and offering training for practitioners. We found positive attitudes towards new technologies amongst the parents we interviewed. When prompted by attitude statements, they were ready to discuss some of the claims about the negative impact of children's interactions with technology, e.g. that inactivity contributes to obesity, or that computer games are addictive. Nevertheless, each family felt that they had achieved a balance between time spent with technology and time with more traditional activities and all were keen to ensure that their children had a broad range of everyday activities and experiences (Plowman et al., 2008a). Their 3- to 5-year-olds had opportunities to use a wide range of technologies at home: digital cameras, Wii, remote-controlled cars, interactive television, games consoles, internet computer games and resources aimed specifically at young children, e.g. the V-tech range of interactive toys. However, these parents reported that their children frequently played in the garden or went to the play park, played with dolls and cars, rode bicycles, used slides and swings and went swimming and to the soft play room (Plowman et al., 2008b).

Exploring preschool children using technology at home

In this chapter, we draw on findings from *Entering e-Society*, one of a series of Economic and Social Research Council-funded studies which we have completed, exploring young children's encounters with new technology. In *Entering e-Society* we focused on the experiences that 3- and 4-year-olds have with new technologies in their own homes. Through case studies of 19 families over a period of one year, we built rich portraits of the children's lives. We explored the perspectives of their parents towards new technologies, the influence of parents' own early experiences with ICT, parental expectations about the place of technology in the children's futures and the ways in which parents try to support children as they use the technological resources available at home. We also took care to ensure that we captured the perspectives of the 3- and 4-year-olds, without which our understanding of young children's use of digital technologies at home would have been incomplete. Through the methods which we developed to explore the perspectives of young learners, we found that they are active and discriminating users of technology with decided preferences and a view of their own competencies (Stephen et al., 2008).

The case study families participating in *Entering e-Society* lived in central Scotland, in or near to urban areas of varying size and economic status. Their socio-economic circumstances varied from comfortable and advantaged to disadvantaged and living on government benefits. In some cases, both parents held jobs with good salaries, the family owned their home and two cars and could afford holidays abroad. In other cases, mothers were bringing up their children alone in public sector housing, with or without the support of their extended family and with little money left after basic needs were covered. Among the group of 24 children whose parents volunteered at the beginning of the case study phase, there were 11 girls and 13 boys: 17 lived in two-parent families and seven in one-parent families. Thirteen were from households with an income greater than £20,000 per annum and 11 from homes where the income was less than £15,000 per annum.

All of the case study children attended a preschool education setting, either for the five half-day sessions each week funded by the government for every 3- and 4-year-old, or for more extended hours while their parents worked. By the time they were ready to start school, most of the children had experience of using and watching others use a broad range of technologies in their own homes and those of friends and relatives, including telephones, computers, electronic musical instruments, MP3, CD and cassette players, televisions, video and DVD players, still and video cameras, games consoles and domestic appliances. Many had toy laptops or digital games bought to support literacy and numeracy and interactive, electronic books.

Creating a digital divide?

There is a widespread concern that the development of digital technology has created another divide between children from different economic backgrounds. However, our data suggest that there is no simple divide between the experiences of economically advantaged and disadvantaged children. For example, in our survey we found that among those who did not have access to the internet at home, 29 per cent had an income of less than £8,500 while 30 per cent had an income of more than £20,000. We found a complex relationship between family circumstances and ICT experiences, one that is the result of family practices, parental attitudes and children's own preferences.

In some economically advantaged families, parents did not prioritise competency with new technology and were happy to wait until their child expressed an interest or when they started school. On the other hand, some families with lower income gave priority to acquiring a computer because they thought this was important for their children's futures. Families with lower income but a positive attitude towards their child engaging with new technology made the most of the resources they had (typically a TV and mobile phone). For instance, Kirsty's mum was a single parent who did not work but she was an able computer user and keen to ensure that her daughter could use digital technologies. Kirsty was able to use the TV controls independently, was an enthusiastic user of her LeapPad, an interactive book console, and accessed children's websites on her grandmother's computer.

A more powerful influence on parental attitudes and behaviour towards technology was the adults' own experience of technology and its value for the kinds of things they did at work (e.g. managing databases or architectural design), at home (e.g. online banking or shopping) and for leisure and entertainment (e.g. using a playstation or watching videos). The examples of Grace and Catriona (Case Study 1) illustrate the influence of their parents' engagement with ICT and their perspective on the value of young children using new technologies. Both girls lived in economically advantaged families and their parents had all had experience of using ICT at school and for work. However, while Catriona had become a competent user of the technology at home, Grace had few technological toys, preferred traditional activities and had little interest in technologies. The experiences and technological competencies of the girls are related to the attitudes of their parents. Grace's mother in particular sees little or no need for her daughter to use technology at present as she argues that early knowledge and skills will become obsolete and she is concerned about the impact of computer games on the behaviour of children and adults. On the other hand, using ICT is very much a part of the everyday life of Catriona's mother and is becoming a very familiar feature of her daughter's experience, too.

CASE STUDY

1 Grace and Catriona: the impact of parental attitudes

Grace and Catriona were two 4-year-old girls from families defined by us as advantaged. Both had 6-year-old brothers and their parents had similar backgrounds. Their fathers had skilled jobs requiring specialist technical competencies. Grace's mother

(Continued)

(Continued)

was a childminder and Catriona's was involved in home care for the elderly. Grace's parents had early experiences of learning to use ICT. Her father had gained a qualification in computing at school while her mother had learned basic programming and the use of accountancy software packages to help with her parents' business. Catriona's mother had gained an HNC qualification in computing immediately after leaving school and had worked as an ICT trainer in the National Health Service. Her father used specialist technologies associated with his work as a marine pilot and more recently had become a competent user of the home computer.

However, the attitudes of the two sets of parents towards children's use of new technologies were very different. Grace's parents had negative views of their early experiences with ICT, describing these as boring and irrelevant, and now very out of date. Grace's mother was concerned that video games make children aggressive and that having internet access at home would encourage her husband to become 'addicted to the internet'. She believed that any technological skills acquired now will quickly become obsolete and that there was therefore no urgency about children learning to use ICT. In contrast, Catriona's parents were confident and enthusiastic users of home technologies, using the internet for shopping and banking. 'How did I ever manage without it?' Catriona's mother asked. They had positive views of technology in the future, and believed that children should take every opportunity to develop the technological skills which would enable them to take advantage of developments.

Grace's and Catriona's own abilities to use new technologies appeared to be related to their parents' attitudes and experiences. Grace had very limited skills. Unusually among our case study children, she could not use the TV controls, and had virtually no technically oriented items, other than a toy Barbie CD player and a toy Barbie laptop. Her favourite activities are playing with Barbie dolls, dressing up, playing outdoors and swimming. At the same age, Catriona was fully competent with TV controls and with a mobile phone. She played computer games with her older brother although she needed some help with setting games up. Her favourite activities included playing with dolls, painting, in the traditional way or on the computer, watching TV and playing computer games. By the end of our visits, Catriona could find favourite websites on the internet, enjoyed the Dancemat, had decreed LeapPads and VTech toys to be too babyish for her, and could take pictures with the digital camera, through she had not learned to review or download them onto the computer yet. Her mother was pleased that she was 'not frightened' of ICT.

Children's preferences

In addition to the influence that their families have on children's engagement with technology, the children's own individual preferences and enduring interests and dispositions play an important part in shaping their use of ICT. Children who were cautious and keen to avoid failure were reported by their parents to take a similar approach to using digital technologies. Others were described as explorers who confidently launched into new games or puzzled over and mastered new devices. If a child had an enduring interest, for example in sport like Alexander, or cars and trucks like

Kenneth, this was often reflected in the ways in which they engaged with technology. Alexander particularly enjoyed computer games on a sports website while Kenneth liked to take digital photographs of vehicles and to use his remote-controlled cars.

The children themselves made it clear that they had distinct preferences among traditional toys and activities and technological resources and there was no evidence that using ICT in leisure and family time dominated the children's choices. All of the children involved in *Entering e-Society* identified traditional activities among the things that they were good at and enjoyed doing. About half of them identified playing on a slide and swimming as activities they enjoyed. Drawing was also a popular choice. Over two-thirds said that playing with the computer made them happy and about half were happy to watch television. The children stopped using a technological resource if it became boring or too hard to be an attractive activity. For instance, Angus did not like the alphabet game because he said it was too hard, and Grace complained about having difficulty making the cursor move on some games. Andy thought that playing with his Gameboy was sometimes boring. The children used technology when it was fun or enjoyable and did not see it as a learning activity or work in the way they often describe adult-initiated activities in school.

In their accounts of using new technologies, and their descriptions about how other children the same age could learn to use the resources, the case study children were able to differentiate between operational competence (knowing how to use the technology) and being able to complete the tasks, games or activities that the technology permitted.

> Using the controller [for the Playstation] can be hard because there are so many buttons it's hard to use them all at once. (Kenneth)

> [it's hard] because you've got to try to use the white one to get the balloons to burst them ... you've got to catch them. (Grace, referring to Disney Plug 'N' Play)

Not only did the children have decided preferences, they were also able to evaluate their own competencies, indicating which technologies they were good at using and those with which they struggled. Catriona told the researchers that she was good at the Bob the Builder computer game. Freddie said that he was good at the Pokemon computer game but failed with a Toy Story game: 'I die on that one, it's rubbish, too hard'.

The children most frequently nominated their parents as a source of help with technology and parents clearly provided opportunities for the children, supported their emergent skills and interests and purchased equipment that they thought would give their children pleasure. Nevertheless, although their parents and siblings could provide a context that encouraged the use of particular resources, perhaps using the webcam or downloading and listening to music, the 3- and 4-year-olds resisted playing with technology which they did not find attractive or which did not fit with their interests. Stuart (Case Study 2) was growing up in a household with ample technological resources and his family are keen users of ICT. However, the presence of technology at home (and in his nursery) did not drive Stuart's interests. He chose not to engage in these activities but followed his own interests in outdoor and physical play.

> ### CASE STUDY
>
> #### 2 Stuart: no interest in digital technologies
>
> Four-year-old Stuart was described by his mother as a very active boy who loved the outdoors, cycling and playing action games. He had little interest in computers or playing electronic games or even watching TV or DVDs. The family lived in a technology-rich home and both parents made use of ICT in their work and for leisure and household activities. Chris, Stuart's 6-year-old brother, had developed an early interest in new technologies. By the time he was 3 years old, Chris was able to use the TV and DVD player and was now quickly picking up the skills he needed, such as internet surfing. In contrast, Stuart remained fundamentally uninterested in using digital technologies. At the age of 5 years, he finally learned to use the TV and DVD remote controls by himself, but had little interest in or ability to use the computer, or the X-box.

Learning with technology

In our earlier study of children learning with ICT in preschool settings (Stephen and Plowman, 2008), we identified three kinds of learning:

- operational learning (how to use the technology);
- learning about areas of the curriculum through using technology (e.g. about animals or cities, identifying rhymes, sorting and categorising);
- acquiring positive learning dispositions such as confidence and persistence.

The children learned as they used technology at home, too. Here, the key areas of learning were operational, social and cultural. They developed operational skills, such as learning how to switch on and off, select channels or use icons, rewind or record and how to store and retrieve data. They learned, too, about the social uses of the technologies as they joined their families in communicating with friends and relatives by talking or sending texts on mobile phones, using webcams or sending photographs by email. Cultural learning opportunities came through engaging with a wide range of activities facilitated by digital technologies, ranging from watching and interacting with television or DVDs, playing games or creating scenarios on websites to creating pictures or photographs and video clips.

Digital literacy can be defined as being able to understand and employ a range of technological sources to develop knowledge and potential and achieve goals. In these terms, the children in our study were developing digital literacy likely to be important for future success. Print literacy and digital literacy seem to be mutually enhancing as they offer children experience of alternative forms of symbolic representation (words, numbers, icons). Print, sound and visual representations are increasingly integrated in the multi-media world of digital technology and this offers opportunities to develop interlinked competencies and complementary forms of expression (Yelland et al., 2008).

At home, learning was driven by participating in authentic, shared activities that allowed the child to become a participant in the practices of the family and community. Parents and other family members did sometimes give direct instructions to their 3- or 4-year-olds about how to use equipment but more often they talked of how the children just 'picked it up' as they participated in everyday family practices (Plowman et al., 2008b). This contrasted with their experiences in preschool settings where the children seldom saw practitioners using technology to communicate or acquire information and were much less likely to be involved in using the technology to achieve personal goals (Plowman and Stephen, 2007; Stephen and Plowman, 2008). In addition, at home the range of resources is likely to be richer and more frequently available to any individual child than at nursery or playgroup where some resources such as computers are sometimes old or handed down and children may have to share one digital camera with 15 or 20 others.

In educational settings, particularly when children move on to primary school, the focus tends to be on learning how to use resources or on completing activities in carefully prescribed ways which can fail to take account of the social and cultural learning and skills developed at home and children's individual preferences and strengths. In our study, none of the parents with a child moving to school reported being asked how their child used technologies at home; indeed, one mother told us that her child's teacher said that at school children would be taught how to use the keyboard and mouse 'properly'. This approach risks failing to build on the operational, problem-solving and creative competencies children have developed as they use digital technologies at home, and does not maximise the potential of their existing funds of knowledge (Gonzalez et al., 2005).

Conclusion

In this chapter, we have described how preschool children engage with new technologies at home. The concern that technology is opening another divide between children from different socio-economic backgrounds is not supported by our evidence. Our findings suggest that parents' own encounters with and expectations of ICT, and their family values and practices, are likely to have a stronger influence than economic factors on the experiences that children have with technologies at home. Parents do have some anxieties about exposing children to the negative influences associated with technology, such as physical inactivity, or the endorsement of aggressive behaviour. However, most families were confident that they were achieving an appropriate balance of traditional or technological play, entertainment and risk or opportunity. They took steps to regulate encounters with technology if they felt it was necessary (e.g. limiting the length of time watching DVDs or playing computer games).

The children themselves were active and influential agents in the activities they undertook at home. All of the children in our study selected traditional activities amongst the things that they preferred to do and felt they were good at, and there was no evidence that using technologies dominated their play. As they participated in family life, the children were able to learn how to operate technologies and they experienced what could be achieved with particular resources. However, they did not necessarily choose to engage with technology even if their parents and siblings were enthusiastic users. The children were discriminating users of technologies who had decided preferences, were ready to stop if the activity was too difficult or not interesting enough, and were able to evaluate their own performances. Through their interactions with technologies at home, the 3- and 4-year-olds were developing digital literacy and acquiring operational, social and cultural competencies. If this learning is to be built on in preschool and primary school, it is important for preschool practitioners and teachers to be aware of the rich and varied ways in which children use digital technologies at home and the skills and understandings which they bring to school as a result of these encounters with ICT.

[...]

References

Cordes, C. and Miller, E. (eds) (2000) *Fool's Gold: a critical look at computers in childhood*. College Park, MD: Alliance for Childhood.

Gonzalez, N., Moll, L. and Amanti, C. (eds) (2005) *Funds of Knowledge: theorizing practices in households, communities and classrooms*. Mahwah, NJ: Erlbaum.

Palmer, S. (2006) *Toxic Childhood: how the modern world is damaging our children and what we can do about it*. London: Orion.

Plowman, L., McPake, J. and Stephen, C. (2008a) The technologisation of childhood? Young children and technology in the home. *Children and Society*, published online August 2008. Available at www3.interscience.wiley.com/cgi-bin/fulltext/121385522/PDFSTART (accessed May 2009).

Plowman, L., McPake, J. and Stephen, C. (2008b) Just picking it up? Young children learning with technology at home. *Cambridge Journal of Education*, 38(3): 303–319.

Plowman, L. and Stephen, C. (2007) Guided interaction in pre-school settings. *Journal of Computer Assisted Learning*, 23(1): 14–21.

Prensky, M. (2006) *Don't Bother Me Mom – I'm Learning!* St Paul, Minnesota: Paragon House.

Shaffer, D. (2007) *How Computer Games Help Children Learn*. New York: Palgrave Macmillan.

Stephen, C., McPake, J., Plowman, L. and Berch-Heyman, S. (2008) Learning from the children: exploring preschool children's encounters with ICT at home. *Journal of Early Childhood Research*, 6(2): 99–117.

Stephen, C. and Plowman, L. (2008) Enhancing learning with information and communication technologies in pre-school. *Early Child Development and Care*, 178(6): 637–654.

Yelland, N. Lee, L. O'Rourke, M. and Harrison, C. (2008) *Rethinking Learning in Early Childhood Education*. Maidenhead: Open University Press.

16

A cultural–historical theory of children's development

Mariane Hedegaard

Overview

In this chapter, Mariane Hedegaard introduces a model for learning and development that focuses on societal conditions, institutional practices and motives and intentions of children in everyday activities. When Hedegaard's model is used for framing up research, it focuses the researcher's attention on how to gain insights into the developmental conditions from societal, institutional and individual perspectives. Throughout this expansive view of development, a more holistic approach to research is afforded.

[...]

According to our theoretical standpoint, developmental psychology and childhood research need to embrace the child as an individual person and see the child as a participant in a societal collective interacting with others in different settings. A child develops as an individual with unique distinctiveness, and as a member of a society where different institutional practices are evident.

The model in Figure 16.1 illustrates a situated dynamic where a child concurrently participates in several institutional settings and arenas in his or her everyday life, for

Hedegaard, M. (2008) 'A cultural–historical theory of children's development', in Hedegaard, M. and Fleer, M. (eds) *Studying Children: A Cultural–Historical Approach*, Maidenhead: OUP/ McGraw Hill, pp. 10–29. © 2008. Reproduced with the kind permission of Open University Press. All rights reserved.

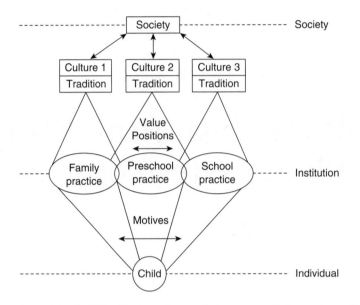

Figure 16.1 A model of children's learning and development through participation in institutional practice, where different perspectives are depicted: a societal, an institutional, and an individual perspective (Hedegaard, 2004)

instance home, day care and extended family, or home, school and community peer group or after-school activities. It can also be seen as a developmental pathway in Western industrialised/information societies, where the dominant institutions in a child's life change from being at home, to day care/infant school, to school. In the following sections, these conceptions of children's development will unfold in relation to three different perspectives: a societal perspective, an institutional perspective and a person's perspective. A wholeness approach to studying children should encompass daily life across different institutional settings and arenas from all three perspectives.

Important conceptions to describe children's development from a societal and cultural perspective are:

- Children's development takes place through participating in societal institutions.
- Institutional practice and children's development are connected to a conception of what constitutes a 'good life' and these vary within the different types of institution and even among those who participate in the practices found within these institutions.
- A child's development can be thought of as a qualitative change in his or her motive and competencies. Development can also be connected to the change in the child's social situation (i.e. when the child moves from one institution to the next or as a result of change in a particular practice within an institution).

A societal perspective that relates to qualitative changes in development

Differences in how children are brought up are reflected in their developmental competencies. Descriptions of such differences can be found in anthropological literature. These are richly illustrated by Barbara Rogoff (2003) in her book, *The Cultural Nature of Human Development* and in Rogoff's (1990) longstanding research documented in *Apprenticeship in Thinking*. Margaret Mead (1956/2001) has also nicely shown how cultural differences in upbringing can differ radically even within the same small society over a generation. In her anthropological research on *New Lives for Old: Cultural Transformation – Manus 1928–1953*, a radical change took place in adult work culture in this period. The American troops in the the Second World War contributed to a fast change in material, cultural and religious traditions in the Manus society, which in turn influenced both work relations and everyday social relations between adults. Mead writes that cultural traditions that were central in the old Manus traditions – for instance, sharing of goods – lived on in children's peer relations longer than among the adults and could be found even after they were abandoned by the adults. The change in Manus traditions influences the way children grow up. In connection with this study Mead points out that 'Every new religion, every new political doctrine, has had first to make its adult converts, to create a small nuclear culture within whose guiding wall its children can flourish …' (1956/2001, p. 150). She writes further, 'Such changes in adult attitudes come slowly, are more dependent upon specially gifted or wise individuals than upon wholesale educational schemes' (1956/2001, p. 151). According to Mead, the adult community creates the conditions for children's development.

Cross-cultural research provides us with a broader understanding of beliefs and expectations of children's development. For example, in some parts of West Africa the principle underpinning child development is social rather than biological, as noted by Nsamenang and Lamb in their study of Nso children in the Bamenda Grassfields of Cameroon, West Africa:

> [C]hildren are progressively assigned different roles at different life stages depending on their perceived level of social competence rather than on their biological maturation. (Nsamenang and Lamb, 1998, p. 252)

Assumptions about development as constructed in one community do not necessarily transfer to other communities. Critically examining one's assumptions about development is important for researchers interested in studying the development of children as anchored in concrete historical settings, institutional practices and the general everyday living conditions of children and their families.

Developmental pathways

In a cultural–historical perspective on children's development, the focus of attention is on the person and the caregiver's perspective in relation to life opportunities and possibilities. In this approach, the formulation of possible trajectories has been very important, although I prefer the concept of pathway, because it surpasses the 'bird's eye' view on children's development and anchors what happens in the person's activities. The conception of developmental pathways takes the focus away from a particular course of development and gives room for a forward-directed approach where children can influence their own developmental pathways. Developmental trajectories have been formulated as an opposition to the 'course–reason' description of children's development and also have this forward-directed perspective.

Klaus Riegel (1975), in his critique of the more traditional theories, formulated the concept of developmental trajectories as an alternative to a more simple environmental influence and pointed to four interacting trajectories: the inner biological, the individual psychological, the cultural-sociological and the outer *physical*. Riegel showed how conflicts or harmony between the different types of trajectories in a person's life could lead to either a positive or a negative development, where timing is a central factor. Examples of conflict between biological lines and individual psychological lines can be found when girls in some cultures, get married very early or between individual psychological and cultural sociological developmental lines, when girls become underage mothers while still at school or when boys become soldiers in war zones.

Riegel argued that, in development, it is the dialectical interaction between inner biological/individual psychological factors and cultural–sociological/outer physical factors that is important.

Glen Elder (1998) has also outlined how a person's lines of development can be represented as social trajectories within families, education and work. Central to Elder's theory of a person's life course development is his conceptualisation of the historical aspect of societal trajectories and their change over generations. His conceptualisations, based on longitudinal research, show differences between children/ youth growing up during the depression of the 1930s and children/youth growing up during the Second World War. How these conditions work together with economic hardship is influenced by timing. An example of timing is when children and youth enter education and work. Here, Elder points out that timing has a greater influence on a person's life trajectory than socially and culturally different life conditions. The relations between people have also been shown to influence how a person's life course will develop.

Elder's and Riegel's concepts of developmental trajectories and life course are structural theories that can be applied to, but not anchored in, practice in institutions and therefore even though they specify how interaction between conditions can take place, they cannot identify how new social relations are formed or what characterises the child's concrete social situation.

Vygotsky (1998) also introduced the concept of developmental lines, but the meaning is quite different to that of Elder and Riegel. Vygotsky points to the importance of taking the child's social situation of development into consideration. A child's social situation of development changes in relation to different periods in his or her development. The social situation of development indicates that the child's personality and social environment at each age level are in a dynamic relation.

The structure of the child's personality appears, and is formed, in the course of the development of critical time periods. Vygotsky also talks of developmental lines as structural, but he places them within the child's development of personality and consciousness, where the structural changes are related to the development of central functions such as a child's speech. Such developmental lines of function can be diagnosed in relation to the child's social situation of development. The relation of the whole to the part, such as language development, is important at each age level. Vygotsky put forward the view that the developmental lines become central, or peripheral, according to their relationship to the child's developmental age. For example, at the age of 2, speech is a central line of development, while the exploration of fingers and toes is peripheral. During school age, the continuing development of a child's speech has a completely different relation to the central neo-formation of this age (e.g. where the focus becomes written symbols for learning to read); consequently, speech must be considered as peripheral lines of development when at school in relation to learning to read and write (Vygotsky, 1998, p. 197).

In Vygotsky's terminology, developmental lines cannot be separated into biological, environmental and psychological, but rather they are woven together. The environment in this relation must not be conceived as something outside the child, as an aggregate of objective conditions, without reference to the child and how they are affecting him or her by their very existence:

> … at the beginning of each age period there develops a completely original, exclusive single and unique relation, specific to the given age, between the child and the reality, namely the social reality, that surrounds him. We call this relation the *social relation of development* at the given age. (Vygotsky, 1998, p. 198)

The social environment is the source for the appearance of all specific human properties that have been gradually acquired by the child. It is the source of a child's personality development that is grounded in the process of interaction of 'ideal' and 'present' forms of properties. In different periods different developmental lines dominate and these can be thought of as the 'social relations of development':

> Toward the end of a given age, the child becomes a completely different being than he was at the beginning of the age. But this necessarily also means that the social situation of development which was established in basic traits toward the beginning of any age must also change since the social situation of development is nothing other than a system of relations between the child of a given age and social reality. (Vygotsky, 1998, p. 199)

Vygotsky writes that the child's chronological age cannot serve as a reliable criterion for establishing the actual level of development. Determination of the actual level requires research that can diagnose the child's development, and to do this one has to focus on reliable traits or functions that can be used to identify the phase and stage of each age of the development process. In my interpretation, this must mean that one has to formulate ideals of child development that interweave biological lines as well as cultural–historical lines of development, so that caregivers and educators can formulate ideals of cultural development that are specific for a cultural tradition.

In combining Vygotsky's conception of developmental lines and the social situation of development with Riegel and Elder's conceptions of trajectories and life courses into a conception of developmental pathways, this concept can be seen as highlighting the ideals for children's development. But it also highlights that there are several ideal pathways for the development of each child. This is in line with Vygotsky's conception of how the child's social situation is created.

Further, I think it is important to combine the concept of institutional practice, as well as a person's activity, with the concept of developmental pathways.

Learning and development through entering institutional practices

The societal perspective is a macro perspective that perspectivates the conditions for the practices in which children can participate, in home, education and work. Changes in children's relation to the world are first and foremost connected to qualitative changes in what are the dominant institutional practices in a child's life. Entering a new institutional practice, such as going to school, can be viewed from a societal perspective. How a child participates in these different institutional practices, and what he or she learns from these experiences, can lead to developmental changes in a child. These changes need to be analysed in relation to the child's social situation.

Children's efforts and motives are usually directed towards successfully participating in the practice traditions of particular institutions. Children also create their own activities in the specific activity settings within these practices. As such, children's engagements and motives have to be seen in relation to both the traditional practices of the institutions and the activities they generate for themselves in the institutions. The concept of setting is inspired by Roger Barker and Herbert Wright's description of *One Boy's Day* (1951). They use the concept of behavioural setting to describe the context of the boy's activity. The setting is the cultural–material conditions that take the form of city architecture, material characteristic of the institutions, room size, furniture, all sorts of materials including books, TV, etc., that are available to the child. Barker and Wright use the term *behaviour* to describe their *meaning* of the boy's activity. They write that: 'All that is concerned with objectivity of this record must face two facts. One is that behaviour without feeling, motives and meanings is of little significance for the student's personality and social psychology. The other is that motives, feelings and meanings cannot be observed directly' (1951, p. 8).

I agree with Barker and Wright when they state that in order to get a child's perspective on what is meaningful to them, one must focus on a child's activities in everyday practice and differentiate between the different institutional activity settings within which children's everyday activities can be found. Instead of behaviour,

[we] use the concept of *activity*. Activity is a concept developed by Leontiev (1978). This term foregrounds the person's perspective by focusing on the person's intentions and motives in the practice being studied. Conceptualising what is going on in an institutional practice from a person's perspective, we prefer to use the concept of activity, a concept that is defined in relation to its 'motive goal'. An example of the relevance of this differentiation can be seen when a child is playing in a preschool activity setting. The traditional practice in the preschool is for staff to provide a spacious setting with the possibility for using different play materials and for supporting children to play together. [C]hildren's activity can be described as play when their motive is directed towards imagining activities such as when a child is imagining driving a car or being a mother taking care of a baby. It is through the focus on the child's engagement in 'make-believe actions' as he or she plays with other children or plays with special toys that the child's activity, and not the institutional practice, is foregrounded. Here, the research takes the child's perspective. Had the focus of attention been on the materials and the space, then the institutional practice would have been the focus.

Practice and activity are related concepts: we will use *practice* when the institutional perspective is taken and *activity* when the person's perspective is taken (an overview of the conceptual relations can be seen in Table 16.1). Children develop through participating in institutionalised practices that are characterised by communication and shared activities. These forms of practice not only initiate but also restrict children's activities and thereby become conditions for their development. A child's participation in a kindergarten's activity settings such as meals and play lead to different activities for the child in kindergarten than in the home, since the kindergarten setting and its practice traditions give different conditions for learning and development than home traditions for these activities.

Learning activities such as mathematics, eating lunch and playing are done within the practice tradition of the schools. In school, neither meals nor play are expected to be the dominant activities; but learning subject matters, such as mathematics, are seen as the dominant activities in school practices. In kindergarten, however, play is seen as the dominant activity (for many countries such as Denmark, Australia, United Kingdom, USA, etc.).

To describe and understand the conditions for development, one has to ask:

- What kind of institutional practices do children in modern society participate in?
- What activity settings tend to dominate the institutional practices of modern society?
- What demands do these dominant practices put on children?
- What possibilities for activity are generated and how do children act in these activity settings?
- What kind of conflicts can occur between different demands?
- What kind of crises will children meet through conflicting demands and motives (i.e moving from one institution to the next, appropriating the orientation and competence required by these institutions)?

Table 16.1   Levels of analyses

Society	Tradition	Conditions
Institution	Practice	Values/Motive objects
Activity setting	Social situation	Motivation
Person	Activity	Motives/Engagement/Intentions

Children's development seen in relation to values and norms

Development should also be seen in relation to values and norms. For instance, development should be viewed as a process that integrates a person's development of competencies with values. In order to enable caregiving persons and educators to evaluate what competencies and motives children have appropriated, they need a set of descriptive norms for children's development. However, valuable competencies and motives are connected with what is seen as a 'good life' by the caregivers or educators who surround the child and who focus on developing the child.

Conceptions of a 'good life' are anchored in the norms and values that are interwoven in the different cultural traditions in the institutions where daily life is lived and daily activities take place. They are expressed through interaction as well as through the material conditions available to children, such as the type of food, way of dressing, where to live, how to give space to children's activities, environmental designs and the financial costs associated with having a child. Ideas of how to create a 'good everyday life' for children are not so simple, because children participate in several institutional practices every day (i.e. in family, kindergarten/school and perhaps religious institutions, sport and leisure time activities) and also in community life. In such a variety of places, there can be different practice traditions and different values and sometimes these values and traditions are not compatible. For example, some refugee families find that there are multiple 'instances' of what constitutes a 'good life', particularly when families experience institutional traditions in their new society (i.e. school, workplace and community in general) that are different to those known and found in their original home community (Hedegaard, 1999, 2003). Even within an institution, there can be different opinions of what is good practice and a good life. For example, this can be found even among teachers at the same school and can sometimes be noticed explicitly between members of the same family.

Change in institutional practice

Elkonin's (1999) theory of child development especially focuses on the importance of social practice in different institutions. These social practices mark important qualitative changes in children's development. Elkonin describes three periods in children's development and outlines how these are related to the dominant practice traditions in Western industrialised society. I especially draw upon Elkonin's formulation of the dialectic between competence and motives throughout a child's development, as seen within different age periods. I have to state very clearly that a concept of period or stage in a child's development has to be understood in relation to the different types of institutional practice and the activities this affords to children. Through participation in institutional practice a child acquires specific motives and competencies. But it is also important to state that in a shared activity setting with other people, the child's engaged activity is central to what he or she may learn. Parents/teachers/educators evaluate a child's competence and motive appropriation in relation to their ideas about what such participation in institutional practices should lead to – either directly or indirectly. That is, as children participate in the institutional practices, their involvement or activity are oriented towards certain goals and their successful appropriation of these 'goals' is then used to evaluate their competence and motive development.

The child's perspective

When we consider the child's perspective, the activity setting in which the child participates is known as the child's 'social situation'. In the child's social situation, demands from caregivers and the possibility for realising their own intentional activity leads to the appropriation of competencies and motives connected to the activity setting.

In order to take a child's perspective as they enter a new practice, one has to focus on the motives inherent in the activity settings. One has also to relate the activity settings in which the child participates to the projects in which the child is engaged, and the intention the child shows through his or her actions.

The easiest way to understand a child's intention is to note when there is a conflict where the child cannot do what he or she wants to do and cannot realise the projects in which he or she is engaged. As such, a cultural–historical methodology needs to focus on the conflicts between the child's intentions and what he or she is unable to realise. It is important, however, not to over-evaluate conflicts. In the first instance, conflict should be seen as a way to understand the child's motive and to see what he or she is oriented towards. Conflicts also allow the researcher to note the ways in which a child interacts with his or her surroundings and this gives greater insight into the child's perspective.

To be able to take a child's perspective, one has to focus on the intentions that guide the child's actions and from the patterns of actions and communication, interpret the projects and motives in which the child engages.

Children's intentional orientation, projects and motives

Since intention and motives are central in a methodology focusing on the child's social situation, a short overview of how the author understands these concepts will be presented. Inspiration will be drawn not only from Leontiev (1978) and Elkonin (1999), but also from Bruner's (1972) research into children's intentional activities in infancy.

Through shared activity, the child becomes aware of his or her own needs and goals and it is through this interaction that the child's biological needs are transformed into societal needs. That is, the biological needs become attached to a cultural 'motive-object' (Leontiev, 1978). For example, when we follow an infant's development we usually note how the child's biological needs turn into cultural needs and become the child's motives. According to Bruner (1972), from the very first moments of an infant's development, the child is intentionally oriented to its surroundings and from this orientation springs further development of the child's dynamic and cognitive orientation to the world. Building on the cultural–historical approach of Leontiev and Elkonin, one has to conceptualise a child's intentional orientation or projects as a relation between the child's motives in an activity setting and the demands in the institutional practice – i.e. between the motives of the child and possibilities for activity. The child's motives have to be seen in relation to his or her experience and competence and the possibility for realising the child's motives in an institutional practice. Meaningful motives are created for the child through experience and through gaining competencies when participating in new activity settings.

Leontiev (1978) states that a child's development can be viewed in relation to his or her 'hierarchy of motives'. A child's motive hierarchy has to be understood in relation to what is considered to be the most important activity for the child. A child's motive hierarchy changes over time because he or she appropriates new motives and also because practice changes. When practice changes, children are given new possibilities for participating in important activity settings. A motive becomes a leading motive when the activity connected with this is the most meaningful activity for the child. The leading motive in a child's life is related to what is the dominating institutional practice in which the child participates, in a given life period. This means that, for a school child, the dominant practice in school would result in a motive for 'school learning'. When a child's leading motive in school is connected to a meaningful activity setting then it should result in academic learning. This holds in most cases, but it is not always the activity in the school practice that the teacher has in mind that becomes the most meaningful, and thereby the leading motive, for the child. The motive complex related to school practice (as well as to other institutional practices) is complicated because so many activities are going on in school between subject matter teaching, peer group activities, teacher–student relations, student–student relations and all the extra-curricular activities.

To take a child's perspective in research is to ask: What different practice is the child taking part in? What activity settings is the child engaged in? What characterises the child's motives and [social relations] in [t]hese different practices and what projects does the child engage in across different institutional practices? Is it possible for children to engage intentionally in activity settings that are meaningful for them and realise their motives when interacting with others who participate in the same everyday activities?

The child's motives are not always in line with the expectations of caregivers – for instance, when a child is playing and is not happy when other children take his or her toys but the caregivers believe it is important to share. In this example, the caregivers and educators should support the child to accept that other children will interfere with his or her play. If, by the same token, the caregivers accept that each child will have his or her own special toys, such as a special teddy bear, then the caregivers should also help the other participants to respect the child's wish not to share this toy. Conflicts can arise between children during shared activities and it is important to recognise that a shared activity setting can contain different projects for different children, depending upon their engagement and understanding of the activity (an activity can be motivated both by several motives of the single person and by different motives from several persons). From a child's perspective, the child can have a special motive which can be seen as a project or an interest that transcends different activity settings or even practices. This can, for instance, be seen when a child is aiming at the same type of play in different settings or wanting to be with his or her best friend in different activities or both. Trying to see an activity from a given person's perspective gives the possibility for understanding how this person both learns from and contributes to shared activities.

During play the different motives and projects of children intersect. How motives and projects influence each other can be illustrated by an extract from an observation of three children, where the eldest child sets the scene for their play, but the two younger children, who do not really understand the theme of the play, 'disturb' the older child's ideas by introducing simpler play themes.

Torben (5½ years old), *Jorn* (3 years old), *Louis* (3 years old)
Torben announces that he is Superman and says directly to Jorn: You are Peter Pan.

Torben: Come on Superman and Peter Pan (Torben does not ask Louis to participate). Jorn goes with him.
Louis: Can I be in?
Torben: Do you know what you can be? You can be our friend. I am Superman.

Torben runs away to look at the other children, Jorn and Louis watch him.

Louis (to Jorn): Can I have a cup of coffee?
Jorn: Yes, here you are. [He pretends to pour the coffee in a doll's cup and Louis pretends to drink it.]

Jorn (to Torben who has returned): Look, a small child.

Torben: No, we aren't playing that! (He laughs.)
Jorn: Yes we are!
Torben: No! Because he is Superman's dog and we don't have babies with us.

Torben walks away again.

Jorn: So I can be a baby.
Jorn: Look, I am a small baby.
Louis: Then I can be the mother – now the ship is sailing.
Jorn: Yes we can play dad and mum.

They look for a short moment at what the other children are doing and sit quietly next to each other.

Torben comes back and says to Jorn: No! This is not part of it [the play].
Torben kicks at the things the two small boys have played with.
Torben (to Jorn):   Do not become so scabby, you should not be a baby but Peter Pan.

The children separate and play by themselves.

Jorn walks towards Torben.

Torben: Now I pour poison on your head.
Jorn: No! Now I can be Peter Pan's dog.
Torben: No! Do you know what you have to be? Superman's dog!
Jorn: Can I just have a cup of coffee?
Torben: Here! [He throws the imaginary coffee onto Jorn's head. Jorn is grinning.]

All three are now together. Louis looks at the other two and is grinning. They are having fun it seems, because Torben goes on playing that he is throwing coffee at Jorn's head. Jorn goes away and Louis also runs away. Torben runs after them and now he acts as if he is shooting Jorn. Jorn drops down on the floor.

Torben to Louis: Come here, here you will be safe.

Torben builds a fortress of pillows.
Jorn approaches them.
Torben is shooting at him.
Louis is looking with his mouth open.
Torben is shooting and shooting and Jorn is running, Torben runs after him, they end under a
   big table, where Jorn drops down as though he were dead.

The *theme* of Torben's play is superheroes. The *leading motive* in this activity setting for Torben is to be the leader of a shared play and he tries to organise the play in a different way in order to achieve this. He starts out with a play project that he cannot realise but ends up being the one that sets the theme of play by dragging the two younger children into a shooting activity. But he first has to act in relation to Jorn's play and this he does by threatening Jorn in a playful way and keeping the two younger boys apart by protecting Louis and making the play very simple.

   For the two younger children the *leading motive* is to play together. Jorn is the key person to keep the three boys together because he wants to play with both Louis and Torben. Louis proposes an activity of drinking coffee, in order to play with Jorn. This can hardly be called a play project as it is more an act that he proposes. Together Jorn and Louis construct a play theme of being a baby and playing dad and mum in opposition to Torben. They do not succeed with this for long, because they do not really know what to do; they just sit together and also because Torben interrupts them.

Problems and conflicts in children's everyday activities

Problems between a child and other persons can arise. For instance, conflicts can occur between an infant and first-time parents when establishing day and night rhythm. Problems between a mother and child can also arise in relation to breast feeding, such as when the infant will not take the nipple or will not drink as much as the mother wants, resulting in more frequent breast feeding. Later when the child has to be weaned from breast milk, this can create serious frustrations for some parents and their child. But problems like this, or that turn up later in a child's development, such as the conflicts described in the play above, do not have to be seen as negative because they are also an indicator of how the child is developing within a particular cultural tradition. It is the way in which caregivers tackle the problems and help the child to solve these conflicts in the social situation that is important, as they can be positive or problematic.

A child's engaged involvement in activities that seem to promote problems is also a sign that the child is acquiring competencies within a certain domain. The caregivers can therefore make positive use of the problems that turn up in a child's everyday activities to help to develop a child's competencies within the domain to which the problems are connected. This can often be done by providing conditions that enable the child or children to solve their own problematic situations instead of the caregiver making direct interventions into the child's activity. Unfortunately, adults sometimes become upset when seeing children struggle in new activities and they frame these struggles as problems and conflicts. This happens when a social situation is viewed as a problem-creating confrontation between the adult's intentions and the child's intentions. In this situation, the adult does not always help a child to find relevant action possibilities in a shared activity to master the problems. Parents may see their small children as being naughty. Eva Ullstadius (2001) found that mothers change their reaction to their infants over the first year of the infant's life. In following a group of 17 first-born infants through weekly visits from the 1st to the 56th week, asking mothers questions related to the infants' 'difficultness' and the mothers' feelings of impatience and irritation towards the infants, she found that mothers' expression of irritation changes with the age of the infant, reflecting her growing demands on her infant. She used three categories: (1) infant crying/fretting/clinging, (2) sleeping problems, (3) protest/disobedience. The last kind of activity was the one that upset the mothers most from the 9th month, culminating around the 12th month. Ullstadius noted that mothers who were influenced by the Swedish childcare authority's child-centred ambition to fulfil the infant's wishes, were not as irritated by the baby's crying/fretting or by sleeping problems. Clearly, the mothers' demands were mediated by the social conditions of middle-class culture as expressed through the mothers' particular personal and social values of what to expect from an infant. Open conflicts and clashes appeared around 1 year of age, indicating a general crisis as described by Vygotsky (1998). But how this crisis took form can be seen in relation to the cultural tradition, where in this Swedish sample, crying and sleeping problems did not upset the mothers as much.

An adult who does not take the child's perspective or who cannot see the child's motive, may end up in more permanent conflict with the child (i.e. conflict may then show up recurrently in activities such as meals and night-time routines). When they cannot 'understand' the child's intention or motive, caregivers often interpret the child's motive/need in a cultural way and try to establish an interaction on this basis. If the interaction is not successful, it may lead to ongoing conflicts during social interactions when establishing day and night rhythms, when eating and around personal hygiene. If caregivers have to find a way to solve these problems, they have to find a way out of the problematic interaction patterns that they themselves are part of. But if the adult interactions with the child are not productive, then these difficult interactions may form a permanent pattern. As another example, a child may be so interested in other children that he or she pushes or hits them to get their attention. Usually caregivers help the child by developing a better interactional pattern (more acceptable in the institutional culture setting) in order to realise his or her motive to be with other children. But if the child is punished instead, this activity pattern around the content of everyday activities can gradually be reflected in the way the child begins to see itself and may result in a self-conception or self-perception of being incompetent or even 'bad'. The way children learn to realise their motives influences the way they develop motives, conceptions and morals in relation to practices in their everyday lives.

Developmental crises

Vygotsky has introduced a special variation of the 'concept of conflict' known as the 'concept of crises'. This concept directs attention to important developmental events in children's development.

Vygotsky conceptualised his ideas of crises as events that alternate with stable periods in a child's life. A developmental crisis is characterised by three parts: deconstruction, construction and mastering (Vygotsky, 1998, pp. 191 ff). The last part is characterised by what Vygotsky calls central neo-formation, which is the stable part in the dominating activity at a new developmental stage.

Crises have been part of other developmental theories, i.e. Piaget (1968 – disequilibrium) and Erikson (1950 – psychic conflicts). In these theories, crises have been located in the child as either functional–cognitive or emotional. Vygotsky's conception of crises is that they must be viewed as being located in the social situation that the child experiences. The first part of Vygotsky's description of crises in a child's social situation – deconstruction – has not been formulated as part of other theories (i.e. Piaget's or Erikson's theories). What is important here is the deconstruction and reconstruction of the social situation, where we note that the child's competence and motives for development are allowed to proceed. Those dominating conflicts in a child's social situation can be seen as a way forward and not as a drawback. These kinds of conflict, among others, are those that toddlers have when they want to do everything themselves and do not want the parents to help and at the same time cannot handle the problem by their own activity (i.e. as when a 3-year-old wants to cross a street without holding a parent's hand).

A dominating conflict can also be a drawback when the conflict does not proceed to a solution for the child, leading to neo-formation of his or her social situation, but instead becomes a fixed negative interaction pattern for the child in the social situation. An example of a long-lasting conflict can be seen when Western families become fixated on eating behaviour and make strong demands on children. The parents worry that their child does not eat enough or does not eat healthy food and the child objects to the parents' demands and sometimes even turns the eating situation into a power game.

A child's individuality

In the 1970s (Bruner, 1972, 1999) a great deal of research was focused on early infancy where scholars began to acknowledge that young infants were actively and intentionally orienting themselves towards the world. Individual differences between infants also became an important topic (this can be seen in the development of the Brazelton test for newborn infants – see Brazelton and Nugent, 2000).

This research into early infancy shows differences between infants in relation to such things as sleep patterns or sucking patterns. Wolfe (in Schaffer, 1979, p. 46) studied infants' sucking patterns and showed that newborn infants had an individual regularity and individual pattern in nutritional sucking, allowing researchers to predict when each single child would start sucking and how long it would last. Even when a child was given a pacifier, which was then removed, the child continued to make sucking movements according to his or her pattern. But the sucking process can be influenced. The sucking rate increased with an increase in the milk stream and nipple size. Bruner (1972), referring to a range of experiments done with colleagues on infants' sucking patterns, showed that from birth onwards infants are in active interaction with their environment. In some experiments done by Kalnins (Bruner, 1972, pp. 23–24), they were able to show that infants intentionally influence their surroundings through sucking, starting at around 6 weeks. Some of these experiments showed that infants (3 months old) could make a picture of their mother clear by sucking on a pacifier connected by a device to the picture. In the sucking process, there is an in-built competence for adaptation that makes it possible for an infant, at a very early stage, to discover a way of interacting intentionally with his or her surroundings.

From the beginning of a child's life, his or her sleeping pattern, sucking pattern and digestion rate influence the infant's interaction with the mother and other caregivers. How the caregivers experience this influences their interaction with the infant (see Ullstadius, 2001) and this in turn influences the baby's experience. This interaction influences the way in which the infant's primary needs start to find its objects and are cultivated into motives.

In the long run, it is the availability of the possible developmental paths that has the biggest influence on children's development and their experience and appropriation of capacities through imitation and activity with others are very important (Vygotsky, 1998, pp. 2002–2003). A child's biological dispositions are in play as threads in a rope and are easier to see in the early months of the infant's life – e.g. digestion, sleeping rhythm and sucking rate. But later these functions become integrated in the child's activities. It will never be the child's disposition for bowel function or disposition for language that have the decisive influence for the child's relation to hygiene training or appropriation of language, but instead it will be the experience the child gets through his or her activity, starting at the first trials with bowel function and language communication in interaction with other people. Each child's development can be viewed historically and in this history the child's biological disposition is an important part; however, they are *not* frames, but aspects that change and develop together with the child's psychic development.

Each child's specific experiences become the foundations for its motive and competence appropriation; therefore one could expect that a developmental description would be specific for each child. But shared characteristics evolve in children's development because they participate and engage in a shared community and in the same type of cultural events in its institutional practices. A local community is also based on a common and shared material world, which means that most children in a shared community share the same type of experience. In the Western tradition, this can be sleeping arrangements, eating arrangements, the use of a pacifier, types of baby food, objects to play with, kind of [clothes] and values such as the elderly members of Western families (e.g. the grandparents) living apart from their adult children and their grandchildren.

A description of a child's motives, knowledge and competencies demands a description of the activities that are central in children's development. To find the central activities in children's development, it will be relevant to describe children's everyday life in relation to a content description of the activities in which children engage in institutional practices in a society; and how these influence their everyday lives.

Implications for researching children's development

The conceptual ideas about children's development discussed in this chapter have led to the following consideration about cultural–historical oriented research:

- The practice traditions of the institutions in which the child lives his or her everyday life.
- Children's appropriation and display of motives and competencies through entering activity settings and sharing activities with other people within a particular cultural practice tradition.
- Demands in upbringing and education that children meet in these shared activities.
- Norms and values that are explicated by caregivers and educators as demands in the everyday practices they share with children.
- Demands in upbringing and education have to he viewed from the child's perspective, i.e. related to the child's projects and intentions.
- The interaction and conflicts between the child's projects and parents/educators' demands point to what is happening developmentally for the child.
- The trouble that the individual child has with realising his or her projects and intentions, and at the same time considerations for the demands and wishes of his or her parents and educators/teachers, can result in developmental learning.

Some researchers believe that the researcher has to go 'native' in order to be able to study children in their everyday social situations. Those that argue this position suggest that the researcher has to become 'childlike' and 'enter' the children's world to 'play' with them (for a critique of this, see Gullov and Hojlund, 2003). Instead, I want to promote an idea of the researcher and the researched as communication partners. From this position, one would think that spoken language would be the prime medium, but I would argue that this implies a much broader research approach than can be found through interviews and informal conversations – especially when one does research *with* young children.

To research a child's social situation the researcher has to be a participant in the child's social situation. But the researcher is not a full participant in the everyday activities, because the researcher's social situation is also a research situation. A social science researcher both enters the everyday activity settings of a person with the intention of being a communication partner in the researched person's social situation and enters with a special intention of her own as related to the research aim of the project.

[...]

References

Barker, R.G. and Wright, H.F. (1951). *One Boy's Day – A Specimen Record of Behavior.* New York: Harper & Brothers Publishers.

Brazelton, B. and Nugent, K. (2000). *Neonatal Behaviour Assessment Scale*, 3rd edition. Cambridge: Cambridge University Press.

Bruner, J. (1972). *Processes of Cognitive Growth: Infancy* (vol. 3). Heninz Werner Lecture Series. Wouster, MA: Clark University Press.

Bruner, J. (1999). Infancy and culture. A story. In S. Chaiklin, M. Hedegaard and U.J. Jensen (eds), *Activity Theory and Social Practice* (pp. 225–234). Aarhus, Denmark: Aarhus University Press.

Elder, G.H. (1998). The life course of developmental theory. *Child Development*, 69, 1–12.

Elkonin, D.B. (1999). Toward the problem of stages in the mental development of children. *Journal of Russian and East European Psychology*, 37, 11–29.

Erickson, E.H. (1950). *Childhood and Society.* New York: Norton.

Gullov, E. and Hojlund, S. (2003). *Faltarbejdc blandt born. Metodology og etik i etnografisk bomeforskning.* [Field work among children. Methodolgy and ethics in ethnographical research.] Copenhagen: Gyldendal.

Hedegaard, M. (1999). Institutional practice, culture positions, and personal motives: Immigrant Turkish parents' conception about their children's school life. In S. Chaiklin, M. Hedegaard and U. Juul Jensen (eds), *Activity Theory and Social Practice.* Aarhus, Denmark: Aarhus University Press.

Hedegaard, M. (2003). *At blivc fremmed i Danmark. Den modsaetningsfyldte skoletid.* [To become a stranger in Denmark: The contradiction in school.] Aarhus, Denmark: Klim.

Hedegaard, M. (2004). A cultural–historical approach to learning in classrooms. Paper presented at the International Society for Cultural and Activity Research, Regional Conference, University of Wollongong, 12–13 July.

Leontiev, A.N. (1978). *Activity, Consciousness, and Personality.* Englewood Cliffs, NJ: Prentice-Hall.

Mead, M. (1956/2001). *New Lives for Old: Cultural Transformation – Manus 1928–1953.* New York: Perennial, Harper & Row.

Nsamenang, A.B. and Lamb, M.E. (1998). Socialization of Nso children in the Bamenda Grassfields of Northwest Cameroon. In M. Woodhead, D. Faulkner and K. Littleton (eds), *Cultural Worlds of Early Childhood* (pp. 250–260). London: Routledge.

Piaget, P. (1968). *Barnets psykiske udvikling.* [Six studies of psychology.] Copenhagen: Hans Reitzel.

Riegel, K.F. (1975). Toward a dialectical theory of development. *Human Development*, 18, 50–64.

Rogoff, B. (1990). *Apprenticeship in Thinking: Cognitive Development in Social Context.* New York: Oxford University Press.

Rogoff, B. (2003). *The Cultural Nature of Human Development.* Oxford: Oxford University Press.

Schaffer, R. (1979). *Spaedbarnsomsorg* (transl. from *Mothering*). Copenhagen: Hans Reitzel.

Ullstadius, E. (2001). The development of conflicts in mother–child interaction. Paper presented at VII European Congress of Psychology. London: 1–6 July.

Vygotsky, L.S. (1998). *The Collected Works of L.S. Vygotsky. Child Psychology,* Vol. 5. New York: Plenum Press.

Hedegaard, M. (2008) 'A cultural–historical theory of children's development', in Hedegaard, M. and Fleer, M. (eds) *Studying Children: A Cultural–Historical Approach*, Maidenhead: OUP/ McGraw Hill, pp. 10–29. © 2008. Reproduced with the kind permission of Open University Press. All rights reserved.

17

Through a different lens: exploring Reggio Emilia in a Welsh context

Trisha Maynard and Sarah Chicken

Overview

Practitioners in Reggio Emilia have always asserted that what happens in their pre-schools ought not to be viewed as a 'model' of good practice. Although practitioners in the UK may find many aspects of the approach adopted in Reggio Emilia stimulating and inspiring, it is not possible to 'import' Reggio to UK settings as the principles underpinning early years provision in the UK are different to the principles underpinning the pre-schools and infant and toddler centres in Reggio Emilia. In this chapter, Maynard and Chicken explore how the philosophy and practice in Reggio Emilia can be used to help practitioners critically reflect on their own practice and in so doing gain a deeper understanding of the theories and discourses shaping their current practice and provision.

[…]

Maynard, T. and Chicken, S. (2010) 'Through a different lens: exploring Reggio Emilia in a Welsh context', *Early Years*, vol. 30, no. 1, March, pp. 29–39.

Education policy in England and Wales

The early years tradition, drawing on theories proposed by pioneers such as Rousseau, Froebel, Montessori and Dewey, upholds the centrality of 'child-centred', progressive education, which, in broad terms, sees the child as intrinsically curious and capable; values free play and first-hand learning which both stems from individual children's interests and cuts across subject boundaries; and views the teacher as a guide and facilitator (Kwon 2002). While the term 'child-centred' has, over time, been appropriated by different groups of people who have shifted the definition to suit their own interests (Chung and Walsh 2000), within statutory education in the UK, child-centred approaches reached the peak of official acceptance in the late 1960s in the Plowden Report, which stated 'At the heart of the educational process lies the child' (CACE 1967, para. 9). It is questionable how far child-centred approaches – as opposed to the discourse of child-centred ideology – were actually implemented in primary classrooms at the time (Galton et al. 1980; Bennett et al. 1984), although it appears that along with the more direct teaching of basic skills there was, as Plowden suggested (CACE 1967, para. 535), an attempt to integrate some subjects into teacher-planned themes or topics. Nevertheless, child-centred ideology was extensively criticised in the 1970s and 1980s by those who claimed that subjects had been devalued within the curriculum (e.g. Alexander 1984).

Concerns about child-centred approaches were reflected in the establishment of a National Curriculum and Assessment system for children of 5–16 years in England and Wales (Education Reform Act 1988). This initiative, paralleled in many other countries with well-developed systems of compulsory education, set out to raise standards within a global marketplace (Soler and Miller 2003), essentially through putting 'subjects' rather than the 'child' at the centre of the curriculum (Alexander et al. 1992). This was seen to have consequences for the role of the teacher (reframed as instructor) and for pedagogy (refocused on whole-class teaching).

Following devolution in 1999, the Welsh Assembly Government raised concerns that primary school teachers were introducing formal, sedentary activities too soon – particularly those working in reception classes (with children aged 4–5 years) (WAG 2003) – and that this was having a negative impact on children's motivation to learn and, in the longer term, to stay in full-time education (Barton 2002). The subsequent proposals for the Foundation Phase Framework (ACCAC 2004) made clear a commitment to active, play-based experiential learning not only for children in nursery and reception classes but throughout Key Stage One (for children aged 5–7 years).

The current Foundation Phase Framework (WAG 2008) identifies seven areas of learning although it is maintained that these should not be approached in isolation but should form part of a holistic, integrated, cross-curricular approach. Indeed, while retaining learning outcomes, the Framework emphasises that it is personal and social development, well-being and cultural diversity which are 'at the heart of the Foundation Phase' (2008: 15). Similarly, and reflecting the words of Plowden 40 years before, it maintains that the child should be 'at the heart of any planned curriculum' (2008: 6). The official introduction of the Foundation Phase started in nursery classes in September 2008: it is anticipated that roll-out will be completed in September 2011.

The Reggio philosophy and child-led learning

While in England and Wales early years education policy appears to have shifted direction in relation to curriculum, pedagogy and underpinning theories of learning, by contrast the infant and toddler centres of the municipality of Reggio Emilia are rooted in a coherent, well-defined theory of knowledge which resonates with socio-cultural principles. The theory proposes that knowledge is co-constructed between participants through communication and reflection *upon*, and analysis *of*, the learning process itself. This leads to an emphasis on relationships, collaboration, negotiation and, ultimately, meaning-making.

The cornerstone of Reggio ideology is a strong construction of the child, 'rich in potential, strong, powerful and competent' (Malaguzzi 1993: 10). This child is viewed not in isolation but as connected to other society members, in a 'system of education based on relationships' (1993: 10). A rich and social child has major implications for pedagogical practice. The dynamics of the teacher–child relationship changes from the traditional model of expert–novice to that of a 'partnership of learning' (Gandini 1993: 6): practitioners act as co-researchers, co-constructing and deconstructing knowledge (Moss 2006). Collaboration between all participants in the learning process is seen as essential with the child playing the role of protagonist within a community of enquiry, constantly attempting to make sense of his or her world through interaction and collaboration with peers and adults. Young children symbolically represent their ideas through, for example, drawing, painting, dance, singing, speaking, mime and play. Children reflect on their representations in order to clarify meaning and begin to recognise that their actions and representations can communicate meaning to their social group. Over time, developing concepts can be revisited in different media, allowing children to re-examine their thinking in order to gain multiple perspectives.

Reggio pedagogues do not advocate the use of a predetermined curriculum that would undervalue their construction of the child; instead, organic projects are used as a vehicle for learning. The Italian term *progettazione* is used to describe the complex interaction between the projects in which children are engaged, the ongoing processes of planning and the process of documenting the learning process. Teachers often work with small groups of children interested in similar problems whilst other children undertake self-selected activities. These projects do not have pre-determined linear outcomes; rather they are compared to 'a journey, where one finds the way using a compass' (Rinaldi 1998: 119). Value is placed on obtaining a group understanding through constant dialogue, with emphasis on constructing and reconstructing ideas. Diverse, conflicting and different viewpoints are seen as a driving force for learning as children (and adults) are forced to reconsider their own developing interpretations and perspectives.

The multifaceted process of documentation attempts to interpret this voyage of learning (Forman and Fyfe 1998), so making that learning visible. Through group analyses of dialogue, observations and annotated representations there is an attempt to formulate a theory of the child's (or group of children's) theoretical perspective (Forman 2000). This acts not only as a way of understanding and evaluating the thinking of the children but also as a pedagogical tool. In addition, as teachers acting as researchers discuss and justify their own interpretations it can be viewed as a tool for professional development. Documentation can also be seen as a democratic process – a *shared* testimony of the learning journey.

Research aims and methods

Reggio practices are embedded, and continue to develop, within a particular social and cultural context. They have been influenced by an engagement with particular philosophies and theories. As Reggio pedagogues and other commentators (e.g. Abbott and Nutbrown 2001) have pointed out, they cannot be transported wholesale into other cultural settings. This being the case, the aim of our project was to support teachers in using Reggio as a catalyst or mirror in order to gain a greater understanding of their *own* professional practice within the Welsh context. At the same time, recognising the challenges that may be posed by the introduction of the Foundation Phase framework, we were particularly interested in supporting teachers' explorations of child-led learning.

Head teachers in two local authorities (the project funders) were invited to nominate teachers who were interested in becoming involved in this research. The participants – seven teachers working in five schools (four primary schools and one infant school) – were selected by the Early Years Advisers on the basis of their enthusiasm for finding out more about the Reggio Emilia philosophy. Two of the teachers were working in nursery classes (with children aged 3–4 years), two in reception classes (with children aged 4–5 years) and three in year one classes (with children aged 5–6 years). The teachers' professional experience ranged from four to 28 years. None of the schools was involved in the piloting of the Foundation Phase.

Underlying this project, which ran for nine months, was a commitment to socio-cultural approaches: teachers were seen as partners in the research process and we emphasised discussion and collaborative meaning-making. Overall, the project adopted a loosely conceived action research approach: initially the research team identified an aspect of Reggio approach ('projects') that would form the basis of their explorations in schools. The teachers chose how (and how far) this approach would be implemented in their different settings and having tried out a particular strategy, evaluated this and refined and developed their understanding and action.

Initial interviews and one-hour (video-recorded) observations of teachers working with children on 'projects' were undertaken in order to establish a 'baseline' for comparing any changes in the teachers' thinking about Reggio philosophy and in their personal theories. During the course of the project, two further observations and interviews aimed to investigate any shifts in teachers' understanding of the Reggio philosophy and to pinpoint any critical incidents that had occurred which had led to a change in either practice or perception.

The teachers also attended a series of seminars held at the university. These took the form of an initial presentation followed by discussion in which the research team co-constructed key elements of the Reggio philosophy. In order to support their reflective practice, teachers were asked to undertake a number of tasks (such as audio-taping their interactions with children) and to keep a journal. At the end of the project, teachers shared with others *their* story of engagement with Reggio Emilia within their schools. Presentations formed the basis of a report in which teachers reflected on their learning and commented on the uses of Reggio Emilia within the Welsh context.

The interviews and seminars were audio-recorded (approximately 70 hours); these were then transcribed and analysed with codes used to identify themes and to structure, interact with and think about the data (Coffey and Atkinson 1996). In addition, we devised a framework to support the analysis of observed activities. This enabled us to consider and compare specific aspects of observed activity including: whether outcomes were specified by the teacher and, if so, what these were focused on (for example, the learning of phonics or the development of social skills); whether the activity was teacher- or child-initiated and teacher- or child-led; and whether adult–child interactions were essentially 'open' (where children's ideas were encouraged and explored) or 'closed' (where children were rewarded for the right answer). Field notes were made throughout the research period of observations, seminars and internet and telephone communication. These and the documentary evidence collected were analysed and used to build and explore the emergent themes.

Findings

The findings are presented in relation to four of the key themes discussed during the seminars: the image of the child, projects, the role of the teacher and documentation.

Image of the child

In one of the early seminars we discussed what might be meant by the 'strong' child. Some teachers interpreted the word 'strong' in a negative way – as in headstrong – or in relation to academic work – as a high achiever in literacy or numeracy. Others maintained that the strong child was, for example, 'one with self worth, self-belief and not afraid to challenge'. In all cases, strength was a construct applied to particular individuals rather than to all children.

In later seminars the teachers reported that when involved in 'projects', many children whom they had perceived to be 'high achievers' floundered: they found it difficult to make decisions and to frame, analyse and devise solutions for the more complex, conceptual problems they were encountering. The teachers maintained that these children were often concerned when there was no apparent right answer and sought constant reassurance. At the same time, several children whom the teachers maintained had previously been 'invisible' demonstrated a willingness and capacity to engage with projects: they were seen to invent, take risks, collaborate and persevere in finding solutions to the problems they encountered. This led the teachers to question the appropriateness of their own understandings of ability as well as more general views of intelligence. They asked, for example, 'Why is intelligence framed in terms of academic attainment?' and 'Are there other dispositions, attributes and skills that are even more important to consider?'. As one teacher noted:

> Children who I initially thought of as low ability, fidgety boys I now feel have fantastic problem solving skills … this approach has made me question what I thought was a bright child and has turned on its head how I rate the children in my class.

Projects

The teachers decided to allocate a certain time during most days for exploring child-led learning through Reggio-inspired projects. Initially, these projects tended to be framed as 'topics' – teacher-initiated and teacher-led themes which incorporated a range of linked activities focused on meeting predetermined outcomes. Indeed, the idea of projects emerging from children's ideas and interests appeared to be challenging for teachers. The teachers maintained that it was not possible to allow time for children's ideas to clarify and develop (and for them to engage with these) given the time frame within which we were working and the pressures of meeting externally imposed targets. As a result, when identifying the focus of projects, most teachers made use of their pre-planned theme (e.g. 'minibeasts', 'growing' and 'water').

Projects all started with an initial stimulus activity. Most teachers used this opportunity to ask children what they wanted to *know*, with subsequent activities focused on finding out knowledge/factual information (e.g. 'What does this creature like to eat?'). As one teacher later commented: 'I felt we were not exploring or confronting their [the children's] thoughts but asking questions to determine what they didn't know …'. One teacher explored what children wanted *to do*: here the focus was more on practical activity; another asked children about problems they would like to solve. The teachers also acknowledged that, 'in case the children didn't come up with anything' they had already considered how the project might develop and had devised appropriate activities.

During the study the teachers' initial attempts at projects stalled: they felt there was 'nowhere else to go'. One teacher later commented that this may have been because their projects were 'linear and content-focused'. Another maintained that she recognised that while she was trying to allow children some autonomy, she was 'still delivering the content in the background'. As a consequence, most of the teachers decided (in one teacher's words) to 'step back, relax and let the children take the lead', re-launching their projects but this time allowing the children to determine the direction in which these would go and not expecting all children to be involved in all project activity. For some teachers, this acted as an important catalyst in allowing them to see the child as a competent learner. For example, a year one teacher wrote in her reflective journal:

> Wow! Talked to my class about the project. They have so many brilliant ideas and questions they want to answer – I am so enthused by their responses and attitude ... They have come up with starting points that I would not have dreamt of ...

It was noted that this teacher was particularly enthusiastic about encouraging child-led learning and seemed very comfortable 'to let go of the control'. However, she later maintained that it was 'so easy to slip back into thinking about children's activities in terms of targets and outcomes'. She described, as an example, an activity in which she took the children to the beach in order to make sand sculptures using shells, seaweed and stone. She spoke of her increasing frustration with one boy who appeared uninterested in this activity and instead was intent on digging a hole in the sand. Realising that other children were becoming distracted by this, she eventually decided to ask him what he was doing. The boy explained that he had found water in the hole and wanted to find out where it had come from. He was asking questions such as 'What would happen to this water if he dug deeper?' and 'Would sea creatures swim into his hole?' The teacher commented that this incident had made her realise that she had been focusing so closely on meeting her target that she had not been 'listening' to the boy. As a result, she commented, she had missed an important opportunity to support his learning.

Towards the end of our study this teacher became increasingly anxious about the slow-moving nature of projects and was concerned that the children were 'not acquiring sufficient subject knowledge'. As a result, like others, she felt the necessity to supplement project work with the direct teaching of factual knowledge. The teacher maintained, however, that the responses of children to this teaching (of the water cycle) were 'better than ... in previous years'. She concluded that children had benefited in terms of attainment, attitude and enjoyment from having time to explore their own ideas before moving on to 'reality': teacher-led activity focused on the acquisition of factual subject knowledge and basic skills.

Role of the teacher

While the teachers quickly adopted the Reggio discourse, our analysis of observed activities and data collected from recordings of seminars revealed that, while warm and encouraging in their interactions with children, in the early stages of the project most teachers tended to be directive and employ closed questioning. In addition, the teachers found it challenging to support children in following their own interests and exploring their own theories when these were deemed to be 'inaccurate'. Teachers felt that it was not appropriate to allow children to continue with misconceptions ('they need to be told the "right" answer') or to develop themes outside the bounds of what was acceptable within a particular subject discipline (such as when working with the topic of minibeasts, making fans for insects). At the same time, teachers were concerned that it would not be in the 'spirit of Reggio' to correct them. One teacher commented in her final report that there had been a great deal of discussion in her setting about 'when to tell children the correct information'.

Over time there were apparent shifts in the classroom practice of some of the teachers. For example, classroom observations revealed that while activities tended to remain teacher-initiated, some teachers were allowing children input into the direction in which these activities developed and had also begun to make more use of open questions. One teacher reflected on her recognition of significant changes to the way in which she worked when supporting children in their projects; in relation to planning and the desire to meet prescribed outcomes she was much more 'laid back', while in relation to listening to and interacting with children she was 'much more active'.

Documentation

Given the time constraints it was not possible to explore documentation in detail and thus it was not extensively developed by the teachers. In the early stages of the project we noted that documentation was often interpreted as 'display', this being used to celebrate the products of activities and as a form of accountability – for example, to parents, other teachers, the head teacher and the inspectorate. The notion of documentation as a dynamic representation of children's thinking with which adults and children maintained an ongoing dialogue was therefore extremely challenging.

As the project progressed, the idea of using display boards to record the development of the project and children's ideas regarding their explorations was taken on by many teachers. It was unclear, however, whether teachers, either individually or collaboratively, used documentation as a tool for analysis and the development (co-construction) of understandings. However, most of the teachers acknowledged the potential of documentation. One teacher, for example, noted that annotating one piece of graphic representation had given her 'a far greater understanding of the ideas and understanding of the child than the rest of the year's work put together'. This process, she noted, had made her focus on what the child could do rather than on what the child could not do. Another teacher pointed out that documentation was not something that teachers could undertake without the involvement of the child: 'the drawings or notes made by children can be misleading or misunderstood by adults unless they are discussed together'.

Discussion

Looking through a different lens

One of the key aims of this study was to support the development of teachers' under-standings about their own thinking and practice. An engagement with Reggio philoso-phy was experienced cognitively, physically and affectively by teachers, and seemed, at different times, to inspire, confuse, concern and irritate them. Looking 'through a different lens' did appear to help 'make the tacit explicit' (Schön 1983). However, this was not always comfortable for teachers who increasingly recognised the conflict and contradictions between what they did, what they thought they did and what they wanted to achieve.

While the fracture between practitioners' intentions and their actions is unsurpris-ing given the complexity, immediacy and unpredictability of professional practice (Schön 1983) the teachers appeared to be referring to deeper and more significant rifts. For example, while in the seminars they maintained their commitment to tradi-tional 'child-centred' values, many teachers became aware that the activities they devised and the pedagogical approaches they implemented were not consistent with these values. Indeed, in the classroom observations and in the conversations with children that were taped and analysed by teachers, it was noted that although they maintained they were becoming more 'child-centred' in their approach, their interac-tions, while warmer and more encouraging, essentially remained closed. Similarly, while the teachers maintained that they allowed children some 'autonomy' in their learning, it appeared that autonomy was interpreted as choice between several – normally content-focused – planned activities. This being the case, the teachers recog-nised that their practice and the way in which they thought about classroom events was through a lens of 'targets and outcomes'. To a greater or lesser extent, this was the case for all teachers regardless of the age phase in which they were work-ing, or their initial teacher 'training', or the length and nature of their professional experience.

Subject-centred teachers

The dominance of an instrumental and subject-centred discourse was particularly noticeable in the teachers' early interpretations of Reggio philosophy – for example, in their construction of the child (generally as weak and overwhelmingly in relation to academic attainment), in their framing of 'projects' as 'topic work' and of 'docu-mentation' as 'display'. In this respect, and from a constructivist perspective, teachers were interpreting information in relation to what was known (von Glasersfeld 1995); like the practitioners in Edwards's (2006) study, they were 'reading' socio-cultural theory through the lens of their existing understandings.

The embeddedness of this discourse was particularly visible in the way the teachers thought about – and talked about – subject knowledge. First, most teachers indicated that their normal practice predominantly focused on the teaching of factual knowledge and basic skills rather than, for example, concepts and processes. Second, most teachers acknowledged that they were uncomfortable about supporting the development of children's ideas and theories when these were seen as being inaccurate or when activities crossed and blurred recognised subject boundaries. Third, it was noted that even though teachers referred to, and valued, the positive impact that child-led learning appeared to have on the children's attitudes towards learning and their social and communication skills, they still felt the need to continue with or return to their normal outcomes-led activities. Thus, a particular version of subject-centred teaching appeared to have become deeply inscribed in the teachers' thinking and practice. Indeed, as those critiques of 1970s and 1980s child-centred ideology had hoped, it had arguably become part of the teachers' professional identity: the teachers essentially saw their expertise as founded on the teaching of factual knowledge and basic skills and evaluated their own success as a teacher in relation to how effectively they achieved this goal.

It was unsurprising, then, that child-led learning was perceived to be demanding in a number of ways: first, the teachers recognised that it was, for example, easier to tell children what they need to know than set up an experience that extended or confronted their thinking. Second, child-led learning required teachers to loosen their control; given the requirement to meet prescribed targets and outcomes this may have been too great a risk to take. Third, supporting child-led learning appeared to involve the development of complex cognitive processes and skills. These included:

- *reconstructing*: seeing the child as (believing the child to be) a competent person and learner;
- *'listening'*: engaging in concentrated, focused observations of children in different situations and social encounters;
- *letting go*: relinquishing the construction of 'teacher as expert' in favour of 'teacher as partner in a learning process'; and relinquishing tight control over what and how children learn;
- *refocusing*: shifting their attention away from targets, content and outcomes and on to individual children's ideas, interests and their learning;
- *framing*: holding and giving form to the children's streams of thoughts and ideas – to make these visible, so that in terms of future learning possibilities they may be rejected, built on or further explored;
- *restraining*: controlling the desire always to 'tell' children and knowing how and when to set up situations and make use of questions and experiences which aim to extend, consolidate or confront children's ideas;
- *searching*: recognising that there is more than one pathway to understanding and helping the child to explore these pathways.

In our view this requires considerable time as well as courage, commitment and support.

Conclusion

In this research the approach adopted in the pre-schools of Reggio Emilia was not seen as a model of good early years practice but as a means of making visible teachers' thinking and practice and, in the light of the proposed Foundation Phase for Wales, as a catalyst for exploring child-led learning. Looking at their practice 'through another lens' enabled the teachers to gain a greater insight into their implicit and explicit theories of learning and, as a result, exposed their commitment to, and the pervasiveness and embeddedness of, an approach dominated by prescribed and subject-related outcomes (see also Maynard and Waters 2007). Moving away from this approach and supporting child-led learning thus proved to be complex and challenging.

The roll-out of the Foundation Phase Framework began in September 2008; from September 2009 it included all children in reception classes. Given that the Framework (WAG 2008) retains learning outcomes that are cross-referenced to the current National Curriculum level descriptors, it may be – as in the 1970s and 1980s – that some teachers adopt a 'child-centred' discourse, integrate areas of learning into planned topics and continue to teach the basic skills.

References

Abbott, L., and C. Nutbrown. 2001. *Experiencing Reggio Emilia: Implications for pre-school provision*. Buckingham: Open University Press.

Alexander, R., J. Rose, and C. Woodhead. 1992. *Curriculum organisation and classroom practice in primary schools: A discussion paper*. London: HMSO.

Alexander, R.J. 1984. *Primary teaching*. London: Cassell.

Awdurdod Cymwysterau, Cwricwlwm ac Asesu Cymru – Qualifications, Curriculum and Assessment Authority for Wales (ACCAC). 2004. *The Foundation Phase in Wales: A draft framework for children's learning*. Cardiff: ACCAC.

Barton, L. 2002. Better late. *Guardian*, 9 July.

Bennett, S.N., C. Dosfbrges, A. Cockburn, and B. Wilkinson. 1984. *The quality of pupil learning experiences*. London: Lawrence Erlbaum.

Central Advisory Council for Education (CACE). 1967. *Children and their primary schools (Plowden Report)*. London: HMSO.

Chung, S., and D.J. Walsh. 2000. Unpacking child-centredness: A history of meanings. *Journal of Curriculum Studies* 32, no. 2: 315–34.

Coffey, A., and P. Atkinson. 1996. *Making sense of qualitative data*. London: Sage Publications.

Edwards, S. 2006. 'Stop thinking of culture as geography': Early childhood educators' conceptions of sociocultural theory as an informant to curriculum. *Contemporary Issues in Early Childhood* 7, no. 3: 238–52.

Forman, G. 2000. Helping children to ask good questions. Paper presented at ELC Group of Schools, Bangkok, Thailand.

Forman, G., and B. Fyfe. 1998. Negotiated learning through design, documentation, and discourse. In *The hundred languages of children. The Reggio Emilia Approach – advanced reflections*, ed. C. Edwards, L. Gandini, and G. Forman. 2nd ed. Greenwich, CT: Ablex.

Galton, M., B. Simon, and P. Croll. 1980. *Inside the primary classroom*. London: Routedge & Kegan Paul.

Gandini, L. 1993. Fundamentals of the Reggio Emilia approach to early childhood education. *Young Children* November: 4–8.

Kwon, Y. 2002. Changing curriculum for early childhood education in England. *Early Childhood Research and Practice* 4, no. 2. http://ecrp.uiuc.edu/v4n2/kwon.html

Malaguzzi, L. 1993. For an education based on relationships. *Young Children* November: 9–13.

Maynard, T., and J. Waters, 2007. Learning in the outdoor environment: A missed opportunity. *Early Years*, 27, no. 3: 255–65.

Moss, P. 2006. Schools as spaces for political and ethical practice. In *Crossing boundaries: Ideas and experiences in dialogue for a new culture of education of children and adults*, Proceedings of the International Conference, Reggio Emilia, Italy, February 2004, 107–12. San Paolo, Italy: Editzioni Junior S.R.L.

Rinaldi, C. 1998. Projected curriculum constructed through documentation – progettazione: An interview with Lella Gandini. In *The hundred languages of children: The Reggio Emilia Approach – advanced reflections*, ed. C. Edwards, L. Gandini, and G. Forman. 2nd ed., 113–25. Greenwich, CT: Ablex.

Schön, D. 1983. *The reflective practitioner: How professionals think in action*. New York: Basic Books.

Soler, J., and L. Miller, 2003. The struggle for early childhood curricula: A comparison of the English Foundation Stage Curriculum, *Te Whāriki* and Reggio Emilia. *International Journal of Early Years Education*, 11, no. 1: 57–67.

Von Glasersfeld, E. 1995. *Radical constructivism: A way of knowing and learning*. Washington, DC: Falmer Press.

Welsh Assembly Government. 2003. *The learning country: Foundation Phase 3–7 years*. Cardiff: National Assembly for Wales.

Welsh Assembly Government. 2008. *Framework for Children's Learning for 3- to 7-year-olds in Wales*. Cardiff: WAG.

18

Pedagogy: a holistic, personal approach to work with children and young people, across services

Pat Petrie, Janet Boddy, Claire Cameron, Ellen Heptinstall, Susan McQuail, Antonia Simon and Valerie Wigfall

Overview

This chapter focuses on research carried out at the Thomas Coram Research Unit (TCRU) which included cross-national studies on service provision and its quality, the daily practice of staff, their training, education, qualifications, recruitment and retention in the workforce. A central interest has been what, in continental Europe, is often called 'social pedagogy' as a distinctive way of working with children and the basis for policy development.

[...]

Petrie, P., Boddy, J., Cameron, C., Heptinstall, E., McQuail, S. and Wigfall, V. (2009) *Pedagogy – A Holistic, Personal Approach to Work with Children and Young People, Across Services*, Institute of Education, University of London, Thomas Coram Research Unit, pp. 1–13.

Why consider social pedagogy?

Until the end of the last century, in England local and national policy was mostly based on clear boundaries between the fields of education, childcare and social care. These divisions were apparent at many levels: conceptual, professional, organisational, and in relation to training and education. However, over the last decade there has been an administrative reorganisation of responsibility for children's services and a shift in how we envisage provision for children and young people. The following are all of relevance for the subject of social pedagogy.

- Responsibility for childcare (for working parents) and social care (for children in need, including those in need of protection) moved from the Department of Health to what [was] the Department for Children, Schools and Families, with:

  o responsibility for early years education and childcare, out-of-school care, child protection and schooling;
  o a Children's Workforce Unit and a School's Workforce Unit;
  o structural links to other government departments.

- Integrated structures such as Children's Trusts, and local authority Children's Departments, and comprehensive provision – Children's Centres and extended services delivered through schools – have been introduced.
- Parenting and family support has a central role, across government departments. For example, *Every Child Matters* (DfES, 2003) and *The Children's Plan* (DCSF, 2008), have emphasised what is called progressive universalism: 'support for all, with more support for those who need it most' (Balls, 2007). Within this conceptual approach, there is a need for child welfare, childcare, parenting and family support, education and health services to work more closely together. The approach also requires the different occupations involved to be more interconnected, with a core training for workers across the children and young people's sector.

Also relevant, although less recent, since the 1989 Children Act and with the UK becoming a signatory to the United Nations Convention on the Rights of the Child, there is an increasing emphasis on listening to children and there has been the appointment of a Children's Commissioner.

This is a time when the borders and relations between different types of services are changing, workforce issues are to the fore, and there is a desire to find new approaches. Not least, children are being seen as persons in their own right, rather than as 'problems' to be managed. With these changing directions comes the opportunity to seek fresh options and to identify the best possibilities for realising government's intentions. One model for work in the children's sector is that of pedagogy, with workers, whatever their job titles, seen primarily as pedagogues.

What does the term pedagogy include in continental Europe?

In England, we do not often use the term 'pedagogy' except in the context of the classroom and formal education. Our European neighbours often apply it to a much broader set of services, covering, for example, childcare and early years, youth work, parenting and family support services, secure units for young offenders, residential care and play work. A consideration of pedagogic policy and practice in continental Europe could help to clarify the challenges and opportunities inherent in the developing English context.

As used in continental Europe, the word 'pedagogy' can relate to the overall support of children's development. In pedagogy, care and education meet. To put it another way, pedagogy is about bringing up children, it is 'education' in the broadest sense of that word. Indeed, in French and other languages with a Latin base (such as Italian and Spanish) terms like *l'éducation* convey this broader sense, and are interchangeable with expanded notions of pedagogy as used in Germanic and Nordic countries.

Parents are sometimes referred to as the first pedagogues, but pedagogy is also a foundational concept that informs many sorts of services, providing a distinctive approach to practice, training and policy. In continental Europe, the use of the terms such as *l'éducation* and *Pädagoge* and *Sozialpädagogik* imply work with the *whole* child: body, mind, feelings, spirit and creativity. Crucially, the child is seen as a social being, connected to others and at the same time with their own distinctive experiences and knowledge.

> In Sweden, the employment of pedagogues in schools has been central to educational reforms. Educational policy addresses the whole child, rather than the child conceived in narrow cognitive terms. Around one third of school heads have a background in pedagogy, rather than teaching. (Cohen et al., 2004)

The terms pedagogy and social pedagogy

Social pedagogy is sometimes used to mean pedagogy conducted on behalf of society, rather than the more private pedagogy performed by parents. But the term can also denote work with more vulnerable groups in society. Different countries have different emphases and use slightly different terms.

In the countries included in our studies of residential care in different European countries, an organic pedagogic system was identified (e.g. Petrie, 2001, 2002;

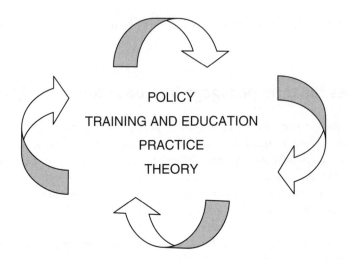

POLICY

TRAINING AND EDUCATION

PRACTICE

THEORY

Figure 18.1   Social pedagogy policy, practice, theory and workforce development form a system

Petrie et al., 2006). The system's components consist of policy and practice, theory and research, and the training and education of the workforce, with each component feeding into, and drawing from, the others.

TCRU research identified the following key principles of pedagogic practice:

- A focus on the child as a whole person, and support for the child's overall development.
- The practitioner seeing herself/himself as a person, in relationship with the child or young person.
- While they are together, children and staff are seen as inhabiting the same life space, not as existing in separate, hierarchical domains.
- As professionals, pedagogues are encouraged to constantly reflect on their practice and to apply both theoretical understandings and self-knowledge to their work and to the sometimes challenging demands with which they are confronted.
- Pedagogues should be both practical and creative; their training prepares them to share in many aspects of children's daily lives, such as preparing meals and snacks, or making music and building kites.
- In group settings, children's associative life is seen as an important resource: workers should foster and make use of the group.
- Pedagogy builds on an understanding of children's rights that is not limited to procedural matters or legislative requirements.
- There is an emphasis on teamwork and valuing the contributions of others – family members, other professionals and members of the local community – in the task of 'bringing up' children.

> Pedagogic theory is specially about relationships, child rearing relationships. (Dutch academic, quoted in Petrie et al., 2006: 23)

The work of the pedagogue is essentially personal. The students and staff, interviewed for recent TCRU research on the applicability of social pedagogy to work with looked-after children, often spoke of the work of the pedagogue in terms of the human person: head, hands and heart – all three being essential for the work of pedagogy. The personal, relational approach is emphasised in students' training and education, where fostering sound pedagogic values and attitudes is seen as at least as important as the acquisition of knowledge and skills.

> When you are holding a person in your hand, you are holding a bit of his life in your hand. (Principal, Danish training college, quoted in Petrie et al., 2006: 2)

Pedagogic principles derive from a highly developed professional training and education, and relate to social policy that is conceived in terms of pedagogy; for example, pedagogic principles can be brought to bear in cases where children are also a concern for youth justice systems.

Education, training and qualification

Some of those working directly with children have undertaken pedagogic studies in the last years of secondary school or colleges or in further education. In our research, these courses were not seen as a sufficient qualification for work with children and young people. Many who have taken them go on to degrees in pedagogy, after working in the field.

Would-be pedagogues usually prepare for pedagogic work in universities and colleges, where first degrees take around three or four years. Courses involve the following:

- As an aid to becoming reflective practitioners, students take a range of theoretical subjects in the behavioural and social sciences, including, importantly, group processes.
- Students are introduced to the skills needed for their work such as group work, working with conflict and challenging behaviour, and teamwork (which is much emphasised).
- Students take courses in creative and practical subjects, such as art, drama, woodwork, music or gardening – interests and skills that they will bring to their work as media through which they can relate to children. Arts and practical subjects are also valued for their general therapeutic effect: they can help children to enjoy life and feel good about themselves.
- There are often optional study modules and practice placements for specific settings, such as work with disabled children or in residential care.
- In some countries pedagogic courses offer specialist options, and qualification, for work with adults (for example, in mental health settings).

> It is a job where every day you must ask questions about yourself and your practice right to the end of your professional life. (French pedagogue working in a residential home, quoted in Petrie et al., 2006: 28)

In Germany, the Netherlands and Flanders, some students take an initial five-year course in pedagogic theory, which includes placements in various agencies and services, resulting in the equivalent of an English Masters degree. This prepares students for further academic work, for research and development posts in government and voluntary organisations, for management jobs, and consultancy and advisory positions in a range of provision. But some of those qualified in this way choose to work directly with children.

Once in employment, people with a background in pedagogy/social pedagogy can have a variety of job titles relating to the work they undertake. Since 1992, Danish pedagogues training for work in, for example, nurseries, out-of-school services, adult services, and children's residential homes have a common training, with optional specialisms. In other countries there may be a more differentiated initial training and work roles. [W]hatever the setting, educational, health, youth services, social services or nurseries, pedagogues usually work alongside other professionals and share the general aims of the establishment, but they bring their own distinctive principles, understandings and skills to bear.

What could adopting a pedagogic approach offer for England?

The possible benefits of taking a pedagogic approach cross the realms of policy development, training and workforce issues This is acknowledged in recent government statements, and the commitment to explore effectiveness of social pedagogy in residential care in England (DfES, 2007):

> Pedagogues are generalists. Their uniquely broad training with its theoretical, personal and practical content ideally fits them for outcome-focused work with children, including those with significant developmental need. (DfES, 2005)

> A new framework of skills and qualifications incorporating the principles of social pedagogy … would offer a competency based approach available to all foster carers and staff and managers in residential homes. (DfES, 2006)

Also, in its move to establish a framework for professional development, the government is exploring how social pedagogy could be applied and promises more detail in the Children's Workforce Action Plan (DCSF, 2008). A pilot project, by which social pedagogues are being employed in English children's residential care homes, is currently being implemented at TCRU.

1. What has social pedagogy to offer social policy?

    a. Pedagogy is an overarching concept that could bring greater coherence to children's services, as expressed in, for example, *Every Child Matters* and *The Children's Plan*.

b. Pedagogy could also provide a framework for discussing aims for children and young people in society as a whole. Social pedagogy also has potential for developing the family support network, for example in relation to Parent Support Advisers in school.

c. Many recent service developments sit well in a pedagogic framework. Schools delivering extended services and Children's Centres are pedagogic provision in that they aim to support children's overall development. Both are sites in which pedagogues could bring their own expertise and values to bear, alongside the work of other professionals, such as nurses and teachers.

2. What has social pedagogy to offer training, education and the children's workforce?

a. Pedagogy degrees and careers are highly popular in the European countries studied, even though pedagogues are not especially well paid. Establishing pedagogy courses in this country could produce a well-equipped, flexible and stable workforce.

b. The breadth of pedagogic training qualifies staff for direct work with children and young people across a wide range of childcare, educational and welfare services. Whether in established or developing services, the key pedagogic principles would hold true, with workers sharing common values, theoretic understandings, skills and practice principles.

c. As well as their broader training, pedagogues can take specialist options such as those which would further many government objectives, for example for a professional workforce, trained in the skills and understandings required for residential settings. Pedagogical approaches may also have something to offer in the training and support of foster parents.

d. Positioning work in the children's sector as pedagogy can provide a framework for rationalising existing qualifications and allowing for career development within the sector.

e. European Community legislation allows the freedom to work throughout EC member states. Adopting a pedagogic approach would allow for a greater harmonisation of professional training and practice with that of other European countries.

3. What has pedagogy to offer children and parents?

The TCRU research found that pedagogy, as practised in the countries studied, had the potential to serve several aspects of government policy towards children and parents.

a. Pedagogy has the potential for an inclusive approach. The main focus of pedagogy is on children as children, but allowing for some children, at some times, to have additional needs. This normalising approach fits well with government's aims for looked-after children and for disabled children and other children with special needs (see, for example, the amended Disability Discrimination Act 1995).

b. While child protection issues are treated with all due seriousness, pedagogic approaches tend to be child-focused, rather than procedure-focused. Attention to appropriate procedures is a necessary part of the work, but not its basis. The professionalism of the worker, transparency of practice, a commitment to team-work and accountability to others in the team, are seen as the best guarantee of child safety.

c. Pedagogues think in terms both of the individual child *and* of the group of children or young people. This allows for richer, more productive work with children, whether in play schemes, the nursery or a residential home.

d. Because they are trained in creative activities, pedagogues are in a position to offer children activities that enhance children's self-esteem and may be thera-peutic, in the widest sense of that word.

e. Above all, pedagogy aims to take a holistic view of children and respects them as fellow human beings, each with a unique point of view and a distinctive con-tribution to make to whatever task is in hand. This stance can support policy that requires the voice of the child to be heard and for children and young people to play their part in, for example, devising care plans.

f. Working with parents has an established place in government policy across the spectrum of a progressive universalist approach to family policy. Pedagogy is the predominant qualification for direct work with parents and families in many other European countries. Pedagogues are trained to consider parents as partners, with whom they can enter a dialogue about the development and well-being of indi-vidual children, as well as providing advice and counselling on parenting.

Social pedagogy provides a framework for discussing the place of children and young people in society, addressing basic questions:

- What do we want for our children, including those who are currently at social disadvantage?
- What is a good childhood?
- How do we support child well-being, and well-becoming?
- What relationship would we wish to promote between children and children, and children and adults?

These are questions that relate to pedagogic aims and values, and should underlie the objectives of the different professionals who are involved with children. Addressing such questions should also underlie policy and practice throughout children's ser-vices, including schools, and should inform their administration.

Problems regarding pedagogy

1. Is pedagogy in competition with social work and other professions?

The greatest difference between social work and social pedagogy is the extent to which social pedagogues are especially trained for work in group settings, where they share the daily lives and activities of children and young people (or indeed adults). This is less true for social work in England. In other European countries, social work and social pedagogy do not appear to be in competition, they have different, complementary, spheres of work (Boddy et al., 2008).

A TCRU survey across training settings in England revealed wide interest in European models of training, and some centres already had exchanges with pedagogic training establishments in Europe (Petrie et al., 2003). There would also be the need to develop specialist training as optional or post-qualifying courses, in addition to general or 'core' training. The development of such courses is under way. For example, at the Institute of Education, University of London, a framework of social pedagogy qualification is being put in place. A foundation degree, Working with Children, received its first students in 2008, to be followed by a Masters degree in social pedagogy, from October 2009.

2. Without publicly funded training opportunities of the duration and comprehensiveness of those to be found in Europe, a profession comparable to that of the pedagogue cannot be developed.

Government policy is to increase the number of graduates, generally, and to make good staff shortages in childcare, early education and social care. These are settings that need the stimulation of new approaches. The European experience is that pedagogy degrees and careers are popular options

There has been no academic field defined as social pedagogy in English universities. However, as mentioned above, such courses are currently in development. Additionally:

- Some existing English qualifications are based on pedagogic principles: for example, the BA in Curative Education at the University of Aberdeen: degrees in Youth and Community Work such as those to be found at the University of Durham and the YMCA George Williams College in Canning Town (Canterbury Christchurch University).
- Some foundation degrees are building on pedagogic curricula.
- Camphill Schools, Steiner schools and Montessori schools build on a continental European pedagogic tradition.
- Danish pedagogy students on six-month full-time placement in English children's services were highly praised by their English supervisors. Reportedly, they accommodated well to existing modes of practice, they developed excellent relationships with children and staff, and they were creative. They were frequently allowed to undertake responsibilities beyond the normal remit of placement students. Some students were said to promote a questioning culture about practice and procedures, which was seen by staff as beneficial to institutional practice overall (Cameron, 2007).

- A UK agency, specialising in recruitment of German pedagogues, has placed over 200 qualified practitioners in local authorities and other agencies, on permanent contracts (Ladbrooke, 2007).
- Pedagogues from new member states of the EU are said to be increasingly employed in England.
- Subjects studied in European departments of pedagogy are available in universities in this country, and research is undertaken that elsewhere would be seen as contributing to pedagogic theory.

Also, existing courses are often influenced by social pedagogic ideas (for example, the Masters Degree in Residential Care at the University of Strathclyde). In addition, there are across the country first degrees in fields such as Early Childhood, Child Development, and Educational Studies that are theoretically relevant, although they do not have the practice placements, artistic or practical components, and the explicit base in pedagogic principles (see above) that are typical of pedagogy courses in Europe.

3. The term pedagogy can be mystifying for English language speakers and the *Oxford English Dictionary* allows for three ways of pronouncing it!

This is true – although using a soft *g* as in psychology may have a more English ring! An existing alternative is the term 'social education' (but this may suggest lessons in citizenship). On the other hand, the relative strangeness of the term 'pedagogy' is also one of its advantages, inviting enquiry, encouraging new thinking and suggesting new opportunities.

Pedagogy for children's services in England: possible starting points

It is impossible to achieve, not to say undesirable to attempt, the transfer of whole systems of training, qualification and practice from one country to another – and while pedagogic systems are similar they are not uniform in the countries we studied. Nevertheless, the TCRU research points to ways in which pedagogy, as a model, fits policy concerns for children, and the development of training and services, in England. Currently, while these are areas that present many problems, there is also much evidence of a political will to effect change in how society serves its children and young people. The social pedagogic approach is well fitted to further English policy concerns.

References

Balls, E. (2007) Childcare and Child Poverty – Delivering Solutions. London: Daycare Trust Conference, 13 June

Boddy, J. McQuail, S. and Statham, J. (2008) International Perspectives on Social Work: Models of Education and Professional Roles. Unpublished briefing paper for DCSF. London: Thomas Coram Research Unit, Institute of Education

Cameron, C. (2007) New Ways of Educating: Pedagogy and Children's Services, Final report to Esmee Fairbairn Foundation, London, Thomas Coram Research Unit, Institute of Education

Cohen, B., Moss, P. and Petrie, P. (2004) *A New Deal for Children – Re-forming Children's Services?* Bristol: Policy Press

Department for Children, Schools and Families (DCSF) (2008) *The Children's Plan: Building Brighter Futures.* London: DCSF

Department for Education and Skills (DfES) (2003) *Every Child Matters.* London: DfES

Department for Education and Skills (DfES) (2005) *Children's Workforce Strategy: A Strategy to Build a World-class Workforce 306 for Children and Young People.* London: DfES

Department for Education and Skills (DfES) (2006) *Care Matters: Transforming the Lives of Children and Young People in Care.* London: DfES

Department for Education and Skills (DfES) (2007) *Care Matters: Time for Change.* London: DfES

Ladbrooke, A. (2007) Children Webmag, 26 May, University of Nottingham, at www. childrenwebmag. com/content/view/369

Petrie, P. (2001) The potential of pedagogy/education for work in the children's sector in the UK, *Social Work in Europe*, Vol. 8, No. 3, pp. 23–26

Petrie, P. (2002) Social pedagogy: An historical account of care and education as social control. In J. Brannen and P. Moss (eds.) Rethinking Children's Care, Buckingham: Open University Press

Petrie, P., Boddy, J., Cameron, C., Heptinstall, E. and McQuail, S. (2003) Working with Children: Social Pedagogy and Residential Child Care in Europe. Unpublished research report for the Department of Health

Petrie, P., Boddy, J., Cameron, C., Simon, A. and Wigfall, V. (2006) *Working with Children in Residential Care: European Perspectives.* Buckingham: Open University Press

Part 4

Leadership and change

Introduction

Linda Miller

The rhetoric of early years policy in England is that workforce reform is required to develop new leaders and to bring about change (DfES, 2006). Some of the barriers to workforce reform are referred to in the introduction to Part 3 of this book, namely lack of sufficient investment by government leading to a workforce that is characterized by low pay, low status, a paucity of male workers and no national agreement about a minimum standard of pay and conditions for those working in childcare and education. However, other factors have contributed to this position. Gill McGillivray in Chapter 19 of this book, in a wider discussion of professional identity, discusses factors such as the lack of one union or professional association for both teachers and those who are not teachers, who work in early years. She remarks on the low take-up of union membership for this group. This suggests that early years workers could have a stronger and more collective voice in enabling change to happen and in developing a sense of agency. The weak position of the early years workforce is echoed across much of Europe. As the OECD (2006) report discusses, the goals of intensive and high-quality training and good working conditions have still not been achieved for many countries, but with some exceptions, as we saw in Chapter 18 of this book.

A new construction of professional identity is the focus of Chapter 19, where Gill McGillivray explores the multiple influences on the professional identity of early years workers. She sets the scene through documenting the background to workforce reform in England and considers both the theoretical and philosophical perspectives that have impacted on how this feminized workforce is shaped and viewed. She concludes that for change to take place, a 'bottom-up' perspective is needed that will enable young people to view working with young children and their families as a worthwhile career. Mary Whalley, in Chapter 20, also discusses some of the policy changes in England and charts journeys to leadership, helpfully illustrating these through two case studies. She explores the distinctive and distinguishing features of both leading and managing in an early years context. She describes and discusses two key roles in the contemporary children's workforce in England: that of leading and managing an organization and leading practice. She argues that these developments are crucial in creating and sustaining successful and effective organizations whilst recognizing the challenges such changes bring.

A number of recent policy initiatives in England have focused on the importance of having one children's workforce and the culture of integrated working. These include a National Qualifications Framework (see www.cwdcouncil.org.uk/iqf) to bring coherence to the qualifications for the children's workforce and to support the vision embedded in the Common Core of Skills and Knowledge (DfES, 2005; CWDC, 2010). A Common Assessment Framework (CAF) was conceived to encourage integration of services (DfES, 2003) to be used by practitioners across all children's services (i.e. health, education and social welfare). The importance of new and integrated ways of working through multi-disciplinary practice is highlighted by Jillian Rodd in Chapter 21. She also analyses the complex and challenging process of team development when leading and managing in an early years context in order to achieve effective and high-quality early years education.

The theme of effective leadership continues in Chapter 22, where Iram Siraj-Blatchford and Laura Manni report on aspects of a major government-funded contemporary research project, *The Effective Provision of Pre-School Education*. This report has been a significant source of evidence for the England workforce strategy in highlighting the relationship between well-qualified leaders and practitioners and high-quality provision and positive outcomes for children and families. The findings show that having trained teachers in a setting is a key indicator of quality; however, new roles in the workforce, such as those described in Chapters 19 and 20, are not taken account of in this research, although the importance of further professional development is recognized. The findings also show, unsurprisingly, that well-qualified leaders were found in the better-funded settings such as nursery schools and classes. Links can be seen here with Chapter 18, in Part 3 of this book, which shows how higher levels of training and qualifications in some countries in Europe are valued across the whole, and not just part, of the children and young people's workforce. Effective leadership practices are identified, including the importance of communication, co-operation and collaboration in relation to home/school partnerships and monitoring and assessing children. As in Chapter 21, effective leadership and appropriate training are seen as crucial factors as the workforce moves towards multi-disciplinary working.

An ethics of care is traditionally assumed to underpin early years practice. Cable and Miller (2011) argue that dominant discourses tend to play down this aspect of early years work in terms of professional behaviours, as it is seen as associated with emotions and emotional labour and therefore as behaviour that is not rational and as of lesser value as it cannot be categorized, regulated or measured. In Chapter 23, Judith Whitmarsh explains why ethics are so important in early years practice. She offers an overview of what ethics are and what they mean for early years workers. Through case studies, she explores ethical codes of practice in three different professional contexts: early years, social work and nursing. She argues for creating a reflective, non-critical space for shared ethical discussion in a multi-agency context.

References

Cable, C. and Miller, L. (2011) A new professionalism. In L. Miller and C. Cable (eds) *Professionalization, Leadership and Management in the Early Years*. London: Sage.

Children's Workforce Development Council (CWDC) (2010) *Refreshing the Common Core of Skills and Knowledge for the Children's Workforce*. Leeds: CWDC.

Department for Education and Skills (DfES (2003) *Every Child Matters: The Green Paper*. London: The Stationery Office.

Department for Education and Skills (DfES (2005) *Common Core of Skills and Knowledge for the Children's Workforce*. Nottingham: DfES.

Department for Education and Skills (DfES) (2006) *Children's Workforce Strategy: Building a World-class Workforce for Children and Young People*. Nottingham: DfES.

OECD (2006) *Starting Strong II: Early Childhood Education and Care*. Paris: OECD.

19

Constructions of professional identity

Gill McGillivray

Overview

Through this chapter, Gill McGillivray explores some of the multiplicity of influences that contribute to the construction of professional identity in the early years workforce arising from influences such as personal histories, spaces and places of work, dominant discourses related to children and families and political ideologies. She includes some theoretical and philosophical perspectives that may contribute to the construction of professional identities, such as communities of practice, self-identity and power.

[...]

Profile of the workforce

Most recent early years workforce data have been collated from surveys undertaken in 2007 by Nicholson et al. (2008). They note that data were collected separately from childcare and early years provision, and have been 'drawn together to highlight

McGillivray, G. (2011) 'Constructions of professional identity', in Miller, L. and Cable, C. (eds) *Professionalization, Leadership and Management in the Early Years*, London: Sage, pp. 93–106.

Table 19.1 Summary of key workforce data (2007)

- 1 in 3 staff in the private sector was aged under 25 years; school-based early years workforce had an older profile.
- There were 165,200 paid and unpaid staff working in full daycare provision; 123,000 paid and unpaid staff working in schools and nursery schools (but equivalent numbers were not available for those working in sessional care, after school care, informal care or holiday clubs).
- 98% of the workforce were women.
- Approximately 50% worked part-time.
- In 2007, average hourly pay for full daycare was £5.90 for staff without supervisory duties; £7.10 for equivalent staff in Children's Centres; £8.70 for equivalent staff in school-based early years provision.
- In 2008, the median take-home hourly pay for women was £10.90; minimum wage was raised in 2006 to £5.30.
- 61% of the workforce in childcare provision had a level 3* qualification.

Note: *equivalent to A' levels; a school leaving qualification at 18 years, and the level required to work without supervision. For early years, qualified staff are required to have a National Vocational Qualification (NVQ) at level 3, a BTEC National Diploma, a CACHE level 3 Diploma or equivalent.

similarities and differences across the sectors, as well as providing details of the whole childcare and early years workforce' (Nicholson et al., 2008: 1; see Table 19.1). This reinforces the continuing divide between childcare and early years provision, a point that is challenged by the Daycare Trust report (2008: 1): 'the Early Years Foundation Stage (EYFS, DfES, 2007) has expanded the role of early childhood care and education workers by merging the concepts of care and education'. However, the divide between care and education has existed for many decades, and it is likely to take more than the merging of curriculum and daycare standards within the EYFS to close the divide. Some data from the workforce survey undertaken by Nicholson et al. (2008), the most recent available, have been summarized in Table 19.1 in order to illustrate features of those who work in the early years sector.

You may wish to consider the data in Table 19.1 and reflect on the following questions: what are the apparent differences across the early years sector and what impact might they have on members of the workforce? The intention to make a level 3 qualification a requirement for all those working in early years has been stated by the government (DCSF, 2009), but for now, one in three staff require supervision because they do not have a level 3 qualification. What are the implications of this for management and leadership in early years settings? Finally, what are the implications of these data for aspiring early years workers?

Workforce reform, since the introduction of the National Childcare Strategy (DfEE, 1998), has attempted to integrate social services daycare and nursery education as well as expand access to qualifications, vertically and horizontally. Attempts to introduce vertical structures in order to create clearer progression routes for early years workers beyond level 3 qualifications was limited for the following reasons. Firstly, the title of Senior Practitioner conferred on those who achieved the Early Years Sector Endorsed Foundation Degree (a work-based degree that conferred 240 credits up to level 5 in higher education) was never established in practice or in its status, so no additional pay or associated roles and responsibilities were attached to it. Miller (2008b) explains and evaluates some of the issues related to Senior Practitioner status as part of the Foundation Degree sector endorsement by Sure Start, the government department in England that had responsibility for early years provision at that time. Also, the increasing numbers in the workforce were mostly located in the private sector where employers were unable to afford rates of pay equal to those in the statutory sector. Secondly, there was no one union or professional association for both teachers and those who were not teachers who worked in early years. Union membership for early years workers was generally low (Cohen et al., 2004), and the position of teaching unions seeks to protect early years work for those with Qualified Teacher Status (QTS) as well as excluding membership of those undertaking support or assistant work (Goff, 2008; NUT, 2006). Other unions were vocal in their advocacy for more equal pay and conditions (GMB, 2003; UNISON, 2006). Thirdly, changes in children's services were made at local, not national, level, and local authorities' reconfiguration of education, health and social care departments were dependent on local needs and resources. The devolved responsibilities for children's services from central to local government was an intentional shift in policy in an attempt to develop local services to meet local needs (DCSF, 2007). This policy however exacerbated the position of no national agreement as to what pay and conditions could be agreed as a minimum standard for those working in childcare.

Penn (2000: 104) contended that 'recruitment into childcare training in the UK is aimed at a particular group of women with low academic achievements and from mainly disadvantaged socio-economic backgrounds'. She continues, 'childcare students in training tend to see themselves as "naturals", building on their personal experiences in looking after children, and see their strength as lying in their everyday practice, rather than in the acquisition and application of knowledge about children' (Penn, 2000: 104).

Penn's argument remains compelling and is reinforced by Colley (2006); most recent data suggest that trends established decades ago are proving stubborn to shift in terms of gender and academic achievement. Cooke and Lawton (2008) reinforce Penn's proposition as to why young women choose the profession. The profile in Table 19.1 maps out a workforce where there are inequalities in pay by sector, variability in terms of a basic level of qualification, a gender imbalance and an age imbalance by sector. Such trends, traditions, expectations and perceptions have existed for decades. An interrogation of texts that relate to the early years workforce spanning the 1970s to the first decade of the millennium (McGillivray, 2008) reveals that the gender stereotypes of 'kind' and 'loving' were attached to those working with young children as recently as 1984. The historical trajectory of the early years workforce has been shaped by events such as the Second World War and the need for women to work and therefore have access to childcare (Bertram and Pascal, 2001). I would argue that the influence of changing societal and psychological expectations of the role of women, particularly those who work, since the 1960s (Crompton, 1997) and by the ideologies and policies of the governing political party (Baldock et al., 2009) perpetuate the stereotype of what it means to be an early years worker and thus the professional identities of the workforce.

I will now consider some ideas as to how such a varied and inequitable profile contributes to professional identities within the early years workforce with a focus on recent policy that sets out the vision for reform.

Workforce reform

When Labour became the party of government in 1997, the publication of the National Childcare Strategy (DfEE, 1998) laid out strategies for local authorities for early years provision. The government began to compile information on the activity, scope and scale of the early years landscape as it had not previously been available in any substantive form. During the intervening years, the rationalization of qualifications has been one part of workforce reform (see Baldock et al., 2009; Sauve Bell, 2004). The policy documents that set out children's workforce reform (DCSF, 2007; DfES, 2005, 2006; HM Treasury, 2004) state the intention for graduates to lead early years provision in all settings with children from birth to 5 by 2015 (in Children's Centres by 2010) as another aspect of reform. A consultation of the proposals for the early years workforce reform took place between February and July 2005 (DfES, 2005) and the government's response (DfES, 2006) claims support for the vision.

The benchmark of a level 3 qualification for a member of staff working in early years to be accepted as 'qualified' is a current goal for the government (DCSF, 2009) and along with the graduate Early Years Professional Status (EYP) (see Miller, 2008a; Miller and Cable; 2008; Nurse, 2007) suggest that changes will need to be made in schools, further education colleges and higher education institutions to accommodate new qualifications. However, Dent and Whitehead (2002: 4) caution that 'Despite the allure of professional status, the pressures driving this new identity formation are clearly not entirely benign', and, in the context of early years, becoming a professionalized workforce brings with it 'macro-systems' that promote standardization and measures of accountability such as the processes of assessment, inspection and regulation of the workforce. The creation of an Integrated Qualifications Framework (IQF) and the Functional Map (CWDC, 2009) are, at the time of writing, intended to rationalize qualification requirements and progression (the IQF), and define shared responsibilities across the children's workforce (the Functional Map). These developments further illustrate the ways in which government generally, but the Children's Workforce Development Council (CWDC) specifically, is continuing to invest in systems and measures that provide a structural overlay across relevant workforces. These initiatives may perpetuate a level of 'passive resistance' and disillusionment if members of the early years workforce do not feel connected to, consulted on or informed of such changes, or feel that the issues of pay and status are not taken seriously (Carey et al., 2009; CYPN, 2009; Murray, 2009). The post-structuralist ideas of Foucault are helpful in understanding the context of resistance. Foucault (1982) saw power as the means by which individuals enact or perform to reinforce their individuality. He suggests that 'These struggles are not exactly for or against the "individual", but rather they are struggles against the "government of individualization"' (Foucault, 1982: 212).

In other words, resistance may already exist, or may emerge, from a model of imposed requirements to acquire specific statuses or qualifications.

So, in terms of imposed government requirements, we can ask ourselves who benefits from such workforce reform? Is the status of early years graduates one that is embraced by all those who currently work with young children (as well as those who are considering such a career)? What are the financial rewards of study and 'professionalization' if any? The purpose of this chapter is not to offer responses to such questions; rather, the questions serve to illustrate some of the potential struggles that may arise from workforce reform, and responses can contribute to an understanding of identities, decisions and aspirations within the workforce. The increase in 'professions' (NSO, 2009) reflects the shift, certainly in England, and the inherent government strategies associated with the 'professionalization' of workforces. Similar reform is underway in nursing, youth work, social work and social care. The measures may reinforce a 'culture of performativity: the belief in the veracity of apparently objective systems of accountability and measurement' (Dent and Whitehead, 2002: 2). The processes of inspection, audit, information storing and managing with decreasing resources are commonplace in the public sector; such practices sustain regimes of regulatory gaze and surveillance (see Osgood, 2006a; Penna, 2005). The ideas of Foucault in relation to power and regimes of truth are again relevant in this context. Dahlberg and Moss (2005: 142) interpret regimes of truth as the 'means by which the ethical and political are transformed into the technical and managerial'. Issues of gender and feminist ideologies (Colley, 2006; Gilligan, 1982; Goldstein, 1998; Osgood, 2006b), the hegemony of 'outcomes', 'effective practice', 'flexible childcare' become the regimes of truth that underpin the reform of the early years workforce. How aspects of these ideas shape the construction of professional identities, alongside the analysis of research, is the focus of the next section.

Professional identity

Tucker (2004) proposes that, any framework that attempts to assist reflection on matters of professional identity construction must be able to:

1. explore the impact of 'ideological effects' on the socio-political terrain and the conditions of existence for those working with young people;
2. assist analysis of those forms of discourse that are used to define particular forms of work;
3. show how ideas are struggled over and contested at various levels of experience;
4. demonstrate how such matters directly impact upon the professional identities which individuals and groups adopt in their everyday work (Tucker, 2004: 84).

I have noted some of the debates about socio-political terrain and dominant discourses already, but Tucker's propositions point to how aspects of self, people and places are influential.

Self identity, personal identity and their potential interface with professional identities is therefore pertinent in this context. Giddens (1991) acknowledges the role of media, mass communication and globalization against a backdrop of modernity in the narratives we construct about 'the reflexive project of the self' (Giddens, 1991: 5). He argues that the self is not passive, but is reflexively constructed in response to external and internal influences as a narrative, or auto-biography. Thus, the phenomenological sense of who we are, cannot be dissociated from our professional identities.

Similarly, Beijaard et al. (2000) and Lave and Wenger (1991) recognize the role that contexts, experiences and situations have to play in constructing identities. The interpretation of experience is important but it requires individuals to have the agency and motivation to undertake it. This may be determined by expectations of the self but also others in the workplace. The role of mentors, managers, leaders and other colleagues who work alongside early years workers becomes critical here. There needs to be a critical mass of early years staff who are able to undertake these roles; how individuals create narratives for interpretation and re-interpretation may be determined by a multiplicity of factors such as space, skills and support. The notion of agency is apparent here, and needs to be examined in terms of the extent to which early years workers and their colleagues have a sense of agency in order to facilitate change.

Kelchtermans (1993) suggests that significant aspects of the professional self are: self image; self-esteem; job motivation; task perception; and future perspectives. There is some congruence here with Giddens (1991) and Williams (2007); how we see ourselves in the workplace and the influence of others in creating a self-image are both significant. The role of mentors, supervisors, managers, leaders, peers and colleagues once again, as well as family and wider society, therefore become apparent in the construction of how we perceive ourselves at work as part of our professional identities. A consideration of how media portray early years work is pertinent, particularly when television programmes in England such as *Supernanny* are at risk of perpetuating a stereotypical image not far removed from a Victorian governess.

Berry et al. (2007) acknowledge how professional identities are shaped by knowledge from a range of different sources but point to stories about ourselves as well. These stories are shaped and told by individuals as 'expressions of cultural values, norms and structures' (Berry et al., 2007: 137). Stories about our professional selves are constructed and evolve. The stories constructed by our families, communities, careers advisers sustain stereotypical images of working with young children, informed by historical and sociological influences. These narratives are the starting point for some entering the workforce, and they will be continued by the working communities and practices they become members of.

Therefore the place, as well as the people where early years practitioners work, is significant in contributing to professional identities; the notion of place (the physical environment, its resources, its symbolism, its architecture and design) can have an impact on how we construct ourselves as employees within the workplace. Thus those early years workers who undertake sessional work in shared premises, for example, have significant constraints in terms of time, space and resources, and thus on how they perceive themselves as having permanence, ownership and status.

Stronach et al. (2002) examine identities of teacher and nurse, suggesting that they are 'located in a complicated nexus between policy, ideology and practice' (Stronach et al., 2002: 109). The deconstruction of professionalism and professional identities as presented in their paper is helpful as it confirms the ephemeral complexity of what is meant by professional identities. They also articulate how 'economies of performance' (as manifested in the dominant discourses of standards, audit and accountability) interact with 'ecologies of practice' (practices, knowledge, beliefs adopted, acquired and implemented by those undertaking specific professional roles) to create a position, or nexus, in which the professional is caught between. This position recurs within the themes of policy, professionalization and professional knowledge and can be compared to what Dahlberg and Moss (2005: 15) propose as the subjectification of the early years workforce, 'whereby we are created as a particular type of subject'.

Similar influences on professional identities have been proposed by Kuisma and Sandberg (2008) who suggest that language is important in identity formation for early years practitioners in Sweden. They suggest that:

> a potential risk is that pre-school teachers can become private if they do not share a common understanding of professional language. To obtain status and legitimacy in society, professional competencies need to be articulated and communicated to the public. (Kuisma and Sandberg, 2008: 193)

Being private in this context contrasts with confidently articulating knowledge to others, and being able to 'concretely describe their professional area with the help of language and professional concepts' (Kuisma and Sandberg, 2008: 192). Reasons for becoming private as reported by Kuisma and Sandberg (2008) were suggested to be limited opportunities to learn from close colleagues, limited self-knowledge and limited knowledge of the role they are expected to undertake, arguably similar to 'cultural values, norms and structures' suggested by Berry et al. (2007: 137). Kuisma and Sandberg (2008) help us think about what early years workers need to do to become visible, and how status and legitimacy will be achieved through having the confidence, power and opportunity to be heard in society. Their research also reinforces the need for a professional community of learning and confidence to describe to others the nature of their work. The existence of communities of learning traditionally have proved a challenge for early years practitioners in England (Hargreaves and Hopper, 2006; Siraj-Blatchford, 1993) as well as Sweden.

In England, formal strategies of support exist for some groups such as mentoring for newly qualified teachers. The closest early years has achieved in terms of formal support for newcomers to the workforce was the attempt to introduce induction standards for early years workers in 2007–2008. However, issues such as sustainability were identified for their successful implementation in private daycare settings (Owens, 2009). Sustainability, resourcing and capacity are essential for effective mentoring, and the day-to-day demands of frontline early years work creates significant pressures for staff. When we think about newcomers, or apprentices, and how they begin to construct professional identities, concepts of communities of practice and legitimate peripheral participation, developed by Wenger (1998) and Lave and Wenger (1991) respectively, are also helpful.

Within communities of practice (Wenger, 1998) apprentices become included through 'legitimate peripheral participation' (Lave and Wenger, 1991) and thus through observing the ways in which the community operates, who operates within it, and how. For an individual to be on a trajectory that takes them towards the community of practice as opposed to being on the periphery, Wenger (1998) states the prerequisites as 'being useful, being sponsored, being feared, being the right kind of person, having the right birth' (Wenger, 1998: 101). It is worth comparing the notion of legitimate peripheral participation with other models of learning in the workplace, which I consider next.

The notion of movement from novice to apprentice, as suggested by Dreyfus and Dreyfus (1986, cited in Eraut, 1994), focuses on experiential learning in a professional context, with less emphasis on theoretical learning. Both take on a uni-dimensional form, and thus do not take account of the interruptions, multi-dimensional influences and uncertainty of the reality of being a newcomer to a profession. The early experiences as one enters a profession can be critical in the co-construction of professional identities as we shape ourselves through interactions with others (children, parents, colleagues, other professionals), with physical spaces and places and through the imposed structures at meso-, micro- and macro-levels of influence. The notions of micro-, meso- and macro-systems derive from the work of Bronfenbrenner (1979), and suggest systems arranged rather like a Russian doll, that exert influences on individuals as well as individuals exerting influences themselves. The level of micro-system is the immediate community within which an individual exists, surrounded by a meso-system of local community. In the context of this chapter, I am referring to the workplace as the meso-system. The macro-system encompasses the wider influences of government, society, culture, history and so on. The way in which early years workers undertake frontline work and the notion of discretion and interpretation of their work, as suggested by Lipsky (1980), contributes to the complexity of factors that interact with each other to influence ways in which individuals within the workforce, but also groups of workers, continually shape, and have shaped for them by others, their professional identities. Indeed, Frost (2005), in a review of research into frontline working with children and families, demonstrated how professional territories, identities (and I would argue professional cultures too) are dynamic, in a constant state of flux and reconstruction. These are particularly exacerbated by relatively new ways of inter-agency working that have been promoted through the reconfiguration of children's services as a result of Every Child Matters (DfES, 2003).

Finally, what factors, implicit or otherwise, *bind* early years workers together to create a community? How do they contribute to personal stories and professional identities? The point made earlier relating to micro-systems in communities of practice at the level of individual settings, and tensions that can emerge from macro-levels of influence, can be applied too in terms of who has right of entry to a workforce; what do they do when they are part of a workforce at micro-level, and how has this any form of interface with macro-levels of knowledge and expectation? If we consider the cultures of practice that may exist in individual settings, how these may be similar or different to other settings, and ask questions about 'why' and 'how', then we can see how professional identities are shaped by others and self and by the stories that are created and narrated in our day-to-day work. Gender is a significant factor in this debate when attributed to the ideologies and values already noted; there seems to be an expectation that those who undertake early years work are caring and loving – traditional prerequisites for entering the workforce (Colley, 2006; Goldstein, 1998). This is an over-generalization, but a point that still needs to be made and has some resonance with Bourdieu's (1993) notion of habitus in its proposition that symbolism and socialization practices perpetuate any constructions of reality and 'this is how it is'. Research shows that those entering the early years workforce are committed to working with children, and that recruits see their work as being rewarding (Cooke and Lawton, 2008), but data suggest that retention and recruitment are problematic in some provider types within the early years workforce (Nicholson et al., 2008) and that workers need to have access to progression opportunities in order to want to stay in the workforce (Cooke and Lawton, 2008). This returns us to the inequalities within the workforce, as noted near the beginning of the chapter, and reminds us of the challenges that those undertaking low-paid, low-status work face in their day-to-day lives, particularly in times of economic uncertainties. These cannot be ignored in any contemplation of the identities, aspirations and changes within the early years workforce.

Final thoughts

The aim of this chapter has been to offer perspectives that may have shaped and contributed to the construction of professional identities, specifically within the early years workforce, by drawing on a range of disciplines. I have argued that some of the significant factors that seem to have an influence on the construction of professional identities are the communities in which workers are located, and that includes the range of colleagues from leaders, parents, allied professionals, the places where they work, and their own families. Children are not too visible in this arena, however, but are significant from a sociological perspective. How children are sociologically constructed has a direct impact on the construction of identities of those who work with them. The impact of gender and the socialization of women into lower paid, lower status work is apparent not just in the early years sector, but these are other key influences on professional identities, as are notions of self and how we construct narratives about ourselves at work.

Looking forward, it might be optimistic to assert that as the early years workforce has increased access to higher level education and qualifications, then passivity and conformity could be replaced by explicit demands and shifted power bases. I suggest that this needs to be seen from a 'bottom up' perspective, starting with how young men and women in secondary education construct working with young children as a worthwhile career. Clear routes for progression for young people are essential, as well as opportunities to demonstrate values, skills, knowledge and a personal, pedagogical philosophy that respects the children and families they will be working with.

References

Adams, K. (2008) 'What's in a name? Seeking professional status through degree studies within the Scottish early years context', *European Early Childhood Education Research Journal*, 16(2): 196–209.

Baldock, P., Fitzgerald, D. and Kay, J. (2009) *Understanding Early Years Policy*, 2nd edn. London: Sage.

Ball, C. (1994) *Start Right: The Importance of Early Learning*. London: The Royal Society for the Encouragement of Arts, Manufacture and Commerce.

Beijaard, D., Verloop, N. and Vermunt, J. (2000) 'Teachers' perceptions of professional identity: an exploratory study from a personal knowledge perspective', *Teaching and Teacher Education*, 16(1): 749–64.

Berry, A., Clemans, A. and Kostogriz, A. (eds) (2007) *Dimensions of Professional Learning*. Rotterdam: Sense Publishing.

Bertram, T. and Pascal, C. (2001) *The OECD Thematic Review of Early Childhood Education and Care: Background Report for the UK*. Available from: www.oecd.org/ (accessed 30 October 2002).

Bourdieu, P. (1993) 'Structures, habitus, power: basis for a theory of symbolic power', in N. Dirks, G. Eley and S. Ortner (eds) *Culture/Power/History: A Reader in Contemporary Social Theory*. Princeton, NJ: Princeton University Press.

Bronfenbrenner, U. (1979) *The Ecology of Human Development: Experiments by Nature and Design*. Cambridge, MA: Harvard University Press.

Cameron, C. (2004) *Building an Integrated Workforce for a Long Term Vision of Universal Early Education and Care*. Policy Paper Number 3. Daycare Trust.

Carey, D., Cramp, A., Kendall, A. and Perkins, H. (2009) *Facilitating Progression: Towards a 'Fit for Purpose' Progression Model for Early Years Practitioners*. Birmingham Black Country and Solihull Lifelong Learning Network Report. HSCEYE 06-09.

Children's Workforce Development Council (CWDC) (2009) *Functional Map of the Children and Young People's Workforce in England*. Available from: www.cwdcouncil.org (accessed June 2009).

Cohen, B., Moss, P., Petrie, P. and Wallace, J. (2004) *A New Deal for Children?* Bristol: The Policy Press.

Colley, H. (2006) 'Learning to labour with feeling: class, gender and emotion in childcare education and training', *Contemporary Issues in Early Childhood*, 7(1): 15–29.

Cooke, G. and Lawton, K. (2008) *For Love or Money? Pay, Progression and Professionalisation in the 'Early Years' Workforce*. London: Institute for Public Policy Research.

Crompton, R. (1997) *Women Who Work in Modern Britain*. Oxford: Oxford University Press.

CYPN (2009) 'Early years round up of the week', *Children and Young People Now*, 23–29 July.

Dahlberg, G. and Moss, P. (2005) *Ethics and Politics in Early Childhood Education*. Abingdon: RoutledgeFalmer.

Daycare Trust (2008) *Raising the Bar: What Next for the Early Childhood and Education and Care Workforce?* Available from: www.daycaretrust.org.uk/data (accessed 26 July 2009).

Dent, M. and Whitehead, S. (eds) (2002) *Managing Professional Identities*. London: Routledge.

Department for Children, Schools and Families (DCSF) (2007) *The Children's Plan: Building Brighter Futures*. London: DCSF.

Department for Children, Schools and Families (DCSF) (2008) *2020 Children and Young People's Workforce Strategy: The Evidence Base*. Available from: www.dcsf.gov.uk (accessed January 2009).

Department for Children, Schools and Families (DCSF) (2009) *Next Steps for Early Learning and Childcare*. Available from: www.cabinetoffice.gov.uk/media/120944/early_learning_childcare_main.pdf (accessed 12 May 2009).

Department for Education and Employment (DfEE) (1998) *Meeting the Childcare Challenge*. London: The Stationery Office.

Department for Education and Skills (DfES) (2003) *Every Child Matters*. London: DfES.

Department for Education and Skills (DfES) (2005) *Children's Workforce Strategy*. London: DfES.

Department for Education and Skills (DfES) (2006) *Children's Workforce Strategy: The Government's Response to the Consultation*. London: DfES.

Department for Education and Skills (DfES) (2007) *Early Years Foundation Stage*. London: DfES.

Eraut, M. (1994) *Developing Professional Knowledge and Competence*. London: RoutledgeFalmer.

Foucault, M. (1982) 'The subject and power: afterword', in H. Dreyfus and P. Rabinow, *Michel Foucault: Beyond Structuralism and Hermeneutics*. New York: Harvester Wheatsheaf.

Frost, N. (2005) *Professionalism, Partnership and Joined Up Thinking: A Research Review of Front-Line Working with Children and Families*. Available from: www.rip.org.uk (accessed 11 October 2007).

Giddens, A. (1991) *Modernity and Self Identity*. Cambridge: Polity Press.

Gilligan, C. (1982) *In a Different Voice*. Cambridge, MA: Harvard University Press.

GMB (2003) *Education's Hidden Professionals: GMB Survey of Teaching Assistants and Nursery Nurses*. London: GMB.

Goff, H. (2008) *Teachers Should Run Nurseries*. Available from: www.bbc.co.uk/go/pr/fr/-/1/hi/education (accessed December 2009).

Goldstein, L. (1998) 'More than gentle smiles and warm hugs: applying the ethic of care to early childhood education', *Journal of Research in Childhood Education*, 12(2): 244–62.

Hargreaves, L. and Hopper, B. (2006) 'Early years, low status? Early years teachers' perceptions of their occupational status', *Early Years*, 26(2): 171–86.

HM Treasury (2004) *Choice for Parents, The Best Start for Children: A Ten-year Strategy for Children*. London: HM Treasury.

Kelchtermans, G. (1993) 'Getting the story, understanding the lives: from career stories to teachers' professional development', *Teaching and Teacher Education*, 9(5/6): 443–56.

Kuisma, M. and Sandberg, A. (2008) 'Pre-school teachers' and student pre-school teachers' thoughts about professionalism in Sweden', *European Early Childhood Education Research Journal*, 16(2): 186–95.

Lave, J. and Wenger, E. (1991) *Situated Learning: Legitimate Peripheral Participation*. Cambridge: Cambridge University Press.

Lipsky, M. (1980) *Street-level Bureaucracy: Dilemmas of the Individual in Public Services*. New York: Russell Sage Foundation.

McGillivray, G. (2008) 'Nannies, nursery nurses and early years professionals: constructions of professional identity in the early years workforce in England', *European Early Childhood Education Research Journal*, 16(2): 242–54.

Miller, L. (2008a) 'Developing professionalism within a regulatory framework in England: challenges and possibilities', *European Early Childhood Education Research Journal*, 16(2): 255–68.

Miller, L. (2008b) 'Developing new professional roles in the early years', in L. Miller and C. Cable (eds) *Professionalism in the Early Years*. London: Hodder Education.

Miller, L. and Cable, C. (eds) (2008) *Professionalism in the Early Years*. London: Hodder Education.

Murray, J. (2009) 'The poor professionals', *The Guardian*, 28 April.

National Statistics Office (NSO) (2009) *The Jobs People Do*. Available from: www.statistics.gov.uk/cci/nugget.asp?id=11 (accessed 29 July 2009).

National Union of Teachers (NUT) (2006) *Early Years Campaigning Section*. Available from: www.teachers.org.uk/story (accessed December 2009).

Nicholson, S., Jordan, E., Cooper, J. and Mason, J. (2008) *Childcare and Early Years Providers Survey 2007*. Research Report DCSF RR047 BMRB. London: DCSF.

Nurse, A. (ed.) (2007) *The New Early Years Professional*. Abingdon: Routledge.

Osgood, J. (2006a) 'Deconstructing professionalism in early childhood education: resisting the regulatory gaze', *Contemporary Issues in Early Childhood*, 7(1): 5–14.

Osgood, J. (2006b) 'Professionalism and performativity: the feminist challenge facing early years practitioners', *Early Years*, 26(2): 187–99.

Owens, C. (2009) *CWDC Induction Standards Field Testing Project 07–08 Summary Report*. Available from: www.cwdcouncil.org.uk (accessed 8 August 2009).

Penn, H. (2000) 'Is working with children a good job?', in H. Penn (ed.) *Early Childhood Services: Theory, Policy and Practice*. Buckingham: Open University Press.

Penna, S. (2005) 'The Children Act 2004: child protection and social surveillance', *Journal of Social Welfare and Family Law*, 27(2): 143–57.

Sauve Bell (2004) *Sure Start Early Years Workforce Development Evidence Paper*. Bedford: Sauve Bell Associates.

Siraj-Blatchford, I. (1993) 'Educational research and reform: some implications for the professional identity of early years teachers', *British Journal of Educational Studies*, 41(4): 393–408.

Stronach, I., Corbin, B., McNamara, O., Stark, S. and Warne, T. (2002) 'Towards an uncertain politics of professionalism: teacher and nurse identities in flux', *Journal of Education Policy*, 17(1): 109–38.

Tucker, S. (2004) 'Youth working: professional identities given, received or contested?', in J. Roche, S. Tucker, R. Thomson and R. Flynn (eds) *Youth in Society*, 2nd edn. London: Sage.

UNISON (2006) *Qualifications, Pay and Quality in the Childcare Sector*. Report for UNISON prepared by the Centre for Economic and Social Inclusion. Available from: www.unison.org.uk/acrobat/B2773.pdf (accessed December 2009).

Wenger, E. (1998) *Communities of Practice*. Cambridge: Cambridge University Press.

Williams, J. (2007) 'Becoming a teacher', in A. Berry, A. Clemans and A. Kostogriz (eds) *Dimensions of Professional Learning*. Rotterdam: Sense Publishing.

20

Leading and managing in the early years

Mary E. Whalley

Overview

Research consistently confirms 'the crucial role of leadership in creating and sustaining successful and effective organisations' (National College for School Leadership, 2007: 4). Two specific roles have emerged in recent years which are seen to be key to transforming early years practice and provision. These are: Integrated Children's Centre Leader and Early Years Professional. In this chapter, Mary Whalley explores the development of these two roles through two case studies which enable reflection on the distinctive differences between them. Within the context of wider reflection on aspects of leadership and management in the early years, some of the challenges of embedding the two roles within the contemporary children's workforce are outlined.

[...]

Defining leadership and management

The terms 'leadership' and 'management' are often used interchangeably – particularly within early years. This is both unhelpful and confusing. Indeed, both these terms

---

Whalley, M.E. (2010) 'Leading and managing in the early years: towards a new understanding', in Miller, L. and Cable, C. (eds) *Professionalization, Leadership and Management in the Early Years*, London: Sage, pp. 13–28.

are often misunderstood across a range of professional disciplines. Law and Glover (2000, cited in Rodd, 2006) offer helpful insights into the different emphases of the two roles. They encourage an understanding of manager as one who plans and makes decisions, organizes and clarifies work roles, coordinates the organization and generally takes responsibility for monitoring its effectiveness. By contrast, the leader's role is to give direction, offer inspiration, build teamwork, set an example and gain the respect and acceptance of other practitioners. However, it is very difficult to separate leadership from management; indeed, Hall's (1996) study on the role of headteachers shows them to be simultaneously leaders and managers, which led her to the conclusion that 'management without leadership was unethical … leadership without management irresponsible' (p. 11). Whilst discussion here focuses primarily on the roles of managers/leaders in private, voluntary and independent pre-school settings, I intend that there will also be some relevance for those in positions of leadership in early years provision within maintained schools.

Learning from research

For the past couple of decades, there has been a groundswell of interest in issues relating to leadership and management in the early years. This interest has been global but within the UK since 1997, it has been driven – in part, at least – by the high priority and huge financial investment of the government into raising the quality and status of early years practice and provision (Moss, 2001).

In developing the Effective Leadership and Management Scheme (ELMS-EY), Moyles (2006) draws on several years of research into early years practice (Moyles and Musgrove, 2003; Moyles et al., 2002). In the ELMS-EY, she uses the metaphor of a tree with four distinct, but commonly-rooted, branches:

- leadership qualities;
- management skills;
- professional attributes;
- personal characteristics and attitudes.

[…] Here, with the subtle distinction between leadership *qualities* and management *skills*, Moyles raises the age-old argument about whether leadership can be 'learned' or is a set of inherent characteristics. […]

Aubrey et al.'s 2005 research study (Aubrey, 2007; Aubrey et al., 2006) offers key insights into contemporary understanding of leadership practice in the early years. Drawing on participant practitioners' own reflections on their leadership and management roles, a picture emerges that highlights the diversity of roles and responsibilities across different types of setting (full day care, voluntary, foundation stage classes in schools, integrated children's centres); but what also emerges is a commonality of understanding about the significance of these. Aubrey's quest for a grounded theory model of early childhood leadership focuses on Spillane et al.'s (2001: 28) concept of 'distributed leadership'. Although originally applied to school leadership, Ebbeck and Waniganayake (2003) argued that early childhood leadership required a paradigm shift towards such a model and Aubrey's findings indicate that a shared core vision, collegial way of working and a climate of trust and openness are integral to effective early childhood leadership. With a growing emphasis on integrated provision, the concept of distributed leadership is one that has strong resonance.

Rodd's work (1997, 2006) is seminal to contemporary understanding of leadership in the early years and points to a clear correlation between effective leadership and quality childhood services (Waniganayake, 2006: xii). Her original study concluded with practitioners identifying their need for leadership and management training and Rodd developed a typology of an early childhood leader which suggests a staged developmental process from 'novice' leader to leading through 'indirect care', each stage characterized by a set of personal traits, professional skills and roles and responsibilities. The professional skills – including pedagogical and curriculum leadership, conceptual ability (which involves critical thinking and advocacy) and interpersonal skills – are elements which Rodd believes can be developed through training.

Siraj-Blatchford and Manni's study (2007) was undertaken in response to the ongoing investment in early years leadership within the Children's Workforce and aimed to address significant questions about effective leadership of this expanded provision. Drawing on insights from wider leadership theory, they conclude that the role of leadership in early years is essentially that of 'leadership for learning' where the fundamental requirements for the role are:

- **contextual literacy** – situational leadership, engaging with the specific place, time and people she is leading;
- **commitment to collaborative practice** – with effective partnerships with families and other professionals;
- **commitment to the improvement of outcomes for all children** – taking a holistic view of children's development, where individual needs are identified and met (adapted from Siraj-Blatchford and Manni, 2007: 12).

The cultural context: international perspectives on leadership in early childhood settings

Although space does not allow for further expansion, we acknowledge the contribution of theories of leadership and management which, although belonging more appropriately to the worlds of finance, commerce, business and government, have nonetheless informed and shaped understanding of leadership and management roles in all organizations. Bolman and Deal's (1997) concept of 'transformational leadership' has particular resonance for early years. The transformational leader, who is seen as a 'change agent', will 'move (colleagues) towards higher and more universal needs and purposes' (p. 314).

The majority of leadership and management theories have come from North America, or are strongly influenced by its culture, thus raising the issue of possible cultural bias. There are, in fact, wide cultural variations in how people address and talk to each other, carry out and respond to different leadership styles and behaviours. Some cultures are more individualistic or value family systems as against more bureaucratic models. Chakraborty's study (2003) suggests that leadership in the East is dominantly 'feminist-intuitive' whereas in the West it is 'masculine-rational'. Other writers (such as Marshall, 1994) have explored different patterns of leadership linked to gender, with the suggestion that women develop a leadership style that is nurturing, caring and sensitive while male leadership is more often characterized by control, power, domination and competition. There is a danger of stereotyping here, for evidence suggests that the leadership styles of men and women may be influenced as much by the situation as by gender (Rodd, 2006). For example, women are more likely to be in management positions in people-oriented sectors so the nurturing style is likely to be emphasized. The theme of women in early years leadership and management is revisited later in this chapter.

The influential work of Rodd, Moyles, Aubrey and Siraj-Blatchford within the UK has been acknowledged, but all four have also gained international respect. There is limited research available internationally though [through] Muijs et al.'s (2004) review of the available literature on early childhood leadership [...] a strong picture emerges that leaders in early years settings have a 'multiplicity of roles which are context specific' (p. 161). Siraj-Blatchford and Manni's 2007 study concurs with this concept of 'contextual literacy'. From the Muijs et al. review, too, interesting insights emerge from studies of the experience of leaders in New Zealand (Hatherley and Lee, 2003) and the USA (Kagan and Hallmark, 2001), which highlight 'community leadership', and show the role of the leader/manager as that of developing a community of learners and strengthening links between setting and community. This links to the concept of 'distributed leadership' (Spillane et al., 2001) considered earlier and which Ebbeck and Waniganayake (2003) suggest should be applied in early years leadership. However, they also express concern about the almost universal lack of leadership training and argue strongly that this is essential for effective 'distribution' of leadership tasks. The Muijs et al. review concludes with reference to Bloom's (2000) study which identifies three core areas of competence required by leaders and managers in early years settings, whatever the context:

- **knowledge** – including child development, pedagogical principles, group dynamics and organizational theory;
- **skills** – including technical, human and conceptual skills (including budgeting);
- **attitudes** – including a sense of moral purpose and inspiring confidence and respect.

The challenges of leadership and management in integrated settings

The government in England recognizes that the quality of services for children and young people depends above all on the quality of the workforce and, 'in particular, on the quality of the leadership' (NCSL, 2007: 1). This is true of all settings, whatever their size and contexts. Social and political drivers within the UK context have resulted in a new emphasis on integrated working which involves everyone who works with children and young people. This is a central part of the Every Child Matters reforms (DfES, 2003, 2004a, 2004b, 2006a), the Children's Plan (DCSF, 2007) and Children's Workforce Strategy (CWDC, 2008a, 2009) and is aimed at ensuring that everyone involved in supporting children and young people works together effectively to 'put the child at the centre, meet their needs and improve their lives' (CWDC, 2008b: 2). [...]

The development of Sure Start Children's Centres since 2004, bringing together childcare, early education, health and family-support services for families with children from birth to 5 and for parents-to-be, continues to be the cornerstone of the government's drive to tackle child poverty, social exclusion and inequalities in order that all children can flourish at home and continue to do so when they get to school. By 2010, there should be a Children's Centre in every community[1] – about 3,500 in total across the country (DfES, 2005), with further targets for 2015. There are wide regional variations in how such centres are organized but the NPQICL was introduced alongside Children's Centre provision as a nationally recognized qualification aimed at supporting leaders in providing 'seamless high quality, integrated services for babies, children and families' (NCSL, 2007: 4). Children's Centre leaders/managers embarking on the NPQICL normally hold an honours degree and achieving it is generally considered by higher education institutions to be equivalent to approximately one-third credit for a Master's degree. Thus, it has equivalency to the National Professional Qualification for Headship in schools.

The six standards for the NPQICL (DfES, 2007) identify the knowledge, skills and attributes which are required by the Integrated Centre Leader (ICL). The standards also have application in informing job descriptions, person specifications and performance management. Usually, the job title associated with the role is 'Children's Centre Manager' although the emphasis in the NPQICL is on *leadership*. In particular, the characteristics of the Integrated Centre Leader role are:

- providing vision, direction and leadership vital to the creation of integrated services;
- establishing and sustaining an environment of challenge and support for children;
- leading the work of the centre to secure success, accountability and continuous improvement;
- working with and through others to design and shape flexible services;
- ensuring that all staff understand children's developmental needs;
- collecting and using all relevant data to gain a better understanding of its local community to inform how services should be organized (adapted from DfES, 2007: 5).

Amanda is a Children's Centre manager and describes how she sees her role:

CASE STUDY

Amanda, Children's Centre manager

Since early in my initial training as a nursery nurse, I have had an interest in young children as part of families and communities and my first post was with Social Services in a large urban local authority. I moved to a development post with a local Sure Start Project within an Early Excellence Centre, during which time I completed a Sector Endorsed Foundation Degree Early Years and then went on to achieve the BA Hons Childhood Studies. My own 'learning journey' was taking place as Sure Start Children's Centres were evolving and I was appointed as manager of a Phase 1 Children's Centre in an area of significant social disadvantage. This was a challenging but exciting time as the concept of integrated Children's Centre provision began to be consolidated and I was able to complete the NPQICL during this initial post which helped me to root my leadership experience in both grounded theory and in a reflective approach to the role. I then decided to take on a fresh challenge as I was appointed to manage Phase 2/3 Children's Centre provision in a large town. Initially I was a 'team of one', with actual provision only at the 'ideas' stage. Over the past two years, I have led and managed the establishment of three sites across the town and now manage a team of 13 staff, coordinating flexible multi-agency provision which includes family support and training, health visiting, midwifery services, early years provision, speech and language and various voluntary sector activities. Provision is thriving – though there are daily challenges and many critical incidents! For me, the key to being effective in the ICL role is keeping the child and family at the heart of what we do. It is important to maintain a positive outlook as so often the families we support have not engaged with 'professionals' for one reason or another. Leadership for me is about creating an ethos where all the above happens; it's about encouraging an environment where all staff sign up to a shared vision and children and families feel valued.

Amanda's approach to leadership here shows both her own commitment to learning and to the learning and development of the families she serves. Indeed, the initial review of the NPQICL (Williams, 2006) was generally very positive and highlights some excellent examples of effectiveness in ICL. However, in much Children's Centre provision there remain challenges and potential barriers to effective inter-professional communication and collaboration, including confusion about parameters of roles and responsibilities, frustration about slowness or lack of change and conflicting priorities and work practices (Anning et al., 2006). Clearly, a shared multi-professional focus on 'the child and family' is critical here.

Leadership of practice: the role of the Early Years Professional

Few of the texts on leadership and management in early childhood settings focus clearly on the role of 'leader of practice', though Siraj-Blatchford and Manni's concept of 'leadership for learning' comes close. In 2005, the role of Early Years Professional was introduced as a 'strategic leadership role ... with a set of core skills, knowledge and values' (DfES, 2006b). The emergence of the graduate EYP role is fundamental to the government's agenda to improve workforce skills, knowledge and competencies (CWDC, 2007) and particularly in leading effective practice across the Early Years Foundation Stage for children from birth to 5 (EYFS) (DCSF, 2008).

Unlike the NPQICL, EYP is a graduate 'status' and not in itself a qualification – thus having some comparability to Qualified Teacher Status. Candidates seeking validation for EYPS not only have to demonstrate that they can meet the 39 EYP Standards through their own practice but also provide evidence that they can lead and support others in these (CWDC, 2007). It is this 'leadership of practice' which is the defining aspect of the EYP role and which distinguishes it clearly from that of leader or manager of a setting. The EYP's main role is to lead and support the learning and development of the children and to lead and improve the practice of others. The challenge is that this model of leadership is one that must fit generically across all types, sizes and locations of early years settings – private, voluntary, independent and maintained (though not maintained schools).

In developing the EYP role, the CWDC acknowledges the influence of the continental European model of the 'social pedagogue' – mooted as one of the possible titles for the new role (CWDC, 2005). In countries such as Denmark and Sweden, it is social pedagogues (or, simply, 'pedagogues') who are the lead workers in pre-school settings. This is a graduate professional role, with favourable comparability in status, pay and conditions to that of teachers in schools in these countries. The role of the pedagogue [...] has evolved to emphasize the relationship of the adult with the child as a whole being – with a body, mind, emotions, creativity, history and social identity (Moss and Petrie, 2002). The pedagogue, thus, supports all aspects of the child's development equally, working individually with each child to establish positive dispositions for learning. Boddy et al. (2005) offer further insights into and understanding of the pedagogue role, describing it as one of strategic leadership, especially in managing change.

Following wide consultation, the government in England rejected the title of 'social pedagogue' for the new professional role of leading practice in favour of Early Years Professional. This writer worked with a group of newly validated EYPs to define a new paradigm of leadership which best fits the new professional status. Arguably, this emerging definition offers some parallels with the Scandinavian social pedagogue role in suggesting that the EYP demonstrates:

- a reflective and reflexive practice;
- skills in decision-making;
- sound knowledge and understanding of: early years pedagogy; the holistic needs of all children from birth to 5; and competence in planning, implementing and monitoring within the Early Years Foundation framework (DCSF, 2008);
- a strong sense of the intrinsic worth of each child and all those in her/his world;
- the ability to role-model, lead and support others in effective practice;
- the ability to define a vision for practice within a setting;
- competence as an agent of change (Whalley, 2008: 12–13).

Claire, a newly validated Early Years Professional, offers an account of her role which exemplifies many of the above skills and traits.

📁   **CASE STUDY**

Claire, Manager and Early Years Professional, private nursery

In the past year, I have gained a BA Childhood Studies degree *and* achieved Early Years Professional Status and I am only 26! From the age of 16 to 18, I completed a level 3 Diploma in Early Years and then explored the opportunity of completing a degree full-time. However, what I really wanted to do was begin work with young children so I worked initially as a nanny and then in day nursery provision, working my way to posts as senior nursery nurse and then deputy manager. When I was 21, I returned to the same college where I had gained my diploma and started a Sector-endorsed Foundation Degree Early Years. During the time I was doing the FD, not only did I acquire much more in-depth knowledge and understanding but I was also able to critically reflect on my own practice. In April 2008, I moved to a deputy manager post at a new nursery and six months later was appointed manager. I have come to realize the importance of effective leadership in early years settings and am grateful for a manager, in my early posts, who role-modelled for me an approachable but confident style of leadership where each team member felt a valuable part of the whole. I have been able to build a new team, plan and organize the learning environment, work very closely with prospective (many now actual!) parents and – most importantly for me – lead on planning a child-led approach to provision for the children, in partnership with their families. This for me is the essence of my pedagogy. I am delighted that early years is now viewed as a profession and am very proud that my achievements are now being recognized.

Claire's experience has been positive, both in terms of her own career development and in the way she is being able to carry out her role as an EYP. Other EYPs' experiences are not so positive. [...] Indeed, the EYP role itself is proving much more difficult to define than previously anticipated and, with around 4000 EYPs already in England at the time of writing (Murray, 2010), a more complex picture is emerging nationally. Whilst the role has always been intended to be contextualized to different types of settings – private, voluntary and independent (including childminders) as well as in maintained Children's Centres – the reality is that there is no consistency in the type of role the EYP has. In addition to the anticipated graduate leader role in early years settings EYPs are employed in roles as diverse as a teaching assistant in the preparatory department of an independent school and a family outreach worker in a Children's Centre. This development can be viewed positively, as it allows the EYPs themselves to shape and establish the role in public consciousness and to 'restructure, rethink and re-envision the future workforce' (Moss, 2006: 31). However, with the challenge to establish a new professional identity, such ambiguity can also be considered unhelpful.

   [...]

Clearly, within the early years workforce, there is some way to go in developing understanding of the EYP role and [...] [c]urrently, there are wider concerns about the lack of clear infrastructures for EYPs and confusions about the role itself. Moreover, there is much uncertainty about the future of the role given the change of government in the UK and the overall sustainability of the EYP programme (Gordon-Smith, 2009). Arguably, there remains something of a gulf between the rhetoric of this 'world class transformational early years sector, with a high quality, fairly paid workforce' (Cooke and Lawton, 2008) and the reality for many EYPs. Questions are rightly being asked about how such transformation can be delivered with existing levels of spending through the current market model which dominates early years provision in the UK.

Towards a new professional understanding of early years leadership and management

At the outset of the chapter, I noted a new sense of professionalism within early years provision and practice. Historically, the early years workforce has been primarily female, with low pay, low status, basic qualification requirements and little or no career structure (Miller and Cable, 2008), reflecting the general position of women and young children in society. Through enhanced knowledge and understanding of the critical importance of the first five years of a child's life, early years practitioners are becoming passionate about and empowered by their own distinctive contribution to children's services. In the past, there may have been some reluctance from a predominantly female workforce to embrace roles of leadership and management (Hennig and Jardim, 1976, cited in Rodd, 2006) though, arguably, this is no longer the case (McGillivray, 2008). Paradoxically, while the glass ceiling remains a barrier to aspiring women leaders in many professions, the great majority of EYPs and ICLs to date are women and there is a growing call to encourage more male leaders and managers in early years to counterbalance the perceived 'feminized culture' by which it is currently characterized (Early Years Stakeholder Group [EYSG], 2008).

Final thoughts

There remain anomalies and inequalities in many aspects of early years practice and provision (EYSG, 2008) which extend to differences in the way settings are led and managed. Yet, despite these, there is a groundswell of welcome for the raised status and opportunities for career development within the early years workforce. Effective leadership and management are critical to this new understanding of 'professionalism'. The government's vision remains the creation of a 'world class workforce in the early years to improve outcomes for children' (CWDC, 2007: 4) through developing a trained bank of graduate workers whose knowledge and competences will be key to effective leadership of integrated services and of EYFS provision. The roles of ICL and EYP are distinct but complementary within this vision. However, there are significant challenges to this vision becoming reality.

[…]

Note

1. For an update, see www.education.gov.uk/childrenandyoungpeople/earlylearning andchildcare/surestart/a0076712/surestart-children%27s-centres. The Early Intervention Grant, announced in December 2010 following the Spending Review, contains enough money to maintain a network of Children's Centres so they are accessible to all, and supporting families in greatest need.

References

Anning, A., Cottrell, D., Frost, N., Green, J. and Robinson, N. (2006) *Developing Multiprofessional Teamwork for Integrated Children's Services*. Maidenhead: Open University Press.

Aubrey, C. (2007) *Leading and Managing in the Early Years*. London: Sage.

Aubrey, C., Godfrey, R., Harris, A. and Dahl, S. (2006) 'How do they manage? An investigation of early childhood leadership', Symposium at British Educational Research Association Conference, University of Warwick, 9 September.

Bloom, P.J. (2000) 'How do we define director competence?', *Childcare Information Exchange*, 138: 13–18.

Boddy, J., Cameron, C., Moss, P., Mooney, A., Petrie, P. and Statham, J. (2005) *Introducing Pedagogy into the Children's Workforce: Children's Workforce Strategy – A Response to the Consultation*. London: Thomas Coram Research Unit/Institute of Education, University of London.

Bolman, L.G. and Deal, T.E. (1997) *Reframing Organisations: Artistry, Choice and Leadership*, 2nd edn. San Francisco, CA: Jossey-Bass.

Chakraborty, D. (2003) 'Leadership in the East and West: a few examples', *Journal of Human Values*, 9: 29–52.

Children's Workforce Development Council (CWDC) (2005) *Children's Workforce Strategy: A Consultation*. Leeds: CWDC.

CWDC (2007) *Early Years Professional Status: Handbook*. Leeds: CWDC.

CWDC (2008a) *One Children's Workforce – A Journey to the End of the Rainbow*. Available from: www.cwdcouncil.org.uk?whats-new/news/1126 (accessed 14 May 2009).

CWDC (2008b) *Integrated Working Explained*. Leeds: CWDC.

CWDC (2009) *One Children's Workforce Tool*. Available from: http://onechildrensworkforce.cwdcouncil.org.uk/about (accessed 22 July 2009).

Cooke, G. and Lawton, K. (2008) *For Love or Money: Pay, Progression and Professionalism in the 'Early Years' Workforce*. London: Institute for Public Policy Research.

Department for Children, Schools and Families (DCSF) (2007) *The Children's Plan: Building Brighter Futures*. Nottingham: DCSF.

DCSF (2008) *The Early Years Foundation Stage*. Nottingham: DCSF.

Department for Education and Skills (DfES) (2003): *Green Paper: Every Child Matters.* Nottingham: DfES.

DfES (2004a) *Every Child Matters: The Next Steps.* Nottingham: DfES.

DfES (2004b) *Every Child Matters: Change for Children.* Nottingham: DfES.

DfES (2005) *A Sure Start Children's Centre for Every Community: Planning Guidance.* Available from: www.dcsf.gov.uk/everychildmatters/earlyyears/surestartchildrenscentres/childrenscentres (accessed 12 August 2009).

DfES (2006a) *Championing Children: A Shared Set of Knowledge Skills, Knowledge and Behaviours for Those Leading and Managing Integrated Children's Services.* Nottingham: DfES.

DfES (2006b) *Children's Workforce Strategy: The Government's Response to the Consultation.* Nottingham: DfES.

DfES (2007) *National Standards for Leaders of Children's Centres.* Nottingham: DfES.

Early Years Stakeholder Group (EYSG) (2008) *Report to the Children's Minister.* Available from: www.teachernet.gov.uk/_.../Early_Years_Stakeholder_Report_FINAL2.doc (accessed 12 July 2009).

Ebbeck, M. and Waniganayake, M. (2003) *Early Childhood Professionals: Leading Today and Tomorrow.* Sydney: Maclennan and Petty Ltd.

Gordon-Smith, P. (2009) 'Analysis: Conservative Party Policy – time for the sector to talk to the Tories', in *Nursery World*, 21 January. Available from: www.nurseryworld.co.uk/.../Analysis-Conservative-Party-Policy-Time-sector-talk-Tories/ (accessed 26 November 2009).

Hall, V. (1996) *Dancing on the Ceiling.* London: Paul Chapman.

Hatherley, A. and Lee, W. (2003) 'Voices of early childhood leadership', *New Zealand Journal of Educational Leadership*, 18: 91–100.

Hennig, M. and Jardim, A. (1976) *The Managerial Woman: The Survival Manual for Women in Business.* New York: Pocket Books.

Kagan, S.L. and Hallmark, L.G. (2001) 'Cultivating leadership in early care and education', *Child Care Information Exchange*, 140: 7–10.

Law, S. and Glover, D. (2000) *Educational Leadership and Learning: Practice, Policy and Research.* Buckingham: Open University Press.

Marshall, J. (1994) 'Revolutionising organisations by developing female values', in J. Boot, J. Lawrence and J. Morris (eds) *Managing the Unknown by Creating New Futures.* London: McGraw-Hill.

McGillivray, G. (2008) 'Nannies, nursery nurses and early years professionals: professional identity in the early years workforce', *European Early Childhood Research Journal*, 16(2): 242–54.

Miller, L. and Cable, C. (2008) *Professionalism in the Early Years.* London: Hodder Arnold.

Moss, P. (2001) 'New Labour's record: end of term report', *Nursery World*, 3 January. Available from: www.nurseryworld.co.uk/news/727177/New-Labours-record-End-term-report (accessed 19 July 2009).

Moss, P. (2006) 'Structures, understandings and discourses: possibilities for re-envisioning the early childhood worker', *Contemporary Issues in Early Childhood*, 7(1): 31–41.

Moss, P. and Petrie, P. (2002) *From Children's Services to Children's Spaces.* London: Taylor and Francis.

Moyles, J. (2006) *Effective Leadership and Management in the Early Years.* Maidenhead: Open University Press.

Moyles, J. and Musgrove, A. (2003) *EEPES (EY) Essex Effective Pedagogy Evaluation Scheme (Early Years).* Chelmsford: APU/Essex County Council.

Moyles, J., Adams, S. and Musgrove, A. (2002) *SPEEL: Study of Pedagogical Effectiveness in Early Learning*, Report No. 363. London: DfES.

Muijs, D., Aubrey, C., Harris, A. and Briggs, M. (2004) 'How do they manage? A review of the research in early childhood', *Journal of Early Childhood Research*, 2: 157. Available from: http://sagepub.com/cgi/content/abstract/2/2/157 (accessed 21 June 2009).

Murray, J. (2010) 'Shaping the future: caring and learning are inextricably linked', *Society Guardian*, in association with the Children's Workforce Development Council, 17 February.

National College for School Leadership (NCSL) (2007) *Guidance to the Standards for Leaders of Sure Start Children's Centres*. Nottingham: NCSL.

Rodd, J. (1997) 'Learning to be leaders: perceptions of early childhood professionals about leadership roles and responsibilities', *Early Years*, 18(1): 40–6.

Rodd, J. (2006) *Leadership in Early Childhood*, 3rd edn. Maidenhead: Open University Press.

Siraj-Blatchford, I. and Manni, L. (2007) *Effective Leadership in the Early Years Sector: The ELEYS Study*. London: Institute of Education, University of London.

Spillane, J., Halverson, R. and Diamon, J.B. (2001) 'Investigating school leadership practice: a distributed perspective', *Educational Researcher*, 30(3): 23–8.

Waniganayake, M. (2006) 'Foreword', in J. Rodd *Leadership in Early Childhood*, 3rd edn. Maidenhead: Open University Press.

Whalley, M.E. (2008) *Leading Practice in Early Years Settings*. Exeter: Learning Matters.

Williams, S. (2006) *Evaluation of the NPQICL Rollout Programme*. Henley-on-Thames: Henley Management College. Available from: www.ncsl.org.uk/media-fd5-c3-final-evaluation-npqicl.pdf (accessed 25 June 2009).

21

Building and leading a team

Jillian Rodd

Overview

The development of effective leadership approaches, team building and multi-disciplinary practice is an important area within early years education and care. In this chapter, Jillian Rodd questions what counts as a team and goes on to discuss the complex features within effective teamwork and leadership practice. This includes a detailed consideration of the stages of development within a team: team leadership, distributed leadership and a framework for team building. This chapter further examines the advantages of collaboration across multi-disciplinary teams and the value of practitioners working together as a team to achieve high-quality early years education.

[...]

> Good leaders build teams by making everyone feel that their contribution matters ...
> (Early education team leader)

In the administration of early childhood settings, considerable emphasis has been placed upon the significance of effective leadership. The quality and qualifications of leaders in these settings helps ensure high-quality provision (Sylva and Siraj-Blatchford, 2003) and helps raise standards and expectations for the other staff to

Rodd, J. (2008) 'Building and leading a team' (Chapter 8) in *Leadership in Early Childhood*, 4th edition, Buckingham: Open University Press, pp. 145–64. © 1994. Reproduced with the kind permission of Open University Press. All rights reserved.

follow. However, numerous studies of work groups suggest that, in groups which successfully meet the demands of goal attainment and harmonious relationships, leadership responsibilities are not placed upon one person, but are shared widely.

[...] Teamwork, in which individual interests and needs are subordinated in order to engage in joint, coordinated activity to achieve the common goals and purposes of a united group, is equally important, particularly in early childhood services which involve people, their relationships and feelings.

Joining together to achieve quality

The team approach is considered by many to be the most appropriate way of meeting the demands of the complex network of early childhood provision – for example, for the development of organisational vision, policy, plans and operational procedures, as well as for effective day-to-day running of the range of early childhood services presently offered. Ebbeck and Waniganayake (2003: 195) comment that 'building effective teams is fundamental to early childhood practice'. A cohesive team is a key resource for the provision of quality childcare and education for young children. According to Whalley (2001: 140), 'working as a team is a process not a technique. It is rooted in an ideology of empowerment, encouraging adults ... to take control of their own lives and giving children the permission to do the same ...'.

Many early childhood practitioners think that leaders should be community-minded because early childhood settings are essentially communities of learners where 'children ... discover and adults rediscover the joys, difficulties and satisfactions of learning' (Law and Glover, 2000: 149). Teams are like small communities, and to do their job effectively they need to be nurtured by the leader. Effective leaders assume an enabling role to build a strong team.

> A leader needs to build the self-esteem of the community ... (Early years/primary adviser)

Effective leadership and collective responsibility – that is, teamwork – can have a major impact on the quality of the service offered. Considerable research evidence reveals a connection between young children's development and the stability of care in early childhood settings. Instability of care, be it a result of frequent changes in a setting or frequent changes of staff within the setting, can have negative effects on children's development (Hennessy et al., 1992). The tone of the working environment can produce a lack of responsiveness and sensitivity among some staff that can lead to high staff turnover rates. Effective leadership and teamwork are considered to be factors which contribute to increased self-esteem, high job satisfaction and staff morale, reduced stress and a decreased likelihood of staff burnout (Schiller, 1987). The end-product of teamwork is an improvement in the quality of care and education for children.

[...] When practitioners talk about the staff at their settings, the word 'team' is often used.

Sharing distributed leadership throughout the setting and emphasis on teamwork are key leadership attributes … (Early years/primary adviser)

Most early childhood leaders and staff appreciate that teamwork is important for the working conditions of their settings, and understand that what constitutes a team can vary. For example, in pre-schools, the team may consist of two adults: the director or leader and an assistant. In long day or occasional childcare settings, the team may consist of the entire staff group or of the staff who work together in a room or with a particular group of children. In family day care and childminding, the team may mean the coordinator, field workers, office staff and a large group of independent providers who are physically isolated from the centralised administration. Depending on the meaning given to the concept of team, parents may or may not be included in the broader definition. Regardless of its definition, the essence of a team is that all participants work together effectively to achieve a common goal.

[…]

Teamwork is considered to be such an important issue for working in early childhood services that ability to operate as a member of a team is an employment criterion specified in job descriptions. Teamwork is also related to the current belief in the value of participatory management and distributed leadership.

Teams are considered to incorporate opportunities to make things happen and offer additional benefits (Woodcock, 1979). These include:

- help and support;
- coordination of individual activities;
- increased commitment;
- a sense of belonging;
- identification of professional development needs;
- learning opportunities;
- better communication; and
- a satisfying, stimulating, pleasant work environment.

Teams can provide social support to members that lessens the strain, stress and tension present in day-to-day activities in early childhood services, and which ultimately can lead to burnout. Interpersonal relationships can become a source of support, satisfaction and stimulation, thereby enhancing general group morale. By using the unique expertise and resources that each member contributes to the team, motivation and job satisfaction are enhanced, which in turn will result in effective accomplishment of the task.

[…]

What is a team in early childhood?

[Elsewhere] research findings (Rodd, 1998: 100–4) reported Australian and English early childhood practitioners' understanding about teamwork. The data showed that practitioners had a good appreciation of teams and teamwork. A team was defined generally as:

> a group of people cooperating with each other to work towards achieving an agreed set of aims, objectives or goals while simultaneously considering the personal needs and interests of individuals.

Research indicates that practitioners continue to associate the following concepts with teams:

- the pursuit of a common philosophy, ideals and values;
- commitment to working through the issues;
- shared responsibility;
- open and honest communication; and
- access to a support system.

Whalley (1994) comments that early childhood practitioners learnt to be strong – that is, became empowered – through working in a team. Practitioners consistently acknowledge the advantages of working in a team and they believe that an autocratic leadership style stifles effective teamwork by fostering competition, lack of respect, resentment, isolation and reduced commitment.

> I was told that I was responsible for organising a training day but the manager would not even let me send a letter out without seeing it first. I couldn't make one decision without referring it to her – she might as well have saved me the trouble and done it herself …
> (Nursery officer)

These factors are thought to diminish early childhood practitioners' ability to get the job done and maintain positive relationships at work.

The concept of teamwork is usually portrayed as positive and optimistic, and many practitioners describe their expectations regarding participation in a team in such a light. However, as Law and Glover (2000: 71) observe, the reality does not always match the rhetoric. Unfortunately, the experience of working in teams is not always consistent with expectations.

> The staff say they like working in a team and they seem to get a lot of positives out of it when it works well … but often there are difficulties and differences that are not resolved …
> (Nursery manager)

Teams are more than groups of people in a workplace, and not all work groups are teams. Effective teamwork grows out of work groups that are transformed into teams by appropriate leadership. Teamwork in practice can be quite a different proposition from teamwork in theory, with a range of negative experiences reported by early childhood practitioners.

It appears that, although many practitioners value the teamwork approach to the administration of settings, some problems exist in turning groups of individual staff members into team members (that is, team-building) and maintaining team spirit once this energy has been fired up.

[…] Team members are considered to hold particular roles and responsibilities in relation to the team's viability and the achievement of its goals.

> Leadership is exercised by the manager when getting the team to complete tasks. (Pre-school development worker)

Most early childhood practitioners understand that teamwork is more than just turning up for work each day. It involves a special understanding of the roles and responsibilities of both the leader and each team member.

> My head teacher calls meetings to 'brief' the staff on what he expects at the beginning of each school year. He raises morale because he encourages us to share ideas and he guides us through group activities. He shares leadership with us because he focuses on the group not the hierarchy. (Teaching assistant)

For leaders, teamwork means acting more as a facilitator than a superior. For staff members, it means taking an active role in the work situation rather than being a passive follower of instructions and directions. Benefits from teamwork are perceived as accruing for both leader and team members. The inconsistency between expectations and reality in teamwork suggests that early childhood leaders have not developed skill in building and leading teams. An exploration of the stages of team development and team leadership can clarify some of the issues relevant to effective teamwork.

Working in multi-disciplinary teams

According to Edgington (2000: 2), early childhood practitioners have always worked within a multi-disciplinary context, given that 'services for children and families have been developed by professionals holding a range of qualifications within the disciplines of education, social work and health, and are funded by and organised by the local authority, by private enterprise or by the voluntary sector'. However, the professionals from the various disciplines have brought their own values, philosophies, agendas, jargon and ways of approaching the needs of young children and their families. These differences have prevented the development of a partnership approach and it is only recently that any move has been made towards developing collaborative or team approaches. Whalley (1994) calls for a holistic approach to the profession, created from consensus derived from shared values about working with children and families.
[…]
Given that there is increasing inter-agency and multi-disciplinary collaboration, many practitioners will find themselves working in a multi-disciplinary team in the early childhood field. Members of such teams will need to overcome a range of barriers to effective inter-professional collaboration, and work together cooperatively to develop shared vision, values and philosophy, goals and objectives, and quality assurance and evaluation protocols. Rather than defending the approach of individual

disciplines, they need to work on understanding and reconciling any differences to create what Abbott and Hevey (2001) call 'a multi-disciplinary ethos'. Staff in such teams need to work participatively in an integrated way with a range of people and agencies to establish mutually agreed principles and priorities. Abbott and Moylett (1997) suggest that multi-disciplinary teamwork is the answer to developing a shared understanding and continuity in early childhood.

The stages of team development

Team development is not an easy task. It requires concerted, ongoing effort on behalf of each member and an even greater effort from the leader who is to move the team from birth to maturity. A number of writers have identified sequences of team development that a group of co-workers will move through over differing periods of time (Adair; 1986; Woodcock, 1979; Woodcock and Francis, 1981). The speed with which each group will accomplish the demands of a particular stage and move on to the next stage is related to the skill possessed by the leader. Consequently, leaders in early childhood settings need to be informed about the stage of team development at which the group currently functions, and they need to possess the skills to assist the group to move as quickly as possible to a higher stage of development (Walker, 1995).

In many ways, the stages of team development are similar to those commonly described for general group development – forming, storming, norming, performing and adjourning (Curran, 1989). The following stages are outlined in terms of the task and relationship requirements for early childhood settings.

Stage 1: connecting – getting together as a team

The first stage in the development of a team is when a group of people become aware that they are going to be working together. This may be when a new setting is established and a completely new group of staff is employed to work together. More likely, a new person or persons will join an existing group of staff or a person may resign and not be replaced, as long as this does not violate the staff-to-child ratio. Whenever there is a different group composition, the start of a new team has been signalled. This will require assimilation of the new person into the team and accommodation by the existing staff to the new conditions. The leader must address the demands of the task and relationships in order to assist staff to be productive and feel comfortable in this initial stage of team development.

In terms of the task, the major concern is with orientation to the work where structured activities such as information-sharing, organising roles and responsibilities and goal-setting are important because they act to alleviate staff members' apprehension about change and anxiety about competence to undertake the job. Staff will focus on the designated figure of authority to provide a blueprint for the direction of the setting and may ask a variety of questions – for example, 'What are we supposed to do?', 'What happens next?' and 'What are our goals?' Conformity to the leader's approach will be high and few challenges can be expected. The leader needs to provide clear directions and guidelines for staff at this point. [...]

The relationship and group morale aspect can be difficult to manage at this initial stage because many staff are concerned about belonging, inclusion and rejection, and some may be unwilling to disclose their personal concerns and weaknesses. They are likely to be concerned with self-protection in what is perceived as an unknown situation, so may keep feelings hidden, display little concern for others and be unlikely to listen effectively because their own needs will dominate their attention. The climate of the setting may be characterised by politeness and a wish to avoid contentious issues or anything that might result in conflict. Woodcock and Francis (1981) call this 'ritual sniffing' because the staff are focused upon getting acquainted with the others in the group, assessing others' strengths and weaknesses, and generally testing out the situation in order to determine the written and unwritten ground rules which operate in the group. The leader needs to provide opportunities for staff to get to know one another professionally and personally, [for instance] [i]ntroducing some kind of informal social function such as coffee after work. [...]

When the group members feel moderately comfortable with one another because a certain level of trust and security in the people and the task has been achieved, a degree of risk-raking in terms of challenging aspects of the task and the expertise of others to undertake the task may emerge. Small indications of conflict may be noticed. The group is now in transition to the next stage of team development.

Stage 2: confronting conflict in the team

It generally comes as some surprise, both to the leader and the team members, when the group which initially appeared to get along so well disintegrates into one which is marked by open and covert displays of antagonism to one another, dispute, dissension and discord. In terms of team development, the honeymoon period is over. The challenges for the team members at this second stage are establishing a niche in the pecking order and negotiation of roles and responsibilities. The direction and activities of the leader are likely to be evaluated and possibly challenged by team members who are feeling more confident about their position in the group.

[...] As group members get to know each other better, they also can identify one another's strengths and limitations. This can bring about confrontation regarding values, beliefs and appropriate practice which can produce an organisational climate that is characterised by criticism. Questions and statements such as 'What authority have you got to make that decision?', 'Who makes the rules here, the staff or the Coordinator?', 'Who are you to tell me what to do? I only take directions from the manager!', 'How is my performance going to be appraised?' and 'The committee can't tell us to do that!' may be heard from staff as they attempt to clarify where the power lies in the setting.

In this second stage, relationships between members of the team become more significant and can be influential in the ways emerging group differences are dealt with. Staff needs for recognition of their unique contribution can be met only in an atmosphere of mutual support and respect. [...]

The effective leader whose team is in this second stage of development will need to employ sophisticated communication skills to manage the conflict in order to move people towards greater acceptance, increased trust and commitment to the task. Active listening, assertion and conflict-management skills are essential, and the leader may need to provide guidelines for handling differences between staff in a professional manner. [...]

Many leaders of early childhood settings have reported that their team appears to be 'stuck' in a cycle of conflict resulting in high levels of stress for all involved, decreased morale and commitment and high staff turnover. As well as the extra energy required to work in a conflict-prone environment, leaders may need to respond to other issues such as staff resignations and staff replacements. In such circumstances, the leader will need to facilitate a sense of closure and reorient the team to the fact that they will be re-forming. The team will return to the first stage of development and begin the process of getting together as a team again. If the leader does not possess the confidence and skills to deal with conflict, the same scenario will probably be repeated when the new team moves into the second stage of confronting conflict. Without competent intervention, the cycle is repeated with the resultant perception that the team is conflict-prone, or 'stuck' in a destructive cycle of discord.

A major disadvantage of extended periods in the second stage is that early childhood settings that experience high staff turnover as a result of unresolved conflict do not capitalise on the training and experience that staff members have gained. The level of service quality that is expected by staff and parents is more difficult to achieve with a high staff turnover. [...]

If the leader manages the challenges of this second stage, the team will begin to resolve personal animosities and to focus back on improving activities and performance related to achieving the setting's goals. The team now is advancing to the third stage.

Stage 3: cooperating as a team

The assumption that a group that starts to evidence consensus and cooperation is now working as a team is generally accurate. While the group may appear to be operating in a more dynamic manner, some members are not yet performing in a unified or methodical way. However, having worked through some of the important issues in the previous stage, the team is now willing to take some risks and experiment with new practices, debate values and assumptions, review methods of operation and discuss issues of management and leadership. New confidence gained from resolving the earlier conflicts produces a receptiveness in team members to new ideas and risk-taking. If a leader has skilfully handled the first two stages, the team will move quickly through this third stage.

The challenges surrounding task performance issues focus on information-sharing, win–win attitudes to problem-solving, and a willingness to take calculated risks and change. These task-related activities are anchored in the new level of trust that has developed through the management of conflict. Individuals trust both themselves in the job and the other group members. This may motivate previously inactive members of staff to become more involved with a broader range of responsibilities. [...]

The focus of the team at the third stage of development continues to be on group relationships. Having been fragmented by conflict, staff members now are interested in achieving cohesion. The beginning of a 'team spirit' is evident, with staff spontaneously referring to themselves and their colleagues as 'the team'. Team members are more open-minded, more willing to listen to and support one another, and able to focus on the needs of the group rather than their own needs. Mutually accepted group norms begin to guide the work and relationships. The word 'we' is heard more often than 'I' or 'you' when the activities of the setting are discussed. The climate of the setting includes a lighthearted aspect where joking and humour illustrate good-natured attitudes in the staff.

Although conflict and disagreements may still occur, they are perceived as less threatening by the staff and handled differently. [...]

At this third stage, the role of the leader is to promote consensus and cooperation. Staff involvement and participation in goal-setting, the development of policies and their implementation in practice needs to be supported by the leader. A willingness to identify and address potential problems is essential. Open communication, constructive feedback and acknowledgement of contributions to the group will facilitate consensus and cooperation in the team. As the group begins to take pride in its achievements, it is truly becoming a team and is advancing into the fourth stage.

Stage 4: collaborating as an effective team

The rate at which a group of individuals will proceed to this fourth stage depends on the effectiveness of the leader in facilitating the transition through the previous stages. It is not until this fourth stage that the group of individuals who committed themselves to working together in the first stage can be said to be operating as an effective team.

At this stage, all members of the team are making a unique but equal contribution to the task. The team shares responsibility for the efficient operation of a quality service with the leader. Leadership style is decided according to the situation. Regular review and evaluation of goals, policies and practice are undertaken with a view to constant improvement of the service. [...]

The relationship aspect of the team is based on mutual respect and support. Team members recognise their interdependence as well as their independence. Individual differences and successes are valued. People are now able to 'agree to disagree' if mutually acceptable solutions to problems are not forthcoming. The climate is marked by concern for other team members, warmth and friendliness.

[...]

A team that reaches this stage of mature development can operate productively for a long period of time, as long as attention is given to ensuring effective working methods and the maintenance of relationships. While self-evaluation should be encouraged in all staff members from the time they join the group, formal evaluation of the team and its performance needs to be introduced at this point. This will ensure that questions such as 'How are we going?', 'Where do we want to go next?' and 'What are our needs now?' are addressed in order to keep the team at its maximum operational efficiency. However, if any of the conditions change, such as a staff member leaving or the dissolution of the group because its purpose no longer exists, the team enters the final stage in its development: that of separation and closure.

Stage 5: closure

This final stage tends to be ignored by many team leaders who, in their haste to move the team back to a more productive and positive stage, fail to acknowledge the team's need to celebrate or mourn its existence and track record. A change in or the disbanding of a team can occur at any stage in a team's development. The sensitive leader will ensure that the team has an opportunity to experience some form of closure so that staff members can deal with any unfinished business that might prevent them from approaching their future working situation positively.

When a team ceases to be operational, the members have to come to terms with two issues: disengagement from the task and separation from and/or closure of relationships. Usually there is a period of time for the team to work these issues through. It is the leader's responsibility to ensure that the team has access to a means of debriefing and bringing closure to the experience. Comments such as 'Remember when Jenny was here? She would have known what to do' or 'Didn't we work well together before all the changes!' suggest that the staff have not had sufficient time to come to terms with the demise of the previous team. These nostalgic memories may interfere with commitment to the new team and acceptance of any new staff members.

If the team has worked well and it has been a satisfying experience for those involved, the staff will be able to celebrate the end of the team by reviewing and evaluating individual development, task performance and work relationships. The team should recognise and celebrate its accomplishments and express its satisfaction with the process. [...]

If the ending of the team is marked by a lack of achievement and/or poor relationships, it is more difficult – but even more important – to engage in a process of closure. Each team member's contribution should be reviewed and evaluated as well as the overall group dynamic in order to identify the problems that prevented the team from operating effectively. In this way, the leader and the group members should gain a basis for planning for the next team experience.

Team leadership

Becoming an effective leader in early childhood has an inherent difficulty that few leaders in other professions have to deal with. In some services – for example, childcare – leaders have to adapt on a daily basis to moving from the position of administrative leader to being a member of a room team responsible for the direct care of children. The way in which the leader's time is allocated officially to combine administration, direct care and teaching ensures that both the leader and the team members have to adapt to the constant changes in the leader's position in the team. This can place a great strain on the resources of the leader, who is required to relinquish the authority of leadership when working as an equal member of a direct care or teaching team and to resume and command that same authority when undertaking administrative functions. Team members can become confused about the appropriate way to interact with the leader when in the direct care and teaching team role. This constant fluctuation between leader and team member requires sensitive management by the leader. Team leadership has some advantages for early childhood leaders who find themselves in this position.

To review the leader's role in relation to the team, the key functions are to provide and communicate a vision to the group, develop the team culture, set goals, monitor and communicate the team's achievements to the team and relevant others, and facilitate and encourage the development of individuals. [...] An effective team leader:

- uses personality to lead by example, thereby stimulating a particular team culture;
- is innovative and is perceived to be making things better by improving team morale and productivity;
- ensures that constructive relationships are established and maintained with the staff and peers;
- focuses attention on behaviour or the situation, not on the person;
- fosters the self-esteem and confidence of team members; and
- coaches team members to improve their performance.

Certain values and approaches have been found to be associated with developing this team leadership orientation. They can assist in matching the leadership style to follower needs and situational demands. Early childhood practitioners will find that the following attributes may be useful in meeting the demands of team leadership:

- adaptable (the capacity to be responsive and innovative);
- energetic (action-oriented and committed to work);
- people-oriented (values people and communicates openly);
- quality-conscious (pays attention to standards of excellence and consumer needs and expectations);
- uniting (clarifies the common purpose and promotes the value of cooperation);
- entrepreneurial (autonomous and able to articulate the uniqueness of the service);
- focused (self-disciplined and predictable);
- informal (a relaxed, straightforward approach to people and situations).

These features, values and approaches of team leadership are fundamental to the early childhood leader making things happen in ways which can increase staff and parent participation. When attempting to build and lead a team, leaders need to be conscious of the positive impact that team leadership can have on a group of individuals who are working together, and incorporate appropriate aspects of the team leadership approach into their style. [...]

A framework for team-building

As discussed previously in the stages of team development, the process of galvanising a group of individuals into a cohesive team is not a quick and painless one. Becoming a team demands effort from every member of the group, and requires that the leader relate to the group in a certain way. [...]

The team-building process basically focuses on the two dimensions of any team: staff morale and task demands. In order to build team morale, the group needs to be able to provide social support for the interpersonal demands that evolve in any work group. [...]

Leaders who want to encourage a team approach in settings can be guided by the following five-step framework for team-building in early childhood settings (Neugebauer and Neugebauer, 1998).

1. *Set achievable goals* which have been mutually agreed upon by members of the team. Ensure that the assertive staff members do not dominate the process, especially during discussion at staff meetings.
2. *Clarify roles*. Team members work most effectively when their roles are clear to all and free of conflict. Each staff member should be aware of who is responsible for what. While it will be easier to clarify the formal roles that need to be fulfilled, the informal roles that relate to the internal functioning of the group should not be forgotten (Johnson and Johnson, 2003). [...]
3. *Build supportive relationships* – that is, build in opportunities for feedback, develop trust and provide resources to stimulate a cooperative team spirit. Teams where members feel supported are more likely to deal with (rather than ignore) common team problems such as role ambiguity, role conflict and group conflict.
4. *Encourage active participation* to capitalise on the knowledge and skills of individual team members. In an atmosphere of acceptance, team members will be encouraged to contribute their ideas, opinions and energies. Being part of a cooperative venture can be extremely motivating for team members, and this will increase productivity.
5. *Monitor team effectiveness*. There is little point in putting time and energy into team leadership and the team-building process if the team is not achieving the goals effectively or if the team is unhappy with the process. Regular opportunities

need to be provided by the leader to assess the extent of goal achievement and how well members are working together as a team. [...]

The success of the team approach relies on open communication, democratic organisation and effective problem-solving skills. An effective team should fulfil staff needs for participation and support and result in efficient and effective approaches to the task.

Bringing it together

Team-building and effective team leadership usually result in high-quality interaction between team members and the leader, which increases trust and openness, the development of interpersonal relationships, joint goal-setting, clarification of roles and responsibilities, and analysis of the appropriate processes related to the team's purpose. The team approach to work in early childhood settings can also assist in staff development and in meeting the challenge of change because it provides the back-drop of support for and commitment to quality service delivery.

References

Abbott, L. and Hevey, D. 2001, 'Training to work in the early years: Developing the climbing frame', *Contemporary Issues in the Early Years: Working Collaboratively for Children*, 3rd edn, ed. G. Pugh, Paul Chapman, London.

Abbott, L. and Moylert, H. eds 1997, *Working with the Under 3s: Responding to Children's Needs*, Open University Press, Buckingham.

Adair, J. 1986, *Effective Teambuilding*, Gower Publishing Company, Aldershot.

Curran, D. 1989, *Working with Parents: A Guide to Successful Parent Groups*, American Guidance Service, Minneapolis.

Ebbeck, M. and Waniganayake, M. 2003, *Early Childhood Professionals: Leading Today and Tomorrow*, MacLennan + Percy Pty Ltd, Sydney.

Edgington, M. 2000, 'Principles of effective collaboration', *Early Years Educator*, vol. 1, no. 10, pp. 2–5.

Hennessy, E., Martin, S., Moss, P. and Melhuish, E. 1992, *Children and Day Care: Lessons From Research*, Chapman Publishing, London.

Johnson, D.W. and Johnson, F.P. 2003, *Joining Together: Group Theory and Process*, international edn, Allyn & Bacon, Needham Heights.

Law, S. and Glover, D. 2000, *Educational Leadership and Learning: Practice*, Policy and Research, Open University Press, Buckingham.

Neugebauer, B. and Neugebauer, R. eds 1998, *The Art of Leadership: Managing Early Childhood Organisations*, vol. 2, Child Care Information Exchange, Perth.

Rodd, J. 1987, 'It's not just talking: The role of interpersonal skills training for early childhood educators', *Early Child Development and Care*, vol. 29, no. 2, pp. 241–52.

Rodd, J. 1998, *Leadership in Early Childhood: The Pathway to Professionalism*, 2nd edn, Allen & Unwin, Sydney.

Schiller, J. 1987, 'Peer supervision: Learning more about what we do', *Australian Journal of Early Childhood*, vol. 12, no. 3, pp. 43–6.

Sylva, K. and Siraj-Blatchford, I. 2003, *Effective Provision of Pre-school Education*, Department for Education and Skills, London.

Walker, E.H. 1995, 'Teamwork in child care: A study of communication issues in forming a team', Masters Thesis, University of Adelaide, Adelaide.

Whalley, M. 1994, *Learning to be Strong*, Hodder & Stoughton, London.

Whalley, M. 2001, 'Working as a team', in *Contemporary Issues in the Early Years: Working Collaboratively for Children*, 3rd edn, ed. G. Pugh, Paul Chapman, London.

Woodcock, M. 1979, *Team Development Manual*, Halstead Press. New York.

Woodcock, M. and Francis, D. 1981, *Organisational Development Through Teambuilding*, Gower Publishing, Adelaide.

22

Effective leadership in the early years sector: the ELEYS study

Iram Siraj-Blatchford and Laura Manni

Overview

Effective leadership in early years education and care is linked to more positive and successful outcomes for children. In the 'Effective Leadership in the Early Years Sector Study' (EYELS study), Iram Siraj-Blatchford and Laura Manni gather extensive qualitative data from a range of early years and primary settings to examine perceptions of leadership and professional practice from different professional perspectives. The development of effective leadership approaches are considered and the importance of collaboration, home/school partnerships, monitoring and assessing, effective communication and ongoing early years professional development are highlighted. These are discussed as significant contributory factors in developing reflective communities of practice.

[…]

Introduction

[…] Early childhood education has undergone extensive changes through the Sure Start and Children's Centre programmes (10 Year Childcare Strategy). A greater

Siraj-Blatchford, I. and Manni, L. (2007) *Effective Leadership in the Early Years Sector (ELEYS) Study*, London: Institute of Education, University of London, pp. 1–31.

emphasis has been placed on accountability and upon the achievement of excellence. A major policy thrust to develop 1,700 children's centres, has made the need for the training of additional early years practitioners and early years leaders particularly urgent. [...] These centres and all other early years provision will need skilled leadership, but where is the firm evidence regarding the characteristics of effective leadership in early years settings? And where are the training opportunities and support required to help leaders from the diverse provisions to prepare for this?

It was within these challenging contexts that the *Effective Leadership in the Early Years Sector* (ELEYS) project was developed as an extension of the *Researching Effective Pedagogy in the Early Years* (REPEY) study (Siraj-Blatchford et al., 2002).

The ELEYS research was designed to explore the following questions:

• What does the extant literature and research tell us about effective educational leadership in the early years?
• What characteristics or patterns of leadership can be identified in the REPEY sample of effective settings?

[...] The Effective *Provision of Pre-school Education* (EPPE) project (Sylva et al., 2004) assessed the attainment and development of 3,000 children that were followed from the age of 3 until the end of Key Stage 1. The children were recruited to the study during 1997–1999 from a random sample of 141 pre-school settings (nursery schools, nursery classes, play groups, private day nurseries, local authority day nurseries and integrated centres). Both qualitative and quantitative methods were applied in EPPE and REPEY to explore the effects of the pre-school experience on children's cognitive attainment and social/behavioural development at entry to school, and any continuing effects on such outcomes up to 7 years of age.

The REPEY study explored the pedagogical practices occurring in a sample of 12 early years settings identified as effective by EPPE (Siraj-Blatchford et al., 2003). Two reception classes were also added to ensure that all the major institutional forms of Foundation Stage group care and educational settings were represented. The REPEY early years settings thus represented 'good' (slightly above average) to 'excellent' (well above average) settings based upon both cognitive and social/behavioural child outcomes. Data from the 14 settings were collected using an analytical framework to ensure comparable data would allow for across-case comparisons. The analysis of qualitative data also offered a basis for what Geertz (1973) has referred to as 'thick description' (Siraj-Blatchford et al., 2003).

The key characteristics of caring and effective settings as established through the EPPE and REPEY studies

The EPPE and REPEY studies have shown that pre-school experience (compared to none) benefits children throughout Key Stage 1 (Sylva et al., 2004). EPPE found that good quality provision was found in *all* types of early years settings, and that there was greater variation within each type than between them. Higher overall quality was however found in settings that integrated care and education, and in nursery schools.

EPPE and REPEY also found that individual pre-schools varied in their 'effectiveness' for influencing a child's development, and that children made better all-round progress in settings where:

- there was strong leadership and relatively little staff turnover;
- the adults formed warm interactive relationships with children;
- settings viewed educational and social development as complementary;
- the adults used open-ended questioning and encouraged 'sustained shared thinking';
- a balance was achieved between adult-supported freely chosen play, and adult-led small group activities;
- the adults used formative assessment to differentiate the curriculum according to the needs of individual children;
- the adults supported children in being assertive while at the same time rationalising and talking through their conflicts;
- the adults had a good understanding of appropriate pedagogical content;
- a trained teacher acted as manager and a good proportion of the staff were (graduate, teacher) qualified.

The EPPE study also found that the quality of the home learning environment (HLE) had a stronger effect on children's intellectual and social development than other important influences, including (notably) their parent's occupation, education or income. The EPPE study has therefore shown that what parents do to support their children's learning is more important than who the parents are.

Methodology of the Effective Leadership in the Early Years Study

[…] A distinctive feature of the ELEYS analysis has also been to explore the issue of leadership within *effective* early years settings *from the bottom up*. […] Semi-structured interviews had been conducted with the leaders from each of the REPEY case study settings but these questions were not explicitly about leadership; rather they prompted the managers to discuss their general practice with respect to the *Curriculum Guidance for the Foundation Stage* (CGFS), staffing ratios, staff training and development, child development, pedagogy, policy development, etc. The re-analysis of REPEY interviews with EY staff and parents has allowed for analysis across the settings, and within the settings it has provided a means of triangulation; where any contradictions or concurrence between theory and practice or between staff, parent and manager perceptions within a setting could be revealed.

In an effort to identify the contribution made by effective leadership to the success of the REPEY settings, the ELEYS study has drawn upon:

- demographic information about managers;
- semi-structured interviews with managers, teachers and other EY staff (e.g. nursery nurses) and parents;
- researcher observations and field notes;
- EY centre policies and documentation;
- child outcome data associated with cognitive and social/behavioural development.

[...]

In addition, an ELEYS focus group was formed from research 'users' to provide further construct validation, and to clarify the research findings. The focus group members included a range of representatives from relevant organisations, including the National Day Nurseries Association, QCA, TDA, Pre-School Learning Alliance and General Teaching Council. The focus group also included several heads of centres immersed in the day-to-day practice of leadership; four of whom were leaders of centres which appeared on David Bell's (2003) list of excellent centres. [...]

The objective of the initial analysis was to identify the leadership approaches adopted within the effective REPEY early years settings. [...]

The following sections are drawn from our analysis of the REPEY case studies and are supported by the extant literature on effective leadership.

The challenge of developing leadership in early years

Over 15 years ago, Beare et al. (1989) stated that 'Outstanding leadership has invariably emerged as a key characteristic of outstanding schools'. This view of leadership continues to be supported by the research today, with the contribution of educational leadership clearly and 'unequivocally' indicating the importance of leadership for 'improving organisational performance and raising achievement' (Muijs et al., 2004; see also Cheng, 1994; Evans and Teddlie, 1995; Leithwood and Riehl, 2003; Sammons et al., 1995; Southworth, 1998). Following on from Ofsted's (2003a) identification of the importance of leadership, the HMI report *Leadership and Management: managing the workforce*, highlighted 'the importance of developing and managing the culture and ethos of the school, providing a good working environment, tackling excessive workloads, providing well-targeted staff development opportunities and introducing change with sensitivity' as key tasks leaders face (Ofsted, 2003b). Parallel concerns have been expressed within the early years sector, where it is increasingly recognised that the quality of programmes and services for young children and their families has been related to effective leadership (Rodd, 1997; see also Jorde-Bloom and Sheerer, 1992; Clyde et al., 1994; Kagan, 1994; Clyde and Rodd, 1995). Particular challenges identified through the literature search and earlier studies that are connected with developing leadership in early years settings are outlined in this section.

1. Training of leaders and others related to the quality of provision

One of the key findings from the EPPE study which is particularly relevant to the current study and to the GTCE is the evidence that demonstrates that having a trained teacher as a leader/manager and a good proportion of trained teachers on staff are key indicators of quality. Looking particularly at the EPPE data regarding leaders, Taggart et al. (2000) found that the early years leaders with the highest childcare qualifications were found predominately in 'education' rather than the 'care' sector (i.e. in nursery schools and classes). They also found higher leader qualification levels in centres combining both care and education (integrated or combined centres). The least qualified managers were located in playgroups, with 50% with Childcare certificates (BTec) or lower, with one in ten having no childcare qualifications at all (p. 25). The EPPE team went on to report that when quality environment profiles (Early Childhood Environment Rating Scale, 1998) were grouped according to the leader's 'childcare qualification level, it was found that the quality of the environment increases with the' leader's childcare qualifications.

[...]

2. Types of training

Rodd (1997) found that although 91.7% of her sample of 76 early childhood professionals reported having taken some form of training to support their leadership roles, the majority of these were general in-service or short courses. Our research supports Rodd's finding. Analysis of the responses given by interviewees (managers, EY staff), and the exploration of policy and other documentation regarding approaches to professional development demonstrates a verbal and written commitment and conviction to the importance of ongoing professional development. However, upon further analysis of these data, it is clear that a great deal of the professional development opportunities experienced by those both in management and staff positions tends to be, as Rodd describes, general in-service or short courses. In a minority of cases, there was evidence that the manager or another member of staff was pursuing more long-term courses (i.e. Diploma course in Management studies, degree courses in Early Years Education), however reports of this were infrequent. In some instances, respondents referred back to their original early years courses when asked either about their involvement in professional development or the training they are relying on to support them in their current work.

3. Reluctance to accept the leadership role

While organisational and societal barriers may exist to prevent many women from realising their ambitions for leadership in the primary and secondary school sectors, this is not the case in early years settings, where the route to leadership is less constricting. Indeed as Rodd (1998) argues, several of those who apply for leadership positions do so reluctantly or are unconsciously ill-prepared. There also appears to be a misconception that one's success as an early years staff member will naturally translate into a successful leader. Sadek and Sadek (2004), for example, argue that early years staff have many of the skills that nursery leaders require; notably experience supporting and supervising other adults (e.g. parents, placement students). Yet Waniganayake et al. (2000) have found that many of those in positions of leadership identify the role of working with and managing adults difficult (see also Bright and Ware, 2003). Those making the transition need to consider how they are prepared to make the change from 'managing' children to 'managing' adults and to handle all of the other administrative tasks that accompany the role.

Rodd (1998, 2005) has highlighted the reluctance amongst leaders in the early years to accept the label 'leader'. Leaders often express an aversion towards the management aspects of the job, which are seen to take them away from their preferred status as educators and child developers. These were concerns clearly shared by many leaders in the ELEYS sample: 'I spend a lot more time in my office now than I ever did … the amount of paperwork you have to do is depressing and it keeps me away from the children and staff' (Leader, Private Day Nursery). [...]

4. National training for early years leaders

While dedicated training (National Professional Qualification in Integrated Centre Leadership – NPQICL) is now becoming available, through the National College of School Leadership (NCSL), for current and aspiring leaders from Integrated Centres, there are still a majority of early years 'leaders', represented in around 30,000 pre-school settings (i.e. playgroups, nursery schools, private day nurseries, etc.), whose specific training needs are not currently being (collectively] met. Many of those leadership and management courses that are on offer to early years leaders also tend to be geared to the primary and secondary school sector. One of the early years leaders who participated in the ELEYS Focus Group gave an account of her experience on a general educational leadership training course where she was the only early years participant. She explained that she felt isolated, because the experiences shared by others on the course were so different from those she'd experienced in her own setting: and as these were often the foundation upon which discussions and activities were based, she struggled to get deeply involved. [...]

Defining leadership for learning in the early years

It is largely female

One aspect that is unique to the early years context is that the workforce is almost exclusively female. The Daycare Trust reports that 97.5% of the childcare workforce is female. Yet much of the current literature on leadership and management has ignored issues of gender and much of the literature and research in the wider context of education has inevitably been based upon men's experiences and male approaches. Cubillo (1999) argues that 'the modes on which the characteristics of effective leaders are based are therefore stereotypically androcentric', often associated with 'masculine' attributes and behaviours such as competitiveness, dynamism, power and agressivity (p. 547). [...]

In her groundbreaking research involving 600 administrators in schools in the USA, Shakeshaft (1987) identified five main features of the female world in school administration. The first three related to their tendency to focus upon the: (1) centrality of relationships with others; (2) teaching and learning; and the (3) importance of building a learning community. She found that women 'communicated more, motivated more, [and] spent more time with marginal teachers and students' (Scrivens, 2002: 27). The other two distinguishing features identified by Shakeshaft were the feeling of marginality in the otherwise male-dominated arena of education; and in the blurring of private and public spheres (where women's behaviour was not found to differ significantly between the two). Shakeshaft's work also suggests that women's leadership style tends to be more democratic and participatory, encouraging inclusiveness and a broader view of the curriculum (Scrivens, 2002). [...]

It is about leading people

It is through relationships that people develop an attachment and a feeling of responsibility, rather than an obligation, towards common goals and objectives (Lewin and Regine, 2000; Fullan, 2001). It is also important that relationships evolve as the organisation they exist within evolves, continually seeking and responding to dissension from inside and outside to ensure the same common goals and objectives are sought. The role of the formal leader in developing and maintaining these networks/relationships within their schools is essential. Kouzes and Posner (1996) go so far as to argue that the feature that separates effective from ineffective leaders is the degree to which they 'care about the people they lead' (p. 149). Kouzes and Posner (1996) identify seven strategies that may be employed by leaders in establishing and promoting relationships: (1) setting clear standards; (2) expecting the best; (3) paying attention; (4) personalising recognition; (5) telling the story; (6) celebrating together; and (7) setting the example (p. 18). Having identified a list of strategies, it is all too easy to represent them as characteristics of effective leaders. But the emphasis that has been placed on leadership 'traits' in the extant research and literature on school leadership has been criticised (Southworth, 2004: 1). Whenever researchers identify the key traits of an 'effective leader', they infer that these should be simply applied, like a recipe, by others in leadership positions. The greatest danger of this is, of course, as highlighted by Southworth, the failure to consider the importance of context. As Spillane et al. (2004) have argued, while there is a generally accepted view that 'where there are good schools there are good leaders', there is very little evidence that illustrates the *'how'* of school leadership; that is knowledge of the ways in which school leaders develop and sustain those conditions and processes believed necessary for innovation.

It is dependent on context

Southworth (1998) presents the notion of *situational leadership*, describing a type of leadership that involves consideration of the situation in which the leader operates, as well as the people s/he is leading and encouraging to lead. In a more recent publication, Southworth (2004) spoke of the importance of leaders themselves being contextually literate. The leader who develops contextual literacy demonstrates an understanding that schools are dynamic organisms continually evolving, rather than static organisations. It also requires a recognition that education contexts differ at every level; they differ between individual children, families [and] local communities defined by socio-economic class, ethnicity, etc. With fluctuating staff morale and energy levels, the arrival of new staff and students and the departure of others, amongst numerous other factors, schools have to continually adjust and make room for new energies, ideas and conflicts.

The socio-economic and cultural context of settings was found to be particularly significant in the EPPE/REPEY studies. While the research provided evidence of a direct association between children's cognitive and social outcomes, and the pedagogic principles applied by the practitioners in effective settings, the evidence also showed that some settings appeared effective even where these pedagogic principles were not consistently applied. The REPEY evidence suggested that in some middle-class settings (notably some of the private day nurseries), it was less the staff's interventions and more the parents' pro-active support of their children's learning in the home, that accounted for the children's greater development. [...]

How do we define leadership?

[...] For the purpose of this [chapter], the authors have adopted two definitions of leadership, one which emerges from the early years literature and another from the social sector literature. Rodd offers a fairly detailed workable definition of leadership, one which attempts to identify the complexity of the leader's role:

> Leadership can be described as a process by which one person sets certain standards and expectations and influences the actions of others to behave in what is considered a desirable direction. Leaders are people who can influence the behaviour of others for the purpose of achieving a goal. Leaders possess a special set of somewhat elusive qualities and skills which are combined into an ability to get others to do what the leader wants because they want to do it. Leaders are able to balance the concern for work, task, quality and productivity with concern for people, relationships, satisfaction and morale. They combine an orientation towards innovation and change with an interest in continuity and stability for the present. They do this by using personal qualities which command respect

and promote feelings of trust and security. They are also responsible for setting and clarifying goals, roles and responsibilities, collecting information and planning, making decisions and involving members of the group by communicating, encouraging and acknowledging commitment and contribution. (Rodd, 1998. 2)

Whitaker offers a more concise, but equally realistic definition of the complexity of a leader's work:

> Leadership is concerned with creating the conditions in which all members of the organ-isation can give of their best in a climate of commitment and challenge. Leadership helps an organisation to work well. (Whitaker, 1993: 74)

In both of these definitions the importance of collaboration and organisational goals are clear. [...]

The ELEYS project has also identified a range of 'categories of effective leadership practice', each of which will be elaborated upon below.

Effective leadership practices identified in the settings

We have found in the REPEY case study data that a key area of leadership practice in the early years involves the identification and co-construction (by children, parents and staff) of shared objectives. It also involves inspiring others with a vision of a better future. It relies on a level of dedication and passion about early childhood care and education, and also upon a capacity to reflect upon and engage with changing con-texts (i.e. the children, families and community); and a willingness to embrace evi-dence-based practice. The provision of direction is promoted by the leader's capacity to identify and articulate an ambitious collective vision; to ensure consistency amongst the staff (shared understanding of setting practices and processes); being a reflective practitioner and encouraging reflective practice in others.

Identifying and articulating a collective vision

In most of the effective settings, better leadership was characterised by a clear vision, especially with regard to pedagogy and curriculum, which was shared by everyone working within the setting. These philosophies varied from being strongly educational to strongly social or a mixture of both, but all were very child-centred. The idea that the staff should develop or promote shared aims and objectives was consistently seen as crucial. All the most successful managers, in terms of child outcomes, demon-strated a strong educational focus. They valued the importance of adult–child interac-tion and they supported their staff in developing better ways of engaging children. Many of the settings were involved in projects such as the Effective Early Learning (EEL) project, and demonstrated interest in a variety of often promoted, international curricula models including Reggio Emilia (Italy), High Scope (America) and Te Whariki

(New Zealand), as well as adopting a sound and positive stance towards Curriculum Guidance for the Foundation Stage (CGFS, 2000). Many of the examples that we found of collective vision were embedded within the various practices described by interviewees. For instance, one leader's explanation of her strategic decision to trade the possibility of two NNEB staff for a qualified teacher revealed her conviction that specialist staff, and the expected skills and knowledge that they brought with them, could promote better quality and child progress. This was supported by this leader's commitment to the ongoing professional development of all the staff in her setting.

Ensuring shared understandings, meanings and goals

The second key capacity of a leader, next to vision or 'direction setting' (Leithwood and Levin, 2005: 14), is the capacity to influence others into action. In order to ensure the achievement of set targets and desired outcomes, a clear vision must exist. Without it, those within an organisation will often be working towards different and at times conflicting goals. [...] But how can a clear vision emerge? We found that staff members in the effective settings were encouraged to attend staff development sessions, although the nature of this varied greatly.

In the DfES (2005) paper entitled *Championing Children: A Shared Set of Skills, Knowledge and Behaviours for those Leading and Managing Integrated Children's Services,* one key aspect of leadership/management that is highlighted is the provision of *direction.* This is echoed by Leithwood and Riehl (2003) who identified, from their summary of the findings from several leadership studies, *providing direction* as one of the overarching functions of leadership. The leader of an organisation is assigned overall responsibility for determining/developing and articulating the vision, in addition to playing an active role in making the vision a reality. The DfES document argues that in addition to having and pursuing a vision, a manager should demonstrate collaborative, open and inclusive behaviour, towards building a common purpose. They go on to list a series of related aims linked to the pursuit of providing clear and purposeful direction. The original list, which is very much directed towards an integrated children's centre, has been adapted here (with additions and omissions) to meet the needs of a more diverse range of providers:

1. Translate strategic vision into specific plans in collaboration with all stakeholders.
2. Make use of the collective knowledge base – challenge [the] status quo and do things differently to meet the specific needs of the children and families within the setting more effectively.
3. Build a shared value base, promote collective knowledge and common purpose.
4. Support others to talk knowledgably about issues concerning their work and area of expertise.
5. Recognise that service performance and quality of provision can be improved via a responsive and flexible service that reflects the needs of the children, young people and families it serves.
6. Work for equality.

7. Develop a culture of, and systems to support, a high level of responsiveness within the setting.
8. Know the legislative frameworks for services to children and young people, and know where to go for detailed interpretation when required.

According to the research literature, one of the main obstacles impeding successful change is resistance/hesitation to change. The effective leader is therefore one who recognises the inevitability of change and is able to plan for and manage change in such a way that those she leads are a part of the process. Change is best seen as a process rather than an event. [...]

We found that one of the common features in the management of change by the effective settings was the explicit attempt made by leaders to make their changes according to the settings' current contexts (including children and families) and circumstances. Any resistance to change appeared to be overcome by the development of a climate and culture for change that was established through the routine collaborative review of current practice and policy. [...]

Effective communication

Effective communication is multi-functional and multi-directional; it involves speaking, encouraging, listening, reflecting, translating, interpreting, consulting, debating, summarising, understanding, acknowledging and verifying. There are also pre-requisites to communicating clearly and effectively, as an educational leader, that reach beyond elocution. These include the possession of general knowledge of early childhood development and education, as well as specific knowledge of the context within which one works. We found several examples which provided evidence of the features and related outcomes of effective communication. These features included leaders providing a level of *transparency* in regard to expectations, practices and processes; reciprocity (dialogue rather than monologue): *consultation*; and *reflection.* One of the most potent examples of effective communication emerged from the comparison of the responses provided by a leader, nursery teacher and nursery officer in one of the EY settings. The level of match in their responses about their practice was both striking and remarkable (Siraj-Blatchford and Manni, forthcoming), the case demonstrated (supported with other evidence) the fact that this leader was an effective communicator and promoted effective communication amongst her staff. Leaders who delivered and encouraged effective communication amongst and between staff were found capable of ensuring that the vision of the setting, in regards to practice, policy and processes, infiltrated the whole ethos of a centre; promoting consistency amongst staff working with children and families.

Encouraging reflection

Summarising the literature on the critical importance of building teams, Bennett et al. (2003) highlight the importance of individual members of a team sharing a common understanding of the organisation (school, early years setting) and possessing a common understanding of its aims and ways of working. A parallel concept linked within this literature concerned with the development of a team culture is the development of a 'community of learners', with a common commitment to reflective, critical practice and professional development. The recently established National Professional Qualification in Integrated Centre Leadership (NPQICL) programme is typical of many other short-and long-term training programmes, in taking as a key aim to encourage reflective practice. When discussing their policy development, a number of the effective early years settings reported on the collaborative reflective processes that were involved in the process. The active involvement in research, and the conscious/articulate consideration of alternative models or methods, showed that the leaders of the effective settings were both reflective in their own practice and encouraged reflection in their staff.

The current aim to 'professionalise' the childcare workforce (Children's Workforce Strategy, DfES, 2006) promotes the importance of professional development in ensuring improving qualifications of staff which have been linked to increased quality (e.g. Sylva et al., 1999). Fullan (2001) argues that 'organisations can transform when they can establish mechanisms for learning in the dailyness of organisational life' (p. 14). Rogoff et al. (1996) talk in a similar way about 'learning as a community process of transformation of participation in socio-cultural activities; viewing learning as collaboratively and socially constructed, rather than as individual possession' (Moore, 2004).
[...]

Monitoring and assessing practice

Reflective practice can be promoted within an early years setting via a routine and consistent system of monitoring and assessment and collaborative dialogue. In most of the early years settings involved in the ELEYS study, monitoring and assessment of staff was regarded as an important and critical feature of the running of the setting. The first and most important goal for the leaders of these effective settings was to support and improve the children's learning and development and their primary focus was therefore upon *teaching and learning*. It was recognised that the day-to-day practical interaction of the adults with the children had a direct effect upon child development. For this reason, it was considered important that this practice was monitored and assessed to continue to improve standards.
[...]

Commitment to ongoing, professional development

We have found that the managers of effective settings provide intellectual stimulation for their staff, along with respectful individualised support. An example taken from the Sunshine Private Day Nursery provides an excellent example of one centre's commitment to the ongoing assessment and development of their staff. This commitment to staff development begins upon entry to the nursery, where all staff members go through an induction programme which focuses on the care and safety of the children. This is followed by an expectation of ongoing training. Ongoing training is provided according to the needs identified through a regular appraisal system that takes place for each individual member of staff every 6–12 months and through other regular reviews by senior staff. The appraisal system itself provides a model whereby both the appraiser and appraisee can develop techniques of assessment and identification of training needs.

Members of the Sunshine staff can also choose to attend one or two courses from the programme circulated by the principal from a training company to which the centre is affiliated. Some of the courses on offer from this source included management, assessment and child protection courses. Other training is provided during regular in-house staff meetings and is conducted by the senior staff themselves. Also, a procedure is in place to ensure that members of staff who attend courses or workshops are given the time and opportunity to report back during staff meetings for the benefit of other staff. The centre manager also subscribes to relevant professional care and educational journals, which are circulated to all staff members, and staff also have access to an 'extensive' library of professional books.

The informal–formal model of monitoring and appraisal is one that was described by several managers within our sample of effective settings; though the frequency and procedures differ. Most informed us that they conducted ongoing, informal observations or discussions in an effort to maintain a grasp on the day-to-day happenings in their settings (and maintain contact with the children and parents); but then supplement these observations with a more formal approach to identifying the strengths and limitations of the staff. A comment made by the manager of Blue Skies Local Authority Day Care highlighted the role feedback could play in promoting more reflective practice. She explained:

> I am always surprised at the insight observers' comments and feedback offer. I think a lot of what we do is intuitive and for better or worse, access to an outside view can be very useful in promoting improved practice or verbalising existing good practice.

[…]

Distributed Leadership

One of the most detrimental implications of the low status experienced by early years staff in some settings has been its effect upon staff commitment [which is] linked to high staff turnover. One important means of raising self-esteem and morale is through directly involving staff in the leadership and management of their setting. Interestingly all the settings involved in the current study reported limited staff turnover. Most of the managers and the staff from the case study sample had been in their respective settings for over 3 years; in most settings, staff, especially at senior management level, had been in the post even longer: 10–20 years was not uncommon. Findings from the EPPE study which looked at a much larger sample of leaders, found that leaders and staff from the private sector suffered the highest degree of staff turnover. However, of the three private day nurseries included in the REPEY and now ELEYS study, all demonstrated a much greater stability and retention of staff, with many reporting 3 to 9 years of service in their respective settings. In each of the early years settings included in the case studies, all the leaders took on a lead role, most notably in regards to curriculum and planning: 'if staff have a really good sense of different curriculum areas then they can be so much more inspiring to the children. They can set tasks that are much harder and they set them on a more regular basis' (Local Authority Day Care Manager). In the DfES (May 2004) 2002–2003 Early Years Workforce Survey, it was reported that the average length of service amongst paid staff is 3 years and 5 months, with a turnover rate calculated at 18%.

A study conducted by Melhuish (2004) has recently suggested that high turnover in day nurseries and other pre-school settings is threatening the language and social skills of children. Melhuish argues that children learning to communicate often use idiosyncratic speech or gestures and that a caregiver who is familiar with a child learns these idiosyncrasies and is therefore able to respond, whereas a new caregiver is more likely to misunderstand them.

[...]

'Distributed', 'participative', facilitative' or 'collaborative' models of leadership call for a shift away from the traditional vision of leader as one key individual towards a more collective vision, one where the responsibility for leadership rests within various formal and informal leaders. Harris (2002) speaks of distributed leadership involving 'multiple sources of guidance and direction following the contours of expertise in an organisation, made coherent through a common culture' (see also Spillane et al., 2004).

[...]

Distributed leadership should not be seen as a simple panacea. In the case of many early years settings, like Private Day Nursery 413 for instance, where staff are often young, under-qualified and lacking experience (youngest: 18 years old; highest qualification: NNEB), it may be irresponsible for the manager to delegate too much responsibility, especially when funding for training and professional development is limited. Harris and Lambert (2003) usefully discuss leadership capacity building – the creation of opportunities for people, within a school or shared setting, to work together in new ways. The authors highlight the importance of certain conditions to be in place before such capacity building can authentically occur, including the 'internal capacity to manage change and sustain improvement' and the existence of 'collegial relations' between all potential participants. The capacity of the positional leader to manage change and sustain improvement is linked to ensuring that staff who are given leadership responsibilities are also provided with the support and development of skills required in order to meet their new demands. The managers of a number of the effective settings, showed a clear recognition that staff who had been given extra responsibility required ongoing support. For instance, the EEC 225 staff members who were given additional responsibilities were often asked to attend courses. That said, there was also evidence at times of staff members in some settings who were not given appropriate support.

At present, there are few concrete examples of distributive leadership in action within the current literature and indeed this difficulty is augmented by the current blurriness of the concept. A strong, charismatic leader is not necessarily at odds with the emergence of distributed leadership, and at some stages in some settings it may be necessary to achieve the required structural changes to support the emergence of distributed leadership. Harris and Lambert (2003: 31) see this as a paradox.

> ... it appears that the strength of will, vision and values-base required to transform schools as they are currently organised into contexts in which leadership is truly distributed requires strong head teacher leadership.

Though the current data was not collected with a direct interest in identifying distributive leadership in early years settings, some examples did emerge. But from our review of the literature and our analysis of the RELEY data, while 'collaboration', and 'teamwork' appear to be crucial in terms of analysis and practical effectiveness, the use of the term 'distributed leadership' seems to do little to clarify these processes further.

The success of a setting is largely dependent upon the level of dedication, commitment and effort made by the people within it. This commitment and effort will be endorsed and promoted by the positional leader who has high expectations and is able to recognise the current, as well as the potential strengths of all of those staff and children working within their setting. Effective leaders are therefore reflective practitioners who influence and develop people by setting an example, and providing a model, both morally and purposefully.

Building a learning community and team culture

Bennett et al. (2003) argue that 'teams operate best in an open climate, with both intra-group and inter-group relations based on mutual trust and open communication in a supportive organisational climate' (p. 9). They go on to report that this literature stresses the importance of collaboration and the recognition of strengths and expertise amongst staff. But Jackson (2003) highlights an essential point about the challenges that arise in the attempt to encourage collaboration between adults with different roles and status levels. While Jackson was referring to school sectors, it may be argued that the early years sector is currently troubled with far more diversity with regard to the qualifications, ages and levels of experience in its workforce.

In the report of their study of the Coram Community Campus (a multi-agency setting), Wigfall and Moss (2001) identified several factors that appeared to be impeding the integration of the variety of services (health, social services, education, etc.) on offer. They found that there were external forces – government policy and agendas – that appeared to be hampering coordinated work. They argued that these agendas and policies can: ... 'work against effective networks ... [when] introducing too many initiatives, projects, targets, funding schemes and other mechanisms specific to particular services simultaneously'. They also highlighted the lack of attention paid, by funding bodies, to the provision of non-contact time; time required for professional development, as well as that necessary to establish collaborative links with and between working groups/individuals. Another constraint was the idea of 'individual agendas of busy-ness'.

Time and effort clearly needs to be spent in creating the conditions necessary for a collaborative team culture to emerge. There is a need to develop partnerships amongst members of staff, which in turn requires the breaking down of rigid boundaries, the establishment of trust and respect between all those involved (in spite of differing qualifications and experience), and the potential of staff to work flexibly and share expertise. [...]

Encouraging and facilitating parent and community partnerships

As previously noted, the EPPE/REPEY research evidence demonstrates that home educational provisions and consistency across home and early years settings (and between parents and early years staff) promotes achievement for young children (e.g. Sylva et al. 2004). Many other studies highlight family and parent involvement in children's learning as having an influence on their happiness, achievement and learning in schools (see, for example, Epstein, 1989; Coleman, 1991; Epstein and Dauber, 1991; Arvizu, 1996). There is also evidence which demonstrates that this partnership can improve student motivation, behaviour and self-esteem. Sylva et al's (2004) research found that 'work with parents as first educators is an effective strategy' and goes on to argue that 'intervening with parents in early childhood has powerful effects on language, cognition and self-esteem – at least for three and four year olds' (see also Evangelou et al., 2005).

Despite all of this evidence, the relationship between home and many early years settings remains unilateral, with the direction of information about children moving from the early years setting and staff to the parents, and rarely in the opposite direction. One of the main objectives of the Every Child Matters (DfES, 2003) initiative has been to ensure the improvement of the level and degree of support offered to parents and carers. With the increased integration of services revolving around children and their families, such as health services, social care and education, there is a growing need (and expectation) for the development of partnerships with parents and families.

Home–school initiatives in the last two decades have been many and varied and have changed from being largely compensatory in nature to participatory and inclusive of parents, schools and children (Bastiani, 1988). Parent involvement has been interpreted in a number of ways such as: parents in school, teachers at home and parents as governors (Wolfendale, 1992, Siraj-Blatchford and Brooker, 1998). But what is meant by this term 'parental partnership'? Foot et al. (2002) argue that 'partnership goes beyond involvement: it is not just including parents in support and activities of pre-school education. Partnership implies equality and a division of power which inevitably draws parents into decision making and policy issues, not merely helping and information sharing.' It moves towards an empowerment of parents (Ball, 1994) and towards increasing their self-efficacy. Foot et al. (2002) go on to argue that the types of involvement on offer to parents should not be limited to activities which *directly* promote the children or the 'school', but should also move towards making parents the direct recipients of their involvement. Such active participation in attending, for instance, courses offered, planned or advertised by an early years setting (i.e. Nursery School), can promote parents' self-efficacy, which, in turn, can make parents conscious of their influential role over their child's development and therefore improve the quality of both their own interactions with their children and the learning activities that they provide (Bandura, 1997).

Parents are not a homogeneous group and therefore can hold different culturally conceived ideas (social class and ethnic differences) about the role of education, professional educators, and their own role as educators. In some cultures the role of the 'teacher' is seen as quite distinct and separate to the role of parenting.

[...]

[C]entres with good and successful outcomes such as 214 DC and 426 EEC provided regular information through records of achievement and monthly meetings with key workers. In the case of 219 PDN and 421 NS, weekly feedback is provided. What is distinctive about all of these centres is that they focus on what they are teaching the children and report regularly on the children's achievements, offering the opportunity for consistency of learning opportunities between home and school. These centres engage in more regular ongoing assessment of children's learning, and this supports the parents from these centres in engaging more in complementary educational activities in the home.

> We had an induction thing for parents and they went through everything with us. I know they are assessing as they go in and it's continual assessment. They were going to let us know how our child performed in that. Not a standard test but they're watching them. They were going to let us know what stage they're at but I'm not quite sure what form that's going to take whether it's a meeting or written. (501 RC parent 5)

Parents from these centres are pro-active in initiating learning activities at home. Where this was combined with staff encouraging positive dispositions, such as independence, the children often led and initiated the learning activities at home themselves. [...]

The strategies the leaders applied in the development of their parental partnerships varied:

> when our parents are first introduced to the nursery we see them half a term before their children start. And during that time we explain our philosophy and we try to demonstrate some of the ethos of the nursery by inviting them in for visits so that they can see the children working. And we say to them 'look the children are doing science and it looks like this', 'the children here are doing maths, but it looks like this'. (Manager, 106)

In these effective settings, parents were often offered genuine support and encouragement; in setting 017 there was evidence of this in the nursery staff's provision of crèche services for parents attending meetings that were led by counsellors from a nearby health centre. A large parent's room is also available for groups and meetings and a parenting group meets weekly. Also, on open evenings, when parents are invited into the nursery class, the staff put out appropriate toys for the younger siblings of centre children who usually attend.

Leading and managing: striking the balance

Webb (2005) refers to the two dimensions of head teachers as 'leading professional and chief executive manager' (p. 69). The balancing of administrative tasks and tasks associated with teaching and learning is a key responsibility for the formal leaders of organisations (schools and early years settings). However, with the ever-increasing demands for accountability, these two roles are often viewed in conflict by those in positions of leadership, with the mastery of management tasks appearing the clear route to meeting the ever-changing expectations and increasing accountability. This is not helped by the fact that the two terms are often treated as separate concepts within the literature, rather than parallel, Jeffrey and Troman (2004) refer to several research projects (Troman, 1997; Woods et al., 1997; Jeffrey and Woods, 1998) which report 'a growth of constraint, intensification of work and increasing managerialism resulting from school restructuring and Ofsted inspection' (p. 537). The difficulty of balancing these seemingly disparate tasks has often seen one, the administrative role, taking precedence over the other – leading teaching and learning.

[...]

The large majority, almost 88.5%, spoke of their involvement and experience with human beings. When asked about those features they found least satisfying, administrative burdens topped the list, in addition to dealing [with] difficult and demanding aspects of interpersonal relations, external influences and lack of status. Interestingly Rodd found that most of these 'least rewarding' features were also the aspects of the job the respondents found most difficult.

[...]

The feeling of added pressure brought on by the external award of a grant is one shared by the manager of Nursery Class 324. The manager, whose setting had been awarded Beacon status, highlighted her awareness of the potential problems that might arise from attempting to reconcile the demands of the Beacon status on the school, in terms of the number of visitors and training commitments expected, with the maintenance of current provision:

> Somehow or other I will have to decide which I am doing for what purpose. And that won't be easy.

Several of the leaders of our effective settings highlighted their dissatisfaction with the increase in bureaucratic tasks, which have emerged as a result of increased pressure, both external and internal, for change and accountability. [...]

Summary and conclusions

Southworth (2002) argues that much of the existing literature on leadership has been overly prescriptive, disregarding the variation existing between schools, and lacking examples of effective practices. He goes on to argue that the development of taxonomies or lists of what leadership involves, tend to dissect the leaders' work, therefore overlooking the myriad other tasks that they perform. HMI (2003), with others, have argued that the difficulty in identifying what the characteristics of effective leadership are is because different circumstances appear to require different skills and attributes.

We have argued that *contextual literacy*, a commitment to *collaboration*, and to the *improvement of children's learning outcomes* should be considered (by definition) to provide fundamental requirements for *Leadership for Learning*. Each of these leadership qualities was found to be strongly represented in the effective settings that we studied. We also identified a range of 'categories of effective leadership practice' in the effective settings that might be considered valuable in the development of leadership training:

- Identifying and articulating a collective vision, especially with regard to pedagogy and curriculum.
- Ensuring shared understandings, meanings and goals: building common purposes.
- Effective communication: providing a level of *transparency* in regard to expectations, practices and processes.
- Encouraging reflection: which acts as an impetus for change and the motivation for ongoing learning and development.
- Commitment to ongoing professional development: supporting staff to become more critically reflective in their practice.
- Monitoring and assessing practice: through collaborative dialogue and action research.
- Building a learning community and team culture: establishing a community of learners.
- Encouraging and facilitating parent and community partnerships, promoting achievement for all young children.

We also discussed distributed leadership and argued (perhaps paradoxically) that strong leadership may be necessary in the development of the high levels of collaboration and teamwork that are required. It is also necessary for those responsible to reconcile the sometimes competing demands of leadership and management.

The early years sector is experiencing massive change so that it isn't at all surprising that leaders are currently concerned to achieve a better balance of administrative tasks with tasks associated with teaching and learning. It is increasingly recognised that the quality of programmes and services for young children and their families are related to effective leadership. One of the targets set by the childcare workforce strategy is to have one member of staff trained to graduate level by 2015, a target which the Daycare Trust argues 'falls short of the vision of having one of the best childcare services in the world' (Daycare Trust, April 2005). Referring to New Zealand's target of 100% graduate, teacher trained, early years workforce by 2012, the Daycare Trust claim that a similar target is achievable in the UK.

The question of the amount of funding needed to raise the salaries of staff as they raise their qualifications also remains problematic.

However, there is no doubt that effective leadership and appropriate training for the leadership role is an increasingly important element in providing high-quality provision for the early years, especially as we move to larger and sometimes more complex, multi-professional teams of staff (see Siraj-Blatchford et al., 2007) across the early years sector.

References

Arvizu, S. (1996) Family, community, and school collaboration, In J. Sikula (Ed.), *Handbook of Research on Teacher Education* (pp. 814–819). New York, NY: Simon and Schuster Macmillan.

Ball, C. (1994) *Start Right: The Importance of Early Learning.* London: RSA.

Bandura, A. (1997) *Self-efficacy: The Exercise of Control.* New York: Freeman.

Bastiani, J. (1988) How many parents did you see last night? A critical look at some of the problems of evaluating home/school practice. In J. Bastiani (Ed.), *Parents and Teachers 2: From Policy to Practice.* Windsor: NFER-Nelson.

Beare, H., Caldwell, B. and Millikan, R. (1989) *Creating an Excellent School.* London: Routledge.

Bell, D. (2003) www.ofsted.gov.uk/news/index.cfm?fuseaction=news.details&id=1460

Bennett, N., Wise, C., Woods, P. and Harvey, J. (2003) *Distributed Leadership: A Literature Review.* London: National College for School Leadership. Available at: www.ncsl.orq.uk/mediastore/imaqe2/bennett-distributed-leadership-full.pdf

Bright, T. and Ware, N. (2003) *Were You Prepared? Findings from a National Survey of Headteachers. Summary Practitioner Enquiry Report.* Nottingham: NCSL.

Cheng, Y.C. (1994) Teacher leadership style: a classroom-level study. *Journal of Educational Administration* 32(3): 54–71.

Clyde, M. and Rodd, J. (1995) Survey of the perceptions of the definition of caregiving in child care practice. *Australian Journal of Early Childhood Education* 1: 23–30.

Clyde, M., Paramenter, G., Rodd, J., Rolfe, S., Tinworth, S. and Waniganayake, M. (1994) Child care from the perspective of parents, caregivers and children: Australian research. In S. Reifel (Ed.), *Advances in Early Education and Daycare: Volume 6. Topics in Early Literacy, Teacher Prepararion and International Perspectives on Early Care* (pp. 189–234). Greenwich, CT: JAI Press.

Coleman, J. (1991) *Policy Perspectives: Parental Involvement in Education.* Washington, DC: US Government Printing Office.

Cubillo, L. (1999) Gender and leadership in the national professional qualification for head teachers, an opportunity lost? *Journal of In-service Education* 25 (3): 545–555.

Daycare Trust (April 2005) More work needed on workforce strategy. News Release. Available at: www.daycaretrust.org.uk

DfES (2003) *Every Child Matters.* Nottingham: HM Government.

DfES (2005) *Championing Children: A Shared Set of Skills, Knowledge and Behaviours for those Leading and Managing Integrated Children's Services.* Nottingham: DfES.

DfES (2006) *Children's Workforce Strategy: Building a World-class Workforce for Children, Young People and Families. The Government's Response to the Consultation.* Nottingham: HM Government/DfES.

Epstein, J. (1989). Family structures and student motivation: a developmental perspective. In C. Ames and R. Ames (Eds), *Research on Motivation in Education, vol. 3: Goals and Cognitions.* New York: Academic Press.

Epstein, J. and Dauber, S. (1991) School programs and teacher practices of parent involvement in inner-city elementary and middle schools. *The Elementary School Journal* 91: 279–289.

Evangelou, M., Brooks, G., Smith, S., Jennings, D. and Roberts, F. (2005) *The Birth to School Study: A Longitudinal Evaluation of the Peers Early Education Partnership (PEEP) 1998–2005.* London: DfES.

Evans, L. and Teddlie, C. (1995) Facilitating change in schools: is there one best style? *School Effectiveness and School Improvement* 6(1): 1–22.

Foot, H., Howe, C., Cheyne, B., Terras, B. and Rattray, C. (2002) Parental participation and partnership in pre-school provision. *International Journal of Early Years Education* 10(1): 5–19.

Fullan, M. (2001) *Leading in a Culture of Change*. San Francisco: Jossey-Bass.

Geertz, C. (1973) Thick description: towards an interpretive theory of culture. In C. Geertz *The Interpretation of Cultures* (pp 3–30). New York: Falmer.

Harris, A. (2002) *Distributed Leadership in Schools. Leading or Misleading*. Keynote paper. Available at: www.shu.ac.uk/bemas/harris2002.html

Harris, A. and Lambert, L. (2003) *Building Leadership Capacity for School Improvement*. Maidenhead: Open University Press.

HMI (2003) *Children's Workforce Strategy: A Strategy to Build a World-class Workforce for Children and Young People. Every Child Matters: Change for Children. Consultation*. Available at: www.dfes.gov.uk/consltations/downladableDocs/5958-DfES-ECM.pdf

Jackson, D. (2003) Forward. In A. Harris and L. Lambert (Eds) *Building Leadership Capacity for Schoop Improvement*. Maidenhead: Open University Press.

Jeffrey, B. and Troman, G. (2004) Time for ethnography. *British Educational Research Journal* 30(4): 535–548.

Jeffrey, B. and Woods, P. (1998) *Testing Teachers: The Effects of School Inspections on Primary Teachers*. London: Falmer Press.

Jorde-Bloom, P. and Sheerer, M. (1992) The effect of leadership training on child care program quality. *Early Childhood Research Quarterly* 7(4): 579–594.

Kagan, S. (Ed.) (1994) Early care and education. Special Issue: Coming of Age. *Phi Delta Kappan* 76(3): 184–187.

Kouzes, J. and Posner, B. (1996) *An Instructor's Guide to the Leadership Challenge*. San-Francisco: Jossey-Bass.

Leithwood, K. and Levin, B. (2005) *Assessing School Leader and Leadership Programme Effects on Pupil Learning: Conceptual and Methodological Problems*. Research Report RR662. Nottingham: DfES.

Leithwood, K. and Riehl, C. (2003) *What Do We Already Know About Successful School Leadership*. AREA Division A Task Force on Developing Research in Educational Leadership. Available at: www.cepa.gse.rutgers.edu/whateweknow.pdf

Lewin, R. and Regine, B. (2000) *The Soul at Work*. New York: Simon and Schuster.

Melhuish, E. (2004) *Child Benefits: The Importance of Investing in Quality Childcare*. Daycare Trust, June. Available at: www.daycaretrust.orq.uk/mod/fileman/files/Child Benefits.pdf

Moore, P. (2004) *Models of Teacher Education*. Available at: www.readingrecoverv.org/sections/training/models.asp

Muijs, D., Aubrey, C., Harris, A. and Briggs, M. (2004) How do they manage? A review of the research on leadership in early childhood. *Journal of Early Childhood Research* 2(2): 157–160.

Ofsted (2003a) *Leadership and Management: What Inspection Tells Us*. HMI 1646. London: Ofsted.

Ofsted (2003b) *Leadership and Management: Managing the Workforce*. HMI 174. London: Ofsted.

Rodd, J. (1997) Learning to be leaders: perceptions of early childhood professionals about leadership roles and responsibilities. *Early Years* 18(1): 40–6.

Rodd, J. (1998) *Leadership in Early Childhood*, 2nd edn. Buckingham: Open University Press.

Rodd, J. (2005) Leadership: an essential ingredient or an optional extra for quality early childhood provision? A discussion paper. Available at: www.tactyc.org.uk/pdfs/rodd.pdf

Rogoff, B., Matusov, E. and White, C. (1996) *Models of Teaching and Learning: Participation in a Community of Learners*. Oxford: Blackwell.

Sadek, E. and Sadek, J. (2004) *Good Practice in Nursery Management*, 2nd edn. Cheltenham: Nelson Thornes.

Sammons, P. (1998) *School Effectiveness: Coming of Age in the Twenty-first Century*. Lisse: Swets & Zeitlinger.

Sammons, P., Hillman, J. and Mortimore, P. (1995) *Key Characteristics of Effective Schools: A Review of School Effectiveness Research*. London: Institute of Education.

Scrivens, C. (2002) Constructions of leadership: does gender make a difference? Perspectives from an English speaking country. In V. Nivala and E. Hujala (eds) *Leadership in Early Childhood Education: Cross-cultural Perspectives*. Department of Educational Sciences and Teacher Education, University of Oulu, Finland. Available at: http://herkules.oulu.fi/isbn9514268539/isbn9514268539.pdf

Shakeshaft, C. (1987) *Women in Educational Administration*. Newbury Park, CA: Sage.

Siraj-Blatchford, I. and Brooker, L. (1998) *Brent Parent Involvement in Primary Schools Project Report*. London: Institute of Education.

Siraj-Blatchford, I. and Manni, L. (forthcoming) *Managing to make a Difference: Caring and Effective Leadership in the Early Years*. Stoke-on-Trent: Trentham Books.

Siraj-Blatchford, I., Sylva, K. et al. (2002) *Researching Effective Pedagogy in the Early Years (REPEY)*. DfES Research Report 356. London: DfES.

Siraj-Blatchford, I., Sylva, K. et al. (2003) *The Effective Provision of Pre-School Education (EPPE) Project*. Technical Paper 10, Intensive Case Studies of Practice across the Foundation Stage. London: DfES/Institute of Education, University of London.

Siraj-Blatchford, I., Clarke, K. and Needham, M. (2007) *The Team Around the Child: Multi-agency Working in the Early Years*. Stoke-on-Trent: Trentham Books.

Southworth, G. (1998) *Leading Improving Primary Schools*. London: Falmer Press.

Southworth, G. (2002) 'Leading learning and teaching primary schools'. National College of School Leadership, London. Available at: http://www.ncsl.orq.uk/media/F7B/52/kpool-evidence-southworth.pdf

Southworth, G. (2004) *Primary School Leadership in Context: Leading Small, Medium and Large Sized Schools*. London: RoutledgeFalmer/Taylor & Francis Group.

Spillane, J., Halverson, R. and Diamond, J. (2004) Towards a theory of leadership: a distributed perspective. *Journal of Curriculum Studies* 36(1): 3–34.

Sylva, K., Siraj-Blatchford, I., Melhuish, E.C., Sammons, P., Taggart, B., Evans, E., Dobson, A., Jeavons, M., Lewis, K., Morahan, M. and Sadler, S. (1999) *The Effective Provision of Pre-School Education (EPPE) Project: Technical Paper 6A – Characteristics of Pre-School Environments*. London: DfEE/ Institute of Education, University of London.

Sylva, K., Melhuish, E.C., Sammons, P., Siraj-Blatchford, I. and Taggart, B. (2004) *The Effective Provsion of Pre-School Education (EPPE) Project: Final Report*. London: DfES/Institute of Education, University of London.

Taggart, B., Sylva, K., Siraj-Blatchford, I., Melhuish, E.C., Sammons, P. and Walker-Hall, J. (2000) *Characteristics of the Centres in the EPPE Sample: Interviews. Technical Paper 5*. London: DfEE.

Troman, G. (1997) The effects of restructuring on primary teachers' work: a sociological analysis. PhD thesis, Open University, Milton Keynes.

Waniganayake, M., Morda, R. and Kapsalakis, A. (2000) Leadership in child care centres: is it just another job? Special Issue: Management and Leadership. *Australian Journal of Early Childhood* 28(1): 13–19.

Webb, R. (2005) Leading teaching and learning in the primary school: from 'educative leadership' to 'pedagogic leadership'. *Educational Management, Administration & Leadership* 33(1): 60–91.

Whitaker, P. (1993) *Managing Change in Schools*. Buckingham: Open University Press.

Wigfall, V. and Moss, P. (2001) *More than the Sum of its Parts? A Study of a Multi-agency Child Care Network*. London: National Children's Bureau/Joseph Rowntree Foundation.

Wolfendale, S. (1992) *Empowering Parents and Teachers Working for Children*. London: Cassell.

Woods, P., Jeffrey, B., Troman, G. and Boyle, M. (1997) *Restructuring Schools, Reconstructing Teachers*. Buckingham: Open University Press.

23

Negotiating the moral maze: developing ethical literacy in multi-agency settings

Judith Whitmarsh

Overview

In this chapter, Judith Whitmarsh provides an overview of what ethics are, why they are important and what they mean in practice. She explores ethical codes of practice and how practitioners from three different professions – early years, social work and nursing – approach and manage ethical situations in different ways. Principles of ethics are examined in a multi-agency context, identifying the challenges of different views and working practices.

[…]

Introduction

This chapter takes the somewhat abstract notion of ethics and explores its relevance to contemporary practice in the early years, specifically in relation to multi-agency

---

Whitmarsh, J. (2007) 'Negotiating the moral maze: developing ethical literacy in multi-agency settings', in Siraj-Blatchford, I., Clarke, K. and Needham, M. (eds) *The Team Around the Child: Multi-agency Working in the Early Years*, Stoke-on-Trent: Trentham Books, pp. 87–103.

working. It aims to show that ethics is not a dense, philosophical, theoretical concept nor the slavish adherence to a professional code, but that an understanding of basic ethics can clarify problems and help us make decisions that will enhance our practice and our research. The chapter shows how an understanding of ethics can illuminate issues and dilemmas that arise for practitioners, parents and children, and offer some signposts towards joint ethical working. To sum up, ethics concerns the basic values that underpin our relationships with others, whether in a professional or personal context; developing 'ethical literacy' enables us to identify where we, as a multi-agency team, are coming from and to clarify how we can move forward.

Where tensions exist in multi-agency working, they are often caused by misunderstandings about shared language, shared information and mutual practices relating to them. Therefore, first we need to clarify what we mean by ethics and ethical practice: the first section offers a brief history of ethics, exploring the sources of our modern interpretations and how the past influences the present. Next, the why of ethics and ethical practice are investigated: why are ethics important? Why can we not just follow our professional codes and consider our practice therefore to be ethical? The chapter then explores the ethical concept of confidentiality from the perspective of three different disciplines: education, nursing and social work. It shows how professionals from different disciplines may interpret confidentiality differently. Finally, we need to make some decisions about how to develop a joint model of ethical practice that caters for professionals from a variety of backgrounds, for parents, families and, of course, the children who are at the heart of our work. This chapter draws on examples from real-life practice. All names and identifying features have been changed.

Ethical codes of practice

Ethical discussion began with the Ancient Greek philosophers Aristotle, Plato and Socrates. All had meaningful and useful things to say that have informed contemporary ethics. Socrates, for example, devoted his life to a search for the truth about the right way to live (Hogan, 2005: 185). Hogan further argues that Platonic searches for the truth became the foundation for much institutionalised educational thinking, thus the truth became a prescriptive doctrine that headed Christian education through the centuries (Hogan, 2005). Scott (1995) suggests that Aristotle's virtue theory can be applied to health-care ethics. She maintains that from Aristotelian theory we learn that any discussion should begin from what is known about the issues (reflection), followed by clarification of the ethical problem and, finally, consideration of possible ways of addressing the issues. This three-point model would be a useful framework for any potential discussion of an ethical dilemma [see Figure 23.1].

Moving on to more recent times, eighteenth century philosophers such as Kant and Hume critiqued notions of truth, arguing against the metaphysical ideal, which holds that there is one scientific truth that can be observed, held and accounted for. Thus in contemporary modern thought, stances such as postmodernism promote the concept of the truth as relative, conditional and contextual.

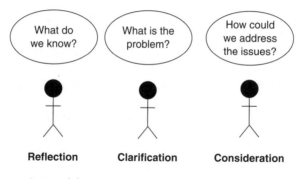

Figure 23.1   Three-point model

📁   **CASE STUDY**

Sara is manager of the Children's Centre. She employs Janet as a nursery nurse. There is an incident, observed by a parent, who states that Janet had been snappy all morning, curt to the children and grabbed Rehaan from the climbing frame, leaving red marks on his arms. Sara needs to find out the truth. Janet denies being snappy and curt; she argues that the parent 'has it in for her' and says that she grabbed Rehaan because she spotted a wasp on the climbing frame just where he was about to place his hand. Whose truth should Sara believe?

Incidents like this demonstrate how the truth can vary, depending on perspective. But if the truth can vary so much, how are we to offer guidance for ethical practices?

[...] Psychological research by Milgram (1974), Zimbardo et al. (1973) and Hofling et al. (1966) all raised questions about what was meant by ethical research and research conduct. The ethical problems raised during this era led the US government to establish the National Commission for the Protection of Human Subjects in Biomedical and Behavioral Research, who, in turn, produced the Belmont Report (1979). From their study of the many codes of conduct and of ethics, the Belmont Report noted three common, basic principles: respect for persons, beneficence – doing good and minimising harm – and justice. These principles were considered equal in importance and were subsequently adopted by the Council for International Organisations of Medical Sciences and its later affiliate, the World Health Organisation (Ensign, 2003). Thus modern-day ethics have their roots in bio-medical scientific research. It is noteworthy that informed consent, confidentiality, privacy and anonymity are seen as integral to the principles of respect, beneficence and justice, whereas much contemporary understanding of ethics focuses on these as separate issues.

What do we mean by ethics?

Ethics is a contested term: most definitions relate, in some sense or other, to guidance about what is considered to be a right and proper way to behave. Gregory (2003: 2) argues that the terms 'ethics' and 'morals' can and should be used interchangeably, whereas Homan (1991: 1) is more specific and argues that 'ethics is the science of morality: those who engage in it determine values for the regulation of human behaviour'. Dahlberg and Moss (2005: 66) have perhaps the most practical and useful definition for early years professionals, when they state that ethics is the 'should question: how should we think and act?'

This raises questions about who decides the right way to think and act. If professionals believe they are acting in an ethical manner, does that make their practice ethical? In order to explore these complex issues further, we need to evaluate the underpinning principles and theories, argued over for centuries by some of the greatest philosophers.

Principles of ethics

The three principles that underpin most codes of ethics are:

- respect for persons: protecting the autonomy of persons, with courtesy and respect for individuals;
- beneficence: maximising good outcomes for science, humanity and the individual while avoiding or minimising unnecessary harm, risk or wrong;
- justice: reasonable, non-exploitative, fair behaviour (adapted from Farrell, 2005: 4).

However, no code of ethics can lay down detailed, absolute guidance for all the complexities that arise during professional practice and research. In some instances, competing moral claims leave the practitioner with an ethical dilemma about which principle is more important than the other (see case study below).

CASE STUDY

Jamie, 4 years old, had a nose-bleed in nursery school. His teacher followed the first-aid guidelines and encouraged Jamie to put his head slightly forward and pinch the soft tissue of his nostrils. This stopped the nose-bleed. The following day, Jamie's mother sent an angry letter to the head teacher stating that:

- Her family are prone to nose-bleeds.
- She has taught Jamie to pinch the bridge of his nose.
- She wants him to deal with his nose-bleeds as she has taught him.
- She refuses permission for staff to treat him otherwise.

There are a number of ethical issues here: first, does the mother have the right to contravene first-aid policy in the setting? Secondly, does the teacher/first-aider have the right to treat Jamie in contravention of his parent's wishes? Thirdly, what effect would the correctly imposed treatment have on (a) Jamie's wellbeing and (b) Jamie's relationship with his mother? Referring back to the ethical principles, we need to consider:

- respect for both Jamie and his mother;
- the mother's right to autonomy and to make decisions about the welfare of her child;
- the head teacher's responsibility to avoid or minimise risk and harm to a child;
- the head teacher's respect for the first-aid knowledge of the teacher and need to protect the teacher from risk and harm;
- Jamie's right to autonomy and to make decisions about treatment that involves his body. Would the teacher be justified in treating Jamie if he refused it?

In this particular case, the competing claims appeared difficult to resolve. Eventually, after negotiation, the mother agreed that Jamie could pinch his nose, as she wished, in the first instance but if the nose-bleed continued for more than a couple of minutes, the teacher would then take over the first-aid. The mother signed a form to this effect. The school is currently considering running first-aid classes for parents and introducing it into the curriculum for pupils.

This particular case introduces the notion that ethical principles may be different to rules and policies: rules tend to be specific (for example, the first-aid treatment for nose-bleeds is …) and less open to interpretation, but the ethical principles underpin the rules (Pring, 2001). Underlying the nose-bleed treatment rules are the principles of 'not doing harm' and 'maximising a good outcome'. Thus principles include values: the nose-bleed rules tell us what to do practically, but the ethical principles give us guidance about what is moral and ethical to do in this situation.

The trouble with codes of ethics

Codes serve a useful purpose as a guide to the ethical behaviour desired by professional bodies; in fact the code of ethics is often seen as 'one of the defining features of a profession' (Banks, 2001: 84). Some professional codes have more power than others: transgressions can lead to the ultimate sanction of removal from the profession. However, as we observed in Jamie's case, codes do not necessarily give us all the answers and, as multi-disciplinary teams become more common in the early years, some codes may conflict with others in their interpretation, as the examples below demonstrate:

CASE STUDY

- Hardeep is a recently qualified health visitor attached to the Children's Centre. She abides by the Nursing and Midwifery Council Code of Practice (NMC, 2002) and is never quite sure how much confidential information about family health issues she should share with the other team members. She is always very cautious; she tends to get her clinical manager's approval to release health information and this delays action and the rest of the team find this delay difficult.

(Continued)

(Continued)

- Tony is a social worker; although careful about client information, his code suggests that this can be shared on a 'need to know' basis and he sees Hardeep's attitude as obstructive, even dangerous, if he has suspicions of child protection issues. He is becoming frustrated with the problem.
- Marge is a nursery nurse with 20 years' experience. While she is careful about record-keeping, she is always ready to share her knowledge of the crèche parents and children at the team meetings, if required. She follows ethical principles of respect and is careful of client privacy.

Rodd (2005) notes the limited impact of ethical codes on the advocacy of children's rights. And while she claims that an ethical code can 'provide guiding principles for decision-making' (p. 141), she acknowledges that ethical codes do not 'attempt to provide prescriptive or "right" answers to the complex questions and ethical dilemmas faced by early childhood practitioners' (p. 142). Furthermore, educational philosophers (see, for example, Greenbank, 2004; Hodkinson, 2004; Homan, 1991) argue that strict adherence to codes can discourage exploration of the values and morality of practice and inhibit morally responsible behaviour.

French (2007) demonstrates how issues of information-sharing and confidentiality frequently create barriers to multi-agency working. Could this be because confidentiality, although not a *prima facie* principle of ethics, is laid down in professional codes and may be thought to have legal ramifications [...]? Breaching confidentiality, therefore, whether consciously or inadvertently, carries risks: sharing information then becomes a risky enterprise. Farrell (2005: 2) suggests that the emergence of ethical codes is a response to an increasing concern with risk, requiring 'heightened accountability, regulation and surveillance'. If children are seen to inhabit a 'risky space' (Farrell, 2005: 3), it is little surprise that the practitioners responsible for their care and education feel themselves vulnerable guardians of a risky enterprise, particularly when ascribed codes do not offer solutions to their ethical dilemmas.

Cultural influences

We have noted that the study of ethics should give us guidance about how to relate to others in a moral way; we have also identified the fact that ethical discourse engages with values and with notions of the truth. This assumes that there is a 'right' way to think and act. But are we sure that our own understandings of the 'right' way and 'truth' are universal? How do we manage our interactions when child, family and other practitioners may have a different understanding of the 'right' way?

Becoming more inclusive

Fleer (2006) draws our attention to the way in which the early childhood centre may not reflect the cultural values and practices of home, school and work. She argues that culturally diverse values and practices need to be integrated and addressed within early years practice and not merely 'added on to mainstream fundamental early childhood education' (p. 136).

French (2007) describes the history and development of the current child-centred pedagogy. She demonstrates how service providers have been required to make a shift to family- and child-centred provision, placing their needs at the heart of professional practice. This may, however, require a shift in the underlying values of multi-agency practitioners. Can we really adapt our own value systems to incorporate diverse, or even opposing, parental beliefs? Clarke and French (2007) highlight how successful partnerships depend on practitioners' ability to accept changes that may be necessary within themselves. In a multi-agency team, the core ethical beliefs and values of the team may be as diverse as those of the general population.

Tackling this dilemma requires us to stop thinking in dualistic terms: that is to halt the dialectic in which something is either true or it is not. Instead, we need to begin thinking more in terms of ethical behaviour as an interaction which can vary according to its context (as we saw in the vignette of Jamie). Considering ethical practice as relational opens up spaces in which we can discuss the issues while trying to weigh up which principle may, on this occasion, be of over-riding use to the specific situation. If we stop thinking in terms of a polarised duality, an either/or situation, we can begin to search for shared understanding. Most of our deeply held values are on a continuum and we will undoubtedly share some of the underlying constituents with others. We can begin by seeking out the similarities during discussion, rather than the differences.

Jackson (2006) suggests that ethical inquiry could begin with developing a consensus on what is not ethical practice and behaviour: identifying this may lead to agreement about what ethical practice would look like. Sharing experiences of ethical dilemmas can feel threatening, so developing ethical literacy may initially be easier if it is not too personal. Setting a few ground rules at the beginning of the discussion, perhaps about privacy, may help those present to feel safer. [...] The three-point model from this chapter could be used to help structure the discussion.

[...]

Moving into an ethical space may enable practitioners to explore taken-for-granted beliefs and practices in order to build an ethos and practice that can encompass diversity. Within that ethical space, we need to listen to parents, carers, families and practitioners, to create a dialogic relationship as a first step along our ethical pathway.

Reviewing the situation

So far, we have considered the origins of ethics and its recent development. This led us into a consideration of ethical principles and an understanding that ethical codes, while useful, may not be able to resolve all the increasingly complex potential dilemmas arising in multi-agency working. If we cannot find simple, straightforward answers to ethical problems, then we need to develop innovative ways of engaging with the issues in order to enable a multi-disciplinary workforce to share understandings and to support each other. One way forward is to avoid thinking in dualisms of either 'I am right and they are wrong', or 'there is one right answer to my problem' and begin to move into the concept of spaces for shared ethical discussion, realising that there may be a number of conflicting priorities, competing ethical principles, and a number of possible solutions; in other words, thinking about ethics as an ongoing process. If we consider ethics as relational, as the basis of our relationships with others, as re-conceptualising our understanding of ethics, it will prepare us for engaging with a personal process of developing ethical literacy. As Martin Needham suggests (2007) the more individuals can see the bigger picture, the better they will be able to help each other deliver the integrated package. [...]

Sharing information within an ethical space

[...] Sharing information is one of the commonest causes of tension in multi-agency teams (Dahl and Aubrey, 2004; Newman, 2000; Rowe, 2003) and frequently perspectives between groups of professionals differ (Anning, 2001; Atkinson et al, 2002; Dahl et al, 2005; Jones, 2000; Milbourne et al, 2003). [...] At the heart of information-sharing lies the concept of confidentiality, and the following section explores this from the viewpoint of an educationalist, a nursing practitioner and a social worker.

Confidentiality and the teacher

Within the discipline of education, confidentiality is most commonly invoked in child protection procedures and in research. The courts have found a common law duty of confidence to exist where, 'there is a special relationship between parties, such as patient–doctor, solicitor–client, teacher–pupil' (DfES, 2005a, Appendix 1: 2.1). However, this consultation document states that the duty is not absolute and information may be shared when:

- the information is not confidential in nature;
- the person to whom the duty is owed has implicitly or explicitly authorised the disclosure;
- there is over-riding public interest in disclosure;
- disclosure is ordered by a court order or other legal obligation.

In a potential child protection case, the guidelines lay out a clear pathway of procedure and the child's best interests must over-ride the duty of confidentiality (see, for example, DfES, 2005b). Few teachers would find difficulties in breaching confidentiality to support an abused child; however, there may be occasions when education practitioners suspect that all is not well, but have no clear-cut evidence of abuse. Many teachers observing cuts and bruises on a child are unsure if these have a natural explanation: children fall over and accumulate injuries through their adventurous and exploratory activities, and young children may not be able to give a clear answer about the origins of injuries. Children have off periods when they may appear unhappy or withdrawn, without necessarily being subject to abuse. Child protection is a risky business, both for the child and the caring adult; teachers, afraid of getting it wrong, anticipate trial by tabloid, disciplinary action, and the worst possible outcome: the death of a pupil. It is little surprise that, as McCullough observes (2007), some practitioners prefer to pass any responsibility for child protection on to nominated local services.

[...]

The advent of the Children Act 2004 and the Every Child Matters policy documentation [...] supported the development of the lead professional in cases of complex need, the development of multi-agency working and the keystone of information-sharing. Ethics and ethical practice underpin these concepts: by becoming increasingly ethically literate, practitioners can share their understanding of confidentiality and their fears and anxieties in a non-threatening space. By considering vignettes of potential child protection scenarios, searching out ethical principles for consideration, and debating risk, we can develop greater confidence in our practice.

Confidentiality and the nurse

Nursing guidelines on confidentiality are framed within a professional code of practice and those who do not follow the guidelines are liable to disciplinary action. The Code of Professional Conduct for nurses states clearly:

- 5.1: You must treat information about patients and clients as confidential and use it only for the purpose for which it was given. As it is impractical to obtain consent every time you need to share information with others, you should ensure that patients and clients understand that some information may be made available to members of the team involved in the delivery of care. You must guard against breaches of confidentiality by protecting information from improper disclosure at all times
- 5.2: If you are required to disclose information outside the team that will have personal consequences for patients or clients, you must obtain their consent. If the patient or client withholds consent, or if consent cannot be obtained for whatever reason, disclosures may only be made where:

  o They can be justified in the public interest (usually where disclosure is essential to protect the patient or client or someone else from the risk of significant harm)
  o They are required by law or by order of a court. (Nursing and Midwifery Council [NMC], 2002: 7)

This appears to give strong, explicit guidance to nurses, midwives and health visitors. However, it raises questions about who is a member of a team: do we include the voluntary workers in the setting? Does the team consist of all the NHS workers: health visitors, midwives, speech therapists, child and adult mental health services and psychologists? How much information can be given to teachers, the early years staff, to the educational psychologist, to the police, Citizens Advice Bureau, the housing department who may be on site? [...]

Confidentiality and the social worker

Let us now consider how a social worker might respond to information sharing and confidentiality.

Clark (2000) describes both a strong and a weak version of confidentiality. In the strong version, nothing the client communicates to the social worker should be passed on to others unless 'good reasons are shown to the contrary' (p. 86) Clark's weak version proposes that client information can be passed on to others but in a way that does not reveal the identity of the client. Thus a case-history, with all identifying features removed, could be passed to a team member for comment and advice. However, Clark then describes how much identifiable client information is

> ... inspected by managers and consulted by supervisors and colleagues who may have to deal with the case in the worker's absence. In practice, files are usually available on demand to virtually any professional member of the agency, even if they have no clear cause for viewing a file. (p. 187)

Open-plan offices, minimal privacy, and informal conversation and gossip all militate against true confidentiality in social work client affairs (Clark, 2000).

Banks (2001) notes how the title 'social worker' covers a diverse range of settings so defining conceptual rules for confidentiality may have different applications in different circumstances. The social worker may belong to a statutory agency or a voluntary agency; they may be attached to a children's centre, a residential unit, an adoption agency or even a rape crisis centre, to name a few. The level of confidentiality may have different importance when dealing with different clients such as people with HIV, offenders, child protection, adoption, or in an independent counselling agency. [...]

Resolving information-sharing dilemmas

The law about confidentiality and sharing information rests on three legal frameworks: the Common Law Duty of Confidence, the Human Rights Act 1998, and the Data Protection Act 1998. The increasingly complex issues regarding confidentiality, viewed – incorrectly – by many as an absolute right in the doctor–patient relationship, have led to the British Medical Association statement that 'patient confidentiality is desirable but not an absolute concept and can be breached if circumstances warrant such action' (BMA, 2004: 3). Montgomery (2003: 270) suggests that 'it is difficult to show that a legal obligation exists' in relation to sharing information about child protection issues, yet it has become part of professional good practice.

This brings us back to the problems of assuming that a policy or code of ethics will answer all our questions about the right way to behave. As this chapter has demonstrated, complex ethical dilemmas require more than a one-size-fits-all ethical code, particularly in multi-agency practice. Banks (2001) proposes that social workers need to develop a capacity to become reflective about their work and its ethical dimensions, which returns us to our notion of ethical spaces:

> Do we want professionals to become more than simply rule-following automata? We do want to develop people who respect confidentiality because they are the kind of people who are trustworthy and respectful in all aspects of life, not just because their agency or professional association has laid down a rule to this effect. (Banks, 2001: 54)

A multi-disciplinary discussion of professional understandings of confidentiality could draw on [...] cross-government guidance (DfES, 2005a) to develop shared reference points on which to build a common understanding of information-sharing and confidentiality. As Nunney notes, 'No inquiry into a child's death or serious injury has ever questioned why information was shared. It has always asked the opposite' (DfES, 2006: 3).

The Department for Education and Skills (2006: 4) suggests that the following principles underpin decisions to share information:

- Is there a legitimate purpose for you or your agency to share the information?
- Does the information enable a person to be identified?
- Is the information confidential?
- If so, do you have consent to share?
- Is there a statutory duty or court order to share the information?
- If consent is refused, or there are good reasons not to seek consent, is there a sufficient public interest to share information?
- If the decision is to share, are you sharing the information in the right way?
- Have you properly recorded your decision?

This brief discussion demonstrates how our understanding of just one key ethical concept, confidentiality, raises a number of questions that will need addressing in a multi-agency setting. The discussion has not begun to engage with issues of autonomy, informed consent, privacy, accountability and anonymity, although these are all inherent within the vignettes: for Jamie's carers, accountability is an over-riding ethical principle; for Hardeep, Tony and Marge, information-sharing is of key importance; for others, child protection may be the over-riding concern. Each profession will have its own knowledge base, its own code-related guidelines, and its own understanding of these. By sharing knowledge, we can perhaps further our understanding of each other's ethical background in order to become ethically literate.

Conclusion

While this chapter has not provided quick-fix answers, it offers some ways to approach ethical dilemmas. Ethical codes offer guidance in professional situations, but they can also inhibit ethical behaviour by their inflexibility. Furthermore, the wide variety of professionals involved in multi-agency working may each have their own code emphasising different rules, principles and values. The voluntary workers and non-professional staff may be left floundering, unsure whose ethical code is paramount.

Moving away from a dualist, polarised way of thinking about ethics, in which there is a right and a wrong answer, and suggesting that ethical codes may be useful in simple situations but cannot respond to complexity, leaves us with our own ethical dilemma: how then do we resolve a situation that appears to have inherent conflicting and competing demands? Our assumptions about what is right and wrong can be culturally determined and historically mediated: can we be sure that children, families and other professionals share our personal viewpoint and, if not, how do we encompass diverse values and beliefs?

The answer to this must lie in the development of reflective, non-critical spaces (Dahlberg and Moss, 2005) in which we explore the labyrinth of ethics and ethical principles and develop our own frameworks for ethical behaviour. Jackson (2006: 4) observes that 'the central question in ethics is: how ought we to live our lives?' New ways of multi-agency working require new ways of thinking and the development of new professional relationships; developing ethical literacy will enable us to make sound, shared decisions about how we want to live our professional lives.

[...]

References

Anning, A. (2001) Knowing who I am and what I know: developing new versions of professional knowledge in integrated service settings. In British Educational Research Association conference. University of Leeds, 13–15 September. Available at: www.leeds.ac.uk/educol/documents/00001877.htm

Atkinson, M. Wilkin, A. Stott, A. Doherty, P. and Kinder, K. (2002) *Multi-agency Working: A Detailed Study*. Slough: NFER.

Banks, S. (2001) *Ethics and Values in Social Work. 2nd ed.* Basingstoke: Palgrave.

The Belmont Report (1979) Ethical Principles and Guidelines for the Protection of Human Subjects of Research. Washington: Department of Health, Education and Welfare. In Small, R. (2001) Codes are not enough: what philosophy can contribute to the ethics of educational research. *Journal of Philosophy of Education*, 35(3), 387–406.

British Medical Association (BMA) (2004) Confidentiality and disclosure of health information. Available at: www.bma.org.uk

Clark, CL. (2000) *Social Work Ethic: Politics, Principles and Practice*. Basingstoke: Palgrave.

Clarke, K. and French, J. (2007) Collaboration with family: the role of the multi-agency setting in working with parents. In Siraj-Blatchford, I. Clarke, K. and Needham, M. (eds) *The Team*

Around the Child: Multi-agency Working in the Early Years. Stoke-on-Trent: Trentham Books, 151–69.

Dahl, S. and Aubrey, C. (2004) Multi-agency working in Sure Start projects: successes and challenges. In British Educational Research Association Early Years Special Interest Group. University of Warwick, 27 May.

Dahl, S. Clarke, L. and Aubrey, C. (2005) Factors facilitating and hindering partnership working: findings from Sure Start local programmes in Coventry. Draft report. In Sharing Research in Early Childhood: A Multi-professional Approach to Education and Childcare: Critical Reflections. University of Warwick, 20–23 March.

Dahlberg, G. and Moss, P. (2005) *Ethics and Politics in Early Childhood Education.* Abingdon: RoutledgeFalmer.

Department for Education and Skills (DfES) (2005a) *Cross-government Guidance: Sharing Information on Children and Young People.* Runcorn: DfES.

Department for Education and Skills (DfES) (2005b) *What to do if you're Worried a Child is being Abused: Summary.* London: DfES.

Department for Education and Skills (DfES) (2006) *Making It Happen: Working Together for Children and Young People.* London: DfES.

Ensign, J. (2003) Ethical issues in qualitative health research with homeless youths. *Journal of Advanced Nursing,* 43(1), 43–50.

Farrell, A. (ed.) (2005) *Ethical Research with Children.* Buckingham: Open University Press.

Fleer, M. (2006) The cultural construction of child development: creating institutional and cultural intersubjectivity. *International Journal of Early Years Education,* 14(2), June, 127–140.

French, J. (2007) Multi-agency working: the historical background. In Siraj-Blatchford, I. Clarke, K. and Needham, M. (eds) *The Team Around the Child: Multi-agency Working in the Early Years.* Stoke-on-Trent: Trentham Books, 47–66.

Greenbank, P. (2004) The role of values in educational research: the case for reflexivity. *British Educational Research Journal,* 29(6), 791–801.

Gregory, I. (2003) *Ethics in Research.* London: Continuum.

Hodkinson, P. (2004) Research as a form of work: expertise, community and methodological objectivity. *British Education Research Journal,* 30(1), February, 9–26.

Hofling, KC. Brotzman, E. Dalrymple, S. Graves, N. and Pierce, CM. (1966) An experimental study in the nurse–physician relationship. *Journal of Mental Disorders,* 143, 171–180. Cited in Gross, R. (1991) *Psychology: The Science of Mind and Behaviour.* London: Hodder and Stoughton.

Hogan, P. (2005)The integrity of learning and the search for truth. *Educational Theory,* 55(2), 185–200.

Homan, R. (1991) *The Ethics of Social Research.* Harlow: Longman.

Jackson, J. (2006) *Ethics in Medicine.* Cambridge: Polity Press.

Jones, H. (2000) Partnerships: a common sense approach to inclusion? In SCUTREA, 30th Annual Conference. University of Nottingham, 3–5 July. Available at: www.leeds.ac.uk/educol/documents/00001456.htm

McCullough, M. (2007) Integrating children's services: the case for child protection. In Siraj-Blatchford, I. Clarke, K. and Needham, M. (eds) *The Team Around the Child: Multi-agency Working in the Early Years.* Stoke-on-Trent: Trentham Books, 7–46.

Milbourne, L. Macrae, S. and Maguire, M. (2003) Collaborative solutions or new policy problems: exploring multi-agency partnerships in education and health work. *Journal of Education Policy,* 18(1), 19–35.

Milgram, S. (1974) *Obedience to Authority.* New York: Harper and Row. Cited in Gross, R. (1991) *Psychology: The Science of Mind and Behaviour.* London: Hodder and Stoughton.

Montgomery, J. (2003) *Health Care Law.* 2nd ed. Oxford: Oxford University Press.

Needham, M. (2007) Keeping people in the big picture: national policy and local solutions. In Siraj-Blatchford, I. Clarke, K. and Needham, M. (eds) *The Team Around the Child: Multi-agency Working in the Early Years*. Stoke-on-Trent: Trentham Books, 67–86.

Newman, J. (2000) Beyond the new public management? Modernizing public services. In Clarke, J. Gewirtz, S. and McLaughlin, E. (eds) *New Managerialism, New Welfare?* London: Sage Publications with Open University Press, 45–61.

Nursing and Midwifery Council (NMC) (2002) *Code of Professional Conduct: Standards for Conduct, Performance and Ethics*. (Online). London: Nursing and Midwifery Council. Available at:www.nmc-uk.org

Pring, R. (2001) The virtues and vices of an educational researcher. *Journal of Philosophy of Education*, 35(3), 407–421.

Rodd, J. (2005) *Leadership in Early Childhood. 3rd ed.* Buckingham: Open University Press.

Rowe, A. (2003) *An Evaluation of the Involvement of Health Visitors in the Sure Start Foxhill and Parson Cross Programme*. (Online). Sheffield University. Available at: www.sheffield.ac.uk/surestart/publns.html (accessed 7.1.05).

Scott, PA. (1995) Aristotle, nursing and health care ethics. *Nursing Ethics*, 2(4), 279–285.

Zimbardo, PG. Banks, WC. Craig, H. and Jaffe, D. (1973) A Pirandellian prison: the mind is a formidable jailer. In *New York Times magazine*, 8 April pp. 38–60.

Index

PROFESSIONALIZATION, LEADERSHIP AND MANAGEMENT IN THE EARLY YEARS

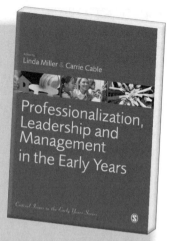

Edited by **Linda Miller** and **Carrie Cable** *both at The Open University*

With the rapid change experienced by the early years workforce over recent times, this book considers what constitutes professionalization in the sector, and what this means in practice. Bringing a critical perspective to the developing knowledge and understanding of early years practitioners at various stages of their professional development, it draws attention to key themes and issues. Chapters are written by leading authorities, and case studies, questions and discussion points are provided to facilitate critical thinking.

Topics covered include:

• constructions of professional identities

• men in the early years

• multidisciplinary working in the early years

• professionalization in the nursery

• early childhood leadership and policy.

Written in an accessible style and relevant to all levels of early years courses, the book is highly relevant to those studying at masters level, and has staggered levels of further reading that encourage reflection and progression.

CRITICAL ISSUES IN THE EARLY YEARS

November 2010 • 184 pages
Cloth (978-1-84920-553-5) • £65.00
Paper (978-1-84920-554-2) • £22.99

THEORIES AND APPROACHES TO LEARNING IN THE EARLY YEARS

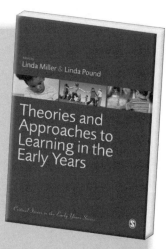

Edited by **Linda Miller** *The Open University* and **Linda Pound** *Education Consultant*

By focusing on key figures in early years education and care, this book considers the influential thinkers and groundbreaking approaches that have revolutionized practice. With contributions from leading authorities in the field, chapters provide an explanation of the approach, an analysis of the theoretical background, case studies, questions and discussion points to facilitate critical thinking.

Included are chapters on:

- Froebel
- Psychoanalytical theories
- Maria Montessori
- Steiner Waldorf education
- High/Scope
- Postmodern and post-structuralist perspectives
- Forest Schools
- Vivian Gussin Paley
- Te Whariki.

Written in an accessible style and relevant to all levels of early years courses, the book has staggered levels of Further Reading that encourage reflection and promotes progression.

CRITICAL ISSUES IN THE EARLY YEARS
December 2010 • 192 pages
Cloth (978-1-84920-577-1) • £65.00
Paper (978-1-84920-578-8) • £22.99

ALSO FROM SAGE